The Paradox of Political Philosophy

Socrates' Philosophic Trial

Jacob Howland

ROWMAN & LITTLEFIELD PUBLISHERS, INC.
Lanham • Boulder • New York • Oxford

ROWMAN & LITTLEFIELD PUBLISHERS, INC.

Published in the United States of America
by Rowman & Littlefield Publishers, Inc.
4720 Boston Way, Lanham, Maryland 20706

12 Hid's Copse Road
Cumnor Hill, Oxford OX2 9JJ, England

British Library Cataloguing in Publication Information Available

Library of Congress Cataloging-in-Publication Data

Howland, Jacob.
　　The paradox of political philosophy : Socrates' philosophic trial /
Jacob Howland.
　　　　p.　　cm.
　　Includes bibliographical references and index.
　　ISBN 0-8476-8975-1 (cloth : alk. paper). — ISBN 0-8476-8976-X
(pbk. : alk. paper)
　　1. Plato. 2. Socrates. I. Title.
　　B395.H85　1998
　　184—dc21　　　　　　　　　　　　　　　　　97-41428

ISBN 0-8476-8975-1 (cloth : alk. paper)
ISBN 0-8476-8976-X (pbk. : alk. paper)

Printed in the United States of America

♾™ The paper used in this publication meets the minimum requirements of American
National Standard for Information Sciences—Permanence of Paper for Printed Library
Materials, ANSI Z39.48–1984.

Contents

Part Two: The Stranger

Preface

I am a part of all that I have met;
Yet all experience is an arch wherethrough
Gleams that untravelled world, whose margin fades
For ever and for ever when I move.

Alfred, Lord Tennyson, "Ulysses"

This book is about Plato's understanding of philosophy. Its guiding hypothesis is that an important part of Plato's thinking about the nature of philosophy emerges over the course of a series of dialogues that contains a philosophic trial of Socrates. This philosophical inquest has several distinctive and intriguing features. It takes place concurrently with Socrates' public trial in Athens, and it focuses on the question of the relationship between philosophy and the political community. It centrally involves a mysterious individual whom we know only as the Stranger from Elea, and who assumes the role of Socrates' prosecutor. And it is an unusually long Platonic drama that fills two days and stretches over five dialogues: the *Theaetetus*, *Euthyphro*, *Cratylus*, *Sophist*, and *Statesman*. The overarching purpose of this series of dialogues is to allow us to judge the activity of Socrates not within the distorting confines of a public court, as in the *Apology*, but with a view to the broadest horizons of human existence. It is only within these horizons that one can adequately pose the question of the best life for both nonphilosophical and philosophically inclined human beings.

The philosophic trial presents us with a unique opportunity to engage in an extended critical exploration of Socrates' speeches and deeds. Here we shall find Plato's deepest reflections about the way of philosophizing dramatized by the protagonist of his dialogues. Yet the length and complexity of the philosophic trial also pose unusual challenges and risks for the interpreter. A fruitful reading must be sensitive to the dramatic shape of the trial as a whole, to the literary subtexts implicated in its moments

vii

of reversal and denouement, and to the range of philosophical and pedagogical possibilities inherent in a sequence of writings in dialogue form. At the same time, the full significance of the philosophic trial emerges only out of a detailed engagement with the relevant texts. But because the Platonic drama studied here encompasses a number of dialogues, including a few that are quite long, important dimensions of some of them must inevitably be ignored. Where compromise has proved necessary, I have attempted to focus on those portions of the text that are most germane to our understanding of the distinct conceptions of philosophy embodied in the characters of Socrates and the Eleatic Stranger.

Scholarly attempts to deal with more than a few Platonic dialogues at one time are uncommon. So, too, are readings that take as their object a dramatic series of dialogues. This book is therefore unusual in its scope and principle of organization. It is not, however, unprecedented. Joseph Cropsey's *Plato's World: Man's Place in the Cosmos* paved the way for the present study by treating as a philosophical whole the dramatic sequence *Theaetetus* through *Phaedo*. It will therefore be helpful briefly to compare my book with Cropsey's insightful and imaginative interpretation.

Plato's World is a short study of seven dialogues that makes use of no secondary literature. The present book is a much longer and more detailed study of five dialogues that attempts to benefit from the best currently available scholarship. Cropsey also ignores the *Cratylus*. Most important, *Plato's World* does not concern the philosophic trial as such, but focuses instead on the cosmology that emerges in the dialogues that take place during the last days of Socrates. While this approach identifies themes of fundamental importance for our understanding of Plato, it also tends to suppress the difference between Socrates and the Eleatic Stranger and so to understate the conflict between philosophy and the political community. As a result, Cropsey paints what I consider to be an insufficiently complex and excessively pious picture of Socrates.

Plato's World has nonetheless planted certain seeds that I have attempted to cultivate in my own reading. Particularly valuable are Cropsey's suggestions that Socrates is distinguished by his exemplary care for human beings, that philosophy is a commingling of incommensurables, and that Plato wishes to correct the Socratic notion that virtue is without parts.[1] Taken together, these ideas point toward a paradox at the heart of philosophy and therefore of virtue in the highest sense, a paradox that is communicated dramatically through the splitting or self-opposition of philosophy that is played out in the rivalry between the characters of Socrates and the Stranger.

Philosophy as it emerges in the philosophic trial of Socrates is inescapably political. It is preeminently concerned with finding the middle ground between extremes, or weaving together the disparate elements of human life—including thought and action, speech and deed, philosophical reflection and political obligation, the highest aspirations of the soul and the most pressing needs of the body—into a whole. These are the terms in which we are given to understand Socrates' care for souls as displayed in the *Theaetetus, Euthyphro,* and *Cratylus.* Socrates' dramatic example of philosophizing in these dialogues provides the backdrop against which we are able to appreciate the fundamental agreement with him that the Stranger consistently evinces, despite initial appearances, in the *Sophist* and the *Statesman.* Like Socrates, the Stranger dwells upon the relationship between philosophy and politics. Indeed, his insistence upon the political responsibilities of the philosopher furnishes the grounds for his fundamental criticism of Socrates. In the end, the Stranger turns against Socrates the characteristically Socratic weapon of internal critique. He makes it clear that the uncompromising pursuit of the knowledge that makes possible the best human life conflicts with the task of weaving together human beings into a political community. In its zealous pursuit of human excellence, Socratic philosophizing undermines the exemplary unity of philosophy and citizenship at which it aims. This is not to say that the Stranger's prudential alternative of philosophical self-suppression is superior to Socrates' path of life, for the Stranger himself teaches that the *phronêsis* or wise insight about human life that Socrates pursues is essential to statesmanship as well. Philosophy that draws back from the pursuit of *phronêsis* is therefore in its own way also at odds with the political community as well as with itself. It is in the light of this profound paradox that we must attempt to understand Plato's own distinctive manner of philosophizing.

This book first took form as a dissertation at the Pennsylvania State University. I owe much to my teacher Stanley Rosen, whose thinking never ceases to inspire me. I wish to acknowledge the long-standing encouragement of Ronna Burger, Michael Davis, Charles Griswold, Mitchell Miller, Carl Page, Paul Rahe, and David Roochnik, and to extend special thanks to Drew Hyland, who read a draft of the manuscript and provided valuable criticism. I would also like to thank the Earhart Foundation for a fellowship research grant that allowed me to pursue work on the manuscript in the spring semester of 1994. The University of Tulsa kindly provided me with summer research support in 1989, 1990, 1992, and 1993 and a sabbatic leave in the spring of 1996. Thanks, too, to the colleagues and students at the University of Tulsa who read Plato with me on Sunday evenings in the spring of 1996, and to Abraham Howland, who produced the figures. My greatest debt of gratitude is owed to Henry V. Hayes, who spent many hours preparing the index. His unstinting support is one of the few certainties of my life. Last but not least, Alicia Mosier, a student of uncommon gifts, provided invaluable assistance in the final stages of production. The book could not have met its production deadline without her extraordinary dedication.

My acquaintance with the notion of a philosophic trial of Socrates goes back to an honors seminar conducted by David R. Lachterman at Swarthmore College almost twenty years ago. It was David who taught me the meaning of philosophical friendship. I continue profoundly to feel both his presence and his absence, and it is to his blessed memory that I dedicate this book.

Introduction

Socrates' Philosophic Trial

Although Socrates did his very best to gain knowledge of human nature
and to know himself . . . he nevertheless admitted that the reason he was
disinclined to ponder the nature of such creatures as Pegasus and the Gor-
gons was that he still was not quite clear about himself, whether he (a
connoisseur of human nature) was a more curious monster than Typhon or
a friendlier and simpler being, by nature sharing something divine (see
Phaedrus, 229e). This seems to be a paradox. But one must not think ill of
the paradox, for the paradox is the passion of thought, and the thinker
without the paradox is like the lover without passion: a mediocre fellow.

Søren Kierkegaard, Philosophical Fragments

There is a passage near the end of Plato's *Phaedo* in which Crito, who
has taken it upon himself to look after Socrates' final affairs, raises the
question of how they are to bury his dear friend. "However you wish,"
Socrates responds, "if indeed you can catch me and I do not flee away
from you" (115c4-5). It is an arresting moment for the reflective reader.
The last bath awaits, the jailer will soon be bringing in the hemlock, yet
Socrates plays. One can only marvel at the lightness of his being. Won-
derful, too, is the way in which his gentle irony invites us to reconsider
our long-standing acquaintance with him—an acquaintance that filters
through a sediment of scholarly editions, translations, and commentaries,
each in some measure reflecting the intellectual preoccupations of its
own epoch. Have we friends of Socrates *ever* held him in our grasp? Is
he not always in flight in the pages of Plato? And as we watch him rise to

bathe, does it not occur to us that we have always already been asking "Who is Socrates?"

*   *   *

The dialogues *Theaetetus, Euthyphro, Cratylus, Sophist, Statesman, Apology, Crito,* and *Phaedo* stand together in dramatic time, in the order in which they have been named, as memorials of Socrates' last days.[1] These eight dialogues—hereafter, the "octology"—constitute the largest single dramatic sequence of writings in the Platonic corpus. In eight out of the thirty-five dialogues listed in the traditional canon of Thrasyllus, Plato concentrates upon the end of Socrates' life. This remarkable fact invites us to ask whether the dialogues of the octology are also linked internally by common philosophical themes and issues. I believe that they are, and that the temporal contiguity of these dialogues is merely the surface of a deeper dramatic and thematic integrity.

This book explores a Platonic drama that I have chosen to call the philosophic trial of Socrates.[2] In Plato's hands, the end of Socrates' life furnishes the occasion for an extended philosophical exploration of the question "Who, or what, is Socrates?" Socrates implicitly asks this question at the beginning of the octology when he says that he will converse with Theaetetus "in order that I may examine myself as to what sort of face I possess" (*Theaetetus* 144d8-9). And Plato indicates in various other ways that the issue of Socrates' identity constitutes the unspoken center of all of the dialogues of the octology. In the first of these, Socrates tells Theaetetus that he would "in no way" converse otherwise than he does, "for I am who I am" (*ôn ge hos eimi, Theaetetus* 197a1); in the last two, he indicates that being who he is is the factor that bears ultimate responsibility for his presence in prison (*Crito* 46b, 49d ff.; *Phaedo* 98c-99a).

In the octology the problem of Socrates' identity is posed and investigated within the dramatic framework of a trial. While this framework plays a major role in the *Euthyphro* and *Apology*, the trial motif is not limited to these dialogues. The *Theaetetus*, as Socrates makes clear at the conclusion of the dialogue (210d), relates a conversation that takes place on the day Socrates goes to the Portico of the King Archon for the preliminary proceedings leading up to his trial. Although in the *Euthyphro* we encounter Socrates immediately prior to his appearance before the King Archon, Plato does not allow us to see any of the judicial proceedings that take place inside the Portico, including Meletus's indictment and Socrates' reply. Nor does he present us with the speeches of Socrates' accusers at his public trial. But he does provide separate dialogues showing Socrates' defense speech (*Apology*), Socrates in prison (*Crito*), and Socrates' execution (*Phaedo*). The *Cratylus*, which occurs immediately after the *Euthyphro*, and the *Sophist* and *Statesman*, which occur on the following day, occupy that place in the story of Socrates' last days left vacant by the omitted proceedings connected with Meletus's indictment and the prosecution phase of the public trial. While the *Theaetetus* and *Euthyphro* are explicitly linked with Socrates' public trial, there is thus also an implicit connection between the *Cratylus*, *Sophist*, and *Statesman* and the public indictment and prosecution of Socrates.[3]

The latter connection has recently been illuminated by the observation that Socrates faces in the *Sophist* and *Statesman* an amplified, philosophical version of the public charges against which he attempts to defend himself in the *Apology*. The Eleatic Stranger most obviously assumes the role of a philosophical plaintiff when in the *Sophist* he implicitly identifies Socrates as a practitioner of a certain kind of sophistry. It seems clear that the Stranger intends to charge Socrates with being not only a bad citizen—the upshot of Meletus's public indictment in the *Apology*—but also a sham philosopher. For the Stranger, both of these accusations are implied in the single designation "sophist."[4]

Insofar as disputes in a court of law center on determining "who is the wrongdoer, and doing what and when [he did wrong]" (*Euthyphro* 8d6), the dramatic device of a trial is well suited to the investigation of the focal problem of Socrates' identity. But Socrates is already on trial in the *Apology*. What accounts for the existence of an additional, philosophical trial? As we shall see, the circumstances of the public trial do not allow for a fair hearing of his case. It therefore becomes necessary to examine the philosophical and political issues raised in the *Apology* within the context of another, extended inquiry, as in a court of appeal. The appeal analogy is of course limited: Socrates' philosophic trial has no formal legal status, and in any case *precedes* his public trial. It is not clear why Plato chose this order of events. Perhaps he did so with the intention of underscoring the finality of the Athenian verdict, or simply because the kinds of encounters represented in the dialogues *Theaetetus* through *Statesman* could not have been reproduced within the confines of a prison cell. In any case, the philosophical trial promises to be much more illuminating for Plato's readers than its public counterpart.

This book begins with a brief examination of the *Apology* and then turns to an exploration of the five dialogues in which the philosophic trial unfolds. The drama studied here falls neatly into two parts, each of which takes place on one of two successive days. For while the Eleatic Stranger's "prosecution" of Socrates occurs in the *Sophist* and *Statesman*, Socrates mounts an anticipatory "defense" that assumes the form of a reflective self-exhibition and that is developed on the preceding day over the course of the *Theaetetus*, *Euthyphro*, and *Cratylus*. The two parts of the philosophic trial dramatically match each other in another way as well: while the first part showcases Socrates' philosophical activity, the second part, in which Socrates is largely silent, constitutes the philosophical self-exhibition of the Stranger.

The order of the parts of the philosophic trial—first the defense, then the prosecution—is unexpected, but not illogical. Two considerations are especially relevant here. First, Plato depicts Socrates in the octology as the possessor of prophetic powers. In the *Cratylus*, Socrates predicts that on the following day (the day on which the *Sophist* will take place) he and his companions will discover a "priest or sophist" who is "clever in purifying" his "daimonic wisdom"—wisdom that he attributes to his earlier conversation with Euthyphro (396d4-397a1). In the *Sophist*, Socrates guesses that the Stranger is an elenchtic god who has come "intending to look over and refute us who are poor in speeches" (216b4-6). Both of these passages anticipate the Stranger's purifying art of diaeresis or division, which attempts to separate the dross of sophistry—including Socrates' "noble" version of the same (*Sophist* 226b-231b)—from philosophy.[5] Second, one need not suppose that Socrates is literally prophetic in order to accept the suggestion that the imminence of his public trial would in any case cause him to concentrate upon the question of how his own activity differs from sophistry. Socrates' self-exploration in the dialogues just prior to the *Sophist* follows naturally and inevitably from his philosophical self-consciousness.

There are independent internal indications that the dialogues explored in the following pages form a distinct group.[6] But what makes this drama *the* philosophic trial of Socrates? The question is pertinent because there are other dialogues in which Socrates may be said to stand trail: the *Cleitophon* and Alcibiades' speech in the *Symposium* spring readily to mind, as do the "indictments" of Socrates by Thrasymachus in the *Republic* and Callicles in the *Gorgias*. Furthermore, the problem of Socrates' identity is arguably at issue in every dialogue in which he takes part.[7] Of the various trials of Socrates in the Platonic corpus, however, the one studied here stands alone in its unusual length and complexity and its unique dramatic and thematic connections with his public trial. Most important, only here is Socrates put on trial by another philosopher.

It would in my opinion be difficult to overemphasize the dramatic character of the philosophic trial. For what is on display in the encounter between Socrates and the Stranger is not ultimately reducible to a set of doctrines or philosophical positions. Rather, these two men come before us as distinct exemplars of a certain orientation of the soul. In the philosophic trial each in his own way bears witness to the depth and power, the sanctity and mystery, of a philosophical way of life. The deepest reason for the existence of the philosophic trial must therefore be sought within Plato's decision to present us with this extraordinary dramatic doubling of philosophy.

Themes and Provocations of the Philosophic Trial

The philosophic trial brings together a group of issues that are raised by Socrates' twofold calling as a philosopher and a citizen, and that thoughtful human beings must inevitably confront when they examine the concrete fabric of their lives. All of these issues are in some way connected with the essential doubleness of human existence as reflected in the tension between autonomy and political obligation, tradition and philosophical discovery, perfecting one's soul and protecting one's body, the irreducible particularity of existence and the universality of human excellence. Hence for each of us the question "Who is Socrates?" ultimately entails the further question "What does it mean to be human?" Like all Platonic dramas, the philosophic trial of Socrates presents us with a rich opportunity for self-examination.

It will be useful to have in prospect some of the main dramatic themes and subtexts that structure the action of Socrates' philosophic trial. The following list is general and introductory; it is not meant to be exhaustive, but merely to orient the reader toward an unusually complex philosophical drama. Additional themes and motifs will emerge when we take up the *Theaetetus*'s prologue in chapter 2.

In subsequent chapters we shall explore:

The encounter between philosophy and the political community. While this encounter is displayed most vividly in the *Apology*, the politically problematic character of Socratic philosophizing is on view from the very beginning of the philosophic trial. In the prologue of the *Theaetetus*, Euclides indicates that he repeatedly visited Socrates during the period between his preliminary hearing and his execution in order to produce an accurate record of Socrates' earlier conversation with Theaetetus. While the slave reads Euclides' transcription of the latter conversation as he and Terpsion rest, Theaetetus, who has been wounded in battle and is sick with dysentery, is being carried to his home in Athens. The *Theaetetus*'s prologue thereby implicitly contrasts the dying patriot Theaetetus, an avowedly noble and good Athenian citizen and a brilliant mathematician, with Socrates, a convicted criminal who seems to possess no positive knowledge. Coupled with the motif of homecoming that runs throughout the philosophic trial, this contrast raises a number of questions. Could the Socratic philosopher ever be at home in the *polis*? What is the home-place or proper domain of the philosopher, both in itself and with respect to the political community? Most important, is Socrates really a philoso-

pher at all—or is he a sophist, meaning both a bad citizen and a bad theoretician?

The intertwining of resemblance and antagonism. Socrates' nature
comes to light in the philosophic trial within a complex play of implicit
and explicit antagonisms. The various antagonists, in turn, are bound together by multiple strands of resemblance. In the *Theaetetus* we learn
that while Socrates looks like Theaetetus, he has the same name as the
lad's companion, a young mathematician who will later serve as the
Stranger's interlocutor in the *Statesman*. Socrates' criticisms of the poeticoreligious tradition in the *Euthyphro* in some ways connect him with
Euthyphro, who indicts his own father, and in other ways with Meletus,
who claims to purify the city of corrupting elements. The Stranger's
philosophical parricide in the *Sophist* against *his* intellectual father, Parmenides (241d), links him with Socrates and Euthyphro as well. In the
Cratylus Socrates uses the names "sophist" and "philosopher" indis-
criminately (403e-404a). On the following day an anonymous visitor (the
Stranger) concerns himself with the question of which of the latter names
apply to Socrates; the issue of whether the Stranger is competent to answer this question is obviously inseparable from the problem of his own
identity. Finally, Socrates, Meletus, and the Stranger all practice arts of
purification, for the Stranger's identification of Socrates' cathartic art in
the *Sophist* (231e) is itself an instance of *katharsis*, or the separation of
the better from the worse—ostensibly, in this case, of a sophist (Socrates) from a philosopher (the Stranger). More generally, Theodorus,
"Protagoras" (as given voice by Socrates in the *Theaetetus*), Meletus,
Euthyphro, the Stranger, and the democratic citizenry of Athens all claim
to be authoritative measures of significant dimensions of human experience, such as the care of souls, the fruitfulness and truth of speeches, and
the nature of piety.

The ambiguity of identities. The identity of the Stranger is at issue
from the moment of his appearance in the *Sophist*. This problem is amplified by the ambiguity of his philosophical procedure. Like the sophist,
the Stranger's appearance is multifarious and unstable. As we shall see,
his explicit pronouncements concerning the method of bifurcatory division regularly conflict with his actual employment of this method. Still
more striking is his suspension of this quasi-arithmetical method in the
Statesman in favor of a distinctly Socratic myth (268e ff.) and his subsequent subordination of technical knowledge to *phronêsis* or wise
judgment.

The identity of Socrates is no less mysterious than that of the Stranger,
for he too seems to defy categorization. In the *Theaetetus* Socrates identifies himself as a patriot (143d), yet he is soon to be executed by his home
city. At his public trial he insists upon his piety, but then recounts his at-

tempts to refute the Delphic oracle. Socrates proclaims his Delphic or Apollonian moderation (*Apology* 23a-b) and maintains that he cares for the souls of others, but the "terrible *erôs*" for naked dialectical exercise to which he admits in the *Theaetetus* (169c1) seems both extreme and self-serving. And while Socrates asserts in the *Apology* that he is concerned above all with virtue (29d-30b), in the *Theaetetus* he speaks of his philosophic *erôs* as a disease and accepts Theodorus' comparison of him with certain savage and monstrous criminals (169a-b). In the *Phaedo* Socrates compares himself with the swans who serve Apollo (84e-85b), but in the *Apology* he associates himself with the gadfly, a species of pestilence (30e). Apollo, we recall from Sophocles' *Oedipus*, has the power to inflict diseases as well as to cure them. Is Socrates a model of reverent shame or hybris, moderate humility or extremism, selfishness or philanthropy, healthy virtue or criminal sickness? Is he a heaven-sent blessing for the Athenians or a divine plague?

Comic and mythological subtexts of the philosophic trial. Numerous allusions to Aristophanes' *Clouds* suggest that versions of, and responses to, Aristophanes' criticisms of Socrates emerge over the course of the philosophic trial. The ambiguity of identities and the play of philosophical antagonisms must furthermore be connected with a Homeric subtext that is highlighted in three main passages. First, the Odyssean theme of *nostos,* or homecoming, is elaborately introduced in the prologue of the *Theaetetus* and echoed in subsequent dialogues. Second, Socrates alludes to the *Odyssey* in speculating about the nature of the Stranger at the beginning of the *Sophist* (216a-b). Finally, the kinship test that Socrates proposes at the outset of the *Statesman* (257d-258a) hearkens back to the mutual kinship test of Odysseus and Penelope in Book 23 of the *Odyssey* as well as to Odysseus's reunion with his father Laertes in Book 24. The polytropic or shifting and shifty character of Odysseus, who was frequently associated with sophistry in the post-Homeric poetic tradition, seems to reflect Socrates' own polytropism, and, more generally, that of the human soul.

The dramatic enactment of philosophy. The Homeric allusions mentioned above suggest that the apparent philosophical antagonisms of the *Sophist* will give way to a demonstration of kinship in the *Statesman*. What is more, there are indications of kinship in the *Sophist* itself. The Stranger maintains that the true dialectician philosophizes "purely and justly" (*Sophist* 253e4-6), and he initially implies that Socrates is ignorant, lacks measure, and may be wild and vicious (*Sophist* 228d, 231a). Yet in tracking the sophist the Stranger repeatedly violates the rules of his own philosophical method, and does so, moreover, in a distinctly Socratic spirit. He also finds it necessary to converse impurely about "that which is not," and worries that such impure speech might look like an act of philosophical parricide against Parmenides (*Sophist* 238e, 241d). In the *Statesman*, the Stranger abruptly begins anew by telling the myth of the reversed cosmos (268e-274e) when it becomes clear that his method of bifurcatory division cannot adequately reveal either the nature of the statesman or that of the human soul. And in its prophetic attempt to understand human life in terms of its place within the cosmos as a whole, the Stranger's myth bears a strong resemblance to other, Socratic myths, such as the palinode of the *Phaedrus* (246a-257a), the myth of Er in the *Republic* (614b-621b), and the topological myth of the *Phaedo* (107d-115a).

The dramatic enactment of identities in Socrates' philosophic trial also gives us a clue as to the whereabouts of the "missing" dialogue *Philosopher*, a text that would seem to have been promised by the Stranger's otherwise fairly full attempt to answer Socrates' threefold question about the sophist, statesman, and philosopher (*Sophist* 217a). On one level, the absence of the Philosopher may indirectly underscore the Stranger's ultimate insistence that the well-being of the political community must take precedence over the unconstrained pursuit of wisdom. But this is not all. For in his dialogues Plato shows that which cannot simply be said, and one thing that cannot simply be said is the nature of philosophy itself. Since the identities of Socrates and the Stranger come to light in terms of their relationship to each other and against the backdrop of the multiple resemblances and antagonisms that structure the philosophic trial, I suggest that we are meant to find the expected clarification of the nature of the philosopher in the drama of the trial itself.[8] The Stranger's style of discourse is no less crucial to this clarification than is the content of his divisions, for the peculiar nature of the soul that makes it resistant to capture by techniques of philosophical analysis nonetheless suits it to being displayed within the medium of philosophical drama. Like the philosopher, the sophist and the statesman cannot be pinned down in a definitive definition; as we shall see, however, a crucial dimension of the Stranger's discourse consists in his mimetic enactments of sophistry and statesmanship. And these enactments will turn out to be essential to Plato's illumination not only of the nature of philosophy, but also of the way in which speech functions as an image of being.

Aims and Methods of the Inquiry

Plato's writings are extraordinarily rich tapestries, and to explore six separate dialogues in a single book seems a daunting task. What are the legitimate aspirations of the present study? More generally, what should one hope to accomplish in writing about the dialogues?

It turns out that one cannot address the latter question without becoming entangled in the very web of issues that binds together the philosophic trial. The nature of reading and writing, the possibility of self-knowledge, the peculiar being of the soul, and the presence of ambiguity and paradox in human life are concerns that inevitably arise for the writer of a book on Plato no less than the reader of the texts of the philosophic trial.

In my view, the most important reason to write about the dialogues is to enhance reading—one's own reading of Plato as well as those of others. The touchstone of an interpretation is therefore the extent to which it allows one to return to the dialogues with germane insights and fresh questions. Be that as it may, the book that follows is necessarily a written demonstration of a certain kind of reading. As such, it reflects a particular understanding of the nature and aims of Platonic writing and the ways or habits of reading that may best allow the Platonic texts to disclose their significance.

In certain crucial respects, the habits of reading called for by the dialogues are literary ones, such as would be appropriate to the narrative of the Hebrew Bible or the plays of Euripides or Shakespeare. This is by no means to deny that the philosophical arguments of the dialogues make interpretative demands upon the reader that are quite distinct from those found in either of the two sorts of texts just mentioned. But in Plato, philosophical argumentation is embedded in a rich literary and dramatic context. For this reason, I have found that the most provocative and insightful interpretations of the dialogues are those that are attuned to the complex interplay between their arguments, their narrative structure, and the three mimetic modes or devices described as follows by Jacob Klein: "ethological mimes, that is imitations of actions in which the speakers reveal themselves both in character and in thought"; "doxological mimes, in which the falsity or rightness of an opinion is not only argued in words but also manifested by the character, the behavior, and the actions of the speakers themselves"; and "mythological mimes . . . [in which] the drama of the dialogue presents, interprets, or replaces a myth."[9] Beyond this, it is a basic interpretative assumption of the present study that Socrates' nature comes to light in the dialogues of the philosophic trial only against the backdrop of the other characters with whom he is dramatically juxtaposed. As Socrates makes clear in the *Apology*, one cannot appreciate the virtues of the philosophic life without exploring the alternatives. "Who is Socrates?" invites the further question "Who are his rivals?"; as we shall see, Plato furnishes us with the resources to address both of these questions. Plato's literary economy allows us to grasp the character of Socrates and of his various interlocutors by attending not only to what they say but also to how they say it, and in particular to the revealing consistencies of tone and emphasis in their speeches. To adapt Heraclitus's famous dictum, one could say that in the Platonic dialogues, as in all great dramatic literature, *logos* (speech) is *êthos* (character) for a human being.[10]

While a Platonic dialogue in some respects resembles a living being (*Phaedrus* 264c), it nonetheless does not display organic harmony on its surface. When we attend to the interrelationships between the mimetic or dramatic modes identified above and the levels of argument and narrative, we typically discover a multitude of tensions and contradictions. Such tensions—which are visible to us as readers of Plato's texts but rarely (one supposes) to the dramatic characters in the dialogues—are what I mean by Platonic irony, and it is Plato's irony that poses for the reader some of the most challenging invitations to philosophical reflection. The philosophical significance of that which is explicitly stated on the level of argument is always enriched by following the interpretative paths that are opened up by Platonic irony. Indeed, it has been well observed that Plato's use of irony is of a piece with his deployment of metaphoric images and the various modes of dramatic mimesis: all of these devices aim to awaken the kind of inquisitive, interpretative reflection that alone can transform bare arguments into ways of active knowing.[11]

The problem of the nature and aims of Platonic writing is implicitly raised at the very beginning of the first dialogue of Socrates' philosophic trial. The *Theaetetus* warns us about the abstract and hence deceptively incomplete character of the written word by pointedly calling attention to the distance between itself as a text and the primary phenomena about which it is written: the dialogue is Plato's writing of a slave's reading of Euclides' transcription of his remembrance of Socrates' narration of his conversation with Theaetetus. As we shall see, the problem of the status of writing is directly relevant to the *Theaetetus*'s guiding question about the nature of knowledge. Most generally, the layered narrative structure of the *Theaetetus* underscores the difference between speeches and beings and thereby anticipates one of the central theoretical concerns of the philosophic trial, for it is the ontological and epistemological gap separating *logos* from beings that makes possible both sophistry and philosophy. Plato's texts, on the other hand, are nonetheless the only route of access we have to the particular beings they bespeak, including the soul of Socrates. They are in this sense a necessary starting point of inquiry for us, but they are not the same as the beginnings, the original and originary beings (*archai*), toward which learning aspires. Here we find something strange, for to open up Plato's writings with an eye toward the disclosure of beings is to discover that in another sense these texts are far from abstract, and that multiple dimensions of significance that are fully available only in writing—including the complexities of wordplay, the relationships between narrative, argument, and dramatic structures, and the employment of mythical or poetic subtexts—endow the dialogues with a richness of meaning that is superabundant in comparison with the spoken discourse of actual conversations. Thus we readers—we *eavesdroppers*—are in a position to learn more from Socrates' conversation with Theaetetus (for example) than Theaetetus ever could, just because we alone can carefully study the text in which this conversation is inscribed.[12]

Interpretative Orthodoxy

These preliminary observations about Plato's writings suggest that readers must submit themselves warily to the text. How warily? The question merits careful consideration, for those who attempt to protect themselves against the distractions of the Platonic texts by simply steering clear of their manifold literary intricacies get nowhere with Plato (although they may accomplish much else that is of interest in its own right). The most common form of this approach is represented by orthodox Plato scholars, a group that includes the majority of Plato scholars writing in English. As I am using the term here, "orthodox" scholars endorse the following theses: (1) The dialogues are primarily intended to advance philosophical theories; (2) The dialogues reflect different stages in Plato's thought; (3) It is possible to distinguish Plato's latest dialogues from the rest, and possibly also his middle dialogues from his earliest works; and (4) The latter chronological distinctions provide an essential interpretative key to the dialogues.[13] The interpretative beginnings of orthodox Plato scholarship thus include not only the Platonic writings themselves, but also the ostensible results of chronological investigation. These "results," together with the assumptions that generate them, determine in advance which sorts of interrelationships between the dialogues are plausible and which implausible, as well as which features of the text can safely be ignored and which must be attended to.

It is important to observe that the commitments of orthodox Plato scholarship militate against the kind of reading pursued in the following chapters. In the first place, the traditional consensus is that the dialogues *Theaetetus, Euthyphro, Cratylus, Sophist, Statesman,* and *Apology* were written at different times, and represent pretty nearly the entire span of Plato's philosophical career.[14] For this reason, it might be objected that our guiding question about Socratic philosophizing is illegitimate, on the ground that changes in Plato's thought preclude the possibility that throughout these six dialogues Socrates exemplifies a unitary conception of the nature and aims of philosophy.[15] Second, my claim that the *Sophist* and *Statesman* must be understood in terms of the overarching dramatic structure of Socrates' philosophic trial may seem extravagant in light of the putative absence of philosophic drama in Plato's "later" dialogues—dialogues that seem didactic and systematic in tone and style, not open-ended and aporetic like Plato's "early," "Socratic" writings.[16]

In response to both of these objections, I would observe that the explicit dramatic arrangement of the philosophic trial argues against any distinction between the Socrates of the *Apology* and the *Euthyphro* and the Socrates of the *Theaetetus*, *Sophist*, and *Statesman*, because in *dramatic* time the intervals between the "earlier" and "later" of these dialogues consist of a few days, a day, or, in the case of the transition from the *Theaetetus* to the *Euthyphro*, perhaps only minutes. It is clear that over the years that he was composing the dialogues of the philosophic trial, Plato was guided by a sense of their dramatic unity. No matter when Plato wrote these dialogues, he evidently wanted his readers to reflect upon the connections—as well as the discontinuities—between them. Insofar as these concinnities and inconcinnities are visible at all, they may be observed in these dialogues only after they have been grouped together in accordance with their shared dramatic and thematic characteristics.[17] Scholars who stand by the interpretative significance of chronological distinctions must therefore assume the burden of explaining why hypotheses about the actual dates or relative order of the dialogues' composition, or about the development of Plato's thought insofar as this is supposedly reflected in general changes in style and emphasis, are relevant to the study of these dialogues.

I have attempted to establish elsewhere that the project of determining the chronology of the dialogues is, in general, and without regard to its particular variants, methodologically and philologically unsound.[18] While my article on chronology is especially concerned with the ancient evidence relevant to the dating of the dialogues, the unfounded character of stylometric analysis, and the paradoxes implicit in the employment of chronological "results" as a key to Plato's development, I also argue that chronological speculation tends to interpose between reader and text a thick layer of interpretative apparatus that serves to obscure subtly drawn features of the Platonic writings. Coming to the dialogues with the canonical works of the History of Western Philosophy in one hand and the chronological studies of philologists in the other, orthodox Plato scholars expect to find, and *can* expect *only* to find, something already familiar to them: Platonism, or a more or less systematic set of developing philosophical doctrines of the sort that philosophers have for more than two millenia been accustomed to inscribe in treatises. But to begin reading the dialogues by granting in advance the interpretative authority of some other, non-Platonic texts is to ignore Plato's warnings about the decep-

tive incompleteness of writing. Seen in this light, the interpretative caution of orthodox Plato scholars—who tend, especially where the "later"
Plato is concerned, to discount the significance of drama, ironic wordplay, and much else that lies beyond the argument proper—is
indistinguishable from rashness. Such scholars commit the characteristic
error of Socrates' interlocutors, who allow what they think they know to
obscure the things of which they are ignorant. Their modes of reading
look like nothing so much as "an outsider's attempt to short-circuit a required initiation." [19]

Derrida and the Deconstructionists

There is to my mind a Scylla that stands opposed to the Charybdis of interpretative orthodoxy. It is another pitfall, to be sure, but one closer to
which my own reading ventures—and *must* venture, if it is to entrust itself to the Platonic text at all. I refer to deconstructionist approaches to
the dialogues, which are worth exploring in some detail precisely insofar
as they highlight the challenge of sophistry that is posed so forcefully in
Socrates' philosophic trial. Let me first explain why I associate deconstructionism with a monster—indeed, with one of the many monsters
who stood in the way of Odysseus's attempt to "win his soul and the
homecoming of his companions" (*Odyssey* 1.5). Plato's dialogues possess certain seemingly sophistical charms, but they are not sophistical
insofar as they call attention to the difference between themselves as
writings and the *archai* that they are meant to evoke. Those who are so
seduced by the dialogues' textual richness that they forget about this difference take the written words themselves to be the *archai*. Plato puts
such readers on stage in the figure of Phaedrus, who comes into the presence of Socrates while clutching the inscribed speech of Lysias beneath
his cloak. The most committed contemporary advocates of the Phaedran
approach to reading and writing rule out the achievement of Socratic
self-knowledge because they embrace the thesis that there is no essential
difference between speaking and writing. The speaker, they argue, is present in discourse only insofar as he is dispersed into a text that is not
even of his own making—only insofar as he is *not* present as the source
and origin of his *logos*, that is, as a *speaker*. It follows that the self we
seek to understand through dialogue is always absent, or that there is in
effect no such self to be known—no Socrates, for example, standing beneath or behind his speeches like a father. Contrary to what Socrates says
in the *Phaedrus* (275d-e), the spoken word is no less an orphan than its
written brother. Socrates' attempt to win his own soul through the
achievement of self-knowledge is doomed to fail. His philosophic journey is Quixotic, not Odyssean.[20]

I believe that these conclusions depend upon a flawed methodology and a number of questionable assumptions about the nature of Plato's philosophic enterprise—assumptions that are surprisingly shared by orthodox Plato scholars. Unlike the latter scholars, however, the deconstructionists are highly sensitive to the literary nuances and the implicit tensions and ambiguities of Plato's texts. This is their special strength. Given their rejection of the possibility of philosophy, however, their delight in paradox reflects professorial cleverness, and so should not be confused with the philosophical *erôs* that characterizes Socratic thinking.[21] Deconstructionist interpretations nevertheless get close to the pulse of the dialogues under consideration here, for the philosophic trial of Socrates dwells on the problem of the relationship between what is present and what is absent. In the *Statesman*, the Stranger links this problem with writing, and thus reiterates a connection that is initially established by the narrative structure of the *Theaetetus*. His remark about the doctor or trainer who writes out prescriptions before he goes abroad (295b-c) evokes the absent authorial figure of Plato and anticipates the impending departure (or, viewed within the narrative frame of the *Theaetetus*, reminds us of the death long ago) of Socrates, who leaves behind either just some versified fables of Aesop or, depending on how one construes a comment of Plato's in the *Second Letter*, the whole Platonic corpus.[22] The peculiar resonance of the Stranger's words within the larger context of the philosophic trial suffices to indicate that Plato recognizes as a fundamental philosophical problem the recovery of the self from its appearances in speech (or writing) and deed.

Plato's general concern with the recovery of the self is intertwined with the more specific problem of uncovering the nature and establishing the identity of Socrates. Socrates also leaves behind another text: Meletus's *graphê asebeias*, his indictment for (literally, "writing of") impiety. As one commentator has noted, "Plato pits his own *graphê* against the *graphê* entered by Meletus."[23] Yet he surely does so as a spur to inquiry into the justice of Meletus's indictment, and not as an implicit admission that nothing stands behind or beyond the text. Anyone taking up this inquiry must ask, on the one hand, questions about what constitutes piety, corruption, and the like, and, on the other, questions about the nature of Socrates. Plato's writing is pitted against that of Meletus just insofar as the dialogues raise and pursue precisely the sorts of questions that might serve as springboards for evaluating Meletus's indictment.

Most important, the philosophic trial fuses the problem of the nature of Socrates with the problem of the identity and integrity of the self or the individual human soul. Throughout the philosophic trial, Socrates is surrounded by speakers, both present and imagined, whose own theoretical commitments in certain respects mirror deconstructionism in that they entail, in different ways and to different degrees, the moral and ontological dissolution and dispersal of the soul. As we shall see, this characterization applies, among others, to Euclides, the founder of the Megarian philosophical school; to Protagoras and the Heracliteans, who are encountered in the *Cratylus* as well as the *Theaetetus*; to the mathematician Theodorus; to Euthyphro and Meletus; and to the Stranger in his initial guise as a practitioner of the universal, technical method of division. Socrates, in turn, is mimetically depicted in relation to these implicit and explicit antagonists as someone who takes his stand upon the ontological and moral integrity of the soul. Socrates emerges from this play of philosophical antagonisms as one who converses and inquires in a way that alone promises to generate, both in speech and in the form of a life of learning, what it is to be human.

The phrase "philosophic trial of Socrates," like the title *Apology of Socrates*, is grammatically ambiguous. Is Socrates the object of indictment, or the subject—the one who is tried, or the one who tries? I have suggested that Socrates and his antagonists are equally implicated in a drama of indictment and counterindictment, accusation and defense. One might even say—anachronistically, but perhaps not too misleadingly— that in the philosophic trial deconstructionism is in the docket right along with Socrates. To take this point seriously one must be willing to accept, at least provisionally, the presuppositions of Platonic writing and of the Socratic quest for self-knowledge. Plato's deconstructionist readers, however, are unwilling to do just this much. The problem is nicely summarized by Charles Griswold in a comment on Jacques Derrida's essay "Plato's Pharmacy," the most well-known and most influential example of the application of deconstructionism to Plato: "Derrida does not ask why Plato wrote *dialogues*."[24] He does not adequately contextualize the passages that he seeks to deconstruct, in large part because he refuses to grant, as a heuristic assumption, that each dialogue is a distinct whole fashioned in accordance with the compositional principle of logographic necessity that Socrates praises in the *Phaedrus* (264b-c). This refusal is connected with Derrida's insistence that neither the written nor the spoken word has a "father." Writing, he argues, has "a dynamics that constantly surprises the one who tries to manipulate it as master and as subject."[25] *Logos* cannot after all be made to say what one wants it to say. The erroneous notion that it *can* is in Derrida's view rooted in an illusory distinction between speaker and speech, signifier and signified, that springs from the play of *logos* itself. But it is Derrida, not Plato, who assumes that the latter distinction is illusory. Plato, Derrida admits, wants us to begin somewhere else—namely, from the presupposition that the study of the dialogues may lead to increased self-knowledge, and so that there *is* a self to be known apart from *logos*. Derrida's supposedly "Socratic," internal critique of Plato fails in its own terms just insofar as it refuses at the outset to occupy Plato's own ground, that is, as Griswold puts it, "to begin by taking seriously the text's claim to articulate the truth." Such a beginning, unlike Derrida's, maximizes one's opportunity to learn from the dialogues, and does so without prejudicing one's reading: "it may still turn out that the text is incoherent." [26]

Deconstructionism curiously mirrors the decisive deficiency of orthodox Plato scholarship: both of these ways of reading evaluate the Platonic writings in accordance with the commitments of extrinsic interpretative schemes. Perhaps most striking in this regard is the manner in which Derrida, like practitioners of the "recognized modes of commentary" from which he claims to slip away, confuses the texts of Plato with Platonism. "Plato's Pharmacy" and the deconstructionist studies of the dialogues that it has spawned perhaps demonstrate the autodeconstruction of the latter, but certainly not of the former. It will nonetheless be worthwhile to try to clarify the nature of this particular confusion, especially because it is shared by orthodox Plato scholars. Such an attempt will also help to specify the paths of self-understanding that Plato opens up for us as we explore the distinction between Socratic philosophizing and sophistry that emerges over the course of the philosophic trial.

Derrida is guided by his perception of the dialogues as intricate, always unraveling tapestries that are connected with one another by a subtle network of filaments. In "Plato's Pharmacy," he traces one such filament, the notion of the *pharmakon* ("drug," "poison," "charm," "remedy," "dye"), as it weaves into and around the problem of the distinction between philosophy and sophistry. Derrida claims that Plato's text itself shows that the latter distinction is ultimately unsustainable, for the fundamental ambiguity of the *pharmakon*—which cannot be comprehended by the logic of opposition or "well computed binarism"—is nothing less than the ambiguity of Platonic writing. "Plato thinks of writing, and tries to comprehend it, to dominate it, on the basis of *opposition* as such." [27] But the resistance of writing to such domination spells the failure of Plato's attempt to inscribe the difference between philosophy and sophistry, a difference that is itself figured as opposition and is expressed in terms of externally opposed contrary values (good/evil, true/false, essence/appearance, and the like). The supposed stability of these oppositions, in turn, reflects the stability of the Platonic *eidos*, or form, the "most worthy object" of philosophic dialogue—"that which is identical to itself, always the same and therefore simple, incomposite (*asuntheton*), undecomposable, invariable," and which, as the *eidos* of the soul, stands at the terminus of the quest for self-knowledge. [28] But the *eidos* itself, the order of forms and Ideas, is nothing other than the result of Plato's attempt to "block" or "stop" the play of opposites within the medium of the *pharmakon*, "the movement and the play that links them among themselves, reverses them or makes one side cross over into the other (soul/body, good/evil, inside/outside, memory/forgetfulness, speech/writing, etc.)."[29] "The *eidos*, truth, law, the *epistêmê*, dialectics, philosophy"—all these are therefore just "antidotes," "other names for that *pharmakon* that must be opposed to the *pharmakon* of the Sophists and to the bewitching fear of death" as "a pharmaceutical force is opposed to another pharmaceutical force."[30]

If Derrida has correctly described the logic of Plato's defense of philosophy, his demonstration of the various ways in which "the parties and party lines [in the battle between philosophy and sophistry] . . . exchange their respective places, imitating the forms and borrowing the paths of the opponent" would seem to be decisive.[31] Neither Socrates' quest for self-knowledge nor the regulative ideal of logographic necessity would then survive Derrida's critique. In deconstructing the notion of simple externality Derrida singles out as "the matrix of all possible opposition" the opposition between inside and outside, and so between the body and the soul. And since the foundational distinction between inside and outside springs from writing, it cannot be used to explain the act of writing: "writing as a *pharmakon* cannot simply be assigned a site within what it situates, cannot be subsumed under concepts whose contours it draws."[32] Thus Derrida writes:

> Plato does not make a show of the chain of significations we are trying progressively to dig up. If there were any sense in asking such a question, which we don't believe, it would be impossible to say to what extent he manipulates it voluntarily or consciously, and at what point he is subject to constraints weighing upon his discourse from "language."

And he concludes: "In a word, we do not believe that there exists, in all rigor, a Platonic text, closed upon itself, complete with its inside and its outside."[33]

Derrida credits Plato, or Platonism—he makes no distinction between these two—with setting up "the whole of Western metaphysics in its conceptuality." In Plato's pharmacy begins "a whole story," "an entire history" that is "full of meaning." If Plato begins by "drawing the curtains over the dawning of the West," Derrida attempts to put an end to Western philosophy by exposing its impure origins.[34] Yet he seems to go wrong precisely insofar as he sees in Plato only what the history of post-Platonic philosophy has prepared him to find there. The Platonic drama explored in the following chapters suggests that Derrida's characterization of Plato is open to criticism on three related fronts.

First, Derrida seems to assume that the kind of self-knowledge Socrates seeks must be in the form of an *epistêmê* of *eidos*—that is, scientific knowledge of a formal structure. But one of the lessons of Socrates' philosophic trial is that the human soul—unlike the souls of animals—cannot adequately be grasped as a formal structure. The reason is that the human soul is incomplete or unfinished and is essentially characterized by desire or *erôs*. As a result of its erotic striving, the soul has no fixed formal nature; like a sophist, it is capable of taking on many different shapes. The kind of self-knowledge Socrates seeks is correspondingly not to be understood as *epistêmê*. In the philosophic trial the distinction between epistemic and nonepistemic modes of knowing human beings, and between the assumptions about the nature of human souls that are implicit in each of these modes, is played out in the encounter between the Stranger and Socrates. The former emphasizes (at least initially) the production of scientific accounts via the method of division; the latter emphasizes a prophetic or recollective familiarity with human souls and the concrete contexts of human life.

Second, Derrida supposes—again, very much in accordance with tradition—that Plato cannot brook ambiguity and paradox. His demonstration that opposed terms cross over into one another has critical value only if he is correct in supposing that, for Plato, philosophy stands or falls with the rigid logic of external opposition. Yet how are we to square his description of Plato's logic with the massive presence within the dialogues of the paradoxical and ambiguous character of Socrates—a figure who, as Derrida suggests, is no less polytropic or aneidetic than *erôs* itself?[35] To put this point in a slightly different way, Derrida does not explore the implications of Socratic irony, which is a mode of being, not just a way of speaking. Socratic irony cannot be understood without coming to grips with *internal* opposition, or the copresence of contrary terms. Socratic irony raises most forcefully the problem of the distinction between philosophy and sophistry. Far from attempting to conceal this fact, as Derrida maintains, Plato repeatedly reminds us of it. Plato's readers hardly need Derrida to show them that in the dialogues philosophy and sophistry "exchange their respective places, imitating the forms and borrowing the paths of the opponent": the latter phrase nicely describes the explicit dramatic action of the *Hippias Minor* (to take perhaps the clearest single example of this point).

Third, Derridean deconstruction reflects more orthodox modes of interpreting Plato in ignoring the extraordinary concreteness of the Platonic dialogues and of Socratic philosophizing. Thus Derrida supposes that Plato and Socrates associate wisdom with the separation of the body from the soul: "The death of the body . . . that is the price that must be paid for *alêtheia* [truth] and the *epistêmê*." And again: "The hemlock has an *ontological* effect: it initiates one into the contemplation of the *eidos* and the immortality of the soul."[36] Now it is true that there is a thrust toward abstraction in Socrates' characteristic requests for essential definitions. Yet there is an equally significant counterthrust toward concreteness in what has recently been called the "situational finitude" of the Platonic dialogues.[37] This opposition produces the characteristic shuttling, up-and-down movement of Socratic philosophizing. Platonic dialogues display the same pattern again and again: the intrinsically questionable nature of concrete human experience leads to the search for an *eidos* or *idea*, but what is revealed in the course of this search is judged by its ability to shed light on the concrete problem that gave birth to the inquiry. Socratic dialogue always begins within, and returns to, the ordinary or everyday contexts in which ensouled bodies—and *only* ensouled bodies—find themselves. So too, we see philosophy, if we see it at all, literally embodied in Socrates. These observations should give pause to those who assume that Plato and Socrates seek to understand philosophy in terms of a *logos* that can meaningfully be abstracted from the concrete circumstances of human life—cirumstances that both engage reflection and provide a context within which to evaluate its worth. They should also give additional credence to the notion that within the Platonic dialogues the nature of philosophy is dramatically displayed or enacted rather than established in argument.

Let us leave the deconstructionists with a question that their interpretations help to call to our attention. To what extent is Socratic philosophizing separable from its original practitioner? Something about Socrates encourages devotion and imitation, although the results are usually absurd or pathetic.[38] Any attempt to imitate Socrates would always turn out to be absurd if his significance were simply equivalent to his uniqueness. But the question "Who is Socrates?" is relevant to Plato's readers just because Socrates takes a stand on behalf of the human soul in general as well as his own soul in particular. In Socrates one finds something that, paradoxically, is wholly his own possession and yet is capable of being shared by others: his life of Socratic philosophizing. Put simply, "Socratic philosophizing" names the most serious aspiration to live up to the Ideas. Although the Ideas of virtue are conceived as universals, the concerted attempt to live up to them is nevertheless, Socrates suggests by example, the only viable route to what is nowadays called "authenticity." A further paradox is that to imitate Socrates in the only essential respect—that is, by embracing Socratic philosophizing as one's own self-defining activity—may be to come into possession of oneself in a way that transforms one from an image into an original. Both of these paradoxes are rooted in the peculiar structure of human being, which emerges in the dialogues not simply as the given nature of all members of the species, but also as an exemplary status that one may strive to achieve by becoming someone in one's own right, an active, reflective center of responsibility that stands apart from other such centers and from the multitudes who resemble plants or drowsy horses in their unreflective passivity.

Socrates' philosophic trial, then, is fundamentally about what makes one a human being—a problem that is no less fresh today than it was in the time of Plato. Socrates' extraordinary devotion to this problem is largely vindicated by the Stranger's attempt to explicate the natures of the sophist and statesman. As we shall see, the Stranger makes it clear that the doubleness of human life—the problematic unity of given nature and exemplary achievement, body and soul, practice and theory, construction and acquisition—lies at the root of the basic issues that philosophy and politics must address. Moreover, the Stranger goes on to give us a Socratic measure for judging Socrates' philosophical activity when he indicates that the ability intelligently to address this doubleness is the touchstone of political wisdom.

To return, finally, to my first question about the purposes of the present inquiry: I do not pretend to offer a comprehensive interpretation of each of the dialogues I discuss in this book. The central aim of this study is to explore the problem of Socrates' identity as it emerges over the course of his philosophic trial. To be sure, this is a large undertaking that involves a host of issues, not the least of which concerns the complex relationship between Socrates and the Stranger. I am furthermore well aware that the act of publishing my thoughts in the form of a philosophical treatise inevitably invests them with an air of authority and finality that is both specious and antithetical to my intentions. This is a paradox of literate education and of Plato scholarship in particular, but the difficulty noted here is surely mitigated by being acknowledged. Reading is no substitute for thinking, but it may be a spur to thinking. If my book helps Plato's reader to interrogate his writings in new and fruitful ways, I shall have achieved my main goal.

PART ONE

SOCRATES

>   . . .   Life piled on life
> Were all too little, and of one to me
> Little remains: but every hour is saved
> From that eternal silence, something more,
> A bringer of new things; and vile it were
> For some three suns to store and hoard myself,
> And this grey spirit yearning in desire
> To follow knowledge like a sinking star,
> Beyond the utmost bound of human thought.
>
>   Alfred, Lord Tennyson, "Ulysses"

Chapter 1

Prelude to the Philosophic Trial: The *Apology*

The wise Plato did not feel free to reveal and uncover the sciences for all men. Therefore he followed the practice of using symbols, riddles, obscurity, and difficulty, so that science would not fall into the hands of those who do not deserve it and be deformed, or into the hands of one who does not know its worth or who uses it improperly. In this he was right. Once he knew and became certain that he had become well-known for this practice, and that all men came to know that this was what he did, he sometimes turned to the subject he intended to discuss and stated it openly and literally; but the one who reads or hears his discussion thinks that it is symbolic and that he intended something different from what he has stated openly. This notion is one of the secrets of his books.

Alfarabi, *Plato's Laws*

The *Apology of Socrates* concerns the relationship between Socratic philosophizing and the political community. So, too, does the philosophic trial of Socrates. One can only conclude that in the *Apology* the issues raised by Socrates' public trial are closed legally and officially, but not philosophically. Why must the case of Socrates be reopened? Why is another philosophical trial necessary? This chapter turns to the *Apology* for answers to these questions.

The *Apology*, I shall argue, indicates that the question "Who is Socrates?" cannot be resolved in a public and political forum. Socrates is unable to convey an accurate impression of himself under such circumstances. As he observes in the *Sophist*, philosophers do not look like philosophers to nonphilosophers, but instead appear in the guise of statesmen, sophists, or madmen (216c-d). Beyond this, the matter of whether Socrates is in fact a sophist cannot be resolved without inquiring into the nature and possibility of philosophy, and such an inquiry is impossible within the confines of a public trial. If philosophy turns out to be impossible, then there is no alternative to sophistry. But even if Socrates' quest for wisdom is theoretically sound, he might still be guilty of sophistry in the practical sense of bad citizenship. The latter possibility is raised by Socrates' failure in the *Apology* to demonstrate that his philosophical way of life is compatible with the well-being of the political community, a failure that leaves intact the jury's preliminary impression that Socratic philosophizing goes hand in hand with corrupting politics. Perhaps philosophy and sophistry are indistinguishable; perhaps they are, paradoxically, distinct and yet inseparable.

The problems adumbrated above stand at the center of Socrates' philosophic trial. Moreover, Socrates' attempt in the *Apology* to define himself in relation to philosophy's antagonists anticipates the structure of exposition that Plato employs in the dialogues *Theaetetus* through *Statesman*. In its dramatic form as well as its content, the *Apology* provides a fitting introduction to our study.

Socrates' Rhetorical Challenge

Cicero maintained that Socrates "was the first to call philosophy down from the heavens and set her in the cities of men, and bring her also into their homes, and compel her to ask questions about life and morality and things good and evil" (*Tusculan Disputations* 5.4.10-11). Cicero's remark has a double significance. It means that Socrates was the first philosopher who did not view human life as an epiphenomenon of the physical cosmos, thereby neglecting man's difference from inanimate beings.[1] It also means that he was the first to make philosophizing a public, political affair that took place within the walls of the *polis* and actively involved its citizens.

Whatever its historical merits may be, Cicero's remark aptly describes the behavior of Plato's Socrates and the major emphasis of the dialogues. Socrates refers to his twofold turn toward the human things on two occasions very near the end of his life. In the *Phaedo*, he explains that his disappointment with the doctrines of Anaxagoras led him to abandon the direct examination of beings and to take up the investigation of them in and through speeches (97b-99e). He offers a somewhat different account in the *Apology*, in which he claims that Chaerephon's consultation with the Delphic oracle led him to begin examining others in discourse (20e ff.). It is fair to say that Socrates' introduction of philosophy into the *polis* stands at the center of the dialogues: no dialogue depicts Socrates during his "pre-Socratic" days, and he speaks directly about this period of his life only on the day of his execution—the day he suffers the ultimate consequences of his "Socratic" turn.

According to Socrates, the indictment against him ran as follows: "Socrates does injustice by corrupting the young and not acknowledging [*ou nomizonta*] the gods the city acknowledges, but other, new and strange divinities [*daimonia*]" (*Apology* 24b8-c1). Socrates' recapitulation of the charges against him anticipates his later emphasis upon virtue and the care of the soul: he seems to have altered the official wording of the indictment in placing the corruption charge first (cf. Xenophon, *Memorabilia* 1.1.1 and Diogenes Laertius 2.40).

At his trial Socrates is compelled to give a fully public defense of his way of life. This compulsion is rooted in the essentially public or political nature of his philosophic practice. In order to philosophize, Socrates needs to converse with others; although the *Phaedrus* takes place outside of the city, he explains therein that he almost never ventures beyond the walls of Athens because he is able to learn only from the men in town (230c-d). The conditions for his defense, however, are far from ideal. Whereas philosophizing requires freedom from external compulsion and leisure for discourse, Socrates emphasizes that he is constrained by law to make a defense speech, and to do so in a short amount of time before the entire jury (*Apology* 18e-19a; cf. *Theaetetus* 172c-173b). Socrates nonetheless meets this challenge head on. He treats his trial not simply as a dispute between himself and his three accusers—after all, he questions Meletus but spares Anytus and Lycon, probably to his detriment (see his remarks at 36a-b about the tally of votes)—but as an occasion for the philosopher to explain himself before the political community. He therefore begins by addressing the jurors not as "judges" (*dikastai*) but as "Athenian gentlemen," reserving the former, customary address for those who vote not to condemn him to death (17a1, 40a2-3).[2]

It is difficult to tell just what Socrates intends to accomplish in his defense speech. Some have noted that he deliberately turns the tables on the Athenians by putting *their* lives on trial, while others claim that he sincerely attempts to mount an effective self-defense.[3] It seems impossible to have it both ways: Socrates may feel obliged to tell the jurors what he thinks of them as well as of himself, but such honesty is bound to offend a good part of his audience and therefore to work against his case. One thing, at any rate, is clear: Socrates is not primarily concerned simply to avoid conviction and punishment by any available means, as is the case with other defendants. He notes that the speech of his accusers nearly caused him to "forget myself" (17a3; cf. *Menexenus* 235c). While his accusers spoke beautifully but falsely, he claims that he will tell "the whole truth" (17b8). This means that he will not attempt to make the judges forget who he is—or, one should note, who they are (cf. 18a5-6). The rhetoric of the law courts is "foreign" to Socrates (17d3) not because he is unfamiliar with it, for he is not. Indeed, Socrates is well aware that acquittal may turn upon his ability to gratify the judges' appetite for tawdry courtroom drama, but he refuses to play the timeworn role of the pitiable defendant. Instead, he reproaches his fellow citizens for having effectively turned public trials into pathetic tragic spectacles (34b-d, 38d-e).[4]

On the basis of the passages cited above, one might cautiously conclude that Socrates aims to try to defend himself by publicly recollecting the character of his philosophic activity so as to reveal to the judges who he is. Socrates' defense speech is admittedly structured in accordance with traditional forms of forensic rhetoric. But because he is more concerned with getting at the truth than with winning acquittal—the only goal at which the defensive species of forensic rhetoric aims—Socrates reverses the ordinary function of rhetoric, employing what has aptly been called an "inverted parody" of courtroom speech.[5] Socrates approaches his public trial seriously—albeit with a certain theoretical or experimental detachment—insofar as he views the trial essentially as an occasion for the exploration of two philosophically interesting questions: Can Socrates communicate the truth about himself to an assembly of his fellow citizens? And, is telling the truth compatible with winning acquittal?

A potential problem with the preceding interpretation is that, as we shall soon see, Socrates at certain points tells something less than the whole truth about himself. In Eva Brann's words, "There can be no doubt that before the court Socrates deliberately curtails and withholds himself."[6] Yet I would argue that this self-curtailment is also a kind of self-exhibition for philosophically inclined auditors (or readers). Socrates withholds himself in a way that makes it clear that it is impossible for a philosopher to do otherwise in a public forum such as a lawcourt or assembly. In just this fashion, he sheds light upon the nature of philosophical communication and the necessary limits of his engagement, *qua* philosopher, with the city.

How is Socrates to go about "telling the truth" to the jury? Given his characterization of the encounter between philosophers and nonphilosophers in the cave image of the *Republic* (514a-517a) and in the digression of the *Theaetetus* (172c-177c), it would be foolish to expect that he could succeed in justifying his life of philosophizing before hundreds of nonphilosophers in a matter of minutes or hours. Socrates is well aware of this problem. At several points he mentions that it is difficult for the judges to get to know him in the short amount of time provided by the law (18e-19a, 24a, 37a). What is worse, many years of hearing unrefuted accusations against him have prejudiced his auditors. Since Socrates does not have the leisure to question individual members of the jury about the rumors they have heard about him, it is impossible for him to know what specific preconceptions he should seek to dispel.

These facts influence Socrates' defense speech in two ways. First, he must engage in a comprehensive review of his activities; he cannot appeal to what the Athenians already know about him. In addition, it is necessary for him to have recourse to explanations that he might not have used in other circumstances, for the conventions of Athenian litigation impose constraints upon his customary style of discourse. Apart from the time limit, Socrates must address a crowd and so cannot engage each individual in dialogue (cf. *Gorgias* 447c, 449b-c). Furthermore, he must speak to everyone or no one; he cannot utilize his daimonic ability to select appropriate interlocutors. These circumstances severely restrict the options available to him in explaining what he characteristically does and, especially, why he does it.

The preceding observations raise a general question: To what extent, if any, could the truth about the philosophic life be conveyed in a public speech, even under optimal conditions (i.e., with an unlimited amount of time available to the speaker, an attentive audience, the possibility to ask and answer questions, and the like)? It seems obvious that a philosopher could not adequately explain his activity to anyone who has never been moved by the longing for wisdom to engage in philosophical inquiry. Socrates' way of life must remain mysterious to those who lack the direct experience of philosophical endeavor. If this is correct, Socrates cannot avoid speaking in a misleading fashion: the bare truth about philosophy will inevitably be understood in a manner other than that in which he intends it to be understood. To the extent that a true speech is distorted by the misunderstanding of the listener, it becomes falsehood. In this sense Socrates *must* speak falsely, but this does not make him a liar: he desires (even if he does not fully expect) that what is false in his speech be understood as such. One could say that the circumstances of his public trial leave him no choice besides irony. It remains to be seen whether the same is true of his philosophical trial.

Let us call the distortion of Socrates' meaning by the misunderstanding of his listeners "unintentional irony." Socrates at one point explicitly refers to the inevitability of such unintentional irony in order to justify his deliberate or *intentional* employment of irony in the *Apology*. In the same passage, Socrates risks unintentional irony in speaking openly about the rhetorical obstacles to the communication of the truth in the courtroom:

> It is most difficult of all to persuade some of you of this [i.e., why he will not cease philosophizing]. For if I say that this is to disobey the god and that on account of this it is impossible for me to keep quiet, you will not be

persuaded by me on the grounds that I am being ironic. If in turn I say that
this also happens to be the greatest good for a human being—making
speeches every day about virtue and the other things about which you hear
me conversing and examining both myself and others—and that the unexamined life is not livable [*biôtos*] for a human being, you will be persuaded
by me still less when I say these things. Yet this is the way things stand, as
I maintain, gentlemen, but to persuade you is not easy. (37e4-38a8)

Socrates could hardly be more direct in calling attention to the rhetorical
challenge he faces in making his defense speech. He admits what many
of the jurors must already have suspected, namely, that he has been
ironic in appealing to "the god" in order to justify his way of life. Yet he
defends this irony on the ground that the unvarnished truth must be even
less persuasive. Socrates thus illuminates the otherwise perplexing combination of frankness and intentional irony in his defense speech. He also
acknowledges that he will fail either to communicate the truth about
himself or to win acquittal. If his ironic explanations are insufficient to
convince the jurors even of the legitimacy, let alone the worth, of his
philosophic activity, his honest appraisal of his own value to the city (as
in his suggestion at 36e-37a that he be boarded in the Prutaneum, as befits a hero) must seem gratuitously offensive.[7]

Some would maintain that Socrates' references to the god are not
meant ironically, and that in the passage quoted above we should take
"this is the way things stand" to apply not only to his assertion that the
unexamined life is not livable for a human being, but also to his claim
that he philosophizes out of a sense of duty to the god.[8] But several considerations militate against this view. First, Socrates provides no evidence to the effect that he has been commanded to do anything by "the
god." In fact, he begins to examine his fellow citizens with the intention
of *refuting* what he takes, with a certain lapse of logical rigor, to be the
meaning of the Delphic oracle—namely, that "I [Socrates] am wisest"
(*Apology* 21b5-6).[9] One might go so far as to say that this intention be-
trays a spirit of irreverence, insofar as it involves either the impious
assumption that the god may be lying (which is *ou themis*, "not in accordance with divine sanction") or the hybristic assumption that the god
may be ignorant (21b-c).[10] In their enigmatic wording, however, oracles
seem to invite cross-examination, and the imperatives inscribed on the
temple of Apollo at Delphi—"Know Thyself" and "Nothing to Excess"
—suggest that the god who dwells there welcomes critical reflection of a
Socratic nature.[11] Indeed, Socrates implies elsewhere that he took the imperative to "Know Thyself" as a command to lead just the sort of
philosophical life he has chosen (*Phaedrus* 229e4-230a1). Yet when all
is said and done, the latter reading of the Delphic inscription is admit-

tedly no more self-evident than the message Socrates derives from the oracle given to Chaerephon. In sum, neither the oracle nor the Delphic inscription contains, or is equivalent to, a divine command to philosophize. Only Socrates' *interpretation* of these intrinsically vague pronouncements could determine the particular nature of his obligations.

Socrates indicates in other subtle ways that his life of philosophizing is rooted not in respect for the traditional gods but in his own independent reflection. His claim in the passage quoted above that "this is the way things stand" (*ta de echei men houtôs*) calls to mind an earlier passage in which he implicitly assimilates himself to the god by replacing "himself" with "the god" in the following chiastic construction:

> This is the way it stands [*houtô gar echei*], Athenian gentlemen, in truth. Wherever one should station *himself*, believing that it is best, or should be stationed *by a ruler*, it is necessary, as it seems to me, to remain there and run the risk. . . . I therefore would have done terrible deeds, Athenian gentlemen, if when *the rulers* whom you chose to rule stationed me [in battle] . . . I stood fast . . . but when *the god* stationed me . . . I should have deserted my station. (28d6-29a1, emphasis added)

Other passages could be adduced to make the same point. In fact, Cropsey has shown that Socrates begins to substitute himself for the god virtually from the moment he first mentions Chaerephon's visit to Delphi.[12]

It is now possible to appreciate the greatest obstacle to frank communication that Socrates faces in the *Apology*. The claim that the unexamined life is not livable for a human being is authorized by Socrates' own reason, not by the gods of Athens. In order seriously to consider the legitimacy of the philosophic life, the jurors would therefore have to be willing at least provisionally to grant that philosophical reflection might in some cases speak with as much authority as the civic tradition. But the very occasion of Socrates' encounter with the jurors—an impiety trial—presupposes the superior authority of the religious tradition in matters of civic importance. To get a fair hearing, Socrates would first have to bring the jurors to question this fundamental presupposition. In almost all cases, he could hope to do so only through "Socratic" dialogue with individual jurors, and in the present circumstances he has neither the time nor the opportunity to engage in such discussion. This is why he is compelled ironically to rest his defense on the oracle.

To sum up the present line of thought, Socrates is engaged in the *Apology* in an experiment concerning the philosopher's ability to mount an effective defense of himself in a broadly public forum while speaking openly and directly about who he is and what he does. This experiment

sometimes includes commentary upon the conditions and expected outcome of the experiment itself. Finally, Socrates acknowledges the
difficulties associated with frank public speech in a way that both justifies his intermittent recourse to irony and anticipates that his self-
exhibition will prove to be incompatible with self-defense.

It should now be evident that there are good reasons for the existence
of a separate, philosophical trial of Socrates, a trial that takes place
within the context of private conversation. Because it removes or at least
mitigates some of the extraneous obstacles to a successful defense that
Socrates meets in his public trial, private conversation promises to provide a more just forum in which to evaluate the merits of his case. Most
important, in private conversation Socrates could engage in relatively leisurely discourse with a few individuals rather than delivering a brief
speech before a crowd. Under such conditions, he would have a fuller
opportunity both to identify and to answer the concerns of his antagonists. On the other hand, a philosophical version of his public trial would
in certain respects raise the stakes for Socrates. While the proceedings
would be free of extrinsic impediments to his self-defense, Socrates
would encounter accusations that reflect and deepen those he faces in his
public trial. In a philosophical trial, moreover, Socrates might have to
face additional charges stemming from the likely failure of his public
trial, charges having to do with his inability to defend his life in a public
forum.

Erôs and Politics

If irony is, in Griswold's words, "a way of speaking (or writing) which is
meant to point to what is not spoken (or written), to what is silent and
kept in reserve, as it were, by its originator," then the *Apology* is a profoundly ironic text.[13] In accounting for himself before the jury, Socrates
remains silent about many things. I have argued that he cannot do otherwise: after a certain point speech becomes equivalent to silence, because
most if not all of the jurors are not prepared to understand direct talk
about what it is to be a philosopher. But while Socrates' silence effectively bespeaks this rhetorical predicament, it is in other respects more
provocative than communicative. The *Apology* raises a number of unan-
swered questions about Socrates, and leaves us readers with a strong
desire to hear more.

Let us now consider in greater detail what Socrates does and does not
say about himself. Socrates' method of introducing himself to the judges
is largely a negative one: he proceeds by attempting to distinguish himself from others. He is not a philosopher of the legendary sort: he does
not investigate the things under the earth and in the heavens (19b-d; cf.

Theaetetus 173e-174a). He is not a sophist, since he has no teaching and neither attempts to educate others nor makes any money from those who seek knowledge (19d-e). He belongs to none of the groups of men he examines on behalf of the oracle: politicians, poets, and craftsmen. Finally, he acts as if he were neither a gentleman nor a common man: he has no interest in the pursuits of his fellow citizens—moneymaking, household management, popular oratory, political offices, conspiracies, and seditions—and he points out without shame that his manner of life has left him destitute and unable to attend to his family of five (23b-c, 36b).

In the course of explaining who or what he is not, Socrates also tells us something about who he is: he lives, he says, "philosophizing and examining myself and others" (28e5-6). But his explanation of this activity, like the claim that the unexamined life is not livable for a human being—from which one can logically infer nothing whatsoever about the worth of the examined life or lives—is itself thoroughly negative. To begin with, perhaps the most important evidence he offers on his own behalf consists of the recollected report of a dead zealot concerning the negative and ambiguous utterance of an oracle.[14] Chaerephon learned from the Delphic oracle that "no one is wiser than Socrates." Socrates set out to prove that this was not the case; just as in the *Phaedo* he explains his turn toward the *polis* in terms of his desire for wisdom, in the *Apology* he presents it as a consequence of his desire to understand the oracle. He discovered, however, that his supposedly superior "wisdom" consisted precisely in the realization that he was not wise. Socrates accordingly has recourse to images—including laughable ones (30e)—in order to explain his philosophic activity: the god has set him in Athens as on a battlefield, set him upon Athens as a gadfly upon a great horse, or given him to the city as a gift in order that he may exhort to virtue whomever he happens to meet. He also provides two different accounts of how he serves the god. He first explains that in revealing the ignorance of others he helps the god to demonstrate the paltriness of human wisdom (23a-b), but he later maintains that he serves the god as a tireless advocate of virtue (29d-30b). These two accounts are not necessarily incompatible, insofar as the refutation of the interlocutor's claim to possess virtue (and so to know what virtue is, and in this sense to be wise) is presumably integral to Socrates' exhortations. Socrates also mentions as proof of his concern for the city certain deeds which any Athenian would deem honorable (cf. 32a4-5). He did his duty in three battles, in two of which, as we learn in other dialogues, he served with distinction (28d-e; cf. *Symposium* 220d-221c, *Laches* 181a-b). In addition, he served on the Council and as one of the chairmen of the Assembly when chosen by lot, and in spite of the danger of imprisonment and even death he upheld the law of the city both at that time, when the democracy unlawfully condemned the generals who fought at Arginusae, and later, when the oligarchs tried to involve him in the unlawful arrest and execution of Leon of Salamis (32a-e). Even these deeds, however, have a curiously negative character. At Potidaea and Delium he distinguished himself in retreating, while in the assembly and under the oligarchy his virtue consisted in his refusal to act. All of these deeds are defensive: Socrates' "whole care," he explains, "is not to do anything unjust or impious" (32d2-3). In the instances he cites, the counsel of his *daimonion*, his inner, daimonic voice or sign, coincided with his duties as a citizen (cf. 31c-d). But this very coincidence leaves open the possibility that Socrates' defense of his body and soul may sometimes take precedence over his care for the Athenian regime and body politic.[15]

The nature of Socrates' philosophical *erôs* may be inferred from certain remarks that contradict his explanation of the way in which he serves the city. In the first place, many of the judges would not need to get acquainted with Socrates if, as he claims, he really is accustomed to speak with everyone he happens to meet (29d, 30a). That this is not his custom is implied by his references to his *daimonion* (31c-d, 40a-c) and by his earlier testimony: he speaks only of questioning those who are reputed to be wise (21b, 22d, 23b).[16] Furthermore, after the judges have convicted him Socrates requests that he be boarded in the Prutaneum because he needs leisure to exhort the Athenians to virtue, which implies that other concerns now prevent him from doing so (36d). In the same passage, Socrates explicitly states that his judges may hear him talking about matters other than virtue (38a). We may suppose that he also discusses other matters when he speaks in private places where the judges cannot hear him (cf. 17c9). As Socrates suggests in the above ways and as the other dialogues confirm, the truth is that he discusses many things, perhaps even all things, with a few men who stand apart from the many in pretension or promise.[17]

It seems clear that Socrates' philosophical activity is neither motivated nor directed solely by concern for the city's welfare. Nor is it limited by traditional reverence for the gods. Socrates in fact gives the judges good reasons to side with his accusers in concluding that his behavior is both impious and harmful to the city. In revealing the ignorance of the men Athens held in the highest esteem (*hoi malista eudokimountes*, 22a3), he indicates the worthlessness of the beliefs and standards of worth (*hai doxai*) held in common by the Athenians. Yet if Socrates is truly worthless with respect to wisdom, as he claims to be (23a-b), it would seem that he must leave his interlocutors with nothing more than a keen awareness of their own ignorance to guide them toward virtue. That he does just this is precisely the charge leveled against him by the eponymous interlocutor of the *Cleitophon*—a character whom one commentator describes as "stand[ing] first and last for the city as it is," and whose criticism seems presciently to defend the city against Socrates' claim in the *Apology* that Athens "undervalues [both] virtue and himself, the arch exhorter to virtue."[18] In fine, Socrates' public account of himself fosters the impression that he loosens the traditional bonds which bind the Athenians together into a political community, but fashions no new bonds for the *polis*.

The latter point becomes still clearer when we consider the connection between the impiety charges and the corruption charge in the indictment against Socrates. Socrates admits that he is frequently accompanied by youths who enjoy the spectacle of older and supposedly wiser men than themselves being defeated in argument, and that these youths often go on to imitate him in examining others (23c, 33b-c). He remains silent about his association with Alcibiades and with the tyrant Critias, who allegedly took from his public interrogations the same techniques of eristic disputation that the sophists taught for a fee (Xenophon, *Memorabilia* 1.2.12 ff.). The connection between Socratic education and tyranny is, however, a main theme of the *Clouds*, which Socrates singles out for special mention in the course of discussing his "first accusers" (19c; cf. 18b-c). For Aristophanes, the political problem posed by Socrates is not that a potentially tyrannical individual like Pheidippides would choose to enter his *Phrontistêrion* or "Thinkery," but that, having kicked over the traces of convention and armed himself with the weapons of clever speech, he might subsequently choose to *leave* it. In the *Apology*, Socrates does not address his accusers' unspoken implication that he teaches tyranny. Nor does he offer any defense against another, related implication of the indictment—that by reducing to silence the older generation in the presence of young men, he weakens the essential relationship through which civic unity is formed and sustained, namely, the relationship between father and son. And although he asserts that all of the charges against him may be traced to his effect upon young men, Socrates refuses to take responsibility for their actions, arguing that he never taught any of them anything at all (23c-24a, 33b).[19] In order fully to appreciate the damaging import of Socrates' admissions and omissions, one must bear in mind that paternal authority and the religious tradition were mutually reinforcing pillars of the Athenian community: the gods offered special protection to the fathers of families, who were in turn the principal guardians of the heritage of ritual and myth.[20] To undermine the authority of the fathers of Athens is therefore to strike a blow against the city's gods. By failing adequately to defend himself against the corruption charge, Socrates seems virtually to admit the justice of the impiety charges.

In spite of his claim that he has no teaching and takes no money, Socrates fails to show that he is not a sophist (in either the practical or theoretical sense of this term). Let us consider each aspect of the problem of sophistry in turn. In his conversation with Socrates in the *Gorgias*, Gorgias initially refused to take responsibility for any students of his who might use rhetoric unjustly, but Socrates caused him to feel that his manner of teaching was shamefully irresponsible. He implied that one should either teach justice along with rhetoric or accept as students only those who are already inclined never to use rhetoric unjustly (460a). Yet when faced at his trial with the accusation that young men imitate his style of speech for unjust purposes, Socrates can appeal to neither of these principles in his own defense. If anything, he seems both more clever and more shameless than Gorgias when he has recourse to the argument that he has no teaching and therefore no students—only "followers" or "companions" (23c2, 25e3). The judges would surely take this argument to imply that he acknowledges no responsibility to his followers *qua* citizen.

In the *Gorgias*, Socrates boasted to Callicles that "I am one of a few Athenians, not to say the only one, who works at the true political art, and the only one of the men of today who tends to [*prattein*] the political things" (521d6-8). Yet it can hardly be maintained that in his defense speech Socrates offers any evidence of possessing such an art. This brings us to the second, theoretical dimension of the problem of sophistry, which is closely related to the practical problem of Socrates' seemingly bad citizenship. If Socrates works at the true political *technê*, why does he insist that he has no teaching? If Socrates has no teaching, is he in fact a philosopher? And in the absence of hard-and-fast knowledge that can be taught and learned, how can Socrates be sure that his way of life is superior to all nonphilosophic ways of life—so much so that he does not hesitate to expose, and thereby to help undermine, the unexamined foundations of these other lives? Entirely apart from its political consequences, Socrates' total devotion to the quest for wisdom seems exceedingly odd in the light of the apparent fruitlessness of his inquiries. It must seem to the judges that Aristophanes was right: while others may imitate his style of speech, only the strangest men could be attracted to Socrates' way of life.

Whether Socrates is a sophist or a philosopher depends upon what philosophy is, or indeed whether philosophy is at all possible. The *Apology* therefore cannot be understood by itself; it points beyond itself toward a larger inquiry within which its significance may become clear. It is possible that, in a context less constrained by necessity than his public trial, Socrates could successfully defend his claim that he is especially concerned with working at the true art of politics. Even so, the *Apology* would then seem to teach the public indefensibility, not of sophistry, but of the free practice of philosophical politics. It would thus point toward a deep incompatibility between philosophic *erôs* and the political community.

In the *Apology*, Socrates provides hints concerning the nature of his philosophical *erôs* while claiming to do a great service for the *polis*, but he fails to clarify the relationship between his *erôs* and his politics. (Indeed, the word *erôs* never appears in the *Apology* in any of its grammatical forms.)[21] This is perhaps the greatest, albeit unavoidable, shortcoming of his defense speech. Socrates might have been acquitted if he had been able to do the impossible—to fill in for the jurors the conceptual and practical lacunae separating his boast to Callicles from his even greater boast to Theages: "I always say that I happen to know, so to speak, nothing, except a certain small subject of learning, [that of] the erotic things [*tôn erôtikôn*]. Of course, in respect to this learning I deem myself to be clever beyond anyone among human beings past or present" (*Theages* 128b2-6; cf. *Symposium* 177d).

By suggesting that Socrates' failure to clarify the relationship between his *erôs* and his politics may be connected with the inevitable constraints of his public trial, the *Apology* invites unconstrained reflection upon this relationship within the larger context of the problem of sophistry. Our task as participants in Socrates' philosophic trial is to engage in just this sort of reflection.

Socrates' Appeal: The Philosophic Trial

In the middle of the *Theaetetus*, Theodorus has occasion to note that he and Socrates are at leisure—an observation that provokes from Socrates a lengthy digression in which he contrasts the free, peaceful, and unhurried life of the philosopher with the slavish and contentious existence of those who live by the tempo of the water-clock in courts of law (172c-177c). This digression underscores several features of the rhetorical context of Socrates' public trial that we noted earlier in this chapter. First, speech in the lawcourts must be cut to fit the relentless press of business, regardless of how complex or subtle the matter at hand may be. Second, legal talk is structured by the relationship between slaves (litigants) and masters (judges), so that the soul of the free man—which may sometimes be the very point at issue (cf. 172e-173a)—cannot appear under these circumstances without some distortion of its intrinsic look or shape. This will be true whether the one who has been reared as a free man attempts to accommodate himself to these circumstances, in which case he fashions a false image of himself, or whether he does not, in which case he will nonetheless be misunderstood by those who are unfamiliar with his way of life (cf. *Theaetetus* 175d-176a). With the *Apology* in prospect, this passage from the *Theaetetus* suggests that Socrates will be unable to avoid presenting a false image of himself in court. Socrates seems to anticipate this situation also when, at the outset of the *Sophist*, he remarks that "on account of the ignorance of the rest of men" philosophers "sometimes take on the semblance of statesmen, sometimes of sophists, and there are times when they might give some the impression that they are altogether mad" (216c4-d2). False images of the philosopher, in other words, are generated without any effort on the part of the philosopher at producing such semblances. This is the phenomenon I referred to earlier as "unintentional irony."

The dialogues *Theaetetus* through *Statesman* provide the leisure that Socrates lacks in the *Apology*, although this leisure is not unlimited (cf. *Theaetetus* 210d). Nor, unfortunately, can we be sure that a philosophical trial will provide a forum in which the truth about Socrates' way of life may be displayed without distortion. To say nothing of the possible ignorance of Plato's readers, the digression of the *Theaetetus* is itself an example of intentional irony that is motivated by the inevitability of unintentional irony: Socrates fashions a false image of himself in order to accommodate Theodorus's deficient yet inflexible conception of theoretical activity. And Theodorus represents the rule rather than the exception: setting aside the problematic case of the Stranger, Socrates does not encounter a mature philosopher in the course of his philosophical trial.

Does the inevitability of unintentional irony within the conversations dramatized by Plato radically undermine our attempt to answer the question "Who is Socrates?" Deconstructionist readers would argue that it does. In a provocative study that acknowledges Derrida's work on Plato as its most influential antecedent, Jay Farness has argued that Socrates' difficulties in the courtroom highlight the impossibility of his attempt to bespeak his own nature. Farness summarizes the courtroom situation as one "in which speakers re-present audiences, telling people what they want to hear, what they are able to hear, what they have always already heard within the horizon of their common sense." In the Athenian court "one must *play* at one's innocence, as an actor rehearsing a social script; one must pretend to be innocent, even if one really *is* innocent."[22] Farness maintains, however, that Socrates is complicitous in making a dramatic spectacle of his trial, and not just because his rejection of the typical role of the defendant will itself inevitably be perceived by the jurors as a kind of role playing. Socrates' self-presentations in other contexts, he notes, are also theatrical in character. The peculiar circumstances of the *Apology* thus bring to light an ineliminable feature of his "ad hominem conversational rhetoric": like the protean "democratic man" whom he criticizes in the *Republic*, Socrates is "a signifier belonging to anybody, representing the understanding of whoever would think to possess it."[23]

Farness aptly describes the peculiar obstacles presented to interpretation in the *Apology*. Other dialogues, too, reveal a self-consciously dramatic dimension of Socrates' conversational posture; rather like the Clouds of Aristophanes' comedy, he frequently plays to his interlocutors by imitatively reflecting their expectations and modes of understanding.[24] To be sure, we may be victims of unintentional irony whenever we think that we have understood something of Socrates' nature. Anyone who appreciates this point will always remain open to other interpretations of Socrates. But *must* we always be "missing" Socrates? Is it *inevitable*, as Farness maintains, that we will fail to discover who he is, and in this sense to "find" him? For Farness and like-minded readers of Plato, the inevitability of missing Socrates would seem to follow only from the basic presuppositions of deconstructionism. Over the course of the philosophic trial, however, Socrates challenges related presuppositions that entail similar deconstructive consequences—as embodied, for example, in Protagorean sophistry. The question we face, then, is whether the debate between Socrates on the one hand, and Protagoras and other rivals of Socratic philosophizing on the other, is really worth studying. Such study has little point for those who are already certain about the outcome of this debate. It is of course possible that when all is said and done we will fail to find Socrates. But if we are to take the philosophic trial seriously, we must at least begin by supposing that we *might* find him. And the *Apology*, with its multiple provocations of style and substance, its ever-shifting tone and repeatedly enigmatic phrasing, simultaneously offers and withholds Socrates in a way that encourages its readers to take up other texts in an effort to get behind his strangely refractory self-dramatization.

It is important to observe that the measure of Socrates' accomplishment in the philosophic trial is not whether his interlocutors understand or fail to understand him, find him or miss him. For the reader's vantage point is always superior to that of Socrates' interlocutors. In this connection we may note that the negative structure of Socrates' defense speech, whereby he proceeds by attempting to distinguish himself from those who lead other sorts of lives, anticipates the structure of the philosophic trial. In the dialogues *Theaetetus* through *Statesman*, Socrates encounters a variety of antagonists—including metaphysicians, mathematicians, sophists, vigilant citizens, and eccentric prophets—who see themselves as contenders for the prize of wisdom.[25] Plato implicitly asks the reader to make the relevant comparisons. No one else is in a better position to make these comparisons, because no one besides the reader and Socrates is present throughout the whole philosophical trial. This fact suggests that Socrates' success or failure in persuading antagonistic interlocutors is less important than what he shows of himself in the course of encountering them. In the end, we readers are the judges of the philosophic trial. It is us that Socrates must persuade.

We have noted that the *Apology* comes to focus on the apparent incongruity between Socrates' philosophical *erôs* and his politics. It is as yet unclear whether this incongruity is rooted in a false image of Socrates. Perhaps the opportunity to observe him under more favorable conditions than those of his public trial, and against the backdrop of a range of theoretical and practical alternatives to his way of life, will allow us to detect a deeper unity within his speeches and deeds.

Chapter 2

Orienting Anticipations: The *Theaetetus*'s Prologue

And seeing that Euclides had taken a serious interest in eristic speeches, he [Socrates] said: "Euclides, you will be able to get on with sophists, but with human beings not at all."

Diogenes Laertius, *Lives of Eminent Philosophers*

It was recognized in antiquity that Plato took special pains over the opening words of his dialogues.[1] "The beginning," Socrates tells Adeimantus in the *Republic*, "is the greatest part of every work" (377a). In particular, the beginning of a Platonic dialogue seems always to be structured in such a way as to help its readers take their bearings in trying to understand the whole of it. The beginning of the *Theaetetus*, which stands apart from the rest of the dialogue as a prologue, is doubly important for our orientation because it introduces Socrates' philosophical trial as well as the *Theaetetus* itself. One finds in this prologue (142a–143c) the tightly intertwined leitmotifs of prophecy, memory and recollection, writing and reading, homecoming and exile, and familiarity and strangeness.

All of the motifs or themes mentioned above provide avenues of entry into the philosophical trial, and all are visible in even as brief a summary of the prologue as the following. Euclides and Terpsion meet upon returning home to Megara. Euclides has just encountered Theaetetus, who is suffering from wounds and dysentery, as he is being carried home from the army camp at Corinth to Athens. Both men agree that Theae-

39

tetus is *kalos k'agathos*, "a real gentleman," or literally "noble and good" (142b7). After he left Theaetetus, Euclides tells Terpsion, he "remembered and was amazed at how prophetically Socrates had spoken about him as well as other things" (142c4-5). He now invites Terpsion to listen to the conversation Socrates had with Theaetetus shortly before Socrates' death, which Euclides heard from Socrates and wrote down while the latter was awaiting execution in his prison cell. The two men go to Euclides' house and the slave reads this written record aloud for them.[2]

The *Theaetetus*'s prologue is an extraordinarily rich text, the manifold implications of which amply repay careful reading. The close analysis set forth in the following pages is meant to allow the major issues and emphases of the philosophical trial to stand forth as clearly as possible.

Caring for Souls:
Prophecy and Recollection, Writing and Reading

The *Theaetetus* begins with Socrates' care or concern for particular human souls. This concern is manifested in the first speech of the dialogue proper, wherein Socrates asserts that he is eager to learn from Theodorus about any young Athenians of promise—a matter that he investigates on his own as far as possible and about which he asks "all the others with whom I see that the young are willing to associate" (143d6-8). Socrates begins his question about promising youths with an explicit reference to care (*ekêdomên*, 143d1). The theme of care actually frames the octology in that it links Socrates' first words in the *Theaetetus* with his very last words in the *Phaedo*: "Crito, we owe a cock to Aesclepius. Deliver it, and don't overlook it [*me amelêsête*]" (118a7-8)—literally, "don't be careless," a meaning that will have acquired resonance from Socrates' prior puns on the name of Meletus (in which one hears *meletân*, "to care, to study, to practice") in the *Euthyphro* (2c-3a) and the *Apology* (24c ff.).[3]

Socrates' question leads directly to his conversation with Theaetetus, the purpose of which is for the latter to display his soul and the former to examine it (145b6-7). As Socrates' initial inquiry makes clear and as he later indicates to Theaetetus himself, what is at issue is more the potential than the actual state of the youth's soul. Theaetetus is not yet all that he will be: Euclides and Theodorus refer to him as a *meirakion*, a "stripling" (142c6, 143e5), and Socrates at one point seeks to encourage him by pointing out that he is not yet at the peak of his powers (148c).[4] Hence the *Theaetetus* directly raises the problem of how to measure human promise or potentiality, that is, the not-yet-actualized power or *dunamis* of the human soul. Because Theaetetus's face resembles Socrates', Socrates tells the lad that he will converse with him "so that I too may ex-

amine myself, as to what sort of face I possess" (144d8-9). Socrates' remark reminds us that the soul is visible only indirectly through the body,
or more precisely through the speeches and deeds of an ensouled body.
The being of the soul always stands, oracularly, behind or beyond its
perceptible manifestations.[5] In the *Theaetetus*, however, Socrates attempts to bring to light something that is doubly removed from perceptible surfaces, for he seeks to determine what Theaetetus's soul is not yet.
Socrates will try to prognosticate Theaetetus's future on the basis of the
present indications of that which is in itself always partially absent.

Euclides explicitly raises the theme of prophecy in connection with
Socrates' assessment of Theaetetus. "I was amazed," he tells Terpsion,
"at how prophetically [*mantikôs*] Socrates had spoken about him
[Theaetetus] as well as other things. . . . He said there was every necessity that he become renowned, if he should reach maturity" (142c4-5, d1-
3). Euclides' amazement should not surprise us, since as the founder of
the Megarian school he held that there is no potentiality (*dunamis*) apart
from actuality (*energeia*)—which is to say that nothing has the power to
become what it is not yet, or that whatever is, is always.[6] "These
[Megarian] *logoi*," Aristotle writes, "do away with both motion and generation. For that which is standing will always stand and that which is
sitting will always sit; for it will not stand up if it should be sitting, because that which is not able [*mê dunatai*] to stand up will not be able
[*estai adunaton*] to stand up" (*Metaphysics* 1047a15-17). It follows that
human development or maturation, or in general any progressive realization of a goal or purpose, is unintelligible. Strikingly, Protagoras as spoken for by Socrates in the *Theaetetus* adopts a Heraclitean perspective
that directly opposes the Megarian position with regard to motion but
leads nonetheless to the same consequence: Theaetetus will not grow
over time because such growth presupposes an enduring self that is the
subject of change, whereas at each moment a new and different self
comes into being, a self that is furthermore bound up with and relative to
the perception that is coming to be for it (158e-160c; cf. 154a). When we
assert, for example, that "Socrates becomes sick," we are illicitly con-
necting moments that are in themselves totally distinct and independent
of each other: "Socrates sick" is simply other than and dissimilar to
"Socrates healthy" (159b).[7]

Both the Euclidean thesis that there is only being without *dunamis* and
the Protagorean thesis that there is only flux imply that Socrates' inquiry
into the promise of Theaetetus's soul is absurd. Both views, in turn, rest
upon antecedent traditions of thought whose mutual opposition emerges
over the course of the dialogue as a challenging philosophical backdrop
to Socrates' discussion with Theaetetus. By framing the question "Who
is Theaetetus?" (a question suggested by the very title of the dialogue) in

a way that presupposes that Theaetetus's soul simultaneously possesses an enduring identity and is coming to be, Socrates guarantees that he will find himself in the seemingly ridiculous position of having fallen in between two groups of ancient wise men: "the streamers" and "the arresters of the whole" (181a-b).[8] Socrates' theoretically laughable situation, however, is matched by the practically or existentially incongruous speech of those who deny the simultaneity of being and becoming in the human soul. Perhaps most important, both Euclides and Protagoras must hold that the experience of *erôs* as the desire to become what one is not yet is the product of false consciousness. Neither thinker, in other words, can provide us with a coherent way of speaking about the experience of learning—the issue with which Socrates is most concerned, both in the *Theaetetus* and everywhere else. For Euclides as for Protagoras, philosophy as the soul's progress toward wisdom is an illusion.

The dialogue form itself underscores the above distinction between Socrates' potential theoretical preposterousness and Euclides' actual existential incoherence. The association of the "author" of the *Theaetetus* with the philosophical tenets of the Megarian school is the source of a number of ironies. While Euclides' philosophical commitments effectively bring the soul to a standstill, he and Terpsion are shown amidst a virtual flurry of motion. The first words of the dialogue plunge us into the middle of a question concerned with time and movement: "[Did you come] just now, Terpsion, or a long time ago from the country?" (142a1). Prior to his discussion with Euclides, Terpsion returned to Megara from the country and searched for Euclides in the agora, during which time the latter was accompanying Theaetetus to Erineos and then journeying back to Megara. As Euclides and Terpsion speak, Theaetetus is being carried home to Athens (*via* Erineos) from the army camp at Corinth. Within the prologue Euclides and Terpsion return from the agora in Megara to Euclides' home, and Euclides also mentions several round-trips he made to Athens in order to visit Socrates while he was in prison. While the prologue in these ways displays the locomotion of bodies, Euclides' praise of Theaetetus as *kalos k'agathos* also ironically bespeaks the goal-directed movement of Theaetetus's soul. Euclides confirms that Theaetetus deserves to be called "noble and good" because of his exemplary behavior in battle, and not simply because of his important accomplishments as a mathematician (142b7-8).[9] Theaetetus's *erôs* is patriotic as well as theoretical: his final display of virtue is the consequence of his desire to fight and if necessary to die as befits a brave and solid citizen of Athens. Yet Euclides' acknowledgment of the excellence of Theaetetus's timely exertion is out of tune with his theoretical critique of the ordinary self-understanding that motivated this exertion, and, more generally, with his denial of the ontological significance of time.

Euclides is either unaware of or unconcerned by the incongruity between his own distinctively political self-understanding and his theoretical activity. Philosophy falls apart from politics in the character of Euclides.

Anyone seeking a taste of the misery the Athenians inflicted on the Megarians during the Peloponnesian war need only read Aristophanes' *Acharnians*. Given the animosity between these two cities, there is perhaps some irony in Plato's having put in the mouth of Euclides a speech praising Theaetetus's soldierly labor. There are further and deeper ironies in the authorial decisions of both Euclides and Plato. Euclides recorded Socrates' conversation with Theaetetus in the following way: he heard Socrates narrate it, then went home and jotted down memoranda, and later wrote these up while recalling the speech at his leisure. Then on later occasions he questioned Socrates "about whatever I hadn't remembered," and afterwards went back to his manuscript and corrected it. In this way he wrote up "pretty nearly all of the speech" (143a1-5). We have no way of knowing what Euclides forgot to include in his transcription. We do know, however, that in writing up the conversation he turned Socrates' narration into direct discourse—in which the difference between the past and the present is suppressed—so as to avoid unnecessary "trouble" (*pragmata*: 143c1). *Pragmata* are more literally "deeds"— items that Euclides finds troubling in a philosophical sense. Euclides thereby unintentionally points toward the fact that writing in general severs speeches from the timely and time-bound deed of speaking. Like Socrates' critique of writing in the *Phaedrus*, however, this implication emerges from the speech of a character within a written text that is structured in such a way as to reinvoke the *pragmata* that writing tends to suppress, namely, the original contexts of discourse—including the dispositions of the various speakers, the circumstances of the conversation, and the like—within which speeches may be fully understood. The success of the dialogue form in doing just this is confirmed by our ability to see that Euclides must not have intended his words to be understood as a critique of writing.

In reading the *Theaetetus* it will be necessary for us to recover the *pragmata* behind the written speeches of Socrates, Theodorus, and Theaetetus. Plato drives home this point by mimicking Euclides' authorial style in his own manner of writing the prologue. Immediately after Terpsion agrees with Euclides' suggestion that they retire to his house to listen to the slave read, we find ourselves in the presence of Euclides' manuscript (143b). Precisely as it appears in the text, the journey from the agora to Euclides' home is instantaneous, because Plato omits from his account the activity of traveling. In the prologue Plato gives us the speeches of Euclides and Terpsion but not their movements. This omission reminds us that at bottom the *pragmata* we are to retrieve from the text of the *Theaetetus* are souls in motion—the living sources of the various speeches that Euclides has transcribed. Only if we are able to do so can we hope to share in Socrates' investigation of the promise of Theaetetus, and thereby in Socrates' exploration of his own nature.

Plato's writing leaves us with another gap that Socrates seems to have bridged by an act of prophecy. I refer to the space of thirty years between his conversation with Theaetetus, the boy, and the death of Theaetetus, the man. In a manner again reminiscent of Euclides, Plato provides us with a portrait of Theaetetus on the verge of manhood and a glimpse of him just prior to his death, but leaves out of his dialogues the process of maturation by which these two critical periods of his life came to be connected. Because the concerns and activities of Theaetetus at the time of his conversation with Socrates are fundamentally theoretical while the atmosphere of his death is overwhelmingly political, this gap raises the question of whether Theaetetus succeeds any more than Euclides in integrating his theoretical pursuits with his political self-understanding. Is Theaetetus's much-lauded display of courage in battle rooted in philosophic reflection on the proper political dimension of his life, or is it a consequence of his own good breeding plus the press of circumstances? Socrates' prophecy regarding the lad—"There is every necessity that he become renowned, if indeed he reaches maturity" (142d1-3)—is ambiguous: it may suggest that theoretical and political activity are united in Theaetetus's life only by necessity (*anangkê*) in the form of external compulsion. Be that as it may, Euclides, true to his theoretical commitments, entirely overlooks the passage of time in his narration. He renders Socrates' conversation with Theaetetus in direct discourse, and because there are no interruptions during the slave's reading of his manuscript we come to experience the sustained illusion that the conversation is taking place in the present. It is thus not surprising that he obscures in his text the connection between reading and remembering—a connection that is visible in the Greek language, wherein "to read" is literally "to recognize," "to know again" (*anagignoskein*). Euclides is in any case not outstandingly memorious: whereas Phaedo narrates the whole of the *Phaedo* from memory, and Socrates recounts the whole of the *Theaetetus* while awaiting execution, Euclides is emphatic about his inability to recite Socrates' conversation with Theaetetus without written reminders (142d6).

Our interpretative task as readers is not merely to remember what was said, but to understand its meaning. The example of Euclides' slave reading aloud underscores this point, for while he mouths the words of the text he presumably does not genuinely comprehend their significance. The slave's reading is in this respect a complementary image of his master's writing. Both Euclides' writing and the slave's reading anticipate a problem that shows up later in the *Theaetetus* in connection with the thesis that knowledge is perception: in order to understand a language one must be able to grasp the meaning of its component words (163b-c). These examples are intrinsically challenging: how can we avoid merely silently imitating Euclides' slave as we read the dialogues of the philosophic trial?

We are helped by the observation that Euclides' slave is not the only one who speaks aloud the conversation of the *Theaetetus*, for Plato also lets us glimpse the figure of Socrates as he relates the conversation to Euclides in his prison cell. This provocative juxtaposition of speakers suggests that there may be a sort of reading or *listening* that would harmonize with Socrates' original act of narration, just as the slave's experience of reading as simply uttering the written word is well-matched with Euclides' superficial understanding of the act of writing. It seems that we must strive to interpret the dialogue in a manner akin to the way in which Socrates originally understood his conversation with Theaetetus and Theodorus. We must recover retrospectively what Socrates uncovered prospectively.

As we have noted, Socrates' inquiry into Theaetetus's soul requires a certain kind of prophecy or prognostication. The significance of this fact is amplified by the association of Socrates with prophecy throughout the octology (*Euthyphro* 3b-c, *Sophist* 216a-b, *Cratylus* 396d, *Apology* 39c, *Crito* 44a-b, *Phaedo* 84e-85b). Socrates' literal prophecy with regard to Theaetetus's future, however, is rooted in his insight into the nature of the young Theaetetus's soul. Because of the absence or invisibility of the soul, this primary insight may be metaphorically grasped as an extended, philosophical kind of prophecy that does not necessarily involve the prediction of future events. It is possible to draw an analogous distinction between remembering, or retaining in one's soul past experiences, and recollecting, or actively seeking to recover the content internal to that which one once had in one's memory. Socratic inquiry is more like recollection than memory, because the latter is passive and unself-conscious while the former involves an effort spurred by the recognition that one has forgotten something—a recognition that is the equivalent of Socrates' knowledge of ignorance. Because one can recover the content or meaning internal to present experiences as well as past ones, recollection can serve as the image of a philosophic power that is not necessarily or essentially related to the past.[10]

In sum, prophecy and recollection may serve as metaphoric images of the interpretative capability that we must bring to the text of the *Theaetetus* and its companion dialogues if we are to read in a manner that complements Socrates' speech. Since our recollective reading of the *Theaetetus* and Socrates' prophetic insight have the same *pragmata* in view—namely, the souls of Theaetetus and Socrates—we may call this interpretative power *prophetic recollection*. It will be useful to adopt this locution also because Socrates is associated in the octology with the activity of recollecting, no less than with prophesying, the natures of souls. In the *Theaetetus*, Socrates' recollection of Parmenides' "altogether noble depth" (184a1) comes to mind, as well as his account of the difference between philosophic souls and those who dwell slavishly in the courts of law (172c-177c). Prophecy and recollection converge in the *Sophist* when Socrates reminds Theodorus, on the basis of Homer's authority, that his companion (the Stranger) may be a god in disguise (216a-b). In the *Statesman* Socrates reminds Theodorus that the sophist, statesman, and philosopher differ in worth from one another in a way that is mathematically immeasurable—a point to which Theodorus somewhat incongruously responds by praising Socrates' memory (257b). Finally, in the *Phaedo* Socrates accounts for learning in terms of recollection (72e ff.). Still more important, especially when the matter is considered with the *Phaedo* in mind, is what Socrates does *not* say about recollection in the inquiry into the nature of knowledge in the *Theaetetus*. Socrates and Theaetetus construct images of the passive acquisition and retention in the memory of opinions (e.g., as imprints on a wax block or birds taken into and enclosed within an aviary), but do not explicitly address either recollection (*anamnêsis*) or the process of learning through studious effort.[11] These theoretical lacunae, like the textual gaps noted above, can be bridged only by our own interpretative efforts; indeed, one suspects that Plato intends the labor of interpretation itself to teach us something about the relationship between learning and knowing.

Socrates' Outlandishness

Another important theme introduced by the *Theaetetus*'s prologue is that of homecoming and exile.[12] As we have already observed, the prologue invites us to reflect upon the attitudes of the political community toward the returning war hero (Theaetetus) and the condemned criminal (Socrates). The problem of whether and in what sense the political community can be a home for Socrates is complicated by his ambiguous pronouncements in the octology. Socrates identifies himself from the first as preeminently Athenian in his attachments (*Theaetetus* 143d). Even prior to his imprisonment, people come and go—Euclides, Theodorus, Euthyphro, and the Stranger are all visitors to the city—but Socrates remains rooted in Athens. Euthyphro notes that Socrates usually spends his time in the Lyceum rather than in the vicinity of the courts (*Euthyphro* 2a). At the end of the *Cratylus* Socrates stays behind while Cratylus and Hermogenes journey out to the country (440e). In the *Crito* Socrates refuses to flee from Athens, and in speaking for the Laws maintains that he "surpassed all the other Athenians in staying at home" (*Crito* 52b; cf. *Phaedrus* 230c-d). Yet Socrates also implies in the *Crito* and the *Phaedo* that in dying he will conclude a journey to his true home, which is Hades.[13]

Perhaps the most striking instance of ambiguity concerning Socrates' proper place in relation to the Athenian political community occurs in the *Apology*, when Socrates proposes that he be boarded in the Prutaneum. Meals at the community's sacred hearth were granted not only to those who had greatly benefited their fellow Athenians, but also to the *pharmakoi* or human scapegoats who were to be expelled from the city during the Thargelia, a festival of civic purification in which the Athenians cleansed themselves of religious pollution. Given that Apollo presided over the Thargelia and that Socrates was supposed to have been born on the very day of this festival, it is unclear whether Socrates means to imply that he will serve the community more in continuing to live within its walls or in undergoing the permanent exile of death.[14]

The ambiguities and paradoxes that surround the theme of homecoming and exile naturally provoke reflection upon the proper place of the Socratic philosopher, and, more generally, invite us to inquire into the significance of place for Socratic philosophizing. The political community, which is rooted in but not reducible to the physical space of Athenian territory, is in an extended or metaphorical sense one of the "places" that figure problematically in Socrates' identity. "Socrates is an Athenian" says something essential about who the old philosopher is, but just what it says is unclear. This uncertainty arises from the fact that Socratic inquiry involves an intellectual journey that slips the bonds of local attachments and opinions. Socrates travels well beyond the horizons of the Athenian political and religious tradition in thought and speech, even if he rarely sets foot outside of Athenian territory in deed. He occasionally invites us to view this journey as occurring within the larger "space" of the Whole—an encompassing domain with respect to which the dislocation or placelessness of the political community first comes into view. On these occasions—including the palinode of the *Phaedrus* (244a-257b), Diotima's account of the ladder of *erôs* in the *Symposium* (210a-212a), the cave image and the myth of Er in the *Republic* (514a-517a, 614b-621b), and the "oecography of the soul" in the *Phaedo* (107d-115a)[15]—the imagistic topography of the Whole reflects features of human life that are prior to and independent of the ways peculiar to any particular *polis*, namely, the erotic motion of souls in relation to the enduring beings.

In the ways noted above, Socrates indicates that he explores his relationship to the political community in terms of the larger philosophical

problem of charting the region within which a distinctively human life—
a life that is "livable for a human being"—may be generated and sustained. At the same time, however, there is a sense in which Socrates
seems to be tethered to a specific locale: even when mythologizing the
Whole, he never loses sight of the specific human circumstances within
which each conversation first emerges. The visibility of these circumstances in the Platonic dialogues is a constant reminder of the concreteness of Socratic inquiry. Socrates' manner of discourse implies that the
road to the ultimate *archai* of human life is always to be sought for close
to home, in the region of the proximate beginnings of philosophic dialogue. The Socratic journey thus displays the simultaneity of movement
and rest that is characteristic of circular motion, a point that is anticipated
by the many round-trips contained in the *Theaetetus*'s prologue.[16]

If indeed there is a place proper to Socratic philosophizing, it is
marked by numerous oppositions and tensions. And if this place is nothing other than the human place—if, moreover, Socrates' attempt to illuminate the human terrain is a paradigmatically human effort—then the
paradoxes of Socrates' extraordinary life simply make explicit the fundamental tensions and oppositions that stand, albeit less visibly, at the
heart of ordinary human existence. A similar pattern of explication and
elucidation is at any rate perceptible in the general structure of Socrates'
elenctic conversations, which repeatedly bring to light the contradictions
hidden within common and deeply held opinions. To undergo Socratic
refutation is to perceive the familiar as strange, to be struck by the absence of that which is present, to hear speech as silence. It is thus to appropriate as one's own inner experience the irony of Socrates, which is
characterized by the copresence of just such antitheses.[17]

Socratic irony appears to be an accurate reflection of the ambiguous
character of human life. One could say that Socrates uses dialogue in order to open the souls of his interlocutors to the mysterious wonderland
that we all already inhabit. This brings us to a caveat: taken literally,
geometrical and geographical concepts cannot do justice to what we
mean by the human place or the place of Socratic philosophizing. The
precise, nondialectical language that is appropriate to the tidy sphere of
spatial relations is simply not suited to ambiguity and paradox. My employment of spatial terms to describe the domains of Socratic philosophizing and human life, and of geometrical terms to describe the "shape"
of Socrates' activity, must therefore be understood metaphorically.

Socrates' Strangeness

Socrates' peculiarly circular style of discourse is connected with the final
theme of the philosopher's simultaneous strangeness and familiarity.

While we shall explore this connection in the following chapters, we may observe here that the statement "Socrates is an Athenian" is in interesting ways analogous to the claim "Odysseus is an Ithacan." To be sure, Ithaca is the home that Odysseus sets out from, for which he longs, and to which he ultimately returns. Yet Homer identifies Odysseus first and foremost not by his hometown but by his laborious and circuitous travels: Odysseus is a *polutropos anêr* (*Odyssey* 1.1), a "much-wandering" man "of many turns and wiles," a shifting individual who is able to persevere thanks to his own shiftiness. Odysseus's polytropism, however, serves his unwavering desire to get home and thereby "to win his soul [*psuchê*] and the return of his companions" (*Odyssey* 1.5). Just as Odysseus comes into possession of himself only by leaving home, his profound strangeness when he finally reappears in Ithaca disguised as a beggar is a mark, not of foreign indifference, but of deep devotion to those who have guarded his memory and thereby allowed him to (re)claim both his home and his identity.[18] So too, I wish to suggest, Socrates' strangeness is—paradoxically—a measure of his care for the souls of his interlocutors as well as for his own soul. To sustain this claim, it will be necessary to show that, for Socrates, a certain kind of strangeness is essential to genuinely philosophic pedagogy. This will be a main aim of our treatment of the *Theaetetus*'s midwife image in chapter 3.

It might seem far-fetched to advert to the situation of Odysseus in the course of reflecting on Socrates' philosophical activity, were it not for the fact that the dialogues themselves regularly invite us to do so. In the *Republic*, for example, Socrates and his companions undertake a philosophic journey whose structure reflects that of the *Odyssey*.[19] In the *Protagoras* Socrates names the sophists in the home of Callias as though he were Odysseus identifying the shades that approach him during his visit to Hades in Book 11 of the *Odyssey* (315b-d). And in the *Hippias Minor* he mimics Odysseus's polytropic deceptiveness in arguing that Achilles is superior to Odysseus on the grounds that Achilles is a better liar.

Most important for our present purposes are the allusions to the *Odyssey* through which Socrates introduces the problem of the philosopher's strangeness at the beginning of the *Sophist*. Socrates uses these allusions to raise questions about the identity of the Stranger, whose proper name is never mentioned in the dialogues. He reprimands Theodorus for failing to notice that the stranger he has brought with him is, "in accordance with Homer's speech, not a stranger but some god." "For he [Homer] declares that . . . the god of strangers in particular is a companion to those human beings who share in a just reverent shame [*aidous dikaias*], and looks down upon the acts of hybris and law-abidingness of human beings" (*Sophist* 216a5-b3). As we shall see, Socrates' remark draws together two different passages from the *Odyssey* in a way that renders his own identity no less uncertain than that of the Stranger. It is also worth noting that the problem of the Stranger's identity, as in the case of Socrates, is connected with a certain vagueness about his proper place: Socrates asks the Stranger to relate the beliefs of "those in that region" concerning the sophist, statesman, and philosopher (*Sophist* 217a1). Indeed, the presence of this unnamed foreigner redoubles, as it were, Plato's emphasis upon the problematic relationship between the philosopher and the political community.

The least that can be said about Plato's employment of Homer in the *Sophist* is that it links the question "Who is Socrates?" with the question "Who is the Stranger?" By asking about the number and natures of certain types of souls immediately after introducing these Homeric allusions, Socrates leads us to expect that we may be able to determine both his identity and that of the Stranger once we understand how to apply the names "sophist," "statesman," and "philosopher." With all of this in mind, it seems plausible to read Socrates' request for an examination of kinship at the beginning of the *Statesman* (257d-258a) as directed not only toward the souls of Theaetetus and young Socrates—who resemble Socrates in body and name, respectively—but primarily toward the Stranger, whose very strangeness may itself be token of kinship with Socrates. The relevant Homeric analogues of the *Statesman*'s kinship test, as Mitchell Miller has pointed out, are Odysseus's meetings with Penelope and his father Laertes in the last pages of the *Odyssey*.[20] Perhaps the final determination of the identities of Socrates and the Stranger will coincide with a philosophic "homecoming" of sorts—one that would somehow have to be reconciled with the brute facts of Socrates' impending conviction and execution.

Looking Ahead: Protagoras and Theodorus

As we unravel the fabric of Socrates' philosophic trial, we shall repeatedly encounter, like bright filaments running throughout a complex pattern, the leading themes of the *Theaetetus*'s prologue—writing and reading, the prophetic recollection of the soul, Socrates' outlandishness and strangeness, and the Odyssean, polytropic character of the philosophic quest. Our specific concern in the following chapter, however, is the *Theaetetus*, the action of which is in an important way foreshadowed by the character of Euclides. Before we turn to the *Theaetetus*, it will be useful to comment very briefly on the specific manner in which Plato's sketch of Euclides anticipates the ensuing philosophical drama.

The characters of Theodorus and Protagoras will occupy much of our attention as we study the *Theaetetus*. At first glance, these two characters seem completely unrelated. Theodorus is a mathematician, and Protagoras is a sophist; the one, a theoretical creature, seems oblivious to the city, while the other is a thoroughly political animal. Theodorus and Protagoras seem respectively to exemplify the opposition between pure philosophy and pure politics. This opposition, however, is a clue to the implicit relatedness of their paths of life. Precisely because they are abstract or one-sided modes of existence, these two paths converge with respect to their political and philosophical implications. Protagoras's anti-theoretical stance rules out the achievement not only of wisdom or knowledge but also of political goods such as justice and virtue, while Theodorus's aloofness from the political community guarantees that he will lack self-knowledge as well as any practical alternative to the politics of sophistry. Philosophy and politics fall apart from each other in the characters of Theodorus and Protagoras, and both of these spheres are thereby corrupted.

The latter, illuminating divorce between philosophy and politics is prefigured in the *Theaetetus*'s prologue by the character of Euclides, whose philosophical theories cannot explain human existence, and whose distinctly political self-understanding gives the lie to his Megarianism. Euclides actually points ahead in two important ways: directly, toward Theodorus and Protagoras, and indirectly, toward the figure of Socrates. For if philosophy and politics seem to his fellow Athenians to be most clearly at odds in the case of Socrates, it is nonetheless Socrates who begins to emerge in the *Theaetetus* as one who exemplifies a most fruitful synthesis of these two fundamental dimensions of human life.

Chapter 3

Midwifing the Soul: The *Theaetetus*

Truly Protagoras was talking in the air in making man the measure of all things, who never knows even his own measure.

Michel de Montaigne, *Essays*

It is a basic principle of contemporary "structuralist" studies of Greek drama that the details of a tragedy, comedy, or satyr play cannot be understood as isolated data, but disclose their full significance only when they are interpreted as part of a complex, often highly dynamic field of meaning that is typically characterized by numerous oppositions and tensions. One interpretation of Euripides' satyr play *Cyclops*, for example, argues persuasively that the political and philosophical significance of this drama turns upon the substantial differences between Odysseus, the satyr Silenus, and the cyclops Polyphemus, and that the identities of these individuals can be determined only by viewing them within an evolving matrix of similarities and differences that encompasses all three of these characters.[1] The most general insights of structuralism in regard to the interpretation of Greek drama may also be applied to the dialogues containing the philosophic trial of Socrates. We have already observed that in the *Apology* Socrates sought to clarify his own way of life by exploring the opposition between himself and other kinds of human beings. Plato employs the same strategy throughout the philosophic trial. In the case of the dialogue now at hand, it has been well observed that Plato presents us with a contest between three characters—Socrates, the mathematician Theodorus, and the self-proclaimed sophist Protagoras—who are engaged in a struggle over Theaetetus's education and so in a

53

sense over his soul. Each of these three characters has a distinct understanding of such fundamental things as the life most worth living, the
nature of theoretical and political activity, what wisdom is, and what
human beings are. The *Theaetetus* invites us to compare these three
modes of understanding, and so of speaking and acting, with respect to a
specific question: which of Theaetetus's three potential "trustees" would
best care for his education? [2]

We learn early on that Theaetetus is an orphan whose legal guardians
(*epitropoi*) have squandered his *ousia*—his "substance" in the sense of
"inheritance," but also, as we are perhaps meant to hear in this passage,
his "being" or "identity" (144c5-d4). This detail suggests that education
involves preserving and developing a soul's intrinsic nature rather than
replacing it with some other nature, a point that will prove to be important in considering the claims of Protagoras. It also alerts us to the
distinct possibility that Theaetetus might fall prey to a sophist who simultaneously lightens his wallet and deprives his soul of its potential excellence. While it is true that "a conspicuous part of the dialogue's plot
. . . [is] the confrontation between philosophy, mathematics, and sophistry," our examination of Theaetetus's potential trustees must take into
account their moral as well as intellectual dispositions.[3] We must famil-
iarize ourselves with their souls, and so discover in the broadest sense
who they are.

The structure of the *Theaetetus* seems especially suited to the interpretative task sketched above. We have already observed that Socrates
asks "Who is Theaetetus?" prior to asking "What is knowledge?", and
that the inquiry into Theaetetus's identity is also meant to serve Socrates'
desire for self-knowledge. But in the *Theaetetus*, the problem of identity
is posed dramatically and comparatively: we learn who Socrates and
Theaetetus are only insofar as we learn who Protagoras is and who
Theodorus is. The central drama of the *Theaetetus* consists in the complex interplay of speeches and deeds whereby the nature of each individual comes to stand out against the backdrop of other natures. This drama,
in turn, acquires philosophical significance through its concern with exploring the human place. Socrates' encounters with Theodorus and Protagoras disclose the extreme nature of certain deceptively familiar paths
of life, and help us to locate other, better ones—paths that cross the middle ground, upon which the human soul may stand out in its intrinsic
character and so best grow toward wisdom and goodness.

Although Protagoras is dead by the year 399, Socrates imagines what
he might have to say and on two occasions in the dialogue speaks in his
voice (162d-163a, 166a-168c; for the sake of simplicity, I shall hence-
forth attribute to the Platonic character of Protagoras the remarks made
by Socrates in these two passages). This detail anticipates Socrates' later

assertion, on another occasion, that philosophers sometimes take on the look of sophists. Socrates' role-playing is also formally appropriate, since Protagoras is in essence an actor. Perhaps most important, we shall see that Socrates' ability to speak for Protagoras indirectly confirms—contrary to the implication of Protagoras's own views—the possibility of philosophic discourse. Yet one must still ask why, within the context of the philosophical trial, Plato has Socrates converse with two mathematicians and imitatively recreate the arguments of a sophist. Why would a dialogue that focuses on the relationship between Socratic pedagogy, mathematical education, and the teachings of Protagoras be an appropriate context for the display of Socrates' nature? In order to address these questions, we need to explore what Theodorus, Protagoras, and Socrates have to offer a youth such as Theaetetus.

Measuring Extremes: Theodorean Mathematics and Protagorean Sophistry

Each of Theaetetus's potential trustees defends the superior worth of his own manner of thinking, and each draws the line separating his own intellectual activity from those of the other two in a different place. Theodorus rejects Socrates' suggestion that he is a guardian of the orphaned myth (*muthos*) of Protagoras, claiming "quickly" to have given up "bare speeches" in favor of geometry (165a1-2). He includes Socrates along with Protagoras as one of those who indulges in bare speeches, as becomes clear when he later suggests that Theaetetus, on account of his youth, would be better able than himself to serve as Socrates' interlocutor and "follow a closely-examined speech" (168e4-5). Protagoras, in turn, ignores mathematics altogether while defending at length his manner of discourse over and against that of Socrates (166a-168c). Finally, in his image of himself as a midwife Socrates separates his pedagogic art from both the teachings of Theodorus and the rhetoric of Protagoras (148e-151d). Socrates also links the mathematician with the sophist when he calls Protagoras Theodorus's "comrade" and "teacher" (161b8-9, 179a10) and states that Theodorus is a "trustee" of Protagoras's orphaned myth (164e4-5). And although he seems to ally himself with Theodorus when in a lengthy digression he compares the lives of free men of theory to those of slaves who live by the art of sophistical oratory (172c-177c), the fact that in important particulars Socrates bears little resemblance to the free men of theory he describes suggests that here, too, he seeks to distinguish himself from both Theodorus and Protagoras.

Just as Theodorus assimilates Socratic philosophizing to Protagorean sophistry, Protagoras is silent about Theodorus's art; the theoretical scientist seems to be unaware of the difference between philosophy and sophistry, while the urbane master of rhetoric seems unconcerned with mathematics. Socrates, on the other hand, combines the mathematician's interest in knowledge for its own sake with the sophist's familiarity with the particulars of everyday life in the *polis* and practical concern with persuasive speech. These reflections suggest the hypothesis that Theodorus and Protagoras represent abstract extremes of theoretical and political existence, and that these extremes help to delimit the intermediate paths of thinking, speaking, and acting that are opened up by Socratic midwifery.

One can begin to explore the latter hypothesis by considering Plato's dramatic characterization of the abstractness of mathematics. Mathematics is represented in the *Theaetetus* by an itinerant merchant of learnings, a fact that has political as well as theoretical implications.[4] Theodorus indicates that he is very pleased with the money he is paid by Theaetetus (144d), and we may suppose that the robustness of the Athenian educational market has more than a little to do with his presence here. He is also relatively indifferent to political attachments; his absence from his home city of Cyrene suggests that he cares no more for the youths there than for the youths of Athens (cf.. 143d). In this respect he resembles the foreigner Protagoras, whom he counts as a "friend" (162a4). Similarly, the content of his mathematical teaching is in significant respects independent of both the specific circumstances in which he teaches and the particular disposition of the learner. The context-neutral character of this teaching is rooted in the nature of the objects studied as well as the strictly theoretical interests of Theodorus and his students. Theodorus's arts of geometry and astronomy concern imperceptible figures and solids that are everywhere the same, and which, precisely in virtue of their purity and universality, allow their perceptible images to stand forth as mathematically intelligible unities (*Republic* 510c-511a, 526c-530a). The mathematical study of figures and solids, as Socrates playfully suggests, is equally well-suited to objects in any region of the cosmos, whether they be located above the heavens or below the earth (*Theaetetus* 173e-174a).

The ability to excel in theoretical mathematics, in turn, is neutral in the sense that it seems to have no significant implications for the moral and intellectual disposition of the soul as a whole or for the understanding of life as a whole. We have just touched upon the apolitical and quasi-sophistical character of the teacher Theodorus. His prize student, in turn, is a highly promising mathematician who nonetheless seriously advances the thesis that knowledge is perception. In Socrates' Protagorean exposition (to the essentials of which Theaetetus fully and immediately consents) this thesis entails that the mathematician's claim to possess scientific expertise is in fact groundless if only it appears to someone that it is groundless (151e ff.; cf. 169a, 170d-e). Theaetetus is thoroughly familiar with the book in which Protagoras announces that human being is the measure of all things (152a), yet neither the boy nor his teacher gives any evidence of having reflected upon the way in which Protagoras's teaching challenges their understanding of what mathematical knowledge is.

If the preceding observations are on the mark, Theodorus (and to a lesser extent, Theaetetus) exemplifies an abstract and unself-conscious turn of mind that is nicely anticipated by the figure of Euclides in the *Theaetetus*'s prologue. Perhaps this explains why Socrates asks Theodorus, of all people, to introduce him to promising young Athenians: any student who seems praiseworthy to Theodorus is likely to combine theoretical brilliance with a lack of self-knowledge and therefore especially to need Socratic examination, which aims first and foremost to help the interlocutor acknowledge what he does not know (210c, *Sophist* 230c-d). While Theaetetus just might profit from an encounter with Socrates, Theodorus refuses actively to wrestle with the problem of his own ignorance and will at best—and only if absolutely necessary—submit limply and painfully to what he regards as a verbal drubbing (162b, 169a-c; cf. 177c, 183c). Socrates, it seems clear, will not "see his own face" in regarding the soul of Theodorus. Yet he is at least able to fashion a rhetorical image that flatteringly reflects the old geometer's self-perception. I refer to the apparent digression at 172c-177c, whose ironic details metaphorically map the abstractness of both the mathematical thinking of Theodorus and the sophistical speech of Protagoras.[5]

Theodorus in the Mirror of Philosophy

Socrates introduces the digression in the context of his discussion with a reluctant Theodorus about Protagoras's relativism. The discussion seemingly changes course after Socrates' remark that "a speech is overtaking us from a speech, a greater from a lesser one" prompts Theodorus to ask whether they are not at leisure (172b8-c2). This is an odd question: if to be at leisure means to be free from compulsion, Theodorus, who engages in the present conversation only under protest, is certainly not at leisure. At any rate, Socrates seizes this opportunity to say something about the proper measure of speeches. He illustrates his point by comparing certain free men with their slavish opposites. The former speak at leisure (*scholê*, the circumstances proper to the scholar) about whatever they please—just as he and Theodorus are doing—and are unconcerned with the length of their speeches relative to one another, but judge them to be adequate "if only they should hit upon that which is" (172d9). The speeches of the latter, on the other hand, are conducted in the course of business (*ascholia*, the absence of *scholê*) and are measured by the flow of water in the "water-clock" of the lawcourt, by the plaintiff's affidavit, and by their adequacy in persuading the judges who sit before them as masters (172d-173a). The digression is Socrates' elaboration of the differences between the lives and souls of these two groups of men.

The digression of the *Theaetetus* anticipates a similar passage in the *Statesman*, in the course of which the Stranger and Young Socrates deviate from the inquiry into the statesman in order to investigate the problem of the proper length of speeches (283c-287b). In the latter passage, the Stranger divides the whole art of measurement into two parts, one arithmetical and one nonarithmetical. While the former is unconcerned with "the coming to be of the mean" and defines the greater as greater only with respect to the less, the latter is relative to "the mean, the fitting, the opportune, and the needful, and all that is settled in the middle ground and away from the extremes" (*Statesman* 284c1, e6-8). A similar distinction is implicit in the *Theaetetus*, for when Socrates introduces the digression he touches upon arithmetical measurement (wherein speeches are judged as greater or less in relation to each other), nonarithmetical measurement in accordance with the suitability of speeches in revealing the nature of being, and the partly arithmetical and partly nonarithmetical measurement of speeches in relation to both the amount of time allowed by the water-clock and their efficacy in persuading judges. The digressions of the *Theaetetus* and the *Statesman*, in turn, are related structurally as well as in terms of content, for each—fittingly enough, given their shared concern with the problem of measurement—stands at the (arithmetically determined) center of the surrounding dialogue.[6]

The preceding observations suggest that the digression of the *Theaetetus* is in the first instance intended to respond to Protagoras's teaching regarding measure. In Socrates' dramatic imagery, Protagoras's doctrine is represented by the Heraclitean flow of the water-clock. Man is indeed the measure of all things in the courtroom, for the adequacy of any speech—at least in the eyes of most litigants, if not of a defendant like Socrates—is determined by the perceptions of the judges, independently of the relationship of these perceptions to the truth of the matter. The thrust of Socrates' comparison is itself, however, ad hominem: if Protagoras were to turn his servile gaze up and away from the flux of human affairs he would see that universal, eternal, unchanging beings, not men, are the proper measures of speech. Yet this is only the superficial implication of the digression. Socrates' speech has partially concealed depths because it is not literally directed toward Protagoras, but toward Theodorus, and is therefore necessarily ironic in certain respects. As we have already noted, Theodorus is not a philosopher, is pained by the prospect of dialogue with Socrates, and has to be compelled to engage in "bare speeches" of the sort in which he is currently involved. Hence Socrates acts somewhat disingenuously, to say the least, in assimilating their present conversation to the activity of free men who speak about whatever pleases them in order to gain philosophic knowledge of being. To put the point in a slightly different way, we may observe that the application to speeches of arithmetical measurement—the sort of measurement that Theodorus exemplifies in his mathematical studies—drops out of the picture after 172c, to be replaced by the nonarithmetical measurement of speeches in accordance with their power to reveal "that which is." This is part and parcel of Socrates' attempt to forge a persuasive link between Theodorus's theoretical activity and that of the philosophers he describes in the digression. In fine, the digression responds to the anti-philosophical posture of Theodorus no less than to that of Protagoras.[7]

Another clue to the irony of the digression is Socrates' description of the free men reared in philosophy as "our chorus" (173b4; cf. the reference to harmony and hymning at 175e-176a). If these free men and their slavish opposites are both choruses, Socrates' speech must be a drama of sorts—a comic drama, to judge by his repeated references to laughter and ridicule (172c6, 174a6, a8, c3, d1, d2; 175b3, b5, d4). The digression's depiction of a mutually disorienting encounter between ethereal philosophers and streetwise orators especially brings to mind Aristophanes' *Clouds*. This implicit dramatic parallel is borne out by Socrates' description of the free man who spends much time in philosophy as one who is oblivious to the common life of the *polis*, who despises the ordinary business of obtaining power, wealth, honor, and physical pleasure, who dwells in the city in body only, and whose thought flies below the earth and above the heavens, engaging in geometry and astronomy and "letting itself down to none of the things nearby" (174a2).[8] Similar language reappears in the portrait of Socrates painted by his first accusers, among whom only Aristophanes is mentioned by name: Socrates is "a ponderer of the things aloft, who has thoroughly investigated all the things under the earth and makes the weaker speech stronger"; he "commits injustice and is meddlesome by investigating the things under the earth and the heavenly things, and making the weaker speech stronger, and teaching others these same things" (*Apology* 18b7-8, 19b4-c1). There are, however, two noteworthy differences between Aristophanes' comic protagonist and the philosopher described in the digression: Socrates assigns to the slavish chorus alone the activity of making the weaker speech stronger (173a), and he portrays the philosopher as someone who is interested (albeit from a purely theoretical perspective) in a whole range of ethical questions with which Aristophanes' Socrates was unconcerned, such as the natures of justice and injustice, human happiness, misery, and kingship, and in general "what a human being is, and how for such a na-

ture it is fitting to differ from all the rest in acting and being acted upon"
(175b-c, 174b3-6).

Theodorus is at first perplexed by Socrates' characterization of the free
man reared in philosophy, which does not quite fit him; he is, after all, a
businessman as well as a theoretician. He assents heartily, however, to
the subsequent account of the conflict between the two choruses, proclaiming that "things happen altogether in the way you are saying"
(175b8) and expressing a wish that others could be persuaded by Socrates just as he himself has been (176a). Socrates' own opinion is another
matter. He acknowledges that the free man he has described is "the one
whom you [Theodorus] call a philosopher" (175e1-2), but he delicately
indicates at the outset of his speech about "our chorus" that he will not be
discussing his own particular manner of philosophizing. "Let's speak,"
he tells Theodorus, "about the leaders of the chorus [*tôn koruphaiôn*]; for
why should one speak of those spending time poorly [*phaulôs*] in philosophy?" (173c6-8). This distinction proves to be a telling one, for it
turns out that Socrates finds it impossible to philosophize otherwise than
"poorly." Later in the dialogue, he admits to Theaetetus that their manner
of conversation has been "shameless" and "impure" and that they are
consequently "no good" (*phauloi*: 197a4), since "we've said thousands
of times 'we recognize' and 'we don't recognize,' and 'we know' and
'we don't know,' as though we somehow understand one another while
still being ignorant of knowledge" (196d10-e5). Socrates nevertheless
will not change his manner of discourse, "for I am who I am" (197a1);
and when the Stranger appears on the following morning Socrates supposes that he is a "refutative god" come "to look us over and refute us
who are poor [*phaulous*] in speeches" (*Sophist* 216b4-6).

Let us pause to see where we stand. In the digression Socrates appro-
priates Aristophanes' image of the Socratic philosopher, purges this image of its association with unjust speech, adds to it a theoretical concern
with human nature and human life, and presents the result to Theodorus
as a portrait of the true philosopher. While Theodorus is persuaded by
this portrait, Socrates subtly dissociates himself from it. Indeed, his ability to characterize *both* philosophers *and* clever orators suggests that he
is a member of neither of the choruses he describes. Unlike the philosophic *koruphaios*, Socrates can find his way to the places of public assembly, knows the laws and decrees enacted therein, is well acquainted
with his neighbors and their habits and opinions, and is intimately familiar with the desires and ambitions that grow within political communities. Socrates' reference to geometry and astronomy (173e5-6) confirms
that he fashions his portrait of the philosopher with Theodorus's nature
in mind. This humorously substantiates the accuracy of something Aristophanes hints at in the *Clouds*: Socrates is capable of imitating in speech

the natures of his interlocutors.[9] In general, however, Socrates invites us to explore the similarities as well as the differences between Theodorus and his transformed version of Aristophanes' Socrates. By distancing himself from the philosopher he describes in the digression, Socrates also suggests that Aristophanes' caricature of philosophy in the *Clouds* may help us to recognize the deficiencies of certain men of theory, men exemplified in the *Theaetetus* by the characters of Theodorus and Euclides.[10]

In the *Clouds*, Socrates and his students are depicted as mathematically inclined theoreticians who engage in geometry and astronomy (178, 194, 200-205, 225; cf. 1503, 1506-1507). Socrates is especially adept at undertaking delicate and precise measurements of such things as the length of a flea's jump and the relative size of the anus of a gnat (144-173). While he and his students examine the heavens and the things beneath the earth (171-173, 188) and are equally interested in the smallest and biggest things (minute vermin and the sun and stars), they are theoretically and practically oblivious to the intermediate, human domain. It is true that Socrates makes the structure of language an object of study (636 ff.), but he seems to view speech as nothing other than a special means of expressing private bodily appetites. Put another way, he does not connect *logos* with the human soul. In theory, he ignores that which elevates humans above animals (1427-1431); in practice, he treats his students as if they were captive beasts or, at best, eager but submissive dogs (184-186, 490-491, 774, 810; cf. 198-199). From the lofty perspective of his basket, Socrates despises both human beings and the things they hold to be divine (223-226).

In sum, Aristophanes' Socrates is a pure scientist who is supremely deficient in the area of self-knowledge. Perhaps most important, his mathematical arts do not allow the human soul to show itself in its distinctive character. Held aloft on the stage by a machine normally reserved for gods, Aristophanes' comic philosopher looks down upon the human things. Yet his philosophical practice results in grotesque inversion of the high and the low, the divine and the bestial, the noble and the base.[11] One suspects that this happens because Socrates treats the high and the low as relative to each other only, and not to the intermediate, human domain. Gods and beasts, it seems, are held apart by human life itself, in that they become difficult to distinguish when one abstracts from the aspirations, standards of worth, and habits of judgment that are peculiar to human beings.[12] The procedure of Aristophanes' Socrates, in turn, must be connected with his preference for mathematical modes of knowledge. Put in terms of the Stranger's crucial distinction, Aristophanes' Socrates is unfamiliar with nonarithmetical measurement relative to the mean. The Stranger speaks in this connection of the *coming to be* of the mean because "nothing, so to speak, of the human things is ever at rest" (*Statesman* 294b3-4). As a consequence of the instability of all things human, the specific being of the mean—that which is fitting, etc., in each concrete instance—changes according to intrinsically variable circumstances. Furthermore, the realization of the mean in a given situation depends upon appropriate action, which in turn requires the prior recognition of that which is appropriate by sound judgment or *phronêsis*. Mathematical expertise is no substitute for *phronêsis*, because the being of the middle ground as middle—and most generally, the distinctive intermediacy of the human place—cannot be detected by the curiously placeless techniques of arithmetical measurement.[13] For Aristophanes' Socrates, however, the mean is neither an object of study nor an aim of action. Both in speech and deed, he is wholly inattentive to the middle ground of human life.

In one respect, Aristophanes' portrait of the philosopher in the *Clouds* seems irrelevant to our interpretation of the digression. As noted above, the digression presents us with a philosopher who differs from the protagonist of the *Clouds* in that he is at least theoretically interested in human life. Furthermore, Socrates seems to connect the philosopher's theoretical interest in human life with practical intelligence: he advises Theodorus to assimilate himself to a god, and so "to become just and pious with *phronêsis*" (176b2-3). Socrates' god-like philosopher, one might suppose, is therefore partly if not wholly immune to the criticism of being oblivious to the intermediate, human domain. Yet a moment's reflection shows that this supposition is indefensible. Socrates describes a thinker who is so detached from everyday life that he hardly knows what his neighbor is doing or even "whether he is a human being or some other nursling" (174b1-3). This theoretician desires to know what human being in general is and does, but is utterly unacquainted with the natures and activities of any particular human beings. He ponders the universal and the eternal, but disdains to descend to the evanescent particulars of human life (174a, 174e-175a; cf. *Clouds* 223). He purports to examine justice and happiness without reflecting on the concrete circumstances in which humans may actually achieve happiness or do what is just. He studies kingship, but is wholly unfamiliar with life in political communities. Moreover, he lacks Socrates' characteristic knowledge of ignorance, for "he doesn't even know that he does not know all these things" (173e1). In a manner reminiscent of his Aristophanean counterpart, he confuses rulers with shepherds and humans with cattle (174d-e).[14] This thinker's detachment from ordinary human experience ensures that he, like Aristophanes' Socrates, will be able neither to discern nor to bring into existence what is fitting, opportune, and needful.

The situation Socrates describes is theoretically as well as practically absurd: the philosopher would not know what he is talking about if he should speak of justice, kingship, and happiness. Socrates' connection of *phronêsis*, justice, and piety with godhood merely highlights this absurdity, for all three of these virtues are rooted in and pertain to the region of "mortal nature" that Socrates advises Theodorus "to flee from as quickly as possibly" (176a7-b1). Scott Hemmenway notes that "two of these virtues [justice and *phronêsis*, respectively] take us right back into the political and practical realm"; we may add that piety is fundamentally the virtue, not of gods or godlike creatures who look down on the mortal realm, but of men who look up toward the divine things from the ground of human life.[15]

Initial appearances to the contrary notwithstanding, Socrates portrays in the digression of the *Theaetetus* a "philosopher" whose interest in human life is an ultimately incoherent extension of abstract, mathematical thinking. The digression is thus on one level a thought experiment that invites us to imagine the results of applying Theodorus's way of thinking to the matters with which Socrates is fundamentally concerned. Among other things, this thought-experiment helps to emphasize the gulf that in fact separates Theodorus from Socrates. In the names "Theodorus" and "Theaetetus" we hear an echo of the Greek words *theos* ("god") and *theôrein* ("to contemplate"). Both of these words, in turn, are audible in the word *theatron* or "theatre," a place where spectators assume the observational posture of gods as they gaze upon the drama below. In listening to Socrates' digression, Theodorus is able, as it were, to view himself on stage. An ironic indication of the applicability of Socrates' image to the character of Theodorus is the fact that the old geometer sees nothing amiss in Socrates' description of the philosopher. Theodorus's passivity guarantees that he will remain unaware of his ignorance; it makes him a poor interlocutor for Socrates but, as we shall see, a good auditor for the likes of Protagoras. Like the leader of the chorus of philosophers, Theodorus looks down upon life in the cities of men from a perspective of godlike contemplation, within which only universal, timeless, unchanging beings—as exemplified by the pure noetic objects of mathematics—are acknowledged to be worthy of attention. Socrates suggests that these Theodorean heights cannot be sustained without due attention to the middle ground of human life, a shifting domain of coming to be and passing away that calls for modes of knowing attuned to the particularity and potentiality of human souls no less than to universal, actualized forms. Theodorus's ignorance of nonarithmetical measurement according to the mean, we may note in passing, is later underscored by Socrates' rebuke of his mistaken belief that the worth of the souls of the sophist, statesman, and philosopher can be measured mathematically (*Statesman* 257a-b).

The present line of reflection helps to bring out one of the issues implicit in Theaetetus's account of his discovery concerning "square" and "oblong" numbers (147c ff.). This discovery involves the geometrical conception of *dunamis*, the "power" or root capable of generating a square of a certain area. Theaetetus divides all numbers into two classes, those that can be formed by multiplying equal factors ("square" numbers like four and nine) and those that cannot ("oblong" numbers like three and five). The square roots of oblong numbers are irrational, but Theaetetus sees that these irrational numbers can be rendered geometrically commensurable with rational numbers if one considers the areas of the oblong figures that represent their squares (147e-148b). He thus finds in geometry a means of thinking about irrational numbers by means of images. Theaetetus's work is especially interesting in the context of the philosophic trial because it suggests that mathematics might after all have something to say about the unique *dunamis* or power of the human soul, which will turn out to be akin to an irrational root (cf. *Statesman* 266a-b). A full investigation of this matter must await the appearance of the Stranger. For now, however, we may note that Theaetetus's research may provide us with an image both of the problem of human *dunamis* and of the indirect treatment of this problem by way of images.[16]

Protagoras and the Chorus of Orators

In certain respects, the imagery of the digression seems especially suited to the representation of Protagoras. When in the *Protagoras* Socrates first catches sight of the dialogue's eponymous protagonist, he describes him as the leader of a chorus of men who became enchanted by his voice as he passed through their cities. In the same passage, Socrates compares Protagoras's powers of enchantment with those of Orpheus (*Protagoras* 314e-315b). Taken together with Socrates' narrative asides at 315b9 and c8, both of which evoke Odysseus's visit to Hades in the *Odyssey*, this passage suggests that Socrates envisions the dance of the sophist's chorus as taking place in the underworld. In the *Theaetetus*, Socrates implies something similar when he has the dead Protagoras pop his head up from beneath the ground in order to defend himself (171d). Here as elsewhere, the *Theaetetus* subtly draws upon a familiar metaphorical topology that is perhaps most vividly and comprehensively employed in the *Republic*. If the flying philosopher of the digression dwells metaphorically in the heavens, the leader of the chorus of orators seems to be at home in the subterranean regions of the cave.[17]

To judge by the "antistrophal precision" with which the two choruses of the digression oppose each other,[18] Protagoras appears to provide a total and striking contrast to Theodorus. Yet as we have seen, there are several indications that the old geometer and the deceased sophist are somehow related. Theodorus admits to being the friend and comrade of Protagoras and does not object to being called his student or even addressed as if he were Protagoras (although he denies that he is the trustee of Protagoras's orphaned myth). Our preliminary reflections on the dramatic structure of the *Theaetetus* suggest that this relationship has some special philosophical or political relevance. What is the link that binds these two characters together? And how does the connection between Protagoras and Theodorus assist us in understanding the nature of Socrates?

The first thing to notice in reflecting upon these questions is that Socrates employs Aristophanes' *Clouds* as a dramatic subtext in characterizing Protagoras as well as Theodorus. Shortly after introducing Protagoras's thesis that "of all things, human being is the measure, of the things that are, how they are, and of the things that are not, how they are not," Socrates suggests that its author is an "all-wise" esotericist whose book *Truth* actually conceals the truth from us, "the multitudinous rabble" (152a2-4, c8-9). The latter remark anticipates Socrates' subsequent characterization of Protagoras as "very much looking down" upon us, so that we are at first "filled with wonder, as if he were a god in wisdom" (161c6-8). Unlike Socrates' own philosophical accomplishments, Protagoras's secret teaching is "not poor" (*ou phaulon*: 152d2). In the sequel, Socrates reveals to Theaetetus "the mysteries" of the "hidden truth" of Protagoras and his philosophical comrades, mysteries that "the uninitiated" are forbidden to overhear (155d ff.).

As with Theodorus, Socrates employs irony in the remarks cited above in order implicitly to connect Protagoras with the comic protagonist of the *Clouds* while simultaneously distancing himself from his Aristophanean counterpart. The passages cited above, however, stand in tension with Socrates' description of the chorus of orators, for they depict Protagoras in terms that echo Socrates' characterization of the flying philosopher: Protagoras is a wise man whose intelligence lifts him up into the region of the gods, from which vantage-point he despises the vast crowds of ignorant mortals. Yet it must also be observed that Protagoras and Theodorus embody different aspects of Aristophanes' Socrates. As noted above, the chorus of orators—but not the chorus of philosophers—knows how to "flatter" in speech and "beguile" in deed (173a2-3), and so possesses the hypocritical practical arts associated with Socrates in the *Clouds*. These arts are more directly, albeit more subtly, associated with Protagoras in two other passages. Just before he calls

Protagoras Theodorus's teacher, Socrates repeats a phrase that Strepsiades utters at *Clouds* 1338: *nê Di', ô mele*: "Yes, by Zeus, my good
man" (178e9).[19] In its original context, the latter phrase expresses the in-
credulity and indignation that Strepsiades feels in response to his son
Pheidippides' offer to prove to him that father-beating is just. Pheidippides has just asked his father to take his pick of the just or the unjust
speech, both of which he has learned at the school of Socrates (*Clouds*
1332-1337). Socrates' employment of the same phrase within the context
of his discussion with Theodorus implies that Theodorus has been corrupted by his association with Protagoras, just as in the *Clouds* Pheidippides was corrupted by his association with Socrates. This suggestion is
obviously somewhat playful, since Socrates takes pains in this context to
exaggerate the nature and extent of Protagoras's relationship with Theodorus. Yet a similar implication surfaces in a later passage. At the earliest
feasible moment Theodorus breaks off his conversation with Socrates, in
accordance with the "contract" the two had made earlier. When Theaetetus urges him to continue the discussion, Theodorus irritably rebukes
the lad: "So young, Theaetetus, and you teach your elders to do injustice
by violating agreements?" (183d3-4). Since Socrates had earlier advised
Theaetetus that he should not disobey Theodorus (146b-c), Plato here
suggests—once again, rather playfully—that even Theaetetus's limited
and indirect association with the doctrines of Protagoras has had a corrupting effect.

The passages cited above invite further reflection on the connection
between Theodorus and Protagoras. Let us first consider the mathematician. Theodorus's appeal to the restrictive authority of previous agreements reminds us that he is truly not at leisure, that is, free from the conventions and common necessities that limit the speech of men in cities.
In fact, the humorless Theodorus (cf. 145b10-c2) is regularly associated
with the serious business of making covenants, fulfilling contracts, and
offering testimony, so much so that it would be fair to say that his understanding of relations with others appears to be thoroughly legalistic (cf.
Theaetetus 145c and 148b with *Sophist* 216a and *Statesman* 257a). It is
tempting to view Theodorus's adherence to the legal and quasi-legal
forms of convention as a direct consequence of his theoretical abstraction
from human life in general and political affairs in particular. Theodorus's
"impractical" turn of mind provides little direct and concrete guidance in
practical affairs. Socrates' flattery of him in the digression proves hol-
low, for Theodorus knows nothing of justice and happiness in themselves. More precisely, his understanding of social intercourse seems to
rest less upon specific conceptions of what is good, noble, or just than
upon a general set of more-or-less well ordered conventions that function
as rules for the establishment and fulfillment of agreements and so gov-

ern a broad range of human interactions. In addition, Theodorus's practical formalism reflects the preference for generality and structure that one might expect from a theoretical mathematician.

If the preceding impressions of Theodorus are on the mark, they suggest an important point of contact with Protagoras. "Human being is the measure of all things" also announces a kind of formalism: Protagoras's doctrine tells us not what is noble or just, but rather what it is that *determines* that things are noble or just. Roughly stated, both Protagoras and Theodorus maintain that the authority of *nomos* (law, custom, convention) inheres in the activity of positing through speech rather than in the intrinsic worth or rightness of that which is spoken about. Indeed, both men are compelled to remain silent about the latter. Both Theodorus's legalism and Protagoras's relativism thereby shift moral and political debate onto a highly abstract plane: what counts in such debate is not content but form, not *what* is said or opined but *how* it is said or opined. Theodorus's claim to have abandoned bare speeches at an early age turns out to be loaded with irony.

Taken to its extreme, the view that what counts is not what is said but how it is said admittedly conflicts with legalism; as Plato suggests in the ways noted above, Protagoras teaches the young to violate *nomos*. But this fact only raises a question about the coherence of Theodorus's practical thinking. For what prevents his legalistic formalism from being taken to extremes? Theodorus does not seem to be in a position to offer any nonarbitrary reason for adhering to the conventions pertaining to social intercourse (rather than, to take the Protagorean alternative, merely appearing to adhere to these conventions). One could perhaps most easily imagine him defending legalism on the ground that it promotes the political stability that makes possible a life of mathematical inquiry. This argument raises once again the question of whether Theodorus is sufficiently reflective and self-conscious to account for the worth of his own theoretical activity. Quite apart from this lingering problem, however, the issue comes down to this: does Theodorus's understanding of the theoretical life in any way militate against the Protagorean alternative mentioned above, especially if this alternative is not obviously inferior from the standpoint of political stability? For Theodorus, the gulf between the domains of godlike theorizing and all-too-human life in political communities seems too wide to support any argument against Protagoras that rests upon an appeal to the good of the community. When these two domains are made to face each other as abstract opposites, the intrinsic worth of each becomes imperceptible from the perspective of the other.

Protagoras is at first depicted by Socrates as looking down on human life from a great distance. As with Theodorus, this distance initially appears to be rooted in Protagoras's contemplative detachment from ordinary life and correspondingly superior wisdom. Yet subsequent developments reverse both of these impressions. Socrates later associates Protagoras with such lowly creatures as pigs, baboons, and tadpoles (161c-d)—a menagerie reminiscent of the fleas, gnats, lizards, chickens, and dogs that populate the *Clouds*. In addition, Protagoras makes it clear that his apparent aloofness vis-à-vis the political community is to be explained not by a preference for the theoretical life, but rather by his desire to possess the common political goods of honor and money (167c-d; cf. 161d-e, 178e-179a). Both of these goods, in turn, are owed to Protagoras on account of his supposed wisdom. In his own way, Protagoras too seeks to flee the mortal region and become a god. But while the flying philosopher of the digression is unaware of the impression he makes upon the city, Protagoras is not: it is crucial that he appear *to others* to occupy great heights of his wisdom and so to be worthy of worshipful esteem. Protagoras is an actor and the city is his audience; as his relativism confirms, he is nothing apart from the way in which he is perceived.

How can Protagoras be the leader of the chorus of orators and yet look (at least initially) like the leader of the chorus of free men raised in philosophy? The answer lies partly in the definitive hypocritical art of the chorus of orators, and partly in the deep similarity between these two choruses and so between Protagoras and Theodorus. The orators are able through guileful speech to appear to be what they are not, or, in the Stranger's later terminology, to produce semblances (*phantasmata*) or false images of themselves (*Sophist* 235b-c). In particular, sophists have the capacity to imitate wise men. Socrates first calls attention to this capacity by unmasking Protagoras as an esotericist who uses writing as a tool of deception, and subsequently by "demoting" him from the level of the gods to the level of beasts. This demotion, however, also highlights a sense in which each of the choruses of the digression shades indistinguishably into its antistrophic opposite. Protagoras's desire to become a god finds expression in his teaching that human being is the measure of all things and his concomitant silence on the question of the gods (162d-e). In one stroke, he effectively divinizes everyone. Protagoras's teaching nevertheless also secures the relative divinity of the orators, since it entails that those who have the power to manipulate the perceptions of others are, as it were, first among equals. But rhetorical godhood is fleeting: as the *Theaetetus* progresses we see Protagoras flying, like the philosopher of the digression, above and then below the human realm. Although his secret teaching that "nothing ever is, but is always coming to be" (152e1) supposedly explains why all things do not "turn upside down" (153d4-5), Protagoras, like Aristophanes' Socrates, cannot prevent the heights from collapsing into the depths.

The cosmic inversion or collapse noted above, which is dramatically echoed in the breakdown of the distinction between the two choruses, is once again rooted in the neglect of the intermediate, human domain. In spite of his intimate acquaintance with everyday pursuits and concerns, Protagoras seems to know no more than Theodorus does about the nature of human beings. Like Theodorus, Protagoras overlooks or ignores the human soul; more specifically, he assimilates the soul to the body. This is the main point of Socrates' many references to animals and plants, which sorts of beings (according to Protagoras) also possess the physiological capacity of perception and so, no less than humans, are measures for themselves of what is and what is not (161c, 167b-c). Like Aristophanes' Socrates, Protagoras severs the connection between *logos* and the human soul; speech does not communicate but at best "expresses," and what it expresses is the private condition of one's own body. Protagoras's most famous dictum seems to privilege human understanding, but this too is an illusion; there remains no significant difference between humans and any other percipient beings (including gods).[20] All the same, Protagoras absurdly persists in regarding himself as radically superior to other humans: while he views others as plants, he envisions himself as a farmer (167b6-7) and therefore as a member of an altogether different species. In a final image, however, Socrates represents Protagoras as something like a head of cabbage (171d1-3). Socrates similarly implies elsewhere that the practitioners of sophistry, far from being farmers or doctors, are themselves diseased plants: he states in the digression that the slavish practice of rhetoric in the law-courts makes the "still tender" souls of the young become "bent" and "stunted" (173a-b). No less than Theodorus, Socrates suggests, Protagoras lacks self-knowledge.

Shortly after Socrates introduces Protagoras's teachings into his conversation with Theaetetus, he observes that eristic sophists—unlike Theaetetus and himself—are untroubled by contradictions between their speeches and their thoughts (154d-e). While Socrates notes that Protagoras's Heraclitean ontology makes such contradictions virtually unavoidable because speech tends to bring things to a standstill (157b), Protagoras's claim to wisdom involves another, profound inconsistency between what he thinks and what he says about the nature of human beings. When he compares himself to a farmer tending sick plants, Protagoras maintains that the sophist accomplishes with speeches what the doctor effects with drugs. Sophistical "education" (*paideia*) accordingly changes bitter perceptions into sweet ones by making a sick man healthy (166e-167a). Learning is therefore coming to experience new tastes (cf. *Protagoras* 313d-314b), and the organ of discrimination is not the soul but—shades of Aristophanes again!—the tongue (cf. *Clouds* 423). It is therefore important, incidentally, that the sophist's "drugs" or transformative speeches seem sweet to his auditors (cf. 157c). To be sick and have sick perceptions and then become healthy and have healthy perceptions is, however, to become a different person. Protagoras teaches that nothing is or becomes in itself, but everything is or becomes relative to or in tandem with something else, and just as perceptions must be or become for someone, I must be or become, so to speak, for my perceptions (160a-c). It follows that the sophist does not "educate" one and the same person but rather brings someone new into being. The sophist is in effect a craftsman who molds new people out of old material. Protagoras correspondingly gives Socrates the telling advice to make others "flee from themselves into philosophy, in order that, having come to be other, they may be rid of who they were before" (168a5-7).[21]

The farmer-doctoring-sick-plants analogy brings out an important dimension of the preceding account of sophistry. Protagoras suggests by way of this analogy that human beings are passive and pliant in the hands of the sophist, and that the sophist possesses authoritative expertise in regard to their care. This seems inconsistent with his public teaching that human being is the measure of all things; to be a measure is actively to determine how things stand, and so to be an expert in one's own right. Here we encounter a contradiction between Protagoras's private thoughts and his public speeches that is smoothed over by his hypocritical art: Protagoras implicitly regards men as plants but leads them to believe that they are active centers of authority. First impressions to one side, the esotericism of Protagoras's famous dictum cannot be understood in purely theoretical terms. Deception is an unavoidable element of Protagoras's manipulative art, for being informed that one is a plant leaves a bitter taste in the mouth. To grasp the necessity of this deception, however, is to see that men are after all different from plants: unlike human beings, plants presumably do not find it sweeter to be told that they are gods than that they are vegetables. Protagoras, on the other hand, is a farmer; one could say that he is a plant that has become truly cognizant of its own active power. Protagorean power is necessarily expressed in relation to an other, and manifests itself not as self-control but as control over others. Protagoras therefore guards his understanding of the nature of this active power as a closely held secret, to be divulged only to those who are willing to pay his high tuition. His "mysteries" are at bottom not a set of ontological doctrines, but the knowledge of a way of speaking that maximizes the passivity or manipulability of one's auditors.

Theodorus and Protagoras as Trustees of the Soul

The connection between Theodorus and Protagoras becomes fully apparent when we attempt to envision these two as trustees of the soul of

Theaetetus. As we have seen, Theodorus embraces a conception of the theoretical life that excludes self-knowledge. For Theodorus, theoretical knowledge is of pure noetic objects. The human soul is not one of these. From Theodorus's lofty perspective, the soul's particularity, potentiality, and changeability make it less worth knowing than the universal, fully actual, unchanging objects of mathematics. Furthermore, the digression begins to suggest that these same characteristics make the soul ill-suited to being grasped by the techniques of mathematical inquiry. Theodorus's theoretical abstraction from the human soul also has practical consequences, including his indifference to political attachments and the empty formalism of his relations with others. In both of these respects, he bears a marked resemblance to Protagoras. At best, Theodorus's narrow conception of theoretical activity leaves his without the resources to challenge sophistry on moral grounds; at worst, it also leaves him without the inclination to do so.

Theodorus holds himself aloof from human life in deed as well as in speech. The fact that he has traveled far from his home city in order to earn fees for his teaching only serves to underscore the superficial and apolitical character of his engagement with human affairs. Theodorus lacks both *phronêsis* and self-knowledge because he has neither the concrete experience of human life nor the theoretical flexibility necessary for the acquisition of either. If both *phronêsis* and self-knowledge are necessary for wisdom and moral excellence, Theodorus represents a path of life that does not lead to substantial human goodness and does not even aim at wisdom. As a student of mathematics, Theaetetus flourishes under Theodorus's tutelage; for all that, the old geometer seems to squander the potential of the youth's soul.

Theaetetus refers at one point to madmen or dreamers who believe they are gods or think they have feathers and are flying (158a-b). This certainly anticipates the situation with regard to Theodorus, whom Socrates cannot awaken to an investigation of the soul and its worth. Socrates elsewhere speaks of geometers as merely dreaming about what is, and he observes in the same context that geometry provides no waking knowledge of the beginning (*archê*), that is, of the Good (*Republic* 533b-c; cf. 534b-d). Moreover, Theodorus is by no means a wakeful and energetic interlocutor; he dislikes being made to answer difficult philosophical questions but clearly enjoys listening to long, preferably flattering speeches (168c, 177c). Theodorus is just the sort of passive and pliant auditor that Protagoras would wish for.

Theaetetus's image of madmen or dreamers who believe they are gods equally suits Protagoras's fantastic vision of active, controlling power, which represents an abstractly political alternative to Theodorus's abstractly theoretical existence. In spite of the impressions generated by his rather sophisticated ontology, Protagoras is not interested in theoretical activity for its own sake; from his thoroughly mundane perspective, the good life consists in the possession of honor and money. Protagoras views himself as a master of the political game, in which the usual sorts of winners include rulers, the wealthy, and the well-born (174d-175b). His superiority in this game rests upon his ability to control the perceptions of others in accordance with his own ends. The situation is the reverse of that which obtains with Theodorus, for in Protagoras's case it is the *practical* imperative of successful rhetorical manipulation that has *theoretical* consequences. Protagoras acquires honor and money not from the city at large, but from a chorus of worshipful and well-heeled followers, all of whom (as is clear from the *Protagoras*) desire to be schooled in the secrets of sophistry. Protagoras must therefore present himself as a master of the art of mastery. His relativism (and as we shall see below, his Heraclitean ontology) is designed to produce just the desired impression. "Human being is the measure of all things" is a theoretical assertion that serves two practical purposes. First, it helps to lull men into the belief that they are all masters, which is a useful illusion for anyone wishing to enslave them. Second, it secures Protagoras's claim to wisdom insofar as it guarantees that he cannot be defeated in argument: any claim you may make against Protagoras is true "for you," but not for Protagoras, and that is where matters must stand. This impenetrable defense is a decided advantage for one who measures discourse in eristic terms (cf. Socrates' comparison of Protagoras to a hard-hitting boxer at *Protagoras* 339e).

If the preceding observations are well-taken, however, it would seem difficult to distinguish Protagorean mastery from slavery, and that in multiple senses. To be a slave is, perhaps first and foremost for the Greeks, to be politically disenfranchised, and therefore to lack the power of speaking a meaningful speech—a speech that counts for something—within the political arena.[22] Protagoras willingly accepts the philosophical equivalent of slavery as a precondition of what he construes to be political mastery, for the relativistic gambit that ensures he cannot be refuted also entails the complete silencing of meaningful philosophic discourse. In a Protagorean universe, there can be no community of inquiry: the giving and receiving of ostensibly philosophical accounts amounts at best to an exchange of reports on the purely private and subjective conditions of the speakers.[23] More broadly, there is in such a universe no common, public space or middle ground upon which otherwise private selves can meet. For this reason, Protagoras's theoretical commitments also rule out the possibility of an authentically *political* community.[24] Here is where the domains of philosophy and politics most clearly intersect: if partnership in discussion and reflection is impossible—if, as

Protagoras hints, the fact of public agreement is always explicable in terms of underlying relationships of domination (activity) and submission (passivity)—then the bonds of common opinion that hold together the *polis* must be forged and sustained by cleverly disguised modes of mastery. But if, as Aristotle maintains, *logos* designates a kind of perception and verbal articulation that is peculiar to human beings and that makes possible the partnership that constitutes a *polis* (*Politics* 1.1.1253a7-18), Protagoras perversely chooses something that is in its essentials hardly distinguishable from literal slavery: he trades for money and honor both his humanity and his share in a genuinely political community.

Finally, it is not quite accurate to say that Protagoras measures the adequacy of his ostensibly theoretical pronouncements in terms of their results in the game of rhetorical mastery, for he is not a fully authoritative or decisive measure even in this arena. In the digression Socrates describes the orators as slaves and the judges of their speeches as masters; so too, Protagoras is at best the servant of his auditors, to whose tastes his speeches must be flavored and upon whom he depends for money and honor. Nor can Protagoras legitimately comfort himself with the reflection that his public speaking is mere role-playing, that he holds part of himself back, and that he is therefore something more than a wage-servant of slaves (actual and potential students) who aspire to be masters. Since none of his thoughts or speeches have theoretical or political significance in any domain beyond the rhetorical context just sketched, he is nothing other than what his auditors make of him. In the last analysis, Protagoras's relative mastery bears a close resemblance to absolute slavery.

Protagoras—like Aristophanes' Socrates—turns out in the end to be a thief and a cheat (cf. *Clouds*, 175-179, 719, 856-859). By his own lights, the usefulness of his wisdom depends upon keeping others ignorant of their capability to cease being plants. Protagoras therefore deliberately conceals from others the knowledge that makes it possible to achieve what he regards as the highest good for oneself. In a deeper sense, however, he also cheats the few to whom he divulges the "Mysteries" of sophistry: like a corrupt guardian, he robs them of their intellectual and moral potential—their distinctively human inheritance or *ousia*—insofar as he seduces them with his vision of wisdom and power. Protagorean measurement is the "subjective" antithesis of the quantitative and "objective" methods of mathematics, yet both turn out to be incongruous with the nature of the human soul. Geometry, however, provides a fitting *image* of Protagorean incongruity. Protagoras understands human being as a multiplicity of discrete, dimensionless selves. His ontology entirely overlooks—or, perhaps more accurately, suppresses for rhetorical reasons—the continuity and depth of the soul. Under these circumstances, the soul cannot, as it were, stand back from itself in order to reflect *upon* itself or attempt to gain knowledge *of* itself; the critical distance of a self from itself becomes the simple otherness of distinct selves. For the same reason, Protagoras indicates that his auditors are changed *in their natures* when they take in the rhetorical "food" or "drugs" that he offers them. This would not necessarily be the case were they able meaningfully to assess the effect of his speeches upon their own souls. Because it implicitly denies the possibility of meaningful reflection upon oneself, Protagoras's ontology, like his relativism, supports his claim to teach a powerful art of mastery. By the same token, however, Socrates' active consideration and ultimate rejection of the doctrines of Protagoras—not to mention his ability to assume the role of Protagoras and to criticize his own arguments from the perspective afforded by this role—provide dramatic counterevidence of the soul's reflective depth and cohesiveness.

Socrates' interpretation of Protagoras's *Truth* is also relevant to the problem of writing and reading. In the absence of suitable and willing "trustees," Protagoras finds it necessary to come to life, as it were, to defend his "orphaned" writings against Socrates' misinterpretations (162d ff., 166c ff.)—a fact that seems to support Socrates' own criticisms of writing in the *Phaedrus* (275d-e). Yet "Protagoras" is actually Socrates, who has mounted a defense of Protagoras's writings entirely without the benefit of their author's presence. A victory for Protagoras in his debate with Socrates would therefore actually be a victory for the possibility of sympathetic and insightful reading. It is also interesting to note that we cannot consistently accept Protagoras's assertion that Socrates is eristic and unjust in argument, since a genuinely eristic disputant would never have put a persuasive criticism of himself in the mouth of his opponent. Just as Protagoras's tendency to take everything personally in his debate with Socrates is a dramatic reflection of his relativism, Socrates' assumption of the role of Protagoras is a dramatic demonstration of the possibility of setting aside the love of one's own things within the context of philosophical discourse.

In the end, Protagoras's famous dictum instantly entitles us to think and speak with authority about "all things," with the massive exception of ourselves. About the latter, we must remain silent. Protagoras can help the young to *flee from* themselves (if only to arrive at a state of vegetal dumbness), but he cannot help them to *become* themselves—that is, to develop and so come into full possession of their distinctively human natures. If the latter fairly describes the main obligation of a trustee of the soul, Protagoras is not even minimally qualified to enter into this relationship with anyone: as concerns the self and the soul, he quite simply does not know what he is talking about.

Theodorus and Protagoras represent abstract and externally opposed ways of life that ultimately converge with regard to their philosophical and political implications. By divorcing philosophy from politics, Theodorus and Protagoras radically diminish the spheres of both theoretical and practical activity. Each consequently embraces a conception of excellence that is neither complete nor, even in its own terms, coherent. The very deficiencies of their distinct ways of life, however, indirectly point toward a middle ground whereupon the philosophical and political modes of existence appear to be complimentary and perhaps even harmonious dimensions of one single way of life. The example of Theodorus teaches that philosophical self-knowledge is inaccessible apart from the concrete familiarity with human souls that comes through serious and continuing engagement with everyday life in a political community. The example of Protagoras, in turn, teaches that the existence of a political space within which the speeches and deeds of individuals may acquire genuinely public significance depends upon the possibility of philosophic inquiry. Taken together, both examples point toward the character of Socrates.

Socratic Midwifery

At a certain point in the course of their discussion, Socrates reminds Theaetetus of one implication of his status as a philosophical midwife:

> Not one of the speeches comes out of me but always from the one who is engaged in dialogue with me. I know nothing more than a small thing: as much as to take a speech from another who is wise and accept it in a measured way (*metriôs*: 161b3-5).

Socrates' assertion is implicitly a sharp rebuke of Protagoras. Far from setting himself up as a measure (*metron*) of all things, Socrates modestly claims to know the measure of only one thing, namely, learning from another through dialogue. Protagoras, in contrast, proves to lack this knowledge: his indignant accusations of injustice against Socrates furnish a good illustration of how *not* to act when one's intellectual wind-eggs are taken away (cf. 151c-d). Protagoras's writings imply in any case that "the whole business of dialogue" is "laughable" (161e5-6); Socrates, however, associates dialogue with the joyful yet intrinsically serious work of giving birth. This difference in tone has more than a little to do with the fact that Protagoras suppresses the connection between speech and *erôs*, and indeed between wisdom and work. Like the ring of Gyges' ancestor in the *Republic*, Protagoras's quick-and-easy teaching is an artificial substitute for the combination of a superior nature and the travail of a philosophical education. The erotic significance of discourse for Socrates, on the other hand, is regularly underscored by Plato. Apart from the prominence of this theme in the midwife image, there is a striking resemblance between the remark quoted above and two other passages: Socrates' claim in the *Symposium* to know "nothing other than the erotic things" (177d7-8) and in the *Theages* to know "nothing except a certain small subject of learning, that of the erotic things" (128b3-4). These two statements, as we noted earlier, must somehow be squared with Socrates' paradoxical assertion that he possesses the art of politics (*Gorgias* 521d) —a claim Protagoras advances as well (*Protagoras* 319a). Does Socrates' knowledge of the proper measure of learning provide the link that we have been seeking between his philosophical *erôs* and his politics?

With the latter question in mind we now take up the midwife image (148e-151d), wherein Socrates turns directly to the elucidation of his qualifications as a trustee of Theaetetus's soul. As we shall see, however, this elucidation continues to take place against the backdrop of the figure of Protagoras.

Socrates' Strange Art

Socrates introduces the midwife image immediately after Theaetetus admits that he is familiar with the sorts of questions reportedly raised by him, and that he has often tried to inquire into the nature of knowledge, but has been able neither to arrive at satisfactory answers nor to "cease from caring [*tou melein*]" about the problem (148e1-5). While this is a good sign, Theaetetus was nevertheless not sufficiently motivated by his intellectual discomfort—or as Socrates puts it, by the "labor pains" that result from being "pregnant" (148e6-7)—to seek out Socrates' company. His hesitation seems to result from a natural aversion to the pain and vertigo that are associated with philosophic wonder (cf. 155c8-d5). In support of this suggestion, we may note that Socrates repeatedly exhorts Theaetetus to approach the inquiry courageously. As it turns out, he is at least somewhat successful in this endeavor. After setting forth the midwife image, Socrates urges Theaetetus to "be manly" in attempting to say what knowledge is (151d5-6; cf. 166a2-4, where Protagoras characterizes Theaetetus as a "little child" who is frightened by Socrates' questions). He later praises Theaetetus's newfound ability to speak "spiritedly" (*prothumos*, or "with *thumos* [spirit] to the fore": 187b8). Still later, Theaetetus himself encourages Socrates to "be bold" (197a6), and at 200d he refuses Socrates' invitation to give up the inquiry.[25]

The opening lines of the midwife passage are worth dwelling upon, especially insofar as they deftly contrast Socrates' and Protagoras's pedagogic styles. Three elements of Socratic learning are already apparent: wonder, pain, and courage. The primary impression generated by Socrates, however, is one of pain. Socrates hurts. Theaetetus has accordingly heard from those who do not truly know Socrates that he is "most strange" (*atopôtatos*: literally, "most out of place") and that he "causes human beings to be at a loss" (*aporein*, to be "without passage" out of perplexity: 149a8-9). Socrates distresses his interlocutors by leading them through speech into a place that is so unfamiliar it seems like nowhere, and from which there appears to be no way out.[26] Yet Socrates neither removes nor softens the source of Theaetetus's discomfort; instead, he will tell the boy that he must face his pain like a man. Furthermore, he proceeds to heighten Theaetetus's puzzlement when he explains his reputation by way of a surprising image that must initially serve to increase his own aura of strangeness.

Socrates' behavior is the exact opposite of what one could have expected from Protagoras. Protagoras gives Socrates advice on how to lessen men's perplexity and so make them love him by replacing bitter or painful perceptions with sweet or pleasant ones (167e-168a; cf. 166e). This is consistent with Protagoras's teaching that perception is the horizon of experience, from which it follows—as is confirmed by the hedonistic calculus that Socrates ironically advances in the *Protagoras*—that pleasure is simply good and pain is simply bad. If knowledge is perception, wonder leads nowhere beyond pain. The mythical genesis of Iris (Rainbow) from Thaumas (Wonder) is therefore entirely misleading: wonder cannot be the *archê* of a heavenly bond that lights the way for men to things divine (155d). There is consequently no good reason to endure the pain that it entails. In any case, the encouragement of boldness is antithetical to the malleability Protagoras prefers in his auditors.

Like Protagoras, however, Socrates has a secret that he at least pretends to guard from "the others" (149a6-7): following in the footsteps of his mother Phaenarete, he practices the art of midwifery. Phaenarete could mean "Revealer of Virtue," which seems to be a good description of Socrates himself. He at any rate describes her as *gennaia* ("noble") and *blosura* ("fierce, intrepid": 149a2), a conjunction of adjectives that he also uses in the *Republic* to characterize the dispositions of potential philosopher-kings.[27] This description is directly relevant to the problem of Socrates' reputation. Even in its ordinary sense, the art of midwifery calls for a kind of unsqueamish toughness that may seem—especially to one in the throes of labor—to verge on brutality, but that is tempered by its subordination to noble ends. The brusqueness of the midwife is forgiven when a healthy infant is born, but the case of psychic labor is far more problematic. To say the least, the fruits of psychic labor are neither as certain nor as obviously beautiful and loveable as those of its biological counterpart. This fact alone is sufficient to explain the common perception of Socrates as a strangely brutal individual. His "secret," unlike that of Protagoras, requires no deceptive effort to maintain; it is rooted in the inherently mysterious nature of his pedagogic activity.

Socrates employs a bewildering cluster of images to explain his secret to Theaetetus: his work involves matchmaking as well as assisting at childbirth and is in certain respects like the arts of farming and prospecting. Socrates differs from ordinary midwives in that his art serves men, not women, and examines their souls in giving birth, not their bodies. He otherwise resembles ordinary midwives in the following particulars. He is especially able to recognize those who are pregnant, and he can arouse and diminish labor pains with drugs and incantations, induce delivery, or cause an abortion. He is also an expert in psychic eugenics, for "midwives are the most terrific matchmakers, since they are all-wise in recognizing what sort of woman must be with what sort of man so as to give birth to the best children" (149d5-8). Like Protagoras, Socrates presents himself as a kind of farmer as well as a kind of doctor: he knows how to care for and harvest "fruits" as well as how to match the "seeds" from which they grow with the "earth" that will best nourish them (149e1-4). Most important, Socrates is able "in every way to assay [as with a touchstone: *basanizein*] whether the thought [*dianoia*] of the young man is giving birth to an image that is false or something fruitful and true" (*eidôlon kai pseudos . . . gonimon te kai alethes*: 150c1-3). Although it may seem to have no counterpart in ordinary midwifery, Socrates insists that "this very thing which belongs to midwives [i.e., the capability of assaying offspring] belongs to me too" (150c3-4). He also identifies the most desirable psychic offspring with wisdom (*sophia*: 150c4) rather than with art or scientific knowledge (*technê* or *epistêmê*).

Even this brief summary of the midwife image is sufficient to convey its extraordinary complexity and to suggest a variety of fundamental questions. Some of these questions center upon Socrates' paradoxical claim to expertise in a *technê* that aims at wisdom but is not itself equivalent to wisdom (cf. 150c-d). This claim raises problems even if the productive dimension of midwifery is given minimal emphasis. Insofar as Socrates' art provides a touchstone for assessing intellectual offspring, it would seem to evaluate such offspring in accordance with antecedent technical standards. Under these circumstances, will not *technê* be the measure and determinant of whatever is to count as *sophia*? Still more troubling, Socrates' art of midwifery does more than simply test ideas. Can we be sure that Socrates' interlocutors—unlike those of Protagoras—are more than just the passive subjects of his technical manipulations (abortion, delivery, matchmaking, planting, and harvesting)?

An equally important question concerns the goal of psychic pregnancy. Why would one wish to become pregnant in soul? Our response will have implications for assessing the worth of philosophy. If it is desirable for human beings to produce offspring of the soul, philosophy is also generally good, but seems to be of little use if it does not yield positive (i.e., fruitful and true) results. But if the generation of such offspring is not a choiceworthy end, then psychic pregnancy is more like sickness than health. In that case, philosophy is beneficial only for the few who happen to be ill, but it is good just insofar as it relieves or wards off labor pains and even if it never produces positive results. Finally, what constitutes the excellence of psychic offspring, and what is the relationship between this kind of excellence and that of biological children? While we cannot answer this question without examining Socrates' conception of fruitfulness, the fact that his art tests for *sophia* raises some interesting possibilities insofar as it suggests that he aims to promote a comprehensive kind of understanding that embraces both self-knowledge and *phronêsis* and therefore entails virtue (cf. *Symposium* 209a) If, for example, to be "best" means (perhaps among other things) to manifest or promote *political* virtue, Socrates and his mother might together possess the knowledge of fashioning divine and human bonds that the Stranger ultimately assigns to the statesman alone (*Statesman* 308d ff.).[28]

Let us approach the questions raised above by first considering the peculiar nature of Socrates' art. Even ordinary midwifery defies easy categorization because of its strange relationship to its objects. It is neither simply productive nor simply acquisitive, and so resists being grasped in accordance with the fundamental division of *technai* introduced by the Stranger at *Sophist* 219a ff. Midwifery stands somewhere in between bringing something new into being and taking possession of what is already there. Without the assistance of a midwife some children would never be born alive and healthy, yet the essential character of the "product" of midwifery is determined by the parents. Furthermore, the circumstances of conception are rarely, if ever, shaped by art. Ordinary midwives, we are told, possess the *technê* of eugenics but shun it so as to avoid the charge of pimping (150a). Nor does Socrates make much use of his putative expertise as a go-between: the only matchmaking he appears to do involves infertile students that he "marries off" to certain sophists (151b). He has not had a hand in Theaetetus's pregnancy, and in this respect the boy is typical of his interlocutors. For these reasons, Socrates' mention of matchmaking seems little more than a boast; his activity as a midwife appears to be limited to controlling labor pains, making relevant diagnoses, inducing abortions and presiding over deliveries, and testing offspring. Socrates' interlocutors are less passive than initial appearances suggest, for the decisive contribution to the event of birth is always their own.

Another feature of midwifery deserves mention. Like medicine and rhetoric, midwifery is a stochastic or fallibilistic *technê*. David Roochnik's distinction between the two basic kinds of *technai* is helpful here. Arithmetic and spelling are paradigms of what Roochnik calls techne$_1$: they are precise, definite, reliable, and teachable, their subject matter is invariable, their rules can be mechanically derived from basic principles or postulates, and their practitioners are easily certifiable as experts. Medicine and rhetoric are examples of techne$_2$: they are somewhat imprecise, indefinite, and unreliable, their subject matter is not invariable, they involve "rules of thumb" and a sensitivity to particulars, they are not wholly teachable, and the expertise of their practitioners is not as evident or publicly certifiable as in the case of techne$_1$.[29] Socrates' employment of midwifery as an image of his care of souls thus suggests that human beings are not to be understood on the model of numbers or letters, and that any attempt to understand human beings along the lines of techne$_1$ will miss the mark. Implicit in Socrates' image is a critique of the quasi-arithmetical method of bifurcatory diaeresis with which the Stranger will attempt to hunt down the sophist.

What about Socrates' apparent employment of technical knowledge to test for the presence of wisdom? Socrates seems here to use the notion of *technê* in an extended or metaphorical sense, even judging by the standards of techne$_2$. This can be seen by examining the analogy between biological and psychic pregnancy. It must first be observed that the scale of appraisal Socrates applies to intellectual offspring is ambiguous. His distinction between "an image that is false or something fruitful and true" is by no means an exclusive disjunction, for an image may be true and a falsehood may perhaps be fruitful. Furthermore, in the same passage (150b ff.) Socrates obscures the possible distinction between "wisdom" and that which is not wisdom but is nonetheless "fruitful and true." We shall return to this important point below. For now, we may note that Socrates subsequently concerns himself primarily with the potential generativity of Theaetetus's offspring: the decisive issue throughout the remainder of the dialogue is whether Theaetetus's ideas are fruitful and so worthy of nurture or mere "wind-eggs" (151e, 157d, 160e-161a, 210b; but cf. 150e and 151c, where Socrates mentions truth). This perhaps explains the apparent disanalogy noted above: while women cannot give birth to false children, they sometimes do give birth to infants that are very sickly or deformed. Ordinary midwives, in turn, evidently possess expertise in identifying such babies, who are not "fruitful" in that they are not likely to grow or (as one would say today) live "productive" lives. Similarly, Socrates' art is somehow able to distinguish those intellectual offspring that have the power to "grow" or otherwise generate good things beyond themselves from those that do not have this power.

But what is involved in making the latter determination? It is doubtful that Socrates views the discrimination of intellectual offspring as a technical problem. Socrates' image of "assaying" understates the difficulty involved in such testing, which is certainly greater in the case of the fruits of the soul than in those of the body.[30] And while mineralogical assaying determines what is, Socratic assaying guesses what will be. Socrates is involved in the business of prognostication with regard to the soul. Such prognostication requires familiarity with the growth of souls and the conditions of their development as well as knowledge of the end promoted by fruitful offspring. It involves a significant measure of self-knowledge as well as *phronêsis*—two components, as we suppose, of *sophia*. Yet because Socrates is a philosopher he is aware of his lack of *sophia*, and so can neither be certain of nor content with either his self-knowledge or his *phronêsis*. He cannot be sure of his expertise even to the limited extent that a doctor can be sure of his medical skill, and he will continue to wonder about the presuppositions of his care of souls in a way that no doctor wonders about the presuppositions of medicine. In sum, Socrates' "art" stretches toward wisdom in a way that ordinary sorts of *technai*—including the arts enumerated by Theaetetus—do not.[31]

In spite of its ambiguous nature, ordinary midwifery shares one crucial feature with the productive *technai*: its worth is strictly instrumental, and can be measured by its work or product alone. Midwives are judged by their ability to bring viable infants into the world while preserving the health of the mother; midwifery that fails to do whatever can be done to bring about these ends is worth little or nothing. So, too, no one would choose to suffer pregnancy and labor for their own sake, and apart from the prospect of having healthy offspring. This brings us to a further respect in which the technical analogy of midwifery fails to capture the nature of Socrates' activity as well as the experience of his interlocutors. Theaetetus agrees at the end of the dialogue that he has given birth only to wind-eggs. Socrates states, however, that the trials of labor have nevertheless improved the boy's character as well as the worth of the conceptions with which he may be pregnant in the future, and he adds that this is all that his art can accomplish (210b-c). The dialogue has not been an unqualified failure: whether or not Theaetetus becomes pregnant in the future, he has been changed in a way that will have positive results. In fine, Socrates indicates that Theaetetus's experience of intellectual labor has been fruitful even though it has issued only in wind-eggs. What is more, Socrates chooses to practice midwifery while acknowledging that his art can accomplish no more than it has in the case of Theaetetus. Does this not suggest that the activity of Socratic midwifery may also be fruitful in itself, quite apart from the worth of the offspring that it midwifes?[32]

The present line of reflection helps to clarify Socrates' rather confusing remarks about his relationship to the gods. "Honoring their similarity to herself," the virgin Artemis—who, "although she is childless, has childbirth as her lot"—appointed (*prosetaxe*) as midwives those who have previously given birth but are now beyond the age of childbearing (149b9-c3). In the *Apology* Socrates uses the same verb, *prostattein*, to characterize the injunction of "the god" that he claims to heed in practicing philosophy (33c7; cf. 28e4), and similar ambiguities appear in both contexts. In the present passage Socrates goes on to speak vaguely of "the god" who "compels" him to midwife and prevents him from giving birth (150c7-8; cf. 150d8, 151d1). It is unclear whether "the god" is Artemis the patroness of midwives, or Socrates' *daimonion* (cf. 151a4), or perhaps even Socrates himself. In partial support of this last possibility, we may note that Socrates' assertion that he has never given birth to wisdom (150c-d) seems to contradict his insistence that "human nature is too weak to grasp an art of whatever things it lacks experience of" (149c1-2)—a point he had appealed to in explaining why Artemis does not choose virgins or sterile women as midwives. If we acknowledge this contradiction and take Socrates' words at face value, he must be more than human, in which case he appears to rival Protagoras in his implicit claim to divinity.

The context in which these seemingly conflicting remarks occur, however, suggests an alternative interpretation. In the first place, we cannot doubt Socrates' assertion that he has never given birth to *sophia*, for otherwise he would be a wise man and not a philosopher or lover of wisdom. There is moreover an important pedagogical reason for him not only to deny that he has ever generated wisdom, but also to blur the distinction between wisdom and other sorts of fruitful intellectual offspring (as he does at 150b-c): to do otherwise would be to imply that he is holding back "the right answers," and therefore to discourage Theaetetus's efforts to think for himself. This is not all. Socrates' precise claim is to be able to distinguish that which is fruitful and true from that which is an image and a lie, and he nowhere explicitly identifies the former sort of offspring with wisdom alone. Indeed, we now have good reason to suppose that pregnancy of the soul may have fruitful and true results that are *not* identical with wisdom and that may even issue from the very experience of undergoing intellectual labor—whether or not the specific ideas born from such labor are themselves anything more than wind-eggs. In sum, Socrates *is* presumably experienced both in generating and assisting in the delivery of offspring that are fruitful and true yet fall short of wisdom. Such offspring lie somewhere in the middle ground between utter ignorance and full-blown wisdom—a region Socrates elsewhere identifies with philosophy (see *Republic* 521c and context). I submit further that the intelligibility of the midwife image, as well as the coherence of Socrates' way of life as a whole, turns upon just this distinction between wisdom and other fruitful births of the soul.

Much more remains to be said about Socrates' understanding of fruitfulness. Without losing sight of this central issue, we may pause to examine a further peculiarity of the midwife image that indirectly sheds light on the nature of those who can benefit from Socrates' art, including Theaetetus. Socrates says that he shares with midwives the ability to discern who is truly pregnant. What is the psychic equivalent of a hysterical or false pregnancy, and how does it differ from a genuine pregnancy that results in unfruitful offspring? It is easy to distinguish the analogous physiological phenomena. In the latter case, the processes of conception and gestation have issued in an offspring that is not worth rearing (as, for example, the runt of a litter); in the former, conception and gestation appear to occur but in actuality do not. There are correspondingly two sorts of indications that would presumably lead Socrates to diagnose a false pregnancy: his services are probably not needed if the would-be parent has not come up with any ideas of his own, and if he does not seem genuinely to be afflicted by perplexity or "labor" (cf. 151a). An interlocutor who can experience neither labor nor birth can benefit from Socrates only insofar as he is capable of acknowledging his sterility. To undergo false pregnancy, however, is to seem to oneself to be capable of giving birth, or to be an active source of potentially fruitful ideas. And it is especially difficult for Socrates to correct this kind of mistake. Since the souls of such interlocutors—to the extent that they are not empty—are occupied by the thoughts of others, it is always easy for them to deny responsibility for any particular ideas that Socrates removes or "exposes." They may therefore be convinced that they have not been correctly understood, so that Socrates' criticisms do not touch them. The fact that Socrates cannot in any way improve such individuals perhaps justifies his practice of giving in marriage to "wise and divinely-sounding men" like Prodicus "those who somehow do not seem to me to be pregnant" (151b2-6). But be it ever so just and artful (cf. 150a), this still looks like pimping, that is, the bringing together of two people for illicit pleasure. For it is certain that the sophists to whom Socrates refers such individuals will refrain from attempting to dispel their happy illusions.[33]

Barring accidents of nature, all women of child-bearing age can become pregnant and can give birth to physiologically "fruitful" children. The same does not appear to be true of the souls of men. There can be little doubt that Socrates simply gives up on those he claims to hand over to the sophists—who are themselves, if one may judge by Protagoras, intellectually sterile. Socrates implies, moreover, that he himself is now beyond the age of childbearing (149b-c), which suggests that there may be a natural period of fertility in the case of the soul as well as the body. Indeed, this period of fertility seems to be associated with the time of life at which Theaetetus now finds himself—a time with which Socrates especially concerns himself in the Platonic dialogues. What accounts for Socrates' special interest in youths on the verge of manhood?

Socrates and Artemis

The latter question brings us around to the figure of Artemis, the crucial civic functions of whom include leading children of both sexes across the thresholds of maturity. Artemis does so in part by presiding over various rites of passage, including mimetic rituals of initiation as well as marriage and childbirth. These activities, in turn, are connected with the goddess's peculiar attachment to the boundaries and border-zones wherein the wilderness touches civilization. Artemis's liminal status may easily be confused with placelessness, but has much to do with helping human beings to assume their proper places. In all of these respects, the figure of Artemis seems to resonate with that of Socrates.

The cultural historian Jean-Pierre Vernant convincingly connects Artemis with "the experience the Greeks constructed of the Other" while explicating her necessary contribution to the domain of the Same—the familiar, identity-conferring sphere of "the human being (*anthrôpos*), the civilized person, the male adult (*anêr*), the Greek, and the citizen."[34] Artemis, Vernant notes, "has two sides": she is "the Huntress, the one who runs in the woods, the Wild One, the Archer," but also "the Maiden, the pure Parthenos, dedicated to eternal virginity," who leads the Nymphs and Graces "in joyous dance, music, and beautiful song." This curious doubleness helps to explain the fact that Artemis is sometimes describes as "*xenê*, stranger," by the ancients—a term that refers, "as in the case of Dionysos, to the 'strangeness' of the goddess, her distance from the other gods by reason of that alterity or otherness she bears." [35]

Artemis's major role in the city is "Kourotrophos par excellence" who "takes all the little ones in charge," and whose "function is to nurture them, to make them grow and mature until they become fully adult." From the perspective of the Greek *polis*, maturation involves being molded and shaped according to the model of citizen-soldier or wife and mother. In coming to assume these social identities, boys and girls leave behind the unformed, natural, or "wild" state of childhood. Maturation therefore turns upon the permeability of the boundaries between the wild and the civilized. Thus, while Artemis "introduces the adolescent [boy] into the world of ferocious wild beasts," the hunt over which she presides is nonetheless a disciplined activity that "constitutes an essential element of his education, of the *paideia* that integrates him into the city." Similarly, in the course of their transition from girlhood to womanhood, the daughters of the *polis* are envisioned as moving from a condition of wild independence to one of tame integration within the community. The virgin goddess "tames" and "civilizes" the sexuality of girls by seeing to its emergence within a conjugal context. The final step in this process, however, is the agony and delirium of childbirth, a "wild and animal side of femaleness" that is paradoxically displayed "precisely at the moment when, by giving the city a future citizen, the wife is reproducing the city itself and therefore seems most integrated into the world of culture."[36]

We saw earlier that the *Theaetetus* begins by calling attention to the problem of how best to care for Theaetetus's *ousia*, his being or identity (144d2). Artemis cares for boys and girls by helping them to cross the threshold of maturity. Socrates' mention of his service and resemblance to Artemis invites us to ask whether Socratic midwifery also provides critical assistance in the development of human beings. If so, what threshold does Socrates help his young interlocutors to cross? A further question concerns the political relevance of Socratic maturation. Artemis exerts a civilizing influence upon the natural wildness of boys and girls. That Socrates does the same is suggested by his claim to have helped to make Theaetetus "less harsh or burdensome [*barus*]" to his associates and "tamer" (210c2-3). It is suggested less directly by his opposition to Protagoras, whose speech is so profoundly unjust as to rule out the existence of the middle ground of publicity upon which political community necessarily rests. Perhaps Socrates' art of midwifery is the "true political *technê*" that he claims to possess in the *Gorgias*. But what exactly are the political implications of being midwifed by Socrates?

These questions remain open throughout the philosophical trial. Some of them will momentarily be taken up in connection with Theaetetus, and some will be explored in detail only when we turn to the *Sophist* and *Statesman*. For now, we may note that the connection Socrates draws between himself and Artemis begins to address the fundamental deficiency of his defense speech in the *Apology*. Socrates' philosophical *erôs*, as we have already observed, propels him beyond the horizons of Athenian life and so is intimately connected with his paradoxical outlandishness—paradoxical, because he seems at the same time to be firmly rooted in Athens. Socrates' outlandishness is also connected with his potential as a teacher: if, like Artemis, he opens up paths from one place to another, it is because he, like this goddess of the margins, is fully at home in no particular place. So, too, if Socrates can civilize young souls while at the same time helping them to grow, it is because he is himself neither simply wild nor simply tame, neither just an Athenian nor just a stranger. The image of Artemis thus points toward the convergence of Socrates' outlandish *erôs* and his politics.

Socrates' Care for Theaetetus: Midwifing the Soul

Socrates repeatedly suggests that the claims Theaetetus has produced are or might be wind-eggs (151e, 157d, 161a, 210b). This image presents certain difficulties because it is drawn from avian physiology. A wind-egg is an unfertilized ovum, such as farmers collect from chickens. While birds can lay unfertilized eggs—which are initially indistinguishable from fertilized eggs, but will simply rot if left in the nest—human beings do not lay eggs at all. Conversely, birds do not become pregnant and do not need assistance (such at that provided by midwives) in laying their eggs.

Perhaps Socrates' references to wind-eggs are meant to remind us of the lingering Protagorean problem of what, if anything, raises the thoughts of human beings above the perceptions of animals or plants. In one respect, however, the analogy of avian reproduction suits Socrates' actual practice better than that of human pregnancy. Human offspring grow into babies in the womb, while eggs are first laid and must subsequently be incubated; only then will they develop or fail to develop into baby birds. So too, Theaetetus comes forth with his ideas ("Knowledge is perception," "Knowledge is true opinion") easily and without much work—just like laying an egg. It is only *after* these thoughts are articulated *in ovo*, as it were, that Socrates midwifes Theaetetus, or assists him with the labor that he associates with intellectual pregnancy.

At the end of the dialogue—after a long discussion of Theaetetus's ideas that knowledge is true opinion or true opinion plus a *logos*, most of which is concerned with the problem of how false opinion is possible (187d ff.)—Theaetetus is judged to have produced nothing but wind-eggs. This disappointing result seems to cast doubt upon the fruitfulness of Socrates' midwifery. If Socrates cannot help a promising youth like Theaetetus to generate substantial intellectual offspring, it is unlikely that he will be able to help many others to do so. One might be willing to accept that the achievement of Socratic midwifery is largely or entirely negative—that it aims simply to reveal ignorance—had Socrates himself not raised our expectations. Has Socrates shown himself to be a worthy trustee of Theaetetus's soul? Has he in any way assisted Theaetetus to cross the threshold of maturity, and so to become himself?

In the remainder of this chapter, I shall attempt to show that both of these questions can be answered in the affirmative. (Because I am specifically interested in establishing the nature of Socrates' trusteeship, we will not examine certain passages, such as the wax image and the aviary image [191c-220d], that bear more directly upon the epistemological concerns of the *Theaetetus*.)

The text of the *Theaetetus* does not support Socrates' conclusion—which is, in fact, cautiously formulated as a question—that Theaetetus has issued nothing but "wind-eggs, unworthy of nurture" (210b9). Let us consider what I take to be the primary instance of learning in the *Theaetetus* as a whole. It requires more than half of the dialogue (151e-186e) for Theaetetus to learn that knowledge is not perception, yet the process of discovering that the thesis "Knowledge is perception" is a wind-egg yields a thought whose fruitfulness is underscored by the unparalleled praise with which Socrates greets it. This thought, which concerns the soul's authoritativeness with respect to knowledge and the independence of its activity with respect to the powers of the body, leads Socrates to comment on the beauty of Theaetetus's speech as well as his soul (185e). What is more, the immediate context of this exchange suggests that Socrates' aim in discussing the thesis that knowledge is perception is to deliver Theaetetus of just this conception of the soul.

Just prior to the digression, Socrates states that Protagoras would not be so bold as to deny that all opinions about what will be beneficial for a political community are equally correct (172a-b). Some perceptions about the future, in other words, cannot count as knowledge. Just after the digression, Socrates wonders whether the thesis that knowledge is perception might be defensible if one considers only present experience (179c). Socrates connects this thesis with Protagoras's secret, Heraclitean teaching that "nothing ever is, but is always coming to be" (182a ff.; cf. 152e). From the hypothesis that all things are in motion, it follows that all things are in flux both with respect to qualitative alteration as well as local motion; otherwise all things would be at rest as well as in motion (181d-182a). Under these circumstances, however, the question "What is knowledge?" cannot be meaningfully asked or answered. Knowledge *is* not, but, like all things, is always coming to be other than it was; hence knowledge is no more knowledge than not-knowledge (182e). *Logos* cannot accommodate this fact, for it brings things to a standstill: to speak of "knowledge" is to posit a stable, self-identical unity that can be meaningfully distinguished from other such unities. The upshot of this disharmony between speech and being (or rather, becoming) is that "every answer, concerning whatever someone should answer about, is equally correct" (183a5-6).

It is at this point that Theodorus drops out of the discussion and Theaetetus reenters it. Theaetetus's willingness to continue to examine the hypothesis that knowledge is perception suggests that he still believes the question "What is knowledge?" is meaningful. This belief has not been shaken by the Heracliteans, even though the Heracliteans have not

been refuted. At best, Socrates has managed to clarify one of the fundamental assumptions of philosophical discourse in a world of motion,
namely, that it is possible to speak of the *sorts* of things that are in flux
(cf. 182c10: *hoia . . . rhei*), so that sorts or kinds must themselves be at
rest. It is likely, however, that Theaetetus has been encouraged by Socrates' remarkable example no less than by his arguments. It would be
natural for Theaetetus to continue to suppose that philosophical discourse
is meaningful, if only because this man of superior intellectual and moral
substance—a man, moreover, who is present for the express purpose of
talking to *him*—has devoted his life to discussing fundamental philosophical questions, bravely persisting even in the face of serious hostility. Like all true teachers, Socrates is a seducer.

In any case, Socrates now reiterates that the main task at hand is "to
attempt, by the art of midwifery, to deliver Theaetetus of whatever he is
pregnant with concerning knowledge" (184a8-b2). Immediately after this
pronouncement, Socrates introduces the soul as a distinct topic of inquiry. He asks Theaetetus whether we see by our eyes and hear by our
ears, or whether we see *through* (*dia*) our eyes and hear through our ears
(184c). Theaetetus favors the latter alternative, whereupon Socrates concurs: for there must be, he supposes, "some one look (*idea*), whether soul
or whatever one should call it," toward which perceptions strain, and "by
which we perceive, through these [i.e. seeing, hearing, and the like] as
through tools, as many things as are perceptible" (184d3-5). The notion
of *idea* in this passage is ambiguous, since it seems to refer both to that
which is apprehended and that which apprehends. On the one hand, it
picks up Socrates' earlier suggestion that perceptually evident flux takes
place against a backdrop of unchanging sorts of things, and points ahead
toward Socrates' introduction of the categories of being, otherness and
sameness, unity and multiplicity, similarity and dissimilarity, beauty and
ugliness, and good and bad (185a-186a).[37] On the other hand, Socrates'
reference to "some one *idea*" calls attention to the unity that discerns
these imperceptible looks.

Because being, otherness and sameness, and the like are common to
the objects perceived through our bodily powers of perception, Socrates
argues that they are perceived through none of these bodily powers
(185b). Through what, then, are they apprehended? Theaetetus's answer—that "the soul itself through itself appears to examine the things
common to everything"—elicits strong praise: "For you are beautiful,
Theaetetus, and not as Theodorus was saying, ugly. For he who speaks
beautifully is beautiful and good (*kalos kai agathos*)." Socrates adds that
the thought that "the soul itself through itself examines some things, and
others through the powers of the body" was his own opinion, "and I
wanted it to be yours as well" (185e3-8). He quickly proceeds to draw

from Theaetetus the claims that being is the object of the soul, and that the soul is especially concerned with the examination and calculation, with an eye to the future, of the beautiful or noble (*kalon*) and the ugly or shameful (*aischron*) as well as the good and the bad (186a-b; cf. Protagoras's distinction between the *kalon* and the good at 167c). Theaetetus also assents to the view that "the calculations [*analogismata*] concerning being [*ousian*] and benefit" come about not through perceptual experience, and not directly by nature, but "in time, through much trouble and education" (*dia pollôn pragmatôn kai paideias*: 186b11-c5). Finally, Theaetetus agrees that truth pertains to being and knowledge pertains to truth, and that there can consequently be no knowledge in perceptual experience but only in the reasoning (*sullogismos*) of the soul by itself (186c-d). The hypothesis that knowledge is perception has now been laid to rest for good (186e).

The notion of the soul adumbrated above leads Theaetetus to formulate the claim that knowledge is true opinion, for opinion is the name he gives to "whatever the soul possesses whenever it troubles itself, by itself, with the beings [*ta onta*]" (187a5-6). This hypothesis, with which Theaetetus answers Socrates' call to begin "once more from the beginning" (*palin ex archês*: 187a9-b1), also proves in due course to be a wind-egg. But what about the insight that leads Theaetetus to generate the latter hypothesis—an insight that merits Socrates' special praise, and that he wanted Theaetetus to come to share? Might not Theaetetus's newly articulated conception of the soul be just the kind of fruitful intellectual offspring "concerning knowledge" that Socrates hoped to bring out of him?

The image of psychic midwifery certainly suits the portion of the *Theaetetus* we have just reviewed. Theaetetus's speech about the soul's nature and its objects articulates a thought that was implicit in his conviction that philosophical discussion is meaningful. In this sense, Theaetetus was "pregnant" with this thought prior to giving voice to it. Socrates' questions, in turn, bring on the pangs of labor, for they make clear to Theaetetus that philosophical *logos* is meaningless if truth pertains only to perceptual experience. More important, a strong case can be made for the fruitfulness of Theaetetus's conception of the soul. As we have seen, his recognition of the being of the soul and its proper objects makes it possible for the discussion about the nature of knowledge to move forward from a new beginning. Theaetetus allows philosophical discourse to proceed just insofar as he provides a basis for understanding how philosophical questions can meaningfully be asked and answered: *logos* is adequate to the soul's objects because, as beings, these objects are stable unities. In addition, he articulates in a general way the relationship between philosophy and the human good, and thereby helps to establish the goodness of Socratic dialogue.

The latter point can best be made by glancing back at the Protagorean alternative to Theaetetus's new insight. Protagoras taught that education (*paideia*) is the process whereby the wise man makes good perceptions appear and be for human beings in the place of bad perceptions. Education thus looks to the future, which is a subject of special interest to the young and those who care about them. Yet the Protagorean thesis that knowledge is perception makes nonsense of Protagoras's teaching on *paideia*. "Knowledge is perception" cannot account for either the goodness of perceptions or the wisdom of the wise. Moreover, Protagoras's Heracliteanism deprives human beings of any future at all. Protagoras cannot consistently maintain that Theaetetus, having been educated, now has better perceptions than he did before; he can hold only that a different man now has different perceptions. "Having come to be other, they may be rid of who they were before" (168a6-7).

Theaetetus, on the other hand, recovers the possibility of education insofar as he recovers the soul and its proper objects from Protagoras's assimilation of this pair to the body and its perceptual objects. In so doing, he effectively gives himself a future. "Human being is the measure of all things" meant that the truth was effortlessly and fully accessible, through perception, to all percipient creatures. Theaetetus now holds that the truth is gradually accessible, through reasoning, to the soul. Education is the philosophical labor of the soul as it learns, by itself, about the beings toward which it "stretches" (*eporegetai*: 186a4). Insofar as the soul and its powers are distinct from the body and its powers, Theaetetus lays the groundwork for an account of education in terms of the growth of one and the same human being, as opposed to a succession of different selves. His speech about the soul thus begins to explain why it made sense to speak, as Socrates, Euclides and Terpsion did in the *Theaetetus*'s prologue, of who Theaetetus was and what he would become—or did in fact become—as he matured.

Although Socrates challenges the thesis that knowledge is true opinion, he does not attempt to refute the conception of the soul that gives rise to this thesis. Socrates, we recall, welcomes Theaetetus's conception of the soul by saying that Theaetetus is beautiful. Theaetetus would be ugly, however, if he were nothing apart from his body. In commenting on Theaetetus's physical ugliness, Socrates seems to refer to the ugliness of Protagoras's assimilation of human being to the human body. Conversely, Theaetetus's speech is beautiful because it will help to encourage him to continue to care for the development of his soul.

The preceding reflections help to establish Socrates' credentials as a trustee of Theaetetus's soul. Socrates helps Theaetetus to mature by assisting him in understanding what education is and why it is possible. Put another way, Socrates helps to make intelligible for Theaetetus the very possibility of human maturation and growth. In so doing, he guides Theaetetus across a most significant intellectual threshold. On one side of this threshold stands Protagoras, as an emblem of despair as to the possibility of philosophical teaching and learning. On the other lie the hopeful paths of discussion and inquiry, along which alone the soul—the *ousia* of human being—can come into its own. In an important sense, Socrates helps Theaetetus to give birth to himself in the course of midwifing his conception of the soul.

Emerging Issues: Politics and the Motion of the Soul

To follow Protagoras is to assimilate the soul to the body, and so to the flux of perceptual experience. To follow Theodorus is to assimilate the soul to the beings that are its objects. In either case, the soul's intrinsic nature is obscured and self-knowledge becomes inaccessible, with the practical consequence that there is no alternative to sophistry in the sphere of politics. Theaetetus has moved beyond Protagoras, but still runs the risk of treating the soul as if it possessed a stable structure akin to that of the objects of geometry and arithmetic. Socrates repeatedly calls attention to this problem in the last third of the *Theaetetus*. He does so by reminding us of the paradoxes associated with learning, or with the erotic motion of the soul toward knowledge. In particular, Socrates indirectly underscores the issue of self-knowledge by inquiring into the nature of false opinion in an ironically unself-conscious fashion.

Just after Theaetetus has formulated his hypothesis that knowledge is true opinion, Socrates raises the problem of false opinion. He proposes to attack this problem by considering only the states of knowing and not knowing: "I bid farewell at present to learning and forgetting," Socrates says, "on the ground that they stand between these [viz., knowing and not knowing]; for nothing there is pertinent with respect to our speech" (188a2-4). This statement is notable both because it implicitly associates learning with remembering, and because it rules out of consideration, in a manner reminiscent of Euclides' Megarian doctrines, the motion of the soul between what are here regarded as, in effect, quantum states. Megarianism is harmonious with the study of beings that possess stable structures, including the objects of the sciences taught by Theodorus, but the soul, which "stretches" erotically toward beings, is not such an entity. Remarkably, Socrates dismisses the middle ground between knowledge and ignorance where human beings actually dwell. False opinion can arise only in this middle ground, for opinion is neither simply ignorance nor simply knowledge, but something in between (cf. *Republic* 476e ff.). Moreover, the question "What is false opinion?" can be seriously raised only by those attempting to move from ignorance to knowledge, as Socrates and Theaetetus are now doing. The intermediate region of opinion is the home-place from which Socratic inquiry begins, and to which it seems always to return: Socrates' famous "knowledge of ignorance," with which the dialogues regularly conclude, is neither simply knowledge nor simply ignorance, but a true opinion that somehow stretches, like *erôs* itself, between these two poles (cf. *Symposium* 203e-204b).

The preceding considerations lead us to expect that the present inquiry into false opinion, if it is not utterly absurd, will at any rate be unable to make sense of the phenomenon of philosophic inquiry. As if to emphasize this point, Socrates allows Theaetetus to agree that one cannot believe that what one does not know is what one knows (188b, 192a). Yet the most pernicious species of false opinion—pernicious just *because* it is confident, and not tentative—involves precisely such a belief. Socrates' claim directly contradicts what he has just said, and later repeats, about the potential benefit of the present conversation: if their attempt to define knowledge fails, he tells Theaetetus, they will in any case "less believe we know what we in no way know" (187c2; cf. 210c). In a later passage, Socrates sets forth in the form of a riddle the whole paradox of self-knowledge: how, he wonders, could knowledge ever make one ignorant, or ignorance ever cause one to know (199d)? This riddle cannot be solved without attention to the purposeful motion of the soul in learning. As Seth Benardete has observed, however, the *Theaetetus*'s "most obvious defect seems to consist in its failure to consider knowledge in its relation to learning, intention, and understanding."[38] The riddling character of the last third of the *Theaetetus* thus calls to our attention the as yet unexamined matter of the peculiar being of the soul—an unfinished or incomplete entity that has no stable structure, but is instead essentially characterized by erotic striving.

Our reading of the *Theaetetus*'s prologue began with the problem of the relationship between Socrates' philosophical *erôs* and his politics. The *Theaetetus* itself invited us to consider the latter problem in connection with the question of who can best care for the soul of Theaetetus. In studying the dialogue's characterization of Theodorus's abstractly theoretical existence and Protagoras's abstractly political existence, we found that the paths of life exemplified by these two characters—paths that strangely converge with respect to their political and philosophical implications—seem to circumscribe the middle ground of Socratic philosophizing. We then turned to Socrates' elucidation, in the midwife image, of his qualifications as a trustee of Theaetetus's soul. I suggested that Socrates' art of midwifery may be identical to the true art of politics of which he speaks in the *Gorgias*; at any rate, Socrates' accomplishment in his discussion with Theaetetus seems to support his implicit claim to guide young souls across the threshold of maturity in a manner analogous to Artemis. Socrates cares for souls by helping them to come into their own through the dialogical generation of a mature and fruitful self-conception. Yet the analogy with Artemis remains unexplored to the extent that the political significance of Socratic midwifery is still an open question. The mature self-possession that young men acquire under the tutelage of Artemis is inseparable from their self-understanding as responsible citizens. Is the same true of the young men who are midwifed by Socrates? What stance toward *nomos* is implicit in the autonomy of the Socratically midwifed soul?

The *Euthyphro* is directly concerned with the political implications of Socratic philosophizing. A no less conspicuous theme, however, is the purposefully circular motion of Socrates' philosophical activity, which is in turn connected with the unique potential of the human soul. The *Euthyphro* thus promises to shed light on precisely the questions raised above, and therefore to take up the exposition of the nature of Socrates just where the *Theaetetus* left off.

Chapter 4

Thinking Back to the Beginnings:
The *Euthyphro*

And he [Socrates] was competent both in persuading and in dissuading. Thus, having conversed with Theaetetus concerning knowledge, he sent him away with a god inside of him, as Plato would say. And when Euthyphro had indicted his father on a charge of manslaughter, he led him away after discussing some questions concerning piety.

Diogenes Laertius, *Lives of Eminent Philosophers*

Our reflections on the *Theaetetus* concluded with questions about the relationship between Socrates' care for human beings and the nurture of responsible citizenship. These same questions stand at the center of the *Euthyphro*, which explores in a rather different context the same Socratic conception of care as midwifery. In the *Euthyphro* Socrates is paired with two young Athenians, Meletus and Euthyphro, who are in some sense rivals but nevertheless see themselves as model caretakers of gods and men and, what is more, as interpreters and defenders of the *nomoi* that make up the fabric of the political community. The dramatic juxtaposition of Socrates with the characters of Meletus and Euthyphro thus promises to shed light on the difference between Socrates' and the city's ways of caring for young souls.

In studying the *Theaetetus*, we connected the inadequacies of Protagorean and Theodorean care with the abstractness of their conceptions of human life. The *Euthyphro* represents a logical extension of the inquiry into trusteeship, for one might expect to find in the city's traditional edu-

95

cation and nurture of its citizens a corrective to the deficiencies of the atheoretical and apolitical ways of life exemplified, respectively, in the figures of Protagoras and Theodorus. Yet as we shall see, the *Euthyphro* frustrates this expectation. When measured against the concreteness of the Socratic alternative, the city's manner of caring for human beings strangely proves to be no less abstract than that of stargazing theoreticians and self-divinizing sophists. Hence we should not be surprised to find in Euthyphro and Meletus some telling resemblances to the otherwise antinomian figures of Theodorus and Protagoras.[1]

One such resemblance is worth noting immediately. Like Theodorus and Protagoras, Euthyphro and Meletus both claim to possess a kind of knowledge or insight that raises them above the level of other human beings and thereby allows them to transcend the ordinary limitations of human finitude. Roughly stated, each of these characters presents us with a distinct embodiment of the aspiration, insofar as it is humanly possible, to become a god. The persistence of this theme raises questions about the way in which Socratic care might involve a kind of therapy for misdirected attempts to overcome our human finitude—espeially since, as we shall see, the aggressive attempts at transcendence pursued by Euthyphro and Meletus prove to be no less problematic that the Theodorean and Protagorean versions of godhood we studied in the previous chapter.[2]

Most Platonic dialogues are named for one of Socrates' interlocutors, as if to underscore the point that, for Socrates, every conversation provides an opportunity to get to know the nature of another individual. All Platonic dialogues are faithful to the natural settings of human life: they occur at a specific time and place, and in circumstances in which one might plausibly expect to find this or that particular human being. This point is connected with the previous one, for the soul learns or forgets, grows angry or mild, stays or retreats—in short, reveals its nature through speech and deed—only within the concrete contexts of ordinary experience. The understanding of things that we derive from experience is of course profoundly questionable, a fact that Socrates opportunely exploits so as to learn about, as well as from, his interlocutors. Thus he pointedly asks generals about courage, rhetoricians about justice, and mathematicians about knowledge. If *logos* is a "second sailing" for Socrates (*Phaedo* 99c9-d1), questions are the oars that propel and steer him across the sea of discourse. Ordinary experience, however, is the source of the questions that guide all Socratic voyages; as such, the phenomena of everyday life constitute an abundant and enduring *archê*, a copious origin or beginning, of philosophical inquiry.

The preceding observation helps to explain why Socrates rarely leaves Athens, or even, as Euthyphro observes in the first words of the *Euthyphro*, his "accustomed haunts" in the Lyceum (2a2). Socrates' trust in the reliability of ordinary experience as a launching-point of inquiry keeps him close to home in a philosophical sense: his conversations begin from, and repeatedly return to, questions that first emerge within the everyday contexts of human life. Yet it is the persistence of Socrates' initially disarming "homeliness" in conversation (cf. *Symposium* 221e), the doggedness with which he exposes the perplexing character of familiar phenomena, that frustrates his interlocutors and often causes them to regard him as a strange and even hostile figure. These reflections raise a number of questions. How does the circular movement of Socratic inquiry assist in midwifing human beings? What is it about this dialogical circularity that disturbs the Athenians' sense of where they dwell and who they are? Finally, and following closely upon the latter question, what approach to the claims of *nomos*—itself an important part of the landscape of ordinary experience—is implicit in this circularity?

These questions emerge over the course of the *Euthyphro* as Socrates' interlocutor proceeds to live up to the multiple promises of his name. Euthyphro (*euthus, phrên*) is either Instant Mind or Straight Thinker (*phrên*, the "heart" or "midriff" in Homer, is also the seat of consciousness). Euthyphro's claim to the former title is rooted in his status as a seer or prophet (*mantis*: 3e3), for prophecy is the direct revelation of the mind or will of the gods. Prophecy, like *phronêsis*, is ad hoc: it speaks to what ought to be done here and now, in this or that concrete context. Moreover, knowledge is imparted to the prophet not once and for all and as a whole, but piecemeal and occasionally—as, for example, just prior to a battle. Hence prophetic knowledge resembles *phronêsis* in that it cannot be rendered in the systematic and comprehensive form of an art or science.[3] Oddly, however, Euthyphro also claims to possess an expert knowledge of *ta theia*, the divine things, that is teachable and demonstrable (4e-5c, 5e, 9b), and he is therefore initially quite willing to accede to Socrates' request for a definition of the "form" (*eidos*) or "look" (*idea*) of piety (5c-d, 6d-e). Euthyphro thus turns out also to be a "straight thinker," and that in several ways. On one level, the geometrical resonance of his name hints at the surprising abstractness of his understanding of piety. Euthyphro presents himself as one who is primarily concerned with a practical matter: doing what is *eusebes* or *hosion*, what is "pious" in the sense of being prescribed or permitted by divine law.[4] Yet in spite of his claim to prophecy, he seems to make no distinction between what is pious in general and what is pious in each particular context. At least with respect to the situation involving his father, he measures the correctness of actions by a universal, inflexible, and therefore abstract standard. Put otherwise, he has no sense of the nonarithmetical mean. What is more, in prosecuting his father for murder he seems to act neither piously nor with *phronêsis*; either *phronêsis* is not a function of prophetic divination or Euthyphro is not a prophet. In certain respects, then, Euthyphro is a Theodorus of the agora: he demonstrates the foolishness that results from applying to ethical issues the modes and standards of thought appropriate to mathematical inquiry (cf. Aristotle, *Nicomachean Ethics* 1.3, 6.8). His lack of self-knowledge, however, does not stem from an exclusive (or even primary) concern with theoretical activity. In this crucial respect, Euthyphro is no Theodorus. His ignorance of the human soul and of the proper measures of human life has other roots.

More suggestive is the contrast between the modes of comportment toward the *archai* of understanding, the origins or beginnings of thought, exemplified by Euthyphro and Socrates. Euthyphro's thinking moves straight away from its point of inception, which is to say that he is not inclined to return reflectively to the roots of his opinions. In this respect, Euthyphro—whose conduct is decidedly unconventional, and who sides with Socrates in his dispute with Meletus—nonetheless exemplifies a crucial dimension of the orthodox mode of thinking that the city and its spokesmen suppose to be indispensable to good citizenship. Orthodoxy is "straight" or "correct" opinion (*orthê doxa*), opinion that flows directly from the beginnings of the political community in ancient *nomos*. These archaic beginnings—including especially the *archaioi theoi*, the ancient gods—are deemed authoritative just because they are Athenian and they are old. Orthodox belief is thus unexamined belief; from the Socratic point of view, "straight thinking" is not really thinking at all. As "straight thinkers," Euthyphro and Meletus lack self-knowledge because they do not know where they are coming from. Socrates, on the other hand, is a "circle thinker": he twice bids Euthyphro to start the inquiry "once more from the beginning" (*palin ex archês*: 11b2, 15c11), and is at one point criticized by Euthyphro for causing his speeches to go around in circles (11b-d). The *Euthyphro* thus connects the homebound circularity of Socratic discourse with the philosophical problem of the beginning of learning and the political problem of the foundations of community.

One more theme lends a special richness to the *Euthyphro*. I refer to the complex relationships of resemblance and antagonism that link Euthyphro and Socrates not only with each other, but also with Socrates' prosecutor Meletus—who is absent, but who nonetheless plays a significant role in this dialogue, just as Protagoras does in the *Theaetetus*. Our exposition, in fact, follows the structure of the *Euthyphro* in beginning with Meletus's indictment and only then turning to Euthyphro's prosecution of his father. As we shall see, the multiple threads of resemblance that run throughout the *Euthyphro* extend even to the story Euthyphro tells about the death of his hired laborer. Most important for our purposes, these thematic and dramatic filaments help the reader to see more clearly the issues at stake in the conflict between Socrates' way of caring for individual souls, the civic concern displayed by Meletus, whose very name is "Care," and the strange religious conscientiousness of Euthyphro. These philosophical and political issues, too, come to rest upon the problem of the various *archai* of human opinion, and the different ways in which these distinct beginnings figure in the self-consciousness of Socrates and the self-perceptions of his fellow Athenians.

Place and Drama in the *Euthyphro*

Euthyphro finds it odd to encounter Socrates in front of the Portico of the King Archon or Stoa Basileios in the agora, where judicial proceedings concerning religious matters were initiated. Socrates, we are reminded, is no longer truly at leisure (cf. *Theaetetus* 210d), and can be found in this place only because he has been compelled by law to appear here. Euthyphro is still more surprised when he hears that Socrates is involved in a *graphê*, literally a "writing"—an indictment of the sort that is brought by a citizen of Athens on behalf of the whole political community and that alleges a crime of public significance. (Euthyphro's indictment against his father, on the other hand, is a *dikê phonou*, a private homicide case normally brought to the court by the victim's relatives.)[5] It is just possible that Socrates is present as a prosecutor, but Euthyphro supposes that someone else must have written up an indictment against him (*graphên . . . gegraptai*: 2b1). The repetition in this passage of words connected with writing calls attention to a significant peculiarity of the *Euthyphro*'s setting: evidence suggests that the Stoa Basileios was also the place where the written laws of both Draco and Solon were inscribed on stone tablets, or *stêlai*.[6] The ancestral laws of Athens are thus physically present as a backdrop to the conversation of the *Euthyphro*, a juxtaposition that highlights the difference between the words of the city and those that belong to Socrates.[7]

Socrates, as Euthyphro suggests (2a), is more at home in the Lyceum, a public gymnasium, than in the present setting, which is to say that he is more at home in the company of living, erotically charged youths than that of frozen letters. Socratic speech is correspondingly flexible, intending always to say just what his philosophical midwifery deems appropriate for *this* particular individual in *these* specific circumstances. Yet it is from the universal and relatively inflexible *nomoi* of the city—some of which are written in stone, and some of which are inscribed only in the sediment of custom—that Meletus derives his understanding of care as a kind of mechanical imprinting of opinions upon the soul, and it is these *nomoi* that the Athenian jury will use to measure the speeches and deeds of Socrates. The situation anticipates an analogy of the

Stranger's, wherein the laws are compared to the prescriptions left behind by an absent doctor. Should the doctor return early, it would be absurd to make him adhere to the prescriptions he once wrote. To do so
would be to treat an indefinite, imprecise art with variable subject matter
as if it were a precise, definite art with invariable subject matter (*Statesman* 295b-296a). So, too, even if the laws of Athens were just so many
prescriptions of Socratic midwifery, it would be ridiculous to demand
that Socrates adhere to them in his treatment of individual souls. The
problem pointed out by the *Euthyphro*'s setting has to do with the form
of law, not its content. *Nomos* as such—*nomos* unmediated by a living
sense of the particularity of distinct individuals—is incongruous with
Socrates' conversational practice, because it is too abstract to provide
what he regards as the proper care for individual souls. Socrates aims to
midwife human beings and the city aims to produce good citizens. Are
these goals incompatible?

The particular location of Socrates' conversation with Euthyphro
evokes other, specifically dramatic resonances that emphasize the relevance of the latter question. In the *Euthyphro* Socrates bears at least a
superficial resemblance to the bad citizen Aristophanes makes him out to
be in the *Clouds*. Euthyphro's guess that Socrates has come to the Stoa
Basileios as a defendant is correct, but perhaps only in the most trivial
sense: Socrates later admits that he is displeased by traditional religious
myths (6a), and in the ensuing discussion he proceeds to attack the poeticoreligious tradition with prosecutorial vigor. Euthyphro's attempt to
punish his father parallels what seems to be a Socratic assault upon *Zeus
patrôios* and *Apollôn patrôios*: Zeus and Apollo, the gods of fathers (cf.
Euthydemus, 302c-d). Yet this parallel points toward a still more profound connection between the *Euthyphro* and the *Clouds*. It alerts us to a
counteraccusation that is embedded within the dramatic structure of the
Euthyphro, and that Plato seems to direct against Aristophanes—the
foremost among Socrates' first accusers—no less than against Meletus.

The *Euthyphro* in certain respects reproduces the plot of the *Clouds*,
but it tellingly reverses the roles assigned to the old philosopher and the
spirited youth. In the *Clouds*, Socrates teaches a young man that nature
sanctions his desire to beat his father. In the *Euthyphro*, Socrates encounters a young man who is already convinced that he is justified in
punishing his father. In the *Clouds*, Pheidippides comes to study with
Socrates in a place that stands conspicuously apart from the city that sur-
rounds it (247-249); in the *Euthyphro*, Socrates comes into the agora at
the heart of Athens and encounters a Euthyphro so "wise" that Socrates
proposes to study with *him* (5a-b). The mute presence of laws inscribed
in stone seems to anticipate the doctrinal rigidity and thoughtless repeti-
tiveness of Socrates' interlocutor. Nor can Euthyphro's apparent corrup-

tion easily be blamed on philosophy, for he appeals to the poeticoreligious tradition itself in order to support his actions (5e-6a). Socrates undermines the gods of the fathers in the *Clouds*, but they are shown to undermine themselves in the *Euthyphro*. Most important, Socrates tries to come to the rescue of the fathers and their gods by at least temporarily dissuading his interlocutor from committing injustice. Although his departure may stem more from frustration than genuine doubt, the fact is that Euthyphro leaves the Stoa, perhaps without even having initiated his lawsuit. If the Socrates of the *Clouds* sickens the healthy, the Socrates of the *Euthyphro* tries to heal the morally sick. The dramatic action of the *Euthyphro* answers the accusations of Aristophanes and Meletus by implying that it is the city that corrupts the youth, not Socrates, and that it does so as measured by its own standards of good citizenship. We shall return to this point in due time. For now, we may simply note that midwifing human beings may have something to do with producing good citizens after all.[8]

Meletus and the Care of Plants

In speaking to Euthyphro of Meletus, Socrates admits that "I myself am not even very familiar [*gignôskô*] with the man at all, for he seems to me to be someone young and unknown [*agnôs*]" (2b7-8). Here Socrates twice employs words based on the root *gnô*, as did Euthyphro at 2b2 (*katagnôsomai*). These words connote knowledge that involves familiarity or acquaintance (*gnôsis* or *gnôrisis*) rather than scientific comprehension (*epistêmê*). *Gignôskein* is the term Socrates uses for knowledge of human souls—either those of others, like Theaetetus, or his own, in accordance with the Delphic injunction "Know Thyself" (*gnôthi sauton*; cf. *Phaedrus* 229e).[9] Socrates is able to describe the general physical appearance of Meletus (2b), but he does not really know him because he is not acquainted with his soul. He acquires *gnôrisis* of Theaetetus—"gets to know" him—by conversing with him and subsequently listening to his discussion with the Stranger (*Statesman* 257a), but he has evidently never spoken with Meletus. By Socratic standards, Meletus also cannot claim to know Socrates very well; at best, he may at one time or another have observed Socrates in conversation with others. Perhaps Meletus is *agnôs* not only because he has not yet made a name for himself through important deeds (cf. 3a), but also in the sense that he is willing to bring a capital charge against Socrates even though he does not know who Socrates is. Either Meletus is ignorant of just what is involved in coming to know human beings (including himself), or the possibility that he might be mistaken about Socrates is something about which he simply does not care.

In answer to Euthyphro's question about the nature of the indictment he is facing, Socrates deftly sketches his antagonism with Meletus and employs a Protagorean image in order to illuminate the political and philosophical issues at stake therein.

What sort [of indictment]? Not an ignoble one, as it seems to me. For a young man to have come to know [*egnôkenai*] about such a big matter is no mean feat [*ou phaulon*]. For that one, as he maintains, knows in what way the young are being corrupted, and who are the ones corrupting them. And he may be someone wise, and, looking down upon my ignorance, he is coming to accuse me before the city as before his mother on the ground that I am corrupting those of his own age. And he alone among the political men seems to begin [*archesthai*] correctly. For it is correct to care first for the young in order that they may be as excellent as possible, just as it is fitting for a good farmer to care first for the young plants, and after this for the others. And moreover, Meletus is perhaps first purging us [*ek-kathairei*], the corrupters of the young shoots, as he claims. Then, after this, it is clear that, having taken care of the older ones, he will be responsible [*aitios*] for the most and greatest good things for the city, as is likely to happen for one beginning from such a beginning [*archês arxamenôi*]. (2c2-3a5)

Socrates could scarcely have more strongly emphasized the problem of beginnings. His speech about Meletus's care imitates the movement of Socratic inquiry as a whole: it ends at the beginning. Socrates' characterization of Meletus, I suggest, is designed to help us grasp the implications of his own philosophical circularity. In order to understand Socrates, we must understand his antagonist. Where does Meletus begin in caring for others, and where does he end? With regard to beginnings, our archaeological query is twofold. How did Meletus arrive at his notion of the proper way to care for others? And what is his conception of the living beings for which he cares? [10]

Socrates supposes that Meletus has *gnôsis* about a big matter (*pragma*). He seems to be referring to the corruption and care of human beings, but this would in any case entail another kind of nonepistemic knowledge to which his words apply equally well, namely, familiarity with the ostensibly corrupting deed (*pragma*) of Socratic philosophizing. Socrates does not tell us how Meletus might have acquired such knowledge, and he has in any case already raised a serious doubt about his possession of it. His speculation that Meletus may be wise (*sophos*) implies that his accuser is not a philosopher (*philosophos*): like the gods, he cannot be a lover of wisdom if he is already wise (cf. *Symposium* 204a). The wise do not seek wisdom, and so do not engage in inquiry. One might suppose that Meletus has reached wisdom by way of philosophic inquiry, except that he would not have had sufficient time to do so: he is still young and without much of a beard (2b). If Meletus is wise, he must be either a god or a prophet.

Alternatively, Meletus lacks knowledge, and has acquired his opinion of how to care for human beings from some nondivine source—perhaps from his "mother," the city, which has nurtured him in accordance with *nomos*. This identification of city and mother is particularly interesting. Ordinarily, the family might be expected to play a large role in any account of the care of human beings. Meletus's understanding of care, however, abstracts from the family, as is also implied in the image of citizens as autochthonous "shoots": if the city is the "mother" of the Athenians, biological parents have little role in the rearing of future citizens.[11] This suggestion is supported by Meletus's claim in the *Apology* that it is the *nomoi* that make the young better. In Meletus's encounter with Socrates before the court, it is precisely the *ordinariness* of his conception of care to which he appeals in order to justify the correctness of this conception. Meletus presents himself there as one among many, an average citizen who speaks for the laws that are embraced by all Athenians—except Socrates. His understanding of how to care for the young is equivalent to the knowledge of the *nomoi* that every Athenian citizen possesses (*Apology* 24d-25a). Meletus speaks in the *Apology* as a radical democrat: he extends the formal notion of legal equality into a vision of substantial moral equality that abstracts completely from individual differences of character and ability.[12] To those who share this radical vision, Socrates appears undemocratically contemptuous of the law in suggesting that caring for human beings involves expertise that is not possessed by the many (*Apology* 25a-b). In spite of his democratic attitudes, Meletus seems unsure about whether he is godlike in his knowledge, or merely human. This ambiguity is also reflected in the curious mixture of superficial activity and plantlike passivity that characterizes his prosecution of Socrates. On the one hand, Meletus aspires to political activity of the highest sort: he seeks actively to make a new beginning in caring for the city, and so to become a cause (*aitia*) of the many good consequences that will flow from this beginning. On the other, his indictment originates in an acknowledgment of the authority of archaic ways and beliefs that are, as it were, absorbed by every sprouting citizen through the soil of civic culture. The apparent incoherence of Meletus's self-conception provokes wonder—all the more so, Socrates suggests, because Meletus is in no way extraordinary. Indeed, his confused self-understanding as simultaneously active and passive seems to be emblematic of the condition of politicized human beings in general.

Socrates is particularly interested in the confusion noted above. In characterizing his antagonist, he rehabilitates the central image that he used in the *Theaetetus* to express Protagoras's "wisdom." Meletus begins by caring for young human beings, much like a good farmer cares first for young plants. If the Athenian plants need a farmer, they must be domesticated; wild plants take care of themselves. As cultivated plants, Meletus's fellow citizens cannot even in principle know why they have come together in political community or what constitutes their own excellence: a farmer cultivates plants for purposes that he himself determines, and with respect to which he alone assesses their flourishing or lack thereof. Meletus, like Protagoras, is described as a farmer doctoring sick plants: he seeks to protect the young shoots by purifying or purging (*ekkathairein*) the corruption that threatens them. Meletus's claim to be a caretaker, like that of Protagoras, presupposes that human beings are passive and pliant (and therefore all the more open to corruption), and implies that he alone possesses authoritative expertise in regard to their nurture. And in a distinctly Protagorean fashion, Meletus "looks down" upon Socrates and his fellow citizens as if he were a god among men.

Socrates' horticultural analogy exposes some of the important implications of Meletus's indictment. Meletus is not a "plant" if he is able to think for himself, as he must if he is truly capable of recognizing that Socrates corrupts. In itself, this recognition would seem to be sufficient protection against being corrupted: Meletus refuses to be guided by Socrates' ideas just because he knows that they are bad ones. It would follow that Socrates cannot corrupt those who are able to think for themselves in the way that Meletus can think for himself. But because Socrates does corrupt (according to Meletus), some Athenians must be unable to think for themselves. These endangered Athenians, these plants, are Meletus's agemates. Meletus seems to stand above his peers, and to resemble a farmer in his elevated solicitousness.

If Socrates were a plant, he would presumably be a weed—an unwanted growth that springs up on its own. Socrates suggests as much in the *Republic*: in cities that exist in deed and not, like the Kallipolis, in speech alone, philosophers grow up spontaneously and quite apart from the will of the regime (520b). Good farmers root out weeds because they tend to make the crops bitter and stunted. But if weeds impede the growth of domesticated plants, the reverse is also true. In fact, Socrates uses the horticultural analogy in the *Republic* to turn the tables on those who accuse him of corrupting the young: it is *philosophic* natures that are exposed to an extraordinary risk of corruption, for such natures live in the cities of men like "foreign seed sown in alien ground" (497b3-4; cf. 491d). The same image is at work in the digression of the *Theaetetus*, where Socrates notes that lawcourts deprive young souls of their potential "growth" and "straightness" (173a4). Perhaps this passage points ahead toward the *Euthyphro*. Is Euthyphro a young shoot of a man who is putting his straightness (*to euthu*) at risk by entering court to prosecute his father?

This talk of philosophic natures as plants should not be allowed to obscure the fact that in the passage at hand Socrates does not actually refer to the corrupters of the young as plants. This detail bears emphasis: if Meletus can reasonably take credit for benefitting the city, as he aims to do after caring for his fellow citizens, Socrates, he assumes, can reasonably be held criminally responsible (*aitios*) for harming it. Meletus accepts at least this much of the *Clouds*, even if, as Socrates suggests in the *Apology*, he uses Aristophanes' characterization of him as a pretext (23d). Meletus insists that Socrates corrupts willfully, and he goes so far as to regard him as the sole corrupter of the young among the Athenians (*Apology* 25a, 25d). Even as he "looks down" upon him, Meletus elevates Socrates in his imagination to the status of an antihero. But neither Meletus nor Socrates could be an *aitia*, a responsible factor or cause of either good or bad—much less the sole savior or corrupter of a city—if either were a plant.

Socrates makes the latter point quite clearly when he asks Euthyphro to teach him about the divine things. That way, he explains, he will be able to shift responsibility for his own views onto Euthyphro. If Meletus agrees that Euthyphro is wise, he will drop the charges against Socrates; if not, he will indict Euthyphro on the ground that he is corrupting the old. Socrates' suggestion is a humorous *reductio* of the view that human nature can be adequately imaged as a plant. Because of their plantlike passivity and pliancy, Meletus assumes, the young who have been corrupted by Socrates can bear no responsibility for the bad condition of their characters. Their problems begin elsewhere, for none of them is the author, the *archê*, of his own speeches and deeds. But if to be human is to be intellectually and morally plantlike, Socrates, too, can easily resist blame for his own bad nature. In fact, he cannot consistently do otherwise: to bear responsibility for one's own nature is to be something other than a plant. If all human beings are plants, no single person is responsible for the health or corruption of any other, for each has become what he is through being molded by external factors (the cultural and social equivalents of soil, air, water, rain, sun, shade, and so forth) over which he himself has no control. It would follow that no one—including the "wise" Euthyphro, as we are meant to see—can meaningfully be praised or blamed for his own, or anyone else's, moral or intellectual condition.

Socrates can be pronounced guilty or not guilty of corruption only if he is not a plant and others—the ones he corrupts—are. Of course, the existence of trials by jury provides a good reminder, if any were necessary, that men in general do not wish to regard themselves as plants. This reflection might lead one to suggest that Meletus confronts the same rhetorical challenge as Protagoras did, for in bringing Socrates to trial he must attempt to conceal from the judges the fact that he is treating them as if they were plants. This is perhaps the way many lawyers today might privately describe the challenge they face in examining witnesses and making opening and closing statements before a jury. Yet Meletus seems less sophisticated than Protagoras, whose clever strategy of self-presentation we examined in the previous chapter. Socrates claims only that Meletus is attacking him on behalf of the poets (*Apology* 23e); Meletus is neither a courtroom orator nor a professional speechwriter, and he has doubtless also not studied with any sophists. His brief tussle with Socrates in the *Apology* suggests that he is an unenthusiastic speaker. Unlike Protagoras, Meletus is probably unaware of the rhetorical problems—much less the philosophical ones—raised by his claim to care for human beings.

Meletus may be unreflective, but it does not follow that his indictment is without substance. The terms in which Socrates represents the indictment are by no means wholly uncompelling. Most people would be willing to acknowledge that it is possible to corrupt children, because children *are* in some sense like plants: they cannot (or cannot always) think for themselves and they are likely to be strongly influenced, for better or worse, by their early experiences. Socrates makes just this point in his discussion of the molding of young souls in the *Republic* (376d ff.). Yet it is also a commonplace of political existence that adults are morally responsible for their actions. Actions, in other words, are one's own; they belong to each of us individually because the decisive origin of speech and deed is ultimately nothing other than the individual. Meletus's indictment of Socrates invites us to ponder these widespread perceptions, as does Socrates' own talk of young philosophic natures as exotic plants. Does it make any sense to speak of a "budding" philosopher? We commonly suppose that to be human is at one stage of life to be something like a plant, and at the next stage not. How is this transition— one in which Socrates is intensely interested—effected? *Is* it effected? Are most adults truly responsible agents, or are they all, or almost all, deluded plants—as Protagoras implies?

Socrates and the Care of Human Beings

By raising questions of the latter sort, Socrates' horticultural analogy helps us to see what is truly at stake in Meletus's indictment. The analogy also gives us an inkling of how long a shadow the figure of Protagoras casts over the philosophic trial. Protagoras begins from the assumption that ordinary experience is a kind of false consciousness or dream, albeit one from which we cannot awake. In the terms of the present discussion, human beings are like plants that dream they are farmers. Protagoras concludes that the sorts of philosophical questions that arise within the horizons of ordinary experience are profitless, as is Socrates' practice of employing such questions in order to midwife human beings. This in fact amounts to a serious argument for the justice of Meletus's accusation. Just as one surely does harm to a child in treating it as if it were an adult, Socrates, so the argument goes, does nothing good—for individuals or for the city—in treating his fellow citizens as if they could be something other than plants. Because they cannot be otherwise, the most that Socrates could accomplish would be to "awaken" his interlocutors to the fact that the soul—the active, reflective center of responsibility with which we each identify ourselves, the authoritative *archê* from which our speeches and deeds originate—is a pipe dream of plants. The pain of this realization is unmitigated, for it augurs no fruitful births: all Socratically induced labor is necessarily false labor. Far better to encourage our dreams of authority and agency, as by teaching that human being is the measure of all things. If done properly this will also sustain a politically useful ambiguity, for the city wants citizens that can be cultivated like plants but that will nevertheless accept personal responsibility for their actions.

Socrates acknowledges the strength of the latter argument by making it clear that the challenge he poses to the city has to do precisely with his attempt to arouse the Athenians to inquire into themselves. Yet he rejects the Protagorean assumption upon which this argument rests, namely, that human beings are in truth plants and cannot be otherwise. Socrates explains the Athenians' displeasure with him as follows:

> For the Athenians, as it seems to me, it is not a matter of much concern [*melei*] if they think that someone is clever, unless he is capable of teaching his own wisdom [*tês hautou sophias*]. But they become angry with whomever they believe is able also to make others of such a sort, whether indeed by reason of envy, as you say, or on account of something else. (3c7-d2)

Tês hautou sophias, "the wisdom of himself," is ambiguous. Depending upon how one hears the reflexive pronoun *hautou*, this phrase could be translated as either "his own wisdom" or "wisdom *about* himself." I suggest that we are meant to understand the text in both ways: if Socrates can be said to have any wisdom at all, it has to do with his own soul. Socrates implies here that the cleverness the Athenians think he is able to transmit to others, and about which they care enough to get angry at him, is nothing other than self-knowledge. This interpretation finds further support in the immediate sequel. Socrates tells Euthyphro that they do not grow angry at *him* simply because "you seem to make yourself scarce [*spanion seauton parechein*], and not to be willing to teach your own wisdom [*tên seautou sophian*]" (3d5-6). Once again, the phrase translated as "your own wisdom" is literally "the wisdom of yourself." Euthyphro does not teach self-knowledge, indeed does not possess self-knowledge. Perhaps Socrates even means to suggest that Euthyphro's self is not much in evidence—that he "makes himself scarce"—just *because* he lacks self-knowledge, so that being a self would go hand in hand with knowing oneself.

In the *Theaetetus* Socrates said that he was barren of wisdom (*Theaetetus* 150c), but now he implies that he possesses wisdom. How are we to understand this "wisdom of oneself"? In the *Theaetetus*, *sophia* names an offspring of the soul that is fruitful and true, and so is not final or complete in itself but should be nurtured. Socrates' "wisdom" is certainly incomplete, rooted as it is in a knowledge of ignorance. Yet it also involves a crucial recognition of what it is to be human, which he articulates in the form of a claim about the human impossibility of the unexamined life. In the *Apology*, Socrates asserts that the unexamined life is "not livable" for a human being (*biôtos*: 38a6). In the terms of the present discussion, there is a relationship of mutual entailment between being a plant and leading an unexamined life, and between being human and leading an examined one.[13] The immediate fruit of Socrates' self-knowledge is thus a way of life that is preeminently open to increasing self-knowledge. Living an examined life seems wise at least in a relative sense—wise *for* a human being because it allows one to live *as* a human being. But it would not be a wise way of life for a plant, including one that dreams that it is human. Socrates' "philanthropy" (3d7), his generous sharing of the wisdom of the examined life, thus forces us to confront the peculiar doubleness of human being. Socrates loves others not for the given natures they happen to possess as a matter of biological or cultural inheritance, but for the exemplary humanity that they might, with effort, achieve.

Is the city justified in being angry at Socrates because he does not treat its citizens, and the young men who are its future citizens, like plants? In the *Republic*, Socrates offers a number of images that are meant to represent the political process of education or enculturation (*paideia*): the citizens of the city in speech are to be tamed like animals, stamped and molded like putty, tuned like musical instruments, and dyed like wool with salutary beliefs (375b-c, 377b, 410d, 429d). These technical analogies bring home the point that the city wants its citizens cut to measure. The human material out of which citizens are to be made must therefore be passive and pliant, which is to say that the city dreams of growing the young like plants. The family is at best a necessary nuisance in the process of nurturing straight-thinking plants, as can be seen from the severely limited role of the family in Sparta—the city that, of all Greek cities, came closest to making the latter dream a reality.[14] So too, Socratic circle thinking seems to interfere with abstract, nomological *paideia*, insofar as it awakens young souls to the questions of who they are and where they are coming from. To ask such questions of the city's archaic beginnings is to challenge their *prima facie* claim to authority. To ask such questions of oneself is to acknowledge the possible inadequacy of the city's attempt to define one's end and identity in terms of the homogeneity of citizenship. The Athenians seem to understand at least this much about Socratic inquiry.

From the point of view of the city or of its spokesman Meletus, Socrates would seem to be guilty of corrupting the young shoots whether he succeeds or fails in awakening their latent humanity. If he succeeds in showing them how to take possession of their own souls as active centers of responsibility, he makes them less fit for enculturation and so corrupts them as citizens. And if he fails, he is nevertheless guilty of promoting a politically destructive version of the false presumption of wisdom that he claims to combat. To the extent that the young men who take after Socrates and who imitate his interrogative style in cross-examining the fathers of Athens do not in fact think for themselves, even though they suppose that they do, Socrates becomes complicitous in bringing on false pregnancies of a particularly ugly sort.

Let us consider each part of the above argument in turn. To begin with a logical point, Socrates cannot reasonably be blamed for the badness of anyone else who is genuinely responsible for his own speeches and deeds. If such individuals make for poor citizens, it must be their own fault. Nor is it obvious that thinking for oneself is necessarily morally and politically corrupting. Socrates could defend himself by pointing to the example of Meletus, who would admit to thinking for himself and would nevertheless claim to be a good citizen. More important, Meletus overlooks the critical respect for *nomos* that is implicit in Socratic philosophizing, and that forms part of the examined life to which he attempts to awaken his young companions. This respect is rooted in the recognition that the *nomoi* are genuine beginnings—both of our shared lives and of philosophical inquiry into ourselves. Yet Meletus should perhaps be excused for his failure to credit Socrates with this insight: the respectfulness with which Socrates questions the *nomoi* will not be evident to one who demands unquestioning acknowledgment of their authority, and is in any case easily obscured by the irresponsible politics of his nonphilosophical imitators.

Socrates explores these matters in a passage in the *Republic* in which he addresses the lawlessness (*paranomia*) that philosophical conversation can apparently breed among the young. This passage, 537e-539c, is of special interest because its characterization of the relationship between the city's *nomoi* and its citizens seems in certain respects to support the standpoint of Meletus. Yet Socrates' account qualifies that standpoint in a way that opens up a means of defending his conversational practice against Meletus's charge of corruption.

Socrates first asks Glaucon to consider the hypothetical situation of a *hupobolimaios*, a child of another who is palmed off as one's own heir. Suppose that, "upon becoming a man," such a child should perceive that he does not belong to his alleged parents, but "should not be able to discover the ones who really gave birth to him" (538a2-3). The young man would thereafter be especially vulnerable to the influence of flatterers. So too, there are "convictions [*dogmata*] about the just and the noble things that belong to us from childhood, in which we have been reared just as by our parents, obeying them as rulers [*peitharchountes*] and honoring them" (538c6-8). Those who hold to the middle ground, who are "measured" (*metrious*), will not cease to feel filial devotion toward the ancestral dogmas (*ta patria*: literally, "the things of the father") when they are approached by ordinary practices or pursuits (*epitêdeumata*) that possess flattering pleasures (538d1-4). But philosophical argumentation also possesses pleasures "that flatter our soul and draw it to them" (538d2-3), pleasures to which even "measured" young men are vulnerable. When such a man is asked "What is the noble?" and "answers what he has heard from the lawgiver," the *logos*, "refuting [*elenchôn*] him many times and in many ways, throws him into the opinion that this is no more noble than shameful, and the same concerning the just and the good and whatever he used to hold most in honor" (538d6-e3). If the young man does not subsequently find his true "parents," the beliefs that are truly "worthy of honor and akin to him," he will embrace the life that has flattered him, and he will seem to have changed from a law-abiding man to a lawless or paranomic one (538e5-539a3).

On the one hand, this comparison indicates that the claim of the *nomoi* to *peitharchia*, the obedience due to one's own authoritative beginnings (*archai*), is in a certain respect illegitimate. The laws and customs of the city nurture the citizens as if they were their own children, and they enjoin filial allegiance as their due. Yet this relationship is rooted in deception, for the city's *nomoi* are not, as Meletus implies, the true "parents" of its citizens. The ancestral dogmas are impostors—stand-ins for the truth about what is noble, just, and the like. Moreover, the city blocks the achievement of self-knowledge or of knowledge about one's true beginnings insofar as it suppresses the question "Who am I?": this question need hardly be asked if the answer can be read off from the orthodox ways and beliefs of the political community. Indeed, Socrates' analogy seems to imply that the city *must* promote the unexamined life in order to secure the filial devotion of its citizens.

On the other hand, the analogy suggests that the *nomoi* deserve something like the respect that one would owe to one's adoptive parents. This means that Socratic philosophizing is by no means simply or straightforwardly antinomian—a point overlooked by those who slander "the whole of philosophy" on the basis of the comportment of its puppy-like devotees (539c3). Furthermore, and most interesting, Socrates suggests that respect for the *nomoi* is a *philosophical* requirement of the quest for self-knowledge—not just a morally appropriate way of acknowledging one's debt for their years of nurture. For the adopted child can discover much about himself if he is willing to listen to his adoptive parents—to learn from them by inquiry rather than simply to reject them out of hand. Their nurture, after all, has helped to form his identity; moreover, they may possess valuable clues as to his original affiliation. So too, the *nomoi* reflect what is already common and familiar to the members of a political community. As such, they should be numbered among the proper proximate beginnings of joint inquiry. To be sure, such inquiry may reveal grounds for suspicion about the content of civic education. Yet Socrates implies that if one learns to pose the right questions, or to pose them in the right way, one may discover in the *nomoi* important traces of what is truly "worthy of honor and akin" to oneself.

Republic 537e-539c thus corrects the impression that Socratic philosophizing encourages simple antinomianism. To the contrary, the philosophical pursuit of self-knowledge entails a kind of critical respect for the laws and customs of one's political community. At the same time, the recognition that the *nomoi* are akin to *adoptive* parents opens up a space that radical democrats like Meletus seek to close, a space within which one's particularity as an individual may assume its proper political relevance.

Some might object, however, that the whole point of Socrates' analogy is that early exposure to philosophical arguments causes young men *not* to pursue philosophy in a serious and responsible manner, but rather "to imitate the one who plays and contradicts for the sake of the game" (539c7-8). And yet it is in the course of an extended philosophical discussion with the young brothers Glaucon and Adeimantus that Socrates recommends not introducing young men to philosophical argumentation. This small irony suggests that Socrates finds it reasonable to believe that with his help at least some young men may learn to think for themselves. As for the rest, a plausible line of defense is implicit in the dramatic action of the *Euthyphro*. It is simply this: young men are by nature inclined to rebel against their fathers. Their native spiritedness or *thumos* will drive them to do so quite apart from any encouragement that Socrates may inadvertently offer to them, and in spite of the best efforts of the city to suppress their rebelliousness. The legal actions that Euthyphro and Meletus initiate against their elders may be the best proof of all that the city is dreaming when it supposes that it can grow its citizens like plants.

The Case of Euthyphro

Meletus's self-conception, as we have seen, is in certain respects incoherent. As an incorruptible protector of his corruptible agemates, he claims implicitly to possess special knowledge, and to be exempt from the plantlike pliability that characterizes his peers. Yet he cannot account for this difference. What is more, Meletus rests his indictment of Socrates upon the legitimacy of authority, that is to say, of passive cognition: although he proposes to make a new beginning in caring for the city, his understanding of care is wholly contained in the old beginning—the knowledge of archaic ways and beliefs that is the inheritance of every Athenian citizen (*Apology* 24d-25a). Like Protagoras, that other self-proclaimed farmer of sick plants, Meletus is a self-deceiver.

I suggested earlier that if Meletus is indeed wise he must be either a god or a prophet. This notion might be developed as follows. The farmer is the proper judge of whether his plants are doing well, for he knows the purposes for which he planted them. If his plants could possess any awareness of the goodness or badness of their own condition, it would only be because the farmer has communicated with them. Perhaps the gods stand to human beings as farmers to plants, so that communication from the gods, or prophecy, would be the basis for our knowledge of the condition of our souls. Something like this suggestion is explored in connection with the character of Euthyphro, whose self-understanding as a prophet reflects the same impulse toward self-aggrandizement, the same pretense of intellectual activity, that Meletus exemplifies.

Euthyphro sees Socrates as a kindred spirit, and regards Meletus's lawsuit as an unjust one (3a). He knows well that Socrates' assertions about his *daimonion* make him an easy target of slander, for, as he maintains, he is himself a prophet who has been unjustly ridiculed by the many "on the ground that I am mad [*hôs mainomenou*]" (3c2). Still, he bears a more than passing resemblance to Meletus. Like Meletus, Euthyphro is a young man who claims exceptional wisdom about matters of piety, care, and corruption—wisdom that has the potential to save the city (4b, 14b). Yet his "wisdom" in no way moves beyond the horizon of *nomos*, but instead amounts to a kind of thoughtless reconfiguration and recapitulation of conventional themes. According to Euthyphro, Meletus views Socrates as an "innovator" (*kainotomountos*) in regard to the divine things (3b6). Whatever the merits of this charge, we cannot fail to notice that it fairly describes Euthyphro: it is he who proves to be a "maker" or "poet" (*poiêtês*: 3b2) in religious matters, and who innovates by reshaping the customary material of myth and ritual in accordance with the dictates of his youthful nature.

Euthyphro takes pride in the idea that his wisdom makes him superior to the many, and he readily accedes to Socrates' request to teach him about the divine things (4e-5c). In Socrates' words, Euthyphro sees himself precisely as one who is "capable of teaching his own wisdom" (3c9). Since acquiring this wisdom would allow Socrates to live a better life (16a), Euthyphro supposes that he can do for Socrates what Socrates claimed his philosophic midwifery was unable to do for Theaetetus (*Theaetetus* 210c). But he can convey his wisdom by way of proofs and demonstrations only if it is "his own" in the specific sense that an art or science can be one's own: he must be actively in possession of it in such a way as to be able to call it forth and lay it out at will. That Euthyphro ultimately disappoints Socrates is not surprising, for the knowledge of a seer is a *passive* possession. Indeed, the seer is no more than a mouthpiece of higher powers: he is himself said to be "possessed" (*mantis* is etymologically related to *mainesthai*, "to be mad"), and he can articulate only such visions as have been vouchsafed to him by the gods.[15] One may doubt, moreover, whether the higher power that finds its voice in Euthyphro is anything other than *nomos* itself, for the foundation of his teaching, in spite of its antinomian veneer, turns out to be convention. His putative wisdom is rooted in that which has been implanted by civic education in every Athenian. Like Meletus, Euthyphro justifies his lawsuit by appealing to *nomos*: human beings, he observes, "happen to acknowledge as a matter of custom or convention [*tungchanousi nomizontes*] that Zeus is the best and most just of the gods, and they agree that he bound his own father because he [Cronos] swallowed up his sons unjustly, and that that one [Cronos] in turn castrated his own father on account of other such things" (5e5-6a3). So, too, his various definitions of piety as whatever is dear to the gods (6e-7a) or to all the gods (9e), and as a kind of commerce between human beings and gods (14e), all reflect an operative conception of piety that is implicit in the conventions of religious ritual.

Because Euthyphro draws on the mythopoetic and ritual traditions in addressing the question that Socrates first raises at 5c-d about the pious (*to eusebes, to hosion*), Socrates' criticisms of his responses are also criticisms of this religious heritage. To think through these criticisms is to open up the question of whether becoming a human being (in the Socratic sense) might not actually be a *requirement* of good citizenship.

Precisely because they can be justified by an unreflective, literalist interpretation of the tradition, Euthyphro's antinomian innovations call attention to contradictions at the heart of *nomos* itself. Such contradictions
underscore the need either for genuine prophecy or for philosophical reflection. And in the absence of prophecy, or in a world that has effectively been abandoned by the gods—a world such as our own, according
to the Stranger's myth of the reversed cosmos in the *Statesman*—one
must be able to think for oneself.

We shall return in due time to the considerations raised above. But one
should also not lose sight of the fact that Socrates introduces the problem
of piety in order to shed light on the particular question of whether it is
right for Euthyphro to be prosecuting his father for murder (4e). And as
soon as one asks why Euthyphro is pressing charges, one opens up questions having to do not only with what the young man thinks about religious matters, but also what he feels toward his father. Euthyphro's anger
at his father—who withholds the recognition he craves as a seer and
seems to him unjustly to interfere in his own sphere of activity—is arguably the real impetus behind his legal action, and his talk of piety
something of a pretext. If this is correct, Socrates' discussion with
Euthyphro is centrally concerned with much the same matter of philosophical and political maturity that he explores at *Republic* 537e-539c,
namely, the proper mode of thinking about, feeling, and comporting oneself toward one's father, or, toward that which is father-like in its status
as an *archê*—an origin, authority, or ruling power.

To connect the preceding point with a theme explored in detail by
Drew Hyland, we may say that the *Euthyphro* concerns the proper response to our human finitude. The paradoxical combination of activity
and passivity manifested in the characters of Meletus and Euthyphro is a
mark of finitude, but also of the possibility of transcendence implicit in
human life. Both of these characters exemplify an abstract way of thinking and acting that effectively ignores the complexities of human
finitude, including in particular those connected with one's status as a
member of a family. Both attempt to transcend finitude by adopting an
aggressive strategy that involves turning to the laws, which Arlene Saxenhouse describes as "the abstract institutions of the city that with the
creation of democracy have moved men away from being enmeshed in
the family to equal individuals."[16] Socrates, in contrast, represents an alternative strategy that Hyland calls "finite transcendence," one that exploits the possibilities inherent in our finitude rather than attempting to
demolish the limiting conditions with which are confronted.[17]

Both Socratic and non-Socratic responses to the problem of finitude
are nicely illustrated in the strange story Euthyphro tells about his father.
Euthyphro's story is, strikingly, a kind of unconscious prophecy, and that

on several levels. In the first place, it reveals Euthyphro's hidden motivation in bringing his father to trial. It is also significant that Euthyphro draws a close connection between his father and the authority of conventional opinion or *nomos*. Still more interesting, Euthyphro's story symbolically represents the effect that Socrates hopes to have upon young men like himself.

Just as Meletus envisions his prosecution of Socrates as a kind of civic catharsis of corruption, Euthyphro describes his lawsuit against his father as an act whereby religious pollution (*miasma*) may be expunged (4c1-3). But the details of his story suggest another, psychological description of the same act. While he and his family were farming an allotment of land on the Athenian-held island of Naxos, Euthyphro had a *pelatês*, a dependent laborer of some sort, who got drunk and murdered one of the family slaves.[18] The father tied up Euthyphro's man, threw him in a ditch, and sent to inquire of the exegete (an expounder of Athenian religious law) what he should do.[19] During this time, Euthyphro emphasizes, his father "paid little attention" to (*ôligôrei*) the man and "showed no care" (*êmelei*) for him, and the hired hand died "from hunger and cold and his bonds" (4d1-5). His father and the rest of his family are now angry with him on the ground that: (1) His father did not actually kill the man; (2) Because the man was a murderer, one should in any case not be concerned about him; and (3) It is impious (*anosion*) for a son to proceed against his father for murder. But, he tells Socrates, they all "know badly, in respect to the divine, how things stand concerning the pious and the impious" (4e1-3).

Euthyphro—again like Meletus—justifies his indictment in terms of his care or concern for others as well as his piety. One wonders, however, why he cares more about his hired laborer—who, as a resident of Naxos, would not even have been an Athenian—than about his family's slave (not to mention his own father).[20] One suspects the reason is that it is Euthyphro himself who feels he has been "paid little attention" and "shown no care." Euthyphro's sensitivity to the ridicule of the many, which he tries to turn into a badge of honor by ascribing it to their envy (3c), underscores his as yet unfulfilled longing to be recognized as an outstanding man.[21] Like the many, Euthyphro's father rejects his son's claim to special knowledge in matters of religion and instead consults other experts. To add injury to insult, his father causes the death of a hired hand that Euthyphro sees as his own man: he calls him "*my* day-laborer" (*pelatês emos*: 4c3-4). The murdered slave, on the other hand, belonged to his family—which is to say to his *father*, not to him. Euthyphro's real feelings are perhaps more than hinted at in his appeal to the stories about how Zeus bound his father "because he swallowed up his sons unjustly," and how Cronos "castrated his own father because of other such things" (6a1-3). Zeus's treatment of Cronos, he insists, was not unjust, for "human beings happen to acknowledge that Zeus is the best and most just of the gods" (5e6-6a1). Euthyphro is angry because he believes that his father, like some monstrous, overreaching Titan, has tyrannically arrogated to himself something that properly belongs to his son. Yet insofar as he envisions himself in the role of Zeus to his father's Cronos, he seeks something more than just what is due to him as a son. Like Zeus, Euthyphro wants to shed the limitations that come with being a son to one's father. He wants to usurp the power of his father, and in this sense to become a (fatherless) father in his own right.

Euthyphro's problem is compounded by the fact that the weight of public opinion opposes him. His desires bring him into conflict with the political and religious tradition, whose authoritativeness in the eyes of his family and of most of the Athenians is rooted in a shared respect for *ta patria* or the *patrioi nomoi*—the ways and laws of the fathers. Here we encounter a problem in Euthyphro's conception of piety. Two words for "the pious" occur in the *Euthyphro*: *to eusebes* and *to hosion*. The former has a specific suggestion of reverence and awe, while the latter is related to *to dikaion*, "the just," and "assumes the general moral meaning of what is permitted."[22] More important than these differences, however, is the general point that the criterion of *to hosion* as well as *to eusebes* is nothing other than ancestral tradition.[23] Given the publicity of the social practices and norms of pious behavior, how could Euthyphro's relatives not "know well" what is pious? Precisely insofar as he appears to act without due respect for the tradition—and indeed, in a way that directly contradicts the filial gratitude that stands at the heart of the traditional conception of piety—Euthyphro's claim to be doing what is pious seems absurd.[24] As we have noted, however, there is a place in Athenian society not only for seers but also for others with expertise in religious matters; exegetes, for example, might be consulted in cases where a complex situation is not clearly covered by the existing *nomoi*. Euthyphro implicitly claims to be just such an interpretative expert. The source of his knowledge, in turn, appears to be the special relationship to the divine sphere that he enjoys in his capacity as a *mantis*. And while any such special relationship—as for example the one Socrates seems to claim for himself in virtue of his *daimonion*—opens up the possibility of a conflict between prophecy and the ancestral traditions, Euthyphro is able to appeal to the tradition in order to support the content of his prophecy.

Euthyphro's rhetorical strategy points toward the incoherence of the tradition. Reverence for that which is archaic is unfortunately an inconsistent political principle, for that which is now old was once young, and in its birth brought about the death of that which was older still.[25] What is more, this brutal political fact is enshrined in the stories about Zeus and his progenitors, and so is itself part of the tradition. Euthyphro, of course, does not call attention to this inconsistency, nor does he even seem to recognize it; he merely insists that his family's understanding of religious matters is self-contradictory, and that the religious tradition in fact supports the justice of his indictment.

Whereas an exegete might be needed because *nomos* is too simple to handle a specific situation, Euthyphro's claim is that *nomos* is not simple enough. Here we encounter another important respect in which Euthyphro resembles Meletus: his attempt to transcend his own finitude involves an intentional act of moral and intellectual abstraction from a number of concrete distinctions that ordinarily inform our sense of who we are. Euthyphro's lawsuit on behalf of the dead laborer ignores the differences between a stranger and a family member as well as those between an Athenian and a foreigner. His implicit assumption that what is right for Zeus is right for him furthermore overlooks the ways in which a father differs from a son and a human being from a god. Finally, Euthyphro abstracts from the differences between the gods of Athens and those of other cities, for he justifies his behavior in terms of Hesiodic tales about the gods that are shared by all the Greeks. Plato appropriately emphasizes this dimension of Euthyphro's character by framing his knowledge claims about the pious and the just in abstract, quasi-mathematical language. Thus he and Socrates examine whether he knows "correctly" (*orthôs*: 4a12, 5b1, 5e4, 9a7, 9b2, 12d4, 14d9, 15c9, 15d7), "clearly" (*saphôs*: 5c8, 9b5, 9b9, 15d4, 15e1), and "precisely" (*akribôs*: 4e4, 5a2, 14b1). So, too, Euthyphro at various points claims to possess a "great proof" (*mega tekmêrion*) and to be able to "demonstrate clearly" (*saphôs epideixai*) that his lawsuit is in fact pious (5e2-3, 9b5), and he readily agrees with Socrates' suggestion that piety is a kind of *epistêmê* or scientific knowledge (14c5, d1).

Euthyphro's language calls attention to his misplaced assumption about the degree of clarity and precision with which the character of persons and actions can be known. And this assumption alerts us once again to the Aristophanean backdrop of the present dialogue. In the *Clouds*, Socrates teaches the young man Pheidippides an abstract way of thinking that ignores just the sorts of distinctions that are overlooked by Euthyphro, and that leads to gross impiety and injustice.[26] In the *Euthyphro*, Socrates does just the opposite: he attempts to school Euthyphro in piety and justice by turning his attention back toward the concrete contexts that confer upon him his particular human identity. Socrates thus takes pains to note the difference between questions that can be resolved by arithmetical calculation and those that cannot (7b-d). Arithmetic has great success with the sorts of problems that can be formulated in quantitative terms. And it is the purity or abstractness of the units of counting that makes possible this success, insofar as the "nonsensual" character of these pure monads allows us to apply them to any items whatsoever.[27] But the relationship between the pious, the noble, the just, and the good and particular instances of piety, nobility, justice, and goodness is not analogous to the relationship between pure monads and countable things. If there is something about which even the gods cannot come to an agreement, Socrates observes, it is whether a certain action is just or unjust, noble or shameful, and good or bad (7c10-d9 with 8e6-8). So if the pious is part of the just, as Euthyphro agrees (12d), the piety of particular actions is the kind of thing one *cannot* reckon in an arithmetical or quasi-arithmetical fashion, and about which one cannot provide demonstrations that are universally acknowledged to be conclusive. Socrates does not explain why this should be so, but it is obvious that disputes about the ethical qualities of an action often turn upon differing assessments of the concrete circumstances in which the action in question occurs. At all events, Socrates tries to show Euthyphro that the abstractness of his mode of thinking, together with his claims to quasi-arithmetical correctness, clarity, and precision, are simply out of place where matters of piety and justice are concerned.

The preceding reflections reinforce Hyland's suggestion that Socratic philosophizing seeks transcendence through a reflective confrontation with finitude, that is, with the concrete contexts of ordinary experience. While Socrates seems in certain respects to interfere with the relationship between fathers and their sons, he nevertheless shows himself in the *Euthyphro* to be a defender of the family. But because he regards his status as a family member, a son, and a human being as merely so many limitations, Euthyphro simply ignores these contexts—attempting to fly, as it were, high above them, much like Aristophanes' basket-borne Socrates and his pupil Pheidippides (cf. 4a2-4 with *Clouds*, 1400). He consequently loses his way, and begins to move in a tightening gyre (11b). If Socrates is Daedalus, as Euthyphro insists (11b-d), then Euthyphro is the impetuous Icarus, who ignores his father's warnings about flying too close to the heavens. In the *Euthyphro*, Socrates demonstrates a certain paternalistic concern in trying to clip the wings of his young companion.[28]

Socrates' fatherly care for the young is also prophetically reflected in Euthyphro's story. Euthyphro accuses his father of not caring about the hired laborer, and, more generally, about what is pious (4d-e). Yet his father, unlike Euthyphro, recognizes the relevant complexity of the situation in which he finds himself and is appropriately perplexed. He therefore decides to do nothing until he can learn by inquiry what is the right course of action. This behavior is reminiscent of Socrates, whose care for the souls of others is manifested in a devotion to inquiry that can sometimes seem indefinitely to postpone even the most needful action (cf. *Alcibiades I* 132b, *Alcibiades II* 150d). We have already had occasion to observe that the exigencies of everyday life can impinge upon the leisure required to philosophize. Perhaps we are meant to see in the image of the dying laborer the other side of the coin—the cost of Socratic inquiry in an unleisurely world of pressing necessities, a world of bodies in motion that is governed by the brisk tempo of politics and war.[29] We may note in this connection that what Euthyphro's father does to the body of the hired laborer is a good image of what Socrates does (or is perceived to do) to the souls his interlocutors: he strips them and tries to wrestle them to the ground (*Theaetetus* 169a-c), thereby exposing their ignorance, leaving them "hungry" for answers that he refuses to provide, and sometimes even rendering them intellectually immobile (cf. *Meno*, 80a-b).

Yet the image works in another, more positive way as well. The hired laborer is something that Euthyphro regards as his own, and with which he identifies himself. He is, moreover, a living being. What is imaged in the exposure and subsequent death of Euthyphro's hired laborer, one suspects, is nothing other than the work of philosophical midwifery: Socrates takes from his interlocutors certain "living" possessions that they associate closely with themselves, and allows them to die. These possessions of the psyche typically include highly animated or vital opinions, such as may stand at the center of the conception one entertains of one's own identity. Thus, Socrates will soon force Euthyphro to recognize the unfounded character of his self-understanding as an expert on piety; if Euthyphro learns anything at all, it is that he must struggle to become what he already imagined himself to be. There is more, however. Euthyphro's man is drunk and violent; as such, he is a good image of unbridled, raging aggression. This servant who no longer serves, who no longer works "with us" (*par' hêmin*, 4c5) but instead raises his hand *against* us, is nothing other than *thumos* run amok—angry spiritedness that has rebelled against the fatherly counsels of reason. This point is underscored by the remarkable echo of the deeds of the gods in Euthyphro's story: while Cronos's castration of Uranus is reiterated—with only a slight displacement—in the laborer's slitting the slave's throat, Zeus's binding Cronos and casting him down into Tartarus figures as Euthyphro's father tying up the laborer and throwing him in a ditch. Just such wayward spiritedness, in turn, characterizes the state of Euthyphro's own soul as he sets out in anger to punish his father. It is this disordered moral condition that Socrates seeks to treat in his conversation with the young man. By exposing the incoherence of Euthyphro's claims about piety, Socrates may hope to excise from his soul, or at least to calm, the aggression that he has unleashed against his father. This should not surprise us. At the end of the *Theaetetus*, after all, the only claim Socrates made for his art of midwifery was that it might help to make his young interlocutor more tame.

Piety and Justice: Socrates' Therapy for Gods and Men

Without explicitly admitting the justice of Meletus's charge, Socrates picks up Euthyphro's statement that he is "making innovations" in regard to the divine things and twice suggests that Euthyphro holds the key to his defense against this accusation (3b, 5a, 16a). Socrates further states that Euthyphro's failure to teach him about the divine things has dashed his hopes of refuting Meletus (15e-16a). These passages raise the suspicion that Socrates *is* in some sense a poet or maker of gods—albeit perhaps not the sort that Aristophanes puts on stage in the *Clouds*, much less the sort that Euthyphro proves to be. Whereas Aristophanes' Socrates tells Strepsiades that "there is no Zeus" (*Clouds*, 367), Socrates swears by Zeus when Euthyphro tells him why he is prosecuting his father and later when he asks Euthyphro whether he really believes the poets' tales of divine binding and castration (4e, 6b). And whereas Euthyphro acknowledges the authority of the poets concerning the divine things, Socrates is considerably more skeptical (6a-c; cf. 12a-b). Yet the action of the *Euthyphro* confirms that Socrates is nonetheless an innovator when it comes to the gods.

The nature of Socrates' innovations is perhaps best seen in comparison with those of Euthyphro. As we have seen, Euthyphro exploits the ambiguity of *nomos* in order to satisfy his anger toward his father. Ancestral tradition dictates that religious pollution be cleansed by bringing the wrongdoer to justice, but also that one should show due reverence toward one's father.[30] The death of the laborer thus poses a difficult problem that highlights the inadequacy of *nomos* alone as a guide to right action and thereby underscores the need for wisdom attained either through prophecy or by thinking for oneself. Whereas Socrates approaches this problem as an occasion for reflection, Euthyphro sees in it only an opportunity to act on previously frustrated longings. A different sort of son (or daughter) might not have simply ignored the obligation to honor one's father, which is prima facie no less binding than that of punishing injustice. Euthyphro emulates Zeus in more ways than he knows, as Socrates hints when he asks whether the pious is loved by the gods because it is pious or is pious because it is loved by the gods (10a). If we are to judge by Homer and Hesiod's depictions of the Olympians—depictions that are specially honored because these poets, being first in time, are also first in authority—it seems clear that what is pious is so because it is loved by the gods, and not the other way around; this is indeed the crux of

Adeimantus's critique of the poeticoreligious tradition at *Republic* 362e-367a. So too, Euthyphro does not love the pious because it is pious; rather, that which he alleges to be pious (the act of prosecuting his father for murder) is so in his estimation primarily because he loves it.[31]

Euthyphro is a second-order poet in regard to the divine things: he manages to cloak himself in piety by innovatively cutting out (*kainotomein*, 3b6, 5a7-8, 16a2) and stitching together useful parts of the civic and poetic tradition. In claiming prophetic inspiration Euthyphro seems to ignore his own productive or poetic activity, as well as the fact that the cultural materials upon which he works—the conventions of religious ritual and myth—are themselves fabrications or poems of the city. Hence Euthyphro never manages to get beyond or behind *nomos* to more primordial beginnings. For all his antinomian bravado, he is not much of an original thinker. Socrates, on the other hand, innovates by reweaving the fabric of *nomos* in such a way as to facilitate a deeper and more coherent understanding of the sacred. A nice image of this activity is provided by his reference at 6b-c to the massive robe, embroidered with poetic images of the gods and their adventures, that adorned the statue of Athena on the Acropolis during the Great Panathenaia. Socrates' cross-examination of Euthyphro will effectively unweave at least part of the poetic web that shrouds him, his fellow Athenians, and the gods of the city.[32] This process, as I have already suggested, is part and parcel of Socrates' therapeutic treatment of Euthyphro's unbridled spiritedness. But unlike Aristophanes' protagonist, who delights in exposing our animal nakedness (*Clouds* 497-498, 856-858), Plato's Socrates simultaneously fabricates or hypothesizes a different, "purified" image of the Olympians that harmonizes with his sense of what is required to become a human being. The *Euthyphro* thus repeats a pattern that is visible in other Platonic dialogues: Socrates' therapeutic treatment of aggression and injustice on the level of the human soul is intimately connected with his philosophical catharsis of the traditional myths about the gods.[33] Socrates' new gods, moreover, are prior to the city's gods not in antiquity—the criterion of civic authority—but philosophically, or in the domain of teaching and learning. Socratic circle thinking thereby succeeds in leading us back to genuinely fruitful beginnings, beginnings that best enable the soul to exercise its own "archaic" or originary powers.

In the *Republic*, Socrates transforms the old poems in such a way as to assimilate the god or gods to the Ideas. (His ambiguity about the number of deities perhaps anticipates the possibility of disagreement and strife that is introduced by multiplicity.) His god never departs from his own form (*idea*) and remains forever simply in his own shape, lacks nothing in beauty or virtue and so is without *erôs* (cf. *Symposium*, 202c-204b), is a cause of all good things and nothing bad, and cannot be bribed (380c-d,

381c, 390e). This picture is compatible with the one Socrates sketches in *Alcibiades II*, the traditional subtitle of which is "On Prayer." In that dialogue, Socrates teaches Alcibiades that it is irreverent to offer the gods lavish sacrifices and gifts or to pray for unjust and foolish things, since these actions imply that the gods are susceptible to bribery and that they do not esteem justice and piety (149c-e). On the contrary, the gods resemble philosophers: "for it is probable that both justice and *phronêsis* are especially esteemed by gods and men possessing intellect [*nous*]" (150a6-b1). Socrates' characterizations of the gods in the *Republic* and in *Alcibiades II*, in turn, are an essential part of his treatment of the tyrannical aspirations of Glaucon and Alcibiades.[34]

A similar kind of purifying poetizing takes place in the *Euthyphro*. After Euthyphro adverts to Hesiod's tales about Zeus and Cronos as proof that his own behavior is pious, Socrates wonders whether he himself has become a target of Meletus for the simple reason that "whenever someone says such things about the gods, I receive them somehow with ill favor" (6a6-8). Socrates is bothered by Euthyphro's use of the gods' quarrelsome behavior as a paradigm for his own. It is worth noting in this connection that while Socrates does ask Euthyphro to teach him the *idea* or *eidos* of the pious so that he may employ it as a "pattern" (*paradeigma*: 6e4-5), no such pattern could be read off directly from the gods' deeds. The reason is that piety is not a virtue of gods, but of human beings with respect to the gods; Zeus's treatment of Cronos could conceivably be just, but it cannot be pious. Indeed, getting Euthyphro to agree that there are *ideai* of piety and impiety (5c-d) is the first step Socrates takes toward rendering the mythical lives of the Olympians irrelevant to our own conduct.

At the same time, Socrates "cleans up" the traditional conception of the relationship between human beings and gods, the general outlines of which are clearly voiced by Euthyphro. Euthyphro's first definition of the pious as what is *prosphiles* or "dear" to the gods (6e10) places at the terminus of any inquiry into piety the brute fact that the gods happen to love certain things and—more to the point—*not* to love others. The human importance of divine antipathy is underscored by Socrates when he restates Euthyphro's *mê prosphiles*, "not dear to the gods," more strongly as *to theomisês kai ho theomisês*, "the god-hated thing and the god-hated man" (7a7-8). Socrates' subsequent demonstration that according to Euthyphro the gods' affections and hatreds make the same thing both pious and impious brings out the Protagorean implications of this approach: what is pious for any god is what seems to him to be pious, just because it seems so. ("Or do you believe," Socrates at one point asks Theaetetus, "that the Protagorean measure is said less pertinently with respect to gods than with respect to human beings?" [*Theaetetus* 162c5-

6].) What is more, this relativism is consistent with the operative under-standing of divine power that is embodied or encoded in the traditions of ritual and myth, and that is succinctly expressed by the poetic verse that Socrates later takes issue with: "where there is fear, there is also rever-ence" (12b1). Fear, a passion that encourages unreflective, unquestioning obedience to those with ample power to harm, is the real root of conven-tional piety. As a practical matter, it is irrelevant why Zeus wants this or that, since the fact of his desire is sufficient to dictate the behavior of anyone who knows what is good for him. Like Mafia kingpins, the gods are in the habit of getting what they want. The basic implication of Euthyphro's first definition of piety is still clearer in his last one, in terms of which being pious is knowing how to gratify the gods: for if we fail to please them with prayers and sacrifices they will "overturn and destroy everything" (14b6-7). We Greeks, Euthyphro suggests, love the gods less than we fear them, and it is fear of becoming an object of their hatred that compels us to show reverence for them. In effect, the gods run a protection racket; Father Zeus is truly a Godfather, and prophets like Euthyphro, who tell us what we owe, are his bagmen.

Fear of the gods' wrath is the flip side of Euthyphro's anger at his fa-ther. Neither passion opens one up to the experience of the sacred, for both nourish a narrow self-obsession that turns one inward and away from a reflective encounter with that which is above and beyond oneself. Socrates therefore attempts to suppress Euthyphro's essentially anti-philosophical fear by portraying the gods as beings that neither behave tyrannically toward human beings nor are hostile toward each other. He begins by observing that enmity among human beings springs from an inability to agree upon matters of the just and the unjust, the noble and the shameful, and the good and the bad. Euthyphro then agrees to the ad-ditional claim that the gods would not quarrel unless they differed about these same matters. But Socrates never concedes that the gods do in fact quarrel, or even that they differ with one another: he consistently speaks only about what would be the case *if* the gods disagree or quarrel (7d, 8b, 8d-e). In addition, Socrates gets his interlocutor to agree early on that the gods love whatever they believe to be noble and good and just (7e). The significance of this concession is apparent in the light of Socrates' later question whether the pious is pious because it is loved by the gods. The gods' loves and hates, unlike those of Euthyphro, do not determine what they regard as noble, good, and just; rather, the passions of the gods are ordered in accordance with what reason discloses to be worthy of love. Socrates also emphasizes the gods' philanthropy rather than their puni-tiveness: he tells Euthyphro that "there is for us no good thing that they [the gods] do not give" (15a1-2). Finally, Socrates explicitly rejects the relativism in which Euthyphro's conventional approach to piety effectively terminates. When Euthyphro defines piety as what all the gods love, Socrates asks whether they should reflect on the answer—"or are we to let it go, and in this way welcome both our own claims and those of others, agreeing that something is so if only someone should assert that it is so?" (9e5-7). This question underscores Socrates' critical approach to the traditional distinction between human and divine utterances: while Euthyphro does indeed suggest that whatever the gods say goes, Socrates' characterization of the gods as generous and reasonable beings begins to open up the possibility of questioning even what *they* might say.

Socrates' gods are models for human beings in ways that the poets' Olympians could never be. If one supposes that the gods are wise, it would follow from Socrates' description of them that they do not quarrel. Alternatively, even if Socrates' gods disagree, they nonetheless surely do not fight. For they would differ only on the level of cognition, not *erôs*, and their common love of the noble and the good would inspire them to argue, discuss, and debate, that is, jointly to consider where their beliefs might be at fault. If Socrates' gods are not actually wise—if, that is, there can indeed be gods who are less than wise (cf. *Symposium* 204a)—they are at any rate philosophers. As such, they would not be able directly to teach us what is noble, good, just, or pious, but they could show us by example how to learn about these things.

Socrates' theological exaltation of understanding and inquiry (cf. *Philebus* 28c) is of a piece with his overall rhetorical strategy. From the beginning of the dialogue, he consistently emphasizes teaching and learning in a way that is designed to draw Euthyphro into a philosophical discussion. He initially flatters Euthyphro by pretending to need him as a teacher and thereby offering him an opportunity to win the recognition that he craves. By cleverly contrasting his own high public visibility with Euthyphro's virtual invisibility (3c-d, 5c), Socrates makes Euthyphro all the more eager to play a leading role in his defense against Meletus's indictment. Later, Socrates observes that his interlocutor's claims must be judged with respect to the matter of learning: immediately after Euthyphro attempts to correct his first definition of piety by agreeing that whatever all the gods hate is impious and whatever they all love is pious, Socrates asks him to "consider whether in setting this down as a hypothesis (*hupothemenos*) you will thereby easily teach me what you promised" (9d7-8). He in effect asks Euthyphro to regard his contributions to the discussion as potential springboards toward increased understanding, and it is important to observe that his ability to elicit from Euthyphro a willingness to do so is no less crucial to the progress of the dialogue than was his ability to get Theaetetus past the notion that knowledge is perception. In this respect, the parallel between the two dialogues is striking. The conversation would have ground to a halt had Euthyphro not tried to defend the content of his prophecies, but simply insisted that he possesses prophetic insight—a stance that would have been entirely consistent with the conventional understanding of the relationship between the gods and prophets. Prophecy in its traditional role makes claims that can neither be defended nor decisively refuted in argument, and that for two reasons. First, the simple fact that the gods want something from us is, as we have seen, a sufficient reason for obliging them; nor could other, better reasons be adduced if, as the poets teach, the pious is pious because it is god-loved and the impious is impious because it is god-hated. Second, the prophet enjoys a special, direct revelation of the mind or will of the gods. About any particular prophecy there can be no argument: since no direct insight into what the gods want has been vouchsafed to those who are not prophets, the latter can only accept or reject the pronouncements of their inspired peers. As for the conflict between the gods that Socrates points out, it would make sense simply to follow Zeus, since he is most powerful. A prophet's statement that "Zeus wants this" would thus seem to be final and unassailable.

As conventionally understood, "prophecy is knowledge" is philosophically no more fruitful a claim than "knowledge is perception." But Euthyphro breaches the horizon of *nomos* when at the critical moment of the dialogue he agrees that the pious is loved by the gods because it is pious, rather than pious because it is loved (10d). Only by choosing this alternative does he make possible further inquiry into the nature of piety. Nor is this possibility purchased at the expense of the gods. While it might appear that the choice Socrates poses renders the gods irrelevant because it leads us away from a consideration of their loves and hates and toward the pious in itself, this impression is misleading: we cannot inquire into what it is to be pious without also considering the nature of the gods in *relation* to whom we are pious or impious. Socrates therefore keeps the latter issue in the forefront of our attention.

The argument Socrates goes through at 10a-11b is hardly less dizzying for Plato's readers than for Euthyphro. One detects in the distinction Socrates draws between being carried, being led, being seen, and being loved and carrying, leading, seeing, and loving an indirect reference to the enduring problem of the relationship between activity and passivity in human life. Beyond this, the main conclusions of the argument are as follows. Being loved by the gods is not the *aitia*, the cause or responsible factor, that explains why something is pious. It is rather something that happens to the pious, a *pathos*, and so does not speak to the *ousia* or intrinsic being of piety (11a-b). The virtue of piety, we may surmise, pertains to the soul's own nature and activity—to what the soul is and does in its own right rather than what it passively undergoes or suffers—and so is more like loving than being loved. A further implication of the distinction that Socrates draws between that which is loved by the gods and that which is pious is that one could not safely read off the pious and the impious from the loves and hates even of Socrates' purified gods (let alone the gods of the poets), for the field of things loved or hated by the gods may include much that is neither pious nor impious. Once again, Socrates frustrates Euthyphro's desire to locate the nature of the pious among the things given to passive cognition rather than those discoverable only through the soul's own exertion (cf. 12a).

After spinning Euthyphro in argument in much the same manner that he spun Theaetetus, Socrates helps his interlocutor to begin "once more from the beginning" by introducing the question of the relationship between the pious and the just (11b-e; cf. *Theaetetus* 162c-d). The new beginning Socrates introduces is not the old one of Meletus and Euthyphro: whereas the latter began from the *archaioi theoi*, the ancient gods, Socrates begins from a question that is designed to bring to sight a more fruitful *archê*. His question is also a timely one, given that he is accused of injustice in large part because he is allegedly impious, while Euthyphro, on the other hand, acts unjustly in doing what, from one angle at least, looks pious. With Socrates' help, Euthyphro generates a third and more auspicious definition of piety: "that part of the just is pious [*eusebes* and *hosion*] which concerns the care [*therapeia*] of the gods, while that which concerns the care of human beings is the remaining part of the just" (12e5-8). This remarkable statement accomplishes two things. First, it reminds us that the discussion of piety, like that of knowledge in the *Theaetetus*, is to be approached within the larger context of the problem of the unnamed care of human beings. Second, it helps us to recognize that Socrates has in the course of the present discussion been caring for, or "tending to," the gods in a way that is part and parcel of his care for Euthyphro.

Socrates goes on to compare our care for the gods with the care of horses, dogs, and cattle that is exercised by skilled horsemen, hunters, and herdsmen (13a-c). Euthyphro rejects these analogies on the ground that such care benefits the animals involved, while we human beings cannot conceivably make the gods better by our pious care (13c). But Socrates *does* in effect "work up" better gods (*apergazesthai*: 13c9) by subtly unraveling and reweaving portions of the web of *nomos* wherein their images appear. Euthyphro also fails to notice two other things about Socrates' analogies. In the first place, the care of horses, dogs, and cattle benefits horsemen, hunters, and herdsmen as well, insofar as it helps them to complete the activities they undertake with the help of these animals. Furthermore, these activities contribute to the care of human beings. So, too, Socrates' care for the gods, or for their representation in myth, may be an integral part of his activity as a therapeutic caretaker of young men. As if to extend this thought, Socrates suggests that the odd stands to number as reverent awe (*aidôs*) stands to dread (*deos*) and the pious stands to the just (12c-d). Now while "being loved" did not get at the *ousia* or being of the pious, the odd and the even *do* pertain to the *ousia* of number.[35] But whereas the quality of oddness belongs only to discrete units, or to the countable as such, evenness is a property of continuous magnitudes as well as numbers. Every continuous magnitude can be evenly divided into two parts ad infinitum; hence Socrates' statement that odd is "scalene" and the even is "isosceles" (12d9-10). The odd, then, is prior to the even because it "imposes a limit on unlimited divisibility in the form of an indivisible unit."[36] Might not reverent awe, in turn, be prior to the remaining part of dread, and the pious prior to the remaining part of the just—namely, the care of human beings—as that which gives a kind of unity or integrity to an otherwise indefinite continuum?

Socrates pursues the latter suggestion in connection with the all-important question of the nature of the gods' *ergon* or proper work (cf. *Republic*, 352d ff.). When Euthyphro backs off from the notion that we care for the gods as horsemen care for horses, he suggests instead that we serve the gods as slaves do their masters (13d). This immediately raises the matter of what it is that the gods hope to accomplish with our assistance. Socrates underscores the significance of this question with an oath: "By Zeus, what ever is the altogether noble work or deed [*ergon*] that the gods accomplish [*apergazontai*] using us as servants?" (13e10-11). According to the present formulation, to do justice to the gods and to act piously toward them is to assist them in doing their proper work. But we cannot assist them, we cannot give them their due, unless we know what their proper work *is*. What is more, this approach to piety understands being human in terms of the role that we play, the *ergon* that we enact, in serving the gods. Hence the problem of the nature of our service to the gods bears directly upon the Socratic question of how properly to care for human beings. As if to underscore this point, the examples Socrates adduces in this context—doctoring, shipbuilding, housebuilding, leading an army, and farming—once again all have to do with the *therapeia* of human beings. The suggested connection between care and justice, in turn, has a distinctly Socratic feel: care involves doing justice to souls by enabling them to perform their properly human activity.[37]

If the preceding reflections are on the mark, one cannot acquire the virtues of either piety or justice without inquiring into the place of man in a cosmos that is structured by purposive striving. Only such inquiry can disclose the ends or aims of such striving, together with the activities in which these ends can be realized. Piety implies philosophy—if indeed it is not equivalent to philosophy, as Socrates suggests when he claims in the *Apology* that he serves the god in trying to persuade human beings to care for the well-being of their souls (29d-30b).[38] This is as close to an adequate understanding of piety as we get in the *Euthyphro*, as Socrates makes clear when he asserts that if Euthyphro had answered his question about the work of the gods "I would already have learned piety sufficiently from you" (14c2-3). This conclusion, in turn, bears directly upon the problem of beginnings with which the dialogue itself began. The poet says Zeus "planted all things" (12a9), but he is wrong, for human beings cannot, *qua* human, be plants. Euthyphro's suggestion about piety is in one respect wishful thinking: while slaves and servants need only take orders from their masters, human beings must discover their "orders" for themselves. This requires a kind of care (*meletê*) that neither Euthyphro nor Meletus is willing to exercise. As Socrates says in the *Theaetetus*, the soul's settled disposition (*hexis*) "grows better and is saved" only by "learning and effort" (*mathêseôs kai meletês*: 153b9-11).[39] The proximate beginning of such studious effort is the soul's awareness of the questionable character of its experience. Socrates is an expert at furnishing others with this sort of starting point.[40] The ends or aims of inquiry, in turn, are causes and beginnings of our purposive striving in the way that a lovable object is the cause and beginning, the *aitia* and *archê*, of love. Socrates' purified gods are meant to encourage philosophic inquiry as a labor of love. But the ultimate *archê* of inquiry, and so of the care and nurture of the human soul, is the individual himself.

The latter point is dramatically signaled by Euthyphro's untimely departure. There is nothing that Socrates can do to make Euthyphro heed his renewed request to begin "once more from the beginning" (15c11). While Euthyphro has had enough by the second time Socrates asks him to start *palin ex archês*, Theaetetus thrice responds gamely to the exact same challenge (*Theaetetus* 151d, 187a-b, 200d). The difference between Euthyphro, who walks away after a small dose of Socratic perplexity, and Theaetetus, who returns in the *Sophist* after a much larger one, lies in the intrinsic dispositions of their souls.

Turning to the *Cratylus*:
The Problem of Prophecy

In the *Euthyphro*, Socrates in effect replaces the poeticoreligious myths of Homer and Hesiod with his own myth, in which he gives the gods natures that make them friendlier to philosophy than the traditional deities must be supposed to be. Socrates thus counters Euthyphro's prophecy with a speech that is grounded in his prophetic recollection of what is best for human souls and what is appropriate to the care of his interlocutor's soul. Euthyphro's explicit claim to prophetic insight, however, seems ludicrous. Is Socrates' implicit claim to philosophical prophecy any less so? What philosophical warrants could one provide for the Socratic activity of prophetic recollection?

The latter questions are explored in the *Cratylus*, in which the problem of prophecy is directly connected with that of the circularity of discourse. The *Cratylus* is a patently ironic and comic piece of writing. In particular, Socrates' ridiculous imitation of Euthyphro's "inspired" way of speaking seems at first to be nothing more than a humorous *reductio* of claims to prophetic insight. Yet the ensuing dialogue unsettles this initial perception by focusing on the logical circularity, not only of Socrates' circle thinking, but of all philosophical speech, in such a way as to make manifest the seriousness of the issue of prophecy for all who care about human souls and their growth through learning. For in the absence of prophecy—in the absence of that which Socrates seems, at first blush, only to parody—Socratic discourse becomes just another species of sophistical self-expression. The specter of Protagoras haunts the *Cratylus* as well.

The *Cratylus* also connects the issue of prophecy with that of the proper place of Socrates, and, more generally, of the philosophic soul. In the *Theaetetus* and *Euthyphro*, Socrates has twice shown up in the middle ground between extremes. If anything, however, Socrates' impersonation of Euthyphro in the *Cratylus* makes prophecy seem more extreme than even Euthyphro himself did. As ever, Socrates is hard to place because of his irony. Irony is typically the mark of an immoderate and outlandish character, a slick and cunning trickster who resists being pinned down.[41] But one of the many surprises of the *Cratylus* is that Socrates' ironic doubleness helps us ultimately to see where he stands, so to speak, in the cosmos. As we shall see, Socrates' irony turns out to be an index of the well-placed intermediacy of his prophetic soul.

Chapter 5

Prophetic Play: The *Cratylus*

The gods too are lovers of play.

Plato, *Cratylus*

Diogenes Laertius gives us the following intriguing account of Plato's travels after the death of Socrates:

> When Socrates was gone, he [Plato] attached himself to Cratylus the Heraclitean, and to Hermogenes who professed the philosophy of Parmenides. Then, when he was twenty-eight years old, according to what Hermodorus says, he withdrew to Euclides in Megara along with other Socratics. After that he went away to Cyrene, to Theodorus the mathematician.[1]

If Diogenes is to be believed, Plato wandered restlessly after the death of Socrates in search of the kind of intellectual companionship for which he did not have to leave Athens while his mentor was alive. Interestingly, in the *Theaetetus* and the *Cratylus* Socrates is placed in the company of the four individuals Diogenes mentions as potential teachers of Plato. Especially when considered in the light of the passage quoted above, this dramatic juxtaposition raises the question of what these four stand to learn from Socrates, and vice-versa. Indeed, the theme of teaching and learning is visible from the very beginning of the *Cratylus*, which consists in a reflexive attempt to learn through dialogue about how we learn *dia logôn*—"through speeches."[2]

The *Cratylus* looks back toward the *Theaetetus* and *Euthyphro* as well as ahead toward the *Sophist* and *Statesman* in the course of dramatizing the issue of the ineliminable circularity and consequent uncertainty of philosophical discourse.[3] In the *Euthyphro*, Socrates came to light as a circle thinker whose reflections always lead us back toward the concrete beginnings of inquiry in the everyday contexts of human life and in the soul of the inquirer. The problem of circularity that is raised in the *Cratylus* ultimately brings us back to these same beginnings, but initially presents itself as a logical difficulty. This problem, which is formally evident in the *Cratylus* in Socrates' use of words to inquire into the question of whether words are well-founded, surfaces briefly in the *Theaetetus* when Socrates at one point observes that he and his young companion have for a long time been "conversing impurely" (*mê katharôs dialegesthai*) about the problem of knowledge, since "we've said thousands of times 'we recognize' and 'we don't recognize,' and 'we know' and 'we don't know,' as though we somehow understand one another while still being ignorant of knowledge" (196e1-5). Yet Socrates goes on to say that, although he and Theaetetus are "no good" (*phauloi*), he will nonetheless continue to converse in the same manner: "For I am who I am" (197a1-4).

The impurity of Socrates' conversational practice is perhaps not surprising in view of the midwife image: childbirth, after all, is a bloody and messy business that implicates the midwife as well as the mother in pollution (*miasma*).[4] In the *Cratylus*, however, Socrates suggests that the circularity or impurity of discourse has to do not only with his idiosyncratic way of philosophizing but, more generally, with the paradoxical nature of *logos* itself as it stretches between souls and beings. As Socrates develops this issue, the adequacy of language as a medium of teaching and learning comes to depend entirely upon the possibility of philosophical prophecy or prophetic recollection. This theme, in turn, is connected with the larger issue of Socrates' stance toward *nomos*, since the *Cratylus* stresses the customary and conventional character of actual languages like Greek while nonetheless leaving open the possibility that linguistic custom may in important respects reflect nature (*phusis*). The *Cratylus* is thus fundamentally about philosophical hermeneutics, a problem that Socrates represents as one of communication between human and divine beings.

Herein lies the connection with Euthyphro of which Socrates makes so much in his conversation with Hermogenes and Cratylus. Throughout the central portion of the *Cratylus* (393a-421c) Socrates is engaged in providing playful etymologies for a great variety of words, including the names of gods, human beings, and virtues and vices. Socrates pretends here to speak with prophetic insight, and he attributes his inspiration to Euthyphro, whom he mentions no less than six times over the course of the dialogue (396d, 399a, 400a, 407d, 409d, 428c). The passage in which

Euthyphro's name first comes up is of particular interest to us, because it links the theme of inspiration with that of the impurity of discourse in a way that indirectly recalls the *Theaetetus* and anticipates the imminent arrival of the Stranger. After Socrates remarks on his new-found wisdom, Hermogenes tells him that "you seem to me simply to be uttering oracles, just like those who are suddenly inspired by a god [*hoi enthousiôntes*]." Socrates replies as follows:

> Yes, Hermogenes, and I insist that it [his inspiration] has come upon me from Euthyphro the Prospaltian. For early this morning I was with him for a long time and I lent him my ears. So he, being inspired by a god [*enthousiôn*], probably not only filled my ears with his daimonic wisdom [*daimonias sophias*] but took possession of my soul as well. It seems then that we ought to act in this way: today we should make use of it [his inspired wisdom] and finish the investigation of names, but tomorrow, if you agree, we will avert ill by making an offering of it, and we will get ourselves purified [*katharoumetha*] when we have found someone who is clever at purifying [*kathairein*] such things, either one of the priests or one of the sophists. (396d4-397a1)

Socrates' prediction that his impure inquiry will be purified on the following day by a priest or a sophist seems to presage the arrival of the Eleatic Stranger, whose identity is appropriately uncertain, but who, Socrates suspects, has come "to refute us who are poor [*phaulous*] in speeches" (*Sophist* 216b4-5). In the event, the Stranger does indeed subject Socrates' manner of discourse to a catharsis of the soul (*katharseôn psuchês*: 227c2-3) or of thought (*peri tên dianoian katharmon*: 227c4) that is intended to weed out his peculiar brand of "noble" sophistry from the field of genuine philosophizing (cf. 231b). Socrates' reference to an earlier discussion with Euthyphro furthermore indicates that the *Cratylus* takes place on the same day as the *Theaetetus* and the *Euthyphro*. One might playfully suggest that the Stranger's purification of Socrates is a philosophical analogue of the ritual purification midwives were required to undergo after assisting in childbirth; if so, this impending catharsis has already been necessitated by Socrates' care for the soul of Theaetetus. More seriously, we have seen that the (re)generation of the human soul in and through Socratic dialogue threatens to incur pollution insofar as it involves making innovations in the religious tradition. Perhaps the drama of the *Cratylus*, like that of the *Euthyphro*, incorporates this specific sort of religious impurity as well as the philosophical impurity of circular argumentation.

We shall return to the latter suggestion by way of a slight detour through a more pressing issue, namely, the dramatic placement of the

Cratylus. While some scholars situate the *Cratylus* immediately after the *Euthyphro*, others counter that Socrates' claim to have talked with Euthyphro *heôthen*, "early in the morning" or "from daybreak" (395d5), leaves no room for his conversation with Theaetetus.[5] Yet it is a distinct possibility that the "inspired" Socrates—who is clearly being ironic about Euthyphro's effect upon him—merely *pretends* in the passage quoted above to have forgotten his conversation with Theaetetus, precisely because it would be impossible to be possessed by Euthyphro's prophetic enthusiasm while in any meaningful sense remembering this conversation. Socrates says that Euthyphro's voice, the voice of a man who never questions his own prophetic access to the truth about the gods, "fills his ears." In another ironic passage elsewhere in the Platonic corpus, Socrates remarks that the speech and sound of orators at public funerals "so rings in my ears, that it is scarcely on the fourth or fifth day that I recollect myself and perceive where on earth I am" (*Menexenus* 235c2-3). The latter passage also brings to mind the very beginning of the *Apology*, in which Socrates states that his accusers spoke with such persuasiveness that he almost forgot himself (17a). So, too, Socrates could be filled up like an empty jar with Euthyphro's "wisdom" only if the lessons that were so pointedly brought home in his conversation with Theaetetus, including the deeply problematic character of knowledge and the active effort or labor that is required to bring it forth, had somehow slipped his mind. To fail to recollect these insights—especially for a man who later identifies himself as one "worth nothing with respect to wisdom" (*Apology* 23b3-4)—would indeed be to forget the nature of one's own soul. If this interpretation is correct, Socrates must have also "forgotten" what he failed to learn at the Portico of the King Archon: while in the *Euthyphro* his interlocutor proves utterly unable to teach him what he should say in response to Meletus, in the *Cratylus* Socrates acts as if Euthyphro had succeeded in becoming the father of his *logos*.[6]

One needs to proceed cautiously at this point. Precisely because the *logos* that Socrates attributes to the influence of Euthyphro is a distinctly ironic one, Socrates' apparent forgetfulness about the soul may be the surface of a still deeper kind of recollection. It is especially noteworthy that the *Cratylus* begins by raising the issue of personal identity. Hermogenes tells Socrates that, according to Cratylus, "Hermogenes" is not his name. But, Hermogenes complains, Cratylus "ironizes" (*eirôneuetai*) because he will not explain this claim (384a1). Hence he wonders whether Socrates can "interpret the oracle of Cratylus" or, better yet, can speak to the matter of the correctness of names (384a5-7). Hermogenes is (not unreasonably) disconcerted by Cratylus's behavior, for to be deprived of one's name is in some sense to lose one's self. Posed as it is within in the philosophically charged atmosphere of an encounter with Socrates, the question "Who is Hermogenes?" is in no way innocent; like the question about the orphaned son of Euphronius that Socrates raised earlier in the day ("I don't know the name of the lad," he tells Theodorus [*Theaetetus* 144c8]), it asks not only after a name but also after the intrinsic being, the *ousia*, of the one who is named. In a deep sense, Hermogenes hopes to recover his identity through conversation with Socrates.

The latter observations illuminate the significance of Hermogenes' mention of oracles. In the *Cratylus*, Socrates is invited to explore the thought hidden in Cratylus's soul so as to uncover, and perhaps recover, the identity of Hermogenes. As we suggested in commenting on Euclides' amazement at Socrates' prophetic insight into Theaetetus's nature, to come to know a soul—be it one's own or another's—is in significant ways like interpreting an oracle. An oracle is a perceptible sign (an audible speech) of an imperceptible presence (the god who speaks through the oracle) about that which is yet to come. So, too, the soul that is to be known is doubly removed from that which is directly present to perception. As a soul, it is always coming-to-be and so is in some sense identity-dependent upon what it is not yet; moreover, insofar as the soul is present it is so only to the extent that its nature can be "recollected" through the speeches and deeds of the body.[7] The *Cratylus*, like the *Theaetetus*, thus begins by linking Socratic dialogue with the prophetic recollection of the soul.

Hermogenes' request casts Socrates in the role of a dialogical stand-in for Cratylus, who remains silent for most of the ensuing conversation. Socrates rises quickly to the occasion, suggesting immediately that the complete answer to Hermogenes' question could be purchased from the sophist Prodicus for fifty drachmas, and later that Protagoras's book *Truth* and the Homeric epics would be equally good sources of information about the correctness of names (384b-c, 391b-c). And rather than interpreting Cratylus's oracular utterances, Socrates himself commences "to sing oracles" (*chrêsmôidein*: 396d3, 428c6-7). Plato thus suggests that Socrates' ironic speech is in its own way no less enigmatic, and so no less in need of interpretation, than Cratylus's silence.

What accounts for Socrates' irony in this dialogue? On one level, his irony calls attention to the stark limitations of the ways of thinking exemplified by his interlocutors. As we shall soon see, Socrates' imitation of Euthyphro indirectly underscores the self-forgetfulness of both Cratylus and Hermogenes, each of whom at least initially advocates a way of thinking about names that abstracts from the actual contexts of speech and effectively blinds one to the distinctive being of the soul. Beyond this, it must be observed that Socrates' irony is genuine irony, which is to say that it is neither simply playful nor simply serious, but both simultaneously.

We may bring these introductory reflections to a close by observing that the place of the *Cratylus* in the philosophic trial of Socrates is now reasonably clear. In the *Cratylus*, Socrates prepares for the Stranger's arrival by attempting to disarm the distinction between pure and impure discourse that the Stranger will turn against him in the *Sophist*. While this literal act of prophecy underscores the necessary impurity of *logos* as such—and thus allows us to predict that the Stranger, too, will find himself caught in the web of speech—it also calls our attention to Socrates' dramatic display of the prophetic recollection that in his view fundamentally distinguishes philosophical speech from sophistry. Socrates claims to speak prophetically, but seemingly undercuts this claim by means of his irony. Yet the action of the *Cratylus* makes it clear that if discourse is in no way prophetic—if, in general, there can be no foreknowledge of beings—then philosophical learning is impossible, and there is no alternative to the chatter of Protagoras. Hence Socrates' extravagant imitation of Euthyphro is intended not simply to deflate the pretensions of self-styled authorities on the nature of *logos*, but to help us explore the genuinely daimonic power that graces human speech, and without which it would be indistinguishable from silence.

Let us now turn to the particulars of Socrates' anticipatory self-defense against the charge of philosophical impurity. The first, necessarily fairly detailed section of this chapter reads the *Cratylus* with attention to the ineluctable problem of the impurity of speech. The next two sections address the dialogue's dramatic illumination of the prophetic character of Socratic philosophizing.

The Impurity of Speech

In the *Cratylus* Socrates quickly forces us to confront the ineliminable circularity of philosophical discourse. An examination of the first part of the dialogue, in which Socrates refutes Hermogenes' opinion that no name belongs to anything by nature, but only by convention, agreement, custom, and habit (*sunthêkê, homologia, ethos, nomos*: 384c-d), will begin to show how he does this.

"Name" (*onoma*) is broadly used in the *Cratylus* to designate not only proper names but also nouns, adjectives, and verbs, or names of kinds of things and actions. The *Cratylus* begins with a disagreement about the correctness of applying the proper name "Hermogenes" to Socrates' interlocutor, but the inquiry soon broadens to include the problem of the correctness of the other classes of words just mentioned. These issues are connected, since Socrates later asserts that the question whether the true name of Callias's brother is "Hermogenes" has to do with whether "something of the race [*genesis*] of Hermes befits him" (429c1-2), or, in other words, whether he is a certain *kind* of person. In much of the *Cratylus*, as has often been noted, names are treated as if they had descriptive force; hence Socrates can speak of "the phrases" (*ta rhêmata*) through which a name is formed (421e1).[8] Viewed in this way, proper names would be neither correct nor incorrect in a world in which (a) things are entirely indeterminate, as in accordance with the teaching of Euthydemus (386d), (b) individual things are radically in flux and so possess no stable natures at all, or (c) the natures of individual things are entirely unique, so that one cannot meaningfully speak of stable kinds of entities. Strangely, Cratylus's assertion that "there is a natural correctness of names that belongs by nature to each of the beings" (383a4-5) seems more harmonious with the teaching of Parmenides than with his professed Heracliteanism (cf. 440d-e), while Hermogenes' radical denial of this thesis, on the other hand, is more in tune with Heraclitus's doctrine of flux than with his alleged Parmenideanism.[9]

It is important to observe that in the *Cratylus* Socrates finds himself in the middle of a dispute between two ways of thinking about names, each of which in its own way threatens the practice of philosophical dialogue. For his part, Hermogenes sets forth at least two distinct theses about names. The weaker one is that the correctness of names rests on convention and agreement as to what the names of things are. The stronger is that any individual can by himself change the names of things at will, "just as we change the names of our slaves" (384d5). Thus each of us is a master of names, and a thing's name is whatever I may choose to call it, for just so long as I choose to call it by that name.[10] The latter view is thoroughly monological. Just as the master turns a deaf ear to his slaves when he changes their names in accordance with his whims, there is no question here of fashioning names that answer to the natures of things. It has also been well observed that if human beings actually changed names at will in the manner allowed by Hermogenes, dialogue would be impossible, since the communication of thoughts from one person to another requires that "the sounds that are used as names have a fairly stable relationship to the objects they are meant to denote."[11] Hermogenes' account of naming nonetheless makes an implicit reference to nature, since it seems to presuppose the initial visibility of things (e.g., slaves) as distinct items to be named. Indeed, the logical and ontological priority of visibility both to the act of naming and to speech about names is dramatically suggested by the occurrence of two forms of the demonstrative pronoun *hode* (which picks out something near at hand with a verbal force akin to the act of pointing) in the first four lines of the dialogue, wherein Hermogenes speaks of "this here Socrates" and "this Cratylus here" (383a1, a4).

We shall return in due course to the significance of the primordial visibility of things, but let us now consider the philosophical position of Cratylus. If Hermogenes advances a view of names that threatens to make dialogue impossible, Cratylus advocates a theory that makes it unnecessary. When he finally enters the discussion, he agrees to the proposition that correct names show the nature of the things named (428e). He then goes on to assert that there are no incorrect names; names are either correct or they are not names at all. He also maintains that a speech that others might say employs an incorrect name is not a meaningful speech at all. Thus Cratylus insists that if anyone in meeting him were to say "Greetings, Athenian stranger, Hermogenes, son of Smicrion," that man would be "making inarticulate noise, and putting himself in motion to no purpose, just as if he should go through the motion of striking some bronze pot" (430a4-5; cf. 383b). But if that were truly the case, the angry words "Die, Athenian stranger, Hermogenes, son of Smicrion!" would be equally devoid of meaning when addressed to Cratylus, and for anyone other than Hermogenes to extend his hand in response to the first utterance or to run for his life in response to the second would make no more sense than greeting, or fleeing from, a clattering cauldron. In sum, Cratylus appears wrongly to believe that in speeches names alone do all the semantic work. It seems to follow that any philosophical question of the form "What is x?" invites no further discussion, for "x" is either meaningless noise or, if it is a genuine name, it already reveals the nature of the thing named.[12]

As in the *Theaetetus* and the *Euthyphro*, the dramatic antagonisms of the *Cratylus* prepare us for a demonstration of the concreteness of Socratic philosophizing. Hermogenes and Cratylus both advance accounts of the correctness of names that abstract from the contexts within which names actually function. Not so with Socrates, who in his first speech in the dialogue admits his ignorance about the correctness of names but tells Hermogenes that "I am ready to engage in a common inquiry together with both you and Cratylus" (384c2-3). Neither Hermogenes nor Cratylus begins as Socrates suggests one ought to begin—that is, by considering speech primarily in the mode of dialogue, and with respect to its significance for the soul that speaks and the soul that is spoken to. Conversely, both seem to understand the correctness of names in terms of an absolute relationship between words and beings, and without regard for what it is that speech accomplishes as it helps to weave and unweave the rich tapestry of human life. Cratylus in particular confuses a part of speech for the whole of speech. It is only due to Plato's irony that Socrates seems repeatedly to make the same mistake. We shall see that the wholeness of speech, like Cratylus, is silently present throughout the dialogue—a dialogue named for a character who exemplifies the ease with which we forget about that which merely seems to be absent.

From 385a to 391b Socrates proceeds to argue that names do in fact possess a certain natural correctness, and so can be established well or badly. In the course of this argument Socrates solicits Hermogenes' agreement that there is a difference between wise insight (*phronêsis*) and folly (*aphrosunê*, the privation of *phronêsis*), so that Protagoras must have been wrong when he asserted that human being is the measure of all things—a position that has some obvious affinity with Hermogenes' view that each individual is the measure of the correctness of names (385e-386d).[13] Then too, Euthydemus was wrong in claiming that things are really indeterminate—so that, for example, all men are simultaneously characterized by virtue and vice (386d).[14] In mentioning Protagoras and Euthydemus Socrates merely makes explicit what we have already noted about Hermogenes' view: the activity of naming pays heed to beings that are already visible in their distinctness. Yet Socrates also gets Hermogenes to consent to a series of propositions that have as their unexpressed consequence a Protagorean result. Hermogenes agrees that: (1) A true speech says that which is as it is (*ta onta hôs estin*) and a false speech as it is not (*hôs ouk estin*); (2) The parts of a whole true speech (*holos logos*), including the small parts, are also true, and the parts of a false speech are false; (3) A name is the smallest part of a speech; so (4) A name can be true or false (385b-d). This passage, which to my mind is clearly ironic, is reminiscent of the discussion near the end of the *Theaetetus* of whether a whole is more than the sum of its parts (202d-206c). What Socrates does not point out to Hermogenes is that by the present reasoning one and the same name could be both true and false *simultaneously*, for it could appear at the same time in a true speech and a false speech. This reflection provokes wonder about what it would mean for a name to be true or false, as well as about the relevant wholes and parts in the domain of speech. If a speech in and by itself can be true or false but a name in and by itself cannot, a speech would seem to be a whole that is not identical to the sum of its parts. But perhaps a name is not the smallest part of speech, for Socrates will later suggest that letters are the ultimate elements out of which a whole speech is constructed (424e-425a). Nor is it yet clear what Socrates means by a whole speech. Is a proposition a whole speech? But propositions are themselves situated within larger wholes, with respect to which they disclose their meaning. Is a Socratic conversation a whole speech? The integrity or wholeness of even these kinds of speeches is fully intelligible only within the larger human contexts within which they unfold. The wholeness of *logos*, which Socrates indirectly invites us to consider by misleadingly treating names as if they were whole speeches, is peculiarly open-ended.[15]

Socrates begins to explore the problem of the contexts of speech in the following way. Protagoras was wrong: things (*ta pragmata*) possess their own stable essence (*ousia*). Socrates' choice of terms subtly anticipates his subsequent emphasis upon the use of names as tools to further the goals of teaching and learning. *Ta pragmata* and *ta onta* ("beings") are not exact synonyms, for *pragmata* are literally "things done"; human activity, in other words, furnishes the horizon within which the correctness of names with respect to beings is appropriately examined.[16] Socrates now quietly turns from names to the activity of naming, and therewith begins to situate names within the horizon of human activity. Deeds (*praxeis*) are a kind of beings (*eidos tôn ontôn*), speaking is a deed concerned with things (*praxis peri ta pragmata*), and naming is part of speaking, so naming can be done either correctly and according to nature or contrary to nature and mistakenly (386d-387c). This means that the proper measure of the correctness of speaking is complex, for if speaking is a being in its own right it has its own proper nature, while at the same time it must be in accord with the being(s) with respect to which it is exercised. In the case of the *logoi* Socrates employs in his work as a midwife, for example, speech must be appropriate to the nature of Socrates' interlocutor as well as to the beings that it bespeaks.

Socrates goes on implicitly to compare naming with cutting, burning, weaving, and boring, each of which requires the appropriate tool (387b, 387d-e). Here we begin to see how the problem of correctness is relevant to names in particular, for to name something is to cut, burn, or pierce into reality in such a way as to separate off a piece of it, or perhaps to weave together parts of reality that have already been distinguished in one way or another. At issue is whether what I distinguish or conjoin by naming is in itself a distinct or connected feature of reality. This question has to do not primarily with the application of a name in particular instances, but, more fundamentally, with whether the original act of naming correctly discerns a natural species. Thus I can ask whether this thing before me really is a goblin, but this begs the logically prior question of whether there is in fact something in the nature of reality that answers to the name "goblin."

At one point Socrates told Theaetetus that "the being [*ousia*] of speech is the intertwining [*sumplokê*] of names" (*Theaetetus* 202b4-5), and he now revives this image. When we weave, Hermogenes agrees, we separate the commingled threads of woof and warp. Hence a name, Socrates asserts, "is an instrument of teaching and of distinguishing being [*diakritikon tês ousias*], just as a shuttle is an instrument of separating a web" (388b13-c1). Socrates here ignores the synthetic dimension of speech, or the fact that the shuttle separates the threads of the warp only so as to interweave the woof through them. So, too, with an augur the carpenter bores into pieces of wood only as a means of preparing them to be joined together. Socrates' silence on this point is perhaps a dramatic indication that the present inquiry into names, like the *Theaetetus*, will emphasize the analysis of wholes into parts while leaving to the reader the problem of how to understand their wholeness.[17] The weaving analogy, which the Stranger will employ at much greater length in order to illuminate the work of statesmanship (*Statesman* 279b ff.), is perplexing in other respects as well. Teaching presumably reveals the nature of beings, but the product of the weaver—like the web fashioned by the statesman—is used as a protective cloak to shield us from nature's harshness. It should also be noted that if names are analogous to shuttles, they are not themselves part of the web they help to produce. One wonders whether the web fashioned by the teacher is something other than a web of speech.

The question Socrates now raises has to do with the original act of naming. Where, he asks, do we obtain the tools we call names? His answer is: from *nomos* (388d). The man skilled in teaching (*ho didaskalikos*) therefore uses the work of the lawgiver who establishes names (*tithetai ta onomata*), and in whose very name (*ho nomothetês*) we can hear the word "namegiver" (*onomathetês*). Hence everything depends on the skill (*technê*) of the lawgiver/namegiver, "who is indeed the rarest of craftsmen among human beings" (389a2-3). Just as the weaver makes various sorts of garments and so requires shuttles suited by nature for each kind of weaving, so the lawgiver must produce names suited by nature for each kind of teaching. And just as different smiths forge the same kind of tool out of different pieces of iron, the lawgiver, be he Greek or barbarian, acts skillfully so long as in "looking toward the very thing which is the name" he instantiates "the form of the name that befits each thing" in whatever sounds and syllables he may choose (389d6-7, 390a5-6). But the lawgiver does not act alone. The kithara player knows best whether a kithara is well-made, and the helmsman is the best judge of the work of a shipbuilder. By analogy, the user of names would best superintend and judge the work of the namegiver. This user is the one who knows how to ask and answer questions, namely, the dialectician (390c). So just as it is the work of a carpenter is to make a rudder under the supervision of a helmsman, the work (*ergon*) of the lawgiver is to make a name with a dialectician as his supervisor, if names are to be given well. Therefore, Socrates concludes, Cratylus spoke the truth when he said that names belong to things by nature, and that not everyone is a craftsman of names, "but only that one who looks away toward the name that belongs by nature to each thing, and who is able to establish its form (*eidos*) in letters and syllables" (390d9-e4). It is noteworthy that these natural names are, as John Sallis observes, "inherently unsounded" prior to their being put into sounds and syllables by the lawgiver; like Cratylus at this point in the dialogue, these natural names can be seen but not heard.[18] The dialectician, in turn, must for this reason mediate between seeing and speaking: it is in view of the nature of beings that he knows how to supervise the fashioning of names in a way that best serves the activity of asking and answering questions. The visibility of things once again appears to be prior to their articulation in speech.

The process of asking and answering questions perhaps bears some resemblance to the weaver's work of opening up and tamping down a web. Perhaps, too, a name is like a rudder in that it is properly used to steer dialectical inquiry. This notion seems to fit Socrates' regular practice of orienting dialogue by asking just what we mean, just what kind of *ousia*, *eidos*, or *idea* we are attempting to bespeak, when we call something or someone just, or pious, or courageous—or when we use the word "name." Be that as it may, Socrates' introduction of teaching and learning complicates matters. It looked initially as if the correctness of names had to do simply with their adequacy in revealing the nature of beings. Socrates' subsequent etymology of "name" (*onoma*), in which he finds the meaning "this is the being about which the inquiry happens to be" (421a8), reinforces this impression. However, Socrates has now finished introducing another touchstone of correctness, namely, the adequacy of names to the work of philosophical dialogue. In one respect, it seems clear that these distinct dimensions of correctness need not entail any conflict, since the ultimate goal of teaching surely involves the knowledge of beings. But the connection Socrates posits between dialectics and politics, between namegiving and lawgiving, reminds us once again that dialogue occurs not in an absolute or contextless relationship to beings but in complex human and political contexts—contexts shaped no less by the particulars of time and place and by the characters of the participants than by the goal of revealing the nature of beings.[19] Anyone not under the spell of Euthyphro will recall that Socrates understands the activity of philosophical questioning and answering as a way of caring for souls, much as midwifery cares for the body; it is furthermore evident that a certain vocabulary might from an abstract standpoint appear to furnish excellent tools for revealing the nature of beings, but might nonetheless be useless with respect to the concrete work of midwifing a particular soul. Standing somewhere in the middle ground between souls and other beings, names must be fitted to the natures and purposes of both.[20]

The preceding considerations would seem to militate against any attempt to explain the correctness of names (or speeches) solely by way of an analysis of their constituent elements, and without regard to their use. Yet Socrates employs this mode of explanation in his etymologies (393a–421c), and pushes it still further when he later inquires into the mimetic function of individual letters (426c ff.). The latter, analytical inquiry, which Socrates himself calls "hybristic" and "laughable" (426b6), is clearly a parody of technical philologizing.[21] This parody is occasioned by a question prompted by Socrates' etymological explanations. Etymologizing proceeds according to the principle that a correct name shows the nature of the thing named, and refers to earlier names in order to establish the correctness of later ones. But what can be said, Socrates wonders, about the way in which the first or earliest names show the natures of the things named (422d-e)? In turning toward the mimetic function of letters in order to answer this question, Socrates turns away from the contexts of speech in which names are embedded, and thereby ignores the plain implication of the shuttle analogy. A tool is what it is only within the appropriate context of use; its specific nature as a tool, its *ergon* or proper function, becomes unintelligible in radical separation from this context. (What would the ancient Athenians have made of a can opener?) So, too, Socrates has suggested, names acquire their power to show anything at all only insofar as they are at work within a larger context of *logos*, and they are fully at work as names only when employed as tools of learning through dialectical questioning and answering. When considered in the light of the beginning of the *Cratylus*, Socrates' later recourse to the analysis of names in terms of letters negatively and indirectly calls attention to the hermeneutical circle presented by *logos*, wherein part and whole become intelligible in terms of each other.[22]

The problem of circularity that Socrates self-consciously seeks to avoid is nonetheless intensified by the clear indications he gives of the discrepancy between his normative account of the correctness of names and actual practice. Socrates articulates a position somewhere in between Hermogenes' conventionalism and Cratylus's naturalism. While Socrates agrees that the names we use are given to us by *nomos*, he argues that nature (*phusis*) is the proper measure of the adequacy of linguistic custom. He also sketches a scenario in which linguistic custom would be in accordance with nature. But this scenario, with its mythical lawgiver and dialectician, is both paradoxical and fantastic. Etymology presupposes the inevitable transformation of language over time, which would be unproblematic so long as later names could be traced to earlier, well-given ones. Well-given names are those that have been established by a godlike dialectician who gives speech to human beings in much the same manner as certain legendary legislators are traditionally said to have given laws to the Greek cities.[23] There is, however, a crucial difference: even though it is impossible to specify the nature of the resemblance, the original act of namegiving seems to involve something like the kind of Socratic discourse that names themselves make possible for us. As described by Socrates, the act of linguistic founding presupposes communication between an original dialectician and a subordinate lawgiver, a relationship that in

certain respects parallels that of god and lawgiver in the political traditions of various Greek cities. Furthermore, what must be communicated,
what must be taught by the dialectician and learned by the lawgiver, is
the essential nature of the activity of teaching and learning through asking and answering questions with respect to which the correctness of
spoken names (as opposed to the unsounded, natural names that spoken
names articulate) is to be measured. The lawgiver must learn what
learning is as a whole prior to furnishing human beings with the basic
tools of learning. In the power of their intellects, the dialectician and the
lawgiver are gods or akin to gods: they know the whole of human learning—its end as well as its beginning—and they are able either to communicate without language (cf. 391e3-4) or to speak a language of a sort
that is not accessible to human beings. In either case, the nature of the
original "dialogue" between the dialectician and the lawgiver remains
wholly inaccessible to us.

As a description of the origin of a natural language like Greek, Socrates' account could be nothing other than a kind of prophecy: how otherwise could any human being know that the original act of namegiving
was the work of a lawgiver who was schooled by a dialectician? It soon
becomes apparent, however, that the names employed in natural languages fall far short of the standard of correctness that Socrates has established. In turning to the correctness of particular names, Socrates first
recommends Protagoras as an expert and then, in the face of Hermogenes' objections, offers Homer as an alternative (391b-d). Perhaps
Homer, as the first and foremost Greek poet, has as much claim as anyone else to be the real *nomothetês* and *onomothetês*, the true founder of
nomos and names. Yet Socrates suggests that Homer is no more or less
authoritative on the matter of how speech reveals being than Protagoras—a man who, according to the *Theaetetus*, made a living by depriving
others of their *ousia* (property) in the course of teaching them that neither
they nor any other person or thing has any *ousia* (intrinsic nature or
identity) at all. This reflection should give us pause.[24]

Things deteriorate quickly from this point on. Socrates cites Homer as
an authority on what names the gods use—assuming, as Hermogenes
cautiously does, that "if the gods call things at all, they call them correctly" (391e2-3). Some of this caution seems to rub off on Socrates,
who soon recommends that they seek for correct names with regard to
gods rather than heroes and human beings, since "*perhaps some of them*
were established by a power more divine than that of human beings"
(397c1-2, emphasis added). And three pages later, he bluntly admits that
"concerning the gods we know nothing, neither of them nor of whatever
names they call themselves" (400d8-9). Hence he recommends an inquiry into the second kind of correctness "that is the custom [*nomos*] in

uttering prayers," according to which we call the gods "whatever names and patronymics are gratifying to them" (400e1-3). An investigation of the opinions human beings had in establishing names for the gods is, moreover, safer: "for this will not incur divine wrath" (401a5). This procedure, which amusingly assumes that Euthyphro was correct in equating the pious with that which is gratifying to the gods, obviously begs the question of how we can know what pleases the gods if in fact we know nothing at all about them. If *nomos* has really been established by the lawgiver such as Socrates described earlier, it would appear that he neglected to give us the correct names of the gods. Perhaps learning can take place without them.

Socrates nonetheless goes on to refer to the lawgiver in the course of explaining the names of Hera and Hermes (404c, 408a-b). But if the lawgiver failed to provide us with correct names for the gods, must we not assume that these names are *incorrect* (cf. 431e)? Then again, there is some question about whether the lawgiver established names at all: Socrates at one point states that "the first ones who established names were no mean individuals [*ou phauloi*], but some high-talkers and babblers [*meteôrologoi kai adoleschai*]" (401b6-8). This ironic language recalls a similar distinction in the digression of the *Theaetetus* between the Aristophanean leaders of the chorus of "philosophers"—thinkers who are geometricians as well as meteorologists—and those who, like Socrates himself, philosophize "poorly" (*phaulôs*: 173c7).[25] And indeed, Socrates immediately demonstrates his power to fly "below the earth" as well as "above the heavens" (cf. *Theaetetus* 173e) by providing etymologies of the gods Hades and Pluto as well as Hestia and other heavenly deities (401c-404b). It is in this ironic context, appropriately enough, that he calls Hades both "a perfect sophist" and "a philosopher" without in any way attempting to distinguish the meanings of these names (403e4, 404a2). Socrates further erodes whatever confidence we may have left in his philological authority by resorting to the "contrivance" (*mêchanê*) of declaring certain words to be of foreign origin whenever he is at a loss about their etymology (409d-410a, 416a, 421c-d). Finally, he fully exposes the mythical character of his earlier speech about the dialectician and the lawgiver when he "prophesies" (*manteuesthai*) that names were actually established not by wise divinities but by ignorant, confused men—"very ancient human beings" who, "just like many of our present wise men, always get dizzy on account of twisting around greatly in the course of inquiring into the way things stand regarding beings, and then it seems to them that things [*ta pragmata*] turn round and are borne along in every way" (411b3-c1; cf. 439b-c). One is again reminded of the very recent experience of Euthyphro.[26]

We shall return shortly to the significance of Socrates' playful irony in the central, etymological portion of the *Cratylus*. For now, we may observe that the serious implication of the passages we have just reviewed is that the process of learning through dialogue is unavoidably impure or question-begging. Names are indispensable tools for learning that we use in order to separate and collect beings, to guide our search toward them, or perhaps, as in prayer, to invoke them (cf. 397b). Yet the names we must employ are altered versions of terms originally fashioned by human beings who possessed neither an adequate knowledge of beings nor a complete understanding of the work of learning.

The latter, seemingly quite pessimistic conclusion is not explicitly challenged in the remainder of the *Cratylus*. Indeed, Socrates subsequently focuses on the problem of the inadequacy of names to the work of learning. Cratylus enters the discussion in response to Hermogenes' request that he either "learn from Socrates or teach us both" (427e3-4). The theme of learning resurfaces when Socrates asks Cratylus to state the power (*dunamis*) of names and the work they accomplish, and he replies "to teach." "Whoever knows [*epistêtai*] names," Cratylus adds, "knows also things [*epistasthai ta pragmata*]" (435d5-6). Socrates next wonders whether the one who has discovered names has also thereby discovered the beings of which they are the names, "or is it necessary to investigate and discover [beings] in some other manner?" (436a5). After Cratylus strongly affirms that the investigation and discovery of beings proceeds by way of names, Socrates points out that if he who first established names had an incorrect belief about the nature of the things named, he will have introduced a systematic error into our language (436b-d). He goes on to provide evidence to the effect that Greek is in fact inconsistent with respect to the nature of things: while some names seem to have been established in accordance with the supposition that things are at rest, others, as we have already seen, reflect the belief that things are in motion (437a-c). This contradiction suggests that names might not have been founded, as Socrates claimed earlier and as Cratylus now insists, by "some greater than human power," since in that case "the namegiver himself would have established names in opposition to himself, although he is a *daimôn* or a god" (438c5-6).[27] In any event, names could not have been well-founded by human beings, nor could we now determine which of the two sorts of names are correct, if, as Cratylus has agreed, "it is not possible to learn about things otherwise than from their names" (438b7-8). What is more, names are untrustworthy insofar as they themselves flow and for the most part arise from the supposition that things flow, whereas knowledge (here, *gnôsis* rather than *epistêmê*) and its objects must be stable if there is to be any knowledge at all (439b-440d). For both of these reasons, one must somehow learn about and discover beings "themselves from themselves" rather than "from names" (439b7-8).

While the primordial visibility of beings that has been hinted at in the *Cratylus* might be taken to allow for progress in learning about them directly, it is strange to hear the latter conclusion coming from the mouth of the same man who will soon warn his friends, on the last day of his life, about the risk associated with directly inquiring into or "looking at" (*skopein*) beings—a risk akin to the one incurred by looking directly at the sun during an eclipse. Socrates speaks of this danger to the soul in connection with an anecdote about his discovery of the thought of the natural philosopher Anaxagoras. He was once told that Anaxagoras's book offered an account of how mind (*nous*) "decorously arranges and is responsible for [*aitios*] all things" (*Phaedo* 97c1-2). Socrates understood this to mean that "mind, in arranging all things, orders and establishes each thing in whatever way is best"—a teaching, as he nicely puts it, that was "much to my mind [*kata noun emautôi*]" (97c4-6, d7). But he found that Anaxagoras in fact made no use of *nous* along these lines, instead speaking only of the necessary material preconditions of intelligent action. Anaxagoras thus failed to see that "the real cause [*to aition*] is one thing, and that without which the cause could never be a cause is another" (99b2-4). In the Anaxagorean fashion, Socrates observes, one would explain the cause of his talking with his friends in the prison in terms of such things as bones, sinews, sound, air, and hearing, "while neglecting [*amelêsas*: 'not caring'] to speak of the true causes [*aitiai*], namely, that since the Athenians thought it better to condemn me, it has seemed better to me also to sit here, and more just to remain and undergo whatever penalty they should command" (98e1-5).

Socrates' disappointment with Anaxagoras, a disappointment echoed at *Cratylus* 413c, led him famously to renounce the direct investigation of beings.[28] In what he describes as a "second sailing in search of the inquiry into the cause [*deuteron ploun epi tên tês aitias zêtêsin*]," he turned away from physics or natural philosophy and took refuge in speeches (*eis logois*) so as safely "to examine [*skopein*] the truth of beings in them," much as one might safely look at an eclipse of the sun through its image in water (*Phaedo* 99c9-d1, e5-6). The damage to the psyche that he seeks to avoid in this way is a blindness both of and to the soul (cf. 99e), for the intelligent, teleological activity of the soul becomes effectively invisible to those who, like the pre-Socratic natural philosophers, attempt to examine beings directly and apart from the mediation of speeches. Put more positively, it becomes clear in the context of the *Phaedo* that Socrates believes his recourse to speeches—that is, to philosophical dialogue—allows for a kind of self-knowledge that is not otherwise available. The work of the soul as such, it would appear, is especially made manifest in the arena of philosophical debate. In rising to the challenge of asking and answering philosophical questions in the company of others, the soul becomes visible as an intelligent *aitia* and *archê*, or as the author of speeches and deeds that are undertaken in the light of the good and so are fully intelligible only in terms of the end or *telos* at which they aim. This insight harmonizes with Socrates' metaphor of the "second sailing," which underscores the joint labor involved in Socratic discourse. In an ocean voyage the crew hopes to travel with the sails up, but if the wind fails to blow they sail in the second-best way: they row. The difference between pre-Socratic physics and Socratic dialogue is analogous to the difference between being passively borne along and being compelled by necessity to join together in the work of propelling ourselves forward toward our common goal. It is easier in the former case than in the latter to forget about the soul's self-moving nature, and to imagine that one's own motion is a function of the same external forces that govern non-ensouled beings.

The foregoing observations bring us back to Socrates' suggestion at the end of the *Cratylus* to the effect that learning about beings should take place apart from names. As we have noted, this conclusion follows from the apparent inadequacy of names as tools of learning. Yet the *Phaedo* suggests that this is a self-defeating mode of philosophizing, since abandoning names, and therefore speeches, would involve sacrificing increasing self-knowledge, and therewith the goal of *sophia*. Aristotle reports that as a result of his extreme Heracliteanism Cratylus "in the end thought that one should say nothing, but only moved his finger" (*Metaphysics* 1010a10-15); perhaps we are meant to see in Cratylus's legendary strangeness the absurdity of attempting to implement Socrates' final recommendation. It seems significant that Plato gives the last word in the dialogue to Cratylus, whose detachment from dialogue and ultimate renunciation of speech are dramatically prefigured not only by his long silence during most of the *Cratylus* but also by several other details.[29]

If the ending of the *Cratylus* anticipates silence, it nevertheless also points back toward the silence implicit in its beginning. The first words of the dialogue belong to Hermogenes—who is, to be sure, a veritable fountain of speeches compared to Cratylus.[30] Yet Hermogenes' initial view that names bear no relation to nature effectively reduces all attempts at learning through speech to empty chatter; this is why Socrates' first order of business with him was to reach an agreement concerning the falsity of Protagoras's maxim. In the *Cratylus*, as we have already noted, Socrates enters an ongoing conversation in midstream, and is called upon by Hermogenes to mediate between him and his oracularly ironic companion. He subsequently attempts to find a middle ground between his interlocutors with respect to the roles of nature and convention in the correctness of names: Hermogenes is made to appreciate the need for a natural standard of correctness, while Cratylus is forced to admit the role of convention in the formulation of names (435a-b). Perhaps the *Cratylus*, in its mimetic and dramatic accomplishment if not its explicit argumentation, also helps us to locate some Socratic middle ground between the two sorts of silence exemplified in the characters of Hermogenes and Cratylus—the silence that results from severing speech altogether from beings and the silence of the speechless contemplation of beings. Perhaps, too, the elusive wholeness of *logos* that Socrates repeatedly emphasizes by indirection lies somewhere in this intermediate region between the speaking soul and silent beings. Socrates' account of the origins of names at any rate suggests that, for all its impurity, human philosophical dialogue is nonetheless an image of the original conversation of the gods.

Prophecy and Philosophical Images

The *Cratylus*, like the *Theaetetus* and the *Euthyphro*, seems at first blush only to confirm our ignorance in the face of the philosophical question that motivates the inquiry. But if the preceding reflections are well-taken, the subtext of the *Cratylus* is the adequacy of the way of philosophizing that Socrates characterizes in the *Phaedo* as his "second sailing." What support can be found in the *Cratylus* for examining beings after the manner of this second sailing? And what exactly does Socrates mean when he speaks of examining the truth of beings in speeches?

With regard to the latter question, it is important to consider the philosophical significance of images within Socratic inquiry, and, more broadly, with respect to Plato's own activity as an author of philosophical dialogues. Speeches, Socrates has already noted, are deeds, and as such they are beings that possess their own intrinsic nature (386e-387b). To think about beings through speeches would thus be to consider the nature of some beings in the light of the nature of others, just as one does when thinking through an image. A concrete example is provided by the act of reading Platonic dialogues, wherein one considers such things as piety and justice in the light of the deeds, and especially the speeches, of Socrates and his interlocutors. This means that speeches and deeds are one kind of beings that can be looked at directly, and without fear of damage to the soul that is doing the looking. There is, moreover, no other route of access to the natures of individual souls than through the character of their speeches and deeds—a point that is sharpened by the reflection that the natures of Socrates and his interlocutors are visible only in the speeches and deeds that Plato has inscribed in his dialogues.

Viewed another way, however, these same speeches and deeds are Plato's own, for they are in truth nothing other than written images of speaking and acting that have been fashioned by him as a maker of images. In the *Phaedo*, Socrates compares looking at beings through speeches to viewing an eclipse of the sun through its reflection in water. This image sheds light on Plato's writing as well as Socrates' speech. Water faithfully reproduces the look of the things that are reflected in it just because it has no distinct look of its own; in this respect, Plato's way of writing is indeed like water. But it is important to see that the same is true of Socrates' way of speaking, just insofar as Socrates repeatedly employs philosophically relevant images. Indeed, Socrates' comparison of speech to water is itself an illustration of the very point of the comparison, which has to do with the power of speech to provide us with images through which we can think about beings.

In order even to recognize that an image is an image, one must somehow have access to the original of which it is an image. Put another way, it must to some extent be possible to compare the image with the original. In the *Cratylus*, Socrates exploits this possibility when he introduces the notion that a name is akin to a picture in that it imitates the *ousia* of the thing that it names (423e, 430b ff.). Because this account presupposes the initial visibility of beings apart from names, Cratylus cannot consistently accept the idea that names make the natures of things manifest by way of their likeness to them (430a-b, 434a) and still maintain that we can learn about things only through their names. Socrates' use of pictures as an image of the way in which names function as images may nonetheless teach us more by way of its difference from the original than by way of its similarity to it. For whereas pictures depict perceptible objects, *ousiai* or essential natures are in themselves imperceptible. Certain beings are also more removed from perception than others, which makes the establishment of names more problematic in these cases: that some being is named by the name "body" is clear, but it is less clear that some being is named by the name "soul." Socrates seems to allude to this problem in his very first words in the dialogue, in which he reminds Hermogenes of the ancient proverb that "it is difficult to learn how things stand with respect to the things that are noble or beautiful [*ta kala*]" (384b1). Nor is it easy to learn how things stand with regard to intellectual and moral virtues and vices, the names of which Socrates explores in the concluding part of the etymological section (411d ff.). In sum, our ability to appreciate the limitations of Socrates' image of names as pictures calls attention to the peculiarly indirect visibility of *ousiai*.

As the preceding example shows, images provide a means of access to the truth of beings just insofar as they provoke reflection upon their own adequacy as images. But such reflection could not take place absent the possibility of philosophical prophecy. This consideration encourages us to look more closely at Socrates' dramatic imitation of divination after the manner of Euthyphro, a ridiculous performance that seems at first to be pure comedy. Before doing so, however, we would do well to remind ourselves that the prophetic character of philosophical insight is a recurring theme in the Platonic dialogues, and one that appears in close connection with the subject of *erôs* as well as that of images.

In the *Republic*, Socrates bases his decision to found a city in speech on a kind of divination: his "godsend" (*hermaion*: more literally, a "gift of Hermes") that doing so will illuminate the Idea of justice in the soul (368d6). Socrates' allusion in this context to Hermes, the messenger god who links the human and divine spheres and who has given the name "hermeneutics" to the art of interpretation, is most appropriate, for his procedure is circular on its face. His reason for constructing the city in speech is that the soul is too difficult to see on its own (368c-d), but to recognize that the city resembles the soul one must *already* be familiar with the nature of the soul as well as that of the city. Socrates' presupposition about the connection between the city and the soul is presumably not knowledge, but is rather a philosophical prophecy that is worth testing. Later in the *Republic*, Socrates uses the vocabulary of prophecy to describe the soul's foreknowledge of the Good. Every soul, "while divining [*apomanteuomenê*] that that which it pursues and for the sake of which it does everything is some one thing, is at a loss about it and unable adequately to grasp just what it is"; thus Socrates tells Glaucon that "I divine [*manteuomai*] that no one will adequately know" the just and noble things before it is known in what way they are good (505d11-e2, 506a6-7). Glaucon's response further emphasizes the prophetic character of our awareness of the Good: "You divine beautifully [*kalôs manteuêi*]" (506a8). Socrates subsequently agrees to speak of the Good in an image, yet he warns Glaucon not to be deceived by what he has to say (507a). Once again, it would appear that we are not without prophetic resources in judging the adequacy of philosophical images.

An examination of the images of the divided line and the cave (*Republic* 509c-511e, 514a-517a) would show that the soul's ascent toward the Ideas and the Good is made possible by the ramification of imaging relationships throughout the entirety of human experience, relationships that allow us in some sense to see that which we seek through that which is already present to us. Thus, to take but one example, the image of the divided line makes it clear that the faculty of "reasoning" or *dianoia* that enables geometricians to employ sketches and models in order to illuminate the literally invisible foundations of the visible world is in fact a prophetic way of "thinking" (*noein*) "through" (*dia*) images, and so is a special application of the even more comprehensive power of *eikasia* or imagination—the power of making and recognizing images that enables ascent toward the *archai* that are the ultimate objects of philosophical inquiry.[31]

The prophetic recollection of beings is an important theme in the *Phaedrus* and *Symposium* as well, in which the soul's power of divination is linked with the daimonic intermediacy of *erôs*. In the *Phaedrus*, Socrates has just finished uttering the concealed lover's speech in praise of the sobriety of the nonlover and is about to leave when he explains that his "daimonic [*daimonion*] and customary sign" has forbidden him to do so until he purifies himself from the error he has committed in regard to the god. He goes on to say that he understands his error because he is a "seer" (*mantis*)—"albeit not a very serious one, but, just like those who are poor [*phauloi*] in letters, only good enough for myself." Socrates' power of divination is indeed not particularly special inasmuch as it reflects a capability that inheres in the soul as such, for "the soul," he remarks, "is somehow prophetic [*mantikon*]" (242b8-c7). Prophecy, in turn, is a kind of heaven-sent or divine madness that is closely connected with both *erôs* and philosophy. In a playful etymology reminiscent of the *Cratylus*, Socrates derives the so-called "mantic art" (*mantikê*) from what men of old named the "manic art" (*manikê*: 244c-d). And in his famous palinode in praise of the madness of love, Socrates associates philosophy with the full flourishing of the erotic species of divine madness that carries the soul upward toward the roof of the cosmos, the gods, and the hyperuranian beings that the soul once saw and now strives to recollect (244a-257b; cf. 265a-c).

Aristophanes, echoing Socrates' observation about the prophetic nature of the soul, remarks in the *Symposium* that the soul of one in love "is not able to say, but divines [*manteuetai*] and speaks oracles about what it wants" (192d1-2). The comic poet's speech is followed by Socrates' account of his initiation by the prophetess Diotima into the Mysteries of *erôs* (201d ff.).[32] *Erôs*, Diotima teaches, is in between the ugly and the beautiful and the mortal and the immortal. As such, it is not a god but great *daimôn*: "For all the daimonic [*pan to daimonion*] is in between god and mortal." "Interpreting [*hermêneuon*] and carrying messages to gods from human beings and to human beings from gods," that which is daimonic fills up the middle ground between both "so that the all itself is bound together with itself" (202d13-e7). And not only does *erôs*, as a *daimôn*, serve as a conduit for "the whole art of divination" (202e7), but it is also a lover of wisdom or *philosophos* (203d, 204b).

The passages we have just considered connect philosophy with *daimôn*s and other intermediaries (including *erôs*, Socrates' *daimonion*, and the god Hermes) as well as with the mediating activities of divination and interpretation. In the etymological section of the *Cratylus*, Socrates links speech (*logos*) with the same sorts of intermediate beings and activities. In particular, speech bears a striking resemblance to *erôs* as it is characterized in the *Symposium*, with respect both to its polyeidetic and polytropic nature and its power to bind all things into a whole. In the course of his etymologies Socrates makes manifest this resemblance in deed as well as in speech, for he spins out a tale that mimetically reflects his own erotic and ironic nature even as it weaves together all things into a cosmos of unified meaning. As with the other dialogues of the philosophical trial, the soul of Socrates is the unspoken center around which the drama of the *Cratylus* revolves.

In the preceding paragraphs I have argued that Socrates' second sailing may be understood as a recommendation to examine the truth of beings through images, an examination that depends upon the possibility of philosophical prophecy or prophetic recollection. The *Cratylus*, I have also suggested, shows mimetically what it does not say explicitly about learning through speech. In particular, Socrates' inspired performance in the central, etymological section of the dialogue dramatically displays the daimonic nature of his philosophical speech. It is to this strange drama that we now turn.

Naming Socrates: *Erôs*, Heroes, *Daimôn*s, and Satyrs

Our earlier discussion of the impurity of philosophical speech focused on the unreliability of names. There is, however, another possible threat to the usefulness of speech as a means of learning, and this from the side of the beings that are named: it would seem that names must be compromised to the extent that *ta onta* are in their natures fundamentally ambiguous. That they might be such is suggested by Socrates' twofold etymology of the divine name "Hestia," which is explained with respect to the words *essia* and *ôsia*; the former term is said to be an ancient version of *ousia*, while the latter is connected with *ôthoun*, "to push or thrust" after the manner of the Heraclitean flux (401c-e). Another example of the ambiguity of beings concerns Socrates himself. On the day following the *Cratylus* Socrates will ask the Eleatic Stranger about the relationship between the names "sophist," "statesman," and "philosopher" and the kinds of human beings these names are meant to discriminate. He wonders in particular whether those in the region from which the Stranger hails "were accustomed to hold that all these things are one or two, or, just as their names are three, did they divide them into three kinds [*genê*] and attach a name to each kind individually?" (*Sophist* 217a6-8). The Stranger responds that they believed they were three different kinds, and proceeds to define the sophist in such a way as to suggest that the name "sophist" is properly applied to Socrates. But Socrates' *genos* or natural kind is hard to pin down, so much so that the Stranger hesitates to use the name "sophist" and settles for a paradoxical qualification: such human beings as are described in the sixth division of the *Sophist* are practitioners of "the sophistical art that is noble in kind" (231b7-8). Perhaps Socrates is a sort of hybrid monster such as he imagines he might be in the *Phaedrus* (230a). Or perhaps Socrates is indeed a philosopher, but the *ousia* of the kind of human being that goes by the name of "philosopher" is in itself ambiguous, and is therefore in some respects no less accurately distinguished by the name "sophist." Either way, the difficulty of naming Socrates—and the possibility or likelihood that he will be *misnamed*, as he seems to be by his public accusers—stems not from the basic incorrectness of names, but from the ambiguous character of his intrinsic nature.

If one approaches the *Cratylus* with the problem of the *Sophist* in mind, it becomes apparent that the *Cratylus*, too, is concerned with naming Socrates. Hermogenes, as we know, is in search of his proper name, and we learn immediately that the question of the correctness of Socrates' name was raised by Hermogenes even before Socrates appeared on the scene (383b). It therefore seems more than coincidental that the first example Socrates gives of a thing to be named is a human being. In that context, he imagines a situation in which one calls a human being a "horse" and vice versa (385a). Both human beings and horses come up again when Socrates sets forth the principle that it is just (*dikaion*) to call the offspring of a lion a "lion" and that of a horse a "horse." "I do not mean," he adds, "if, like a monster, something other than a horse is born from a horse, but I am speaking of the offspring of any kind that is according to nature." Thus, he observes, if the offspring of a human being is not itself a human being it should not be called by that name, "and similarly in respect to trees and all the rest" (393b7-c5).

The latter examples are highly suggestive. They are offered in the context of an analysis of the Homeric names Hector and Astyanax, in the course of which Socrates tries to show that both father and son were named for their kingly natures (392d-393a). But as Bruce Rosenstock has pointed out, Socrates seems to overlook the "pathetic irony" of these particular names: "The name of the son does not in the case of 'Astyanax' reveal the *ousia* of the father or, rather . . . it ironically reveals the father's inability to live up to his kingly identity and preserve it for his son."[33] Astyanax ("Lord of the Town") looks to be a monster after all—unless the sort of thing he represents is actually not contrary to nature. To judge by the names Socrates goes on to explore or at least to mention in the immediate sequel—including those of Orestes, Agamemnon, Thyestes, Tantalus, and Pelops, and, among the gods, Uranus, Cronos, and Zeus—the smooth transference of *ousia* from father to son is more exceptional than its disruption.[34] It is also true that the birth from a horse of something other than a horse need not be monstrous: when asses mate with horses they produce mules, as Socrates himself notes in the *Apology* (27d-e). In the same context Socrates also mentions that *daimôn*s may be the bastard children of gods and nymphs; he speaks as well of Homeric heroes or demigods who were born from unions between mortal and divine beings and then goes on to compare himself with Achilles, the son of the goddess Thetis (*Apology* 27d-28d). Socrates also discusses both *daimôn*s and heroes in the *Cratylus* and notes explicitly the mixed parentage of the latter (398d); in addition, his subsequent mention of wearing a lionskin (411a) serves to identify him with Heracles, the heroic son of Zeus and a mortal woman. Also in the *Apology*, Socrates, quoting Homer, observes that "not even I have grown 'from an oak or a rock,' but from human beings" (34d4-5)—a phrase that is uttered by Hector just prior to his death (*Iliad* 22.126), and that seems to be echoed in Socrates' mention of the offspring of "trees and all the rest" at *Cratylus* 393c. Given all of the clues noted above, Socrates' concern in this passage with the mixture of distinct kinds seems to be intended indirectly to call attention to his own eidetic ambiguity, as well as to the problem of the heritability of his philosophic nature—a problem implicitly posed by the presence in the *Theaetetus*, *Sophist*, and *Statesman* of two youths who may resemble him in soul as well as in name (Young Socrates) and looks (Theaetetus).[35]

Heracles, as is well known, strove heroically to rid the world of monsters. In the first portion of the etymological section of the *Cratylus*, Socrates performs the equivalent labor in speech. At 395e to 400d he goes through the cosmos from top to bottom, as it were, starting with Zeus, Cronos, and Uranus and proceeding through the sun, moon, earth, stars, and sky, *daimôn*s, heroes, human beings, the soul, and finally the body. It is just after Socrates has gone through the names of the first three ruling gods that Hermogenes observes that Socrates is uttering oracles; in response, Socrates attributes his inspired wisdom to Euthyphro and suggests that he will later require a purifying catharsis (396d-397a). Socrates' mention of *katharsis* curiously echoes his emphasis upon purity (*to katharon*) in connection with the meaning of the names of Cronos and Uranus (396b6, c2). These observations help us to see that the impurity of Socrates' speech has both religious and philosophical dimensions. What is more, Socrates' twofold impurity is, paradoxically, a function of his purifying speeches—a point that is later confirmed when the Stranger purges him from the ranks of the philosophers on the ground that he is a sophistical "purifier of soul" (*peri psuchên kathartês*: *Sophist* 231e5-6).

Let us consider each dimension of Socrates' impurity in turn. First and most obviously, Socrates is in danger of incurring pollution because he makes religious innovations. The innovative, productive dimension of his speech is conspicuous in the present context. Socrates suggested earlier that words are instruments with which we cut up, bore into, and weave together *ousiai*, and he now indicates that his etymologies reveal what his newfound wisdom can "make" (*ti poiêsei*, 396c6-7; *poiein* can mean simply "to do," but it is also what a poet [*poiêtês*] does when he fashions a poem [*poiêma*]). As in the *Euthyphro*, Socrates here manufactures a poem about the cosmos that cuts up the sphere of the divine things in such a way as to purge or purify the poeticoreligious tradition. The irony of Socrates' attribution of his wisdom to Euthyphro is heightened by the contrast between the violent tales about Uranus, Cronos, and Zeus cited by the prophet (*Euthyphro* 5e-6a) and what Socrates makes of these gods in the *Cratylus*. According to Socrates, the names of the first three ruling gods express the cosmic hegemony of mind or intellect (*nous*). Zeus, whom some call *Dia* and others *Zêna*, is the one "through whom to live [*di' hon zên*] always belongs to all living things" (396b1-2). Nor is it hybristic to call him the son of Cronos, "for *koros* does not signify a child, but rather his purity [*to katharon autou*] and the undefiled nature of his intellect" (396b6-7).[36] So, too, the nature of Cronos derives directly from that of his father Uranus, in whose name we hear *ourania*, or "looking at the things above [*horôsa ta anô*], from which, meteorologists assert, a pure mind [*ton katharon noun*] comes to be present" (396c1-2). One might not have expected anything at all to be above Uranus, whose name *Ouranos* is the Greek word for "heaven"; as in the *Euthyphro*, however, Socrates transforms even the monstrous pre-Olympians into paradigms of philosophical wonder and thoughtfulness.[37]

Second, Socrates' speech is philosophically impure because it is circular on its face: the order that his etymologies impose upon the monstrous natures of the Homeric and Hesiodic gods serves to guarantee that names are themselves well-ordered. Thus Socrates observes that it is fitting for the names of "the beings that are always and by nature" to have been given with the greatest seriousness, and that at least some of them might have been given by a power more divine than that of human beings (397b-c). Yet gods such as those portrayed by Homer and Hesiod would be likely to pay little heed to the serious business of namegiving, for they live without much regard to anything beyond themselves. Correct names are good tools for human learning; why, then, would we expect them to have been given to us by gods who are neither philanthropic nor philosophic?

The latter way of putting the point helps us to see that Socrates has refashioned the gods of the poets in accordance with his own erotic nature.

The same is true of the etymologies he provides for the names *daimôn*, "hero," and "human being." Hesiod says that the first, golden race of men are now called *daimôns*. Socrates interprets "golden" to mean "good and noble," and the good, Hermogenes agrees, are the wise (*phronimoi*: 398b3). Hence Hesiod called the golden race of men *daimôns* because they were wise and "knowing" (*daêmones*: 398b6). Socrates adds that when a good man dies "he possesses a great share of honor and comes to be a *daimôn*, in accordance with the name given to *phronêsis*"; so, too, he maintains, "whoever is good, whether living or dead, is daimonic [*daimonion*], and is correctly called a *daimôn* (398b10-c4). If the daimonic is that which connects the human and divine spheres, then Socrates is just now in the middle of fashioning a daimonic speech—a poem that moves from gods down to human beings in order to bind them together in a single web of meaning. Presumably his own *phronêsis* is on display in his subtle transformation of Hesiod's fabled Golden Age, a lost paradise of easy living: whereas the ancient poet emphasizes the pleasurable and festive atmosphere of the life lived by these first human beings (*Works and Days* 109-120), Socrates emphasizes their goodness and wise insight. Hesiod was wrong about the nature of men in the age of Cronos, just as he was wrong about the nature of Cronos himself: given Socrates' later etymology of the name "human being" (see below), we may suppose that the first human beings acquired goodness and *phronêsis* by using their leisure not for feasting but for philosophical inquiry into the things above them (cf. *Statesman* 272b-c).

Socrates completes his heroic suppression of poetic monstrosities with his etymologies of "hero" and "human being." Whereas heroes traditionally distinguish themselves through great deeds, Socrates equates heroism with *erôs* and a capacity for asking philosophical questions. *Hêrôs* (or, in its old Attic form, *hêerôs*) bespeaks the *erôs* between mortals and gods which leads to the birth of these intermediate or daimonic beings. The *erôs* of the hero, in turn, is directed toward philosophical inquiry of precisely the sort practiced by Socrates: an alternative etymology connects *hêrôs* with the fact that heroes "were wise and clever orators and dialecticians, who were capable of asking questions [*erôtan*]; for to say [*eirein*] is the same as to speak [*legein*]" (398d6-8). Socrates thus connects speaking with philosophical questioning, and questioning with the daimonic *erôs* that links human beings with gods. Philosophical *erôs* furthermore appears to be a distinctive potentiality of man as such, as becomes clear when Socrates interprets *anthrôpos* as an abbreviated phrase that describes our human nature. Other animals, he notes, do not inquire into, calculate, or look up at any of the things they see, but "the human being alone among the beasts has been correctly named *anthrôpos*, for he looks up at that which he has seen [*anathrôn ha opôpe*]" (399c5-6).

The upshot of the etymologies we have just examined is that Socrates' philosophical *erôs* appears to be self-grounding. If his etymological *logos* describes a cosmos that fully supports his heroic (i.e., erotic and philosophical) labors, it is because that *logos* is in truth a poem authored by his *erôs*. In the last chapter we noted a similar circularity in the traditional myths about the gods, which reflect and justify common human desires for pleasure and domination. With respect to this fundamental circularity, one might argue that there is no logical difference between Socrates' cosmological poem and the myths of Homer and Hesiod, or, what is worse, the sophistical poem of Protagoras. In practice, "human being is the measure of all things" means that in speaking one effectively shapes the world in accordance with the desires one already happens to possess. To say the least, the stories of the poets about the happy, self-obsessed, tyrannical lives of the gods do not contradict this teaching. "Philosophy," Nietzsche writes, "is this tyrannical drive itself, the most spiritual will to power, to the 'creation of the world,' to the *causa prima*."[38] Protagoras would doubtless have agreed—as would Aristophanes, who also drew no distinction between Socratic philosophizing and sophistry—and both, it seems, could have adverted to the *Cratylus* as evidence for this claim.[39]

How could Socrates counter the kind of argument adumbrated above? The circularity of his etymologies effectively returns us to the erotic origins of speech, and it is here, on the level of the soul itself, that he would have to make his stand. In this connection it is important to observe that the preceding attempt to assimilate Socratic philosophizing to sophistry makes no distinction between philosophical *erôs* and other sorts of desire. More to the point, it does not take seriously the claim of Socratic, philosophical *erôs* to be genuinely daimonic. If Socrates' *erôs* is daimonic, it is not an ultimate ground in its own right, but is itself grounded in the nature of that which is divine. In that case, Socrates' manner of thinking and speaking would still be circular, but its circularity, unlike that which characterizes the speech of Protagoras, would be nonarbitrary and genuinely hermeneutical.

In order fully to appreciate the latter point, we must turn to the image of speech that Socrates offers a little later in the *Cratylus*. The image comes from Pan, a divine being whom Socrates identifies as "either *logos* or a brother of *logos*" (408d3). Pan's nature, in turn, becomes clear only in connection with that of his father, Hermes, which is where we must begin in exploring this image. After Socrates has finished offering etymologies for the names of various gods, Hermogenes asks him about Hermes; he also makes it clear that his interest in this name has to do with Cratylus's assertion that he is not *Hermogenês*—not a "Son of Hermes," or one who shares in Hermes' nature (407e). Socrates replies that "this Hermes seems to be somehow concerned with speech, and to be the interpreter [*hermênea*] and the messenger and that which is thievish and wily [*apatêlon*] in speeches and an able trader; all this business is concerned with the power of speech" (407e5-408a2). He goes on to claim that the name of this god was given by the lawgiver, who told human beings that he who contrived speech (*eirein emêsato*) should be called *Eiremês*; the name has since been altered somewhat to *Hermês*. Finally, Socrates adds that Iris also seems to have gotten her name from *eirein,* "to speak" (408a-b).

Let us pause here to note several suggestive resemblances. Like Hermes, the oracular Socrates is an interpreter and a messenger who contrives speeches and mediates between human beings and gods. The link Socrates forges between the verb *eirein* and the names of Hermes and Iris, the rainbow that joins heaven and earth, helps to strengthen this association: his earlier etymology of "hero" connected *eirein* with *erôtan*, "to ask questions" after the manner of the dialectician (398d), and in the *Theaetetus* he endorsed the genealogy that made Iris the daughter of Thaumas or "Wonder," which in turn is the beginning (*archê*) of philosophy (155d). Socrates, moreover, is doubtless a wily thief in speeches, as he proves even in his etymology of the name "Hermes." Hermogenes is surprised to discover that his name must not be "Hermogenes" after all, "since I am certainly not a good contriver of speech" (408b7). This leads one to reflect that if anyone deserves the epithet *Hermogenês*, it is Socrates—but only because he has interpreted the name in such a way as to suit his own nature. Contrary to initial expectations, it is Socrates, not Cratylus, who in the end steals Hermogenes' name. Then too, Hermes' nature is closely akin to that of *erôs* as Socrates describes it in the *Symposium. Erôs*, as we have seen, is also an interpreter and messenger who links gods with human beings; what is more, as the grandson of Cunning (*Mêtis*) and the son of Neediness (*Penia*) he is a clever trickster, "always weaving some contrivances [*mêchanas*]," and "a terrific sorcerer and charmer [*pharmakeus*] and sophist" (*Symposium* 203d6-8).[40]

As for Pan, Socrates is uncertain whether he *is* speech (*logos*) or just the brother of speech, which has itself been fathered by Hermes. This ambiguity seems appropriate to a son of the wily Messenger, and particularly to one born of the intercourse between an immortal father and a mortal mother, the daughter of Dryops (*Homeric Hymn to Pan*, 34). Pan is "double-natured" (408b8) in more ways than one. Strictly speaking, this "shepherd god" (*Homeric Hymn to Pan*, 5) is genetically a mixed being or *daimôn*, and as the son of one skilled in trickery, he combines visible surfaces with hidden depths. Finally, elements from the spheres of divine, human, and animal life are fused in him: while his father is a god, his bodily form is a mixture of goatlike and human elements. Given that *pan* means "all," Pan seems to have been well-named; he is a mythical emblem of that which is daimonic as such, through which "the all [*to pan*] itself is bound together with itself" (*Symposium* 202e6-7). But if we read "all" for Pan, then Socrates is uncertain whether speech is the all or the sibling of the all. If the latter, speech is closely akin to all that is; there would be good reason to believe that speech could articulate the all both separately and as a whole, or in its daimonic integrity. If the former, speech is indistinguishable from all that is; what is would therefore be nothing other than what is said to be, and Socratic dialogue would collapse into Protagorean chatter. When Socrates prays to Pan at the end of the *Phaedrus* (279b-c), one must suppose that he addresses himself to something other than speech itself.

In the present context, at any rate, Socrates seems to assume that speech is the brother of Pan. He tells Hermogenes that "speech indicates the all [*sêmainei to pan*] and makes it circle and always moves it around, and is twofold—both true and false" (408c2-3), but it would make no sense to speak of true or false speeches if what is is just whatever is said to be. The true part of speech, Socrates continues, is "smooth and divine and dwells above, among the gods," whereas the false part "dwells below among the many human beings, and is rough and goatish [*tragikon*]." The word *tragikon* nicely illustrates Socrates' point about the duality of speech, for while its lower meaning is "goatish," its "higher" meaning is "tragic." "The greatest part of myths and falsehoods are in that [lower] region," Socrates adds, "in the vicinity of the goatish or tragic life [*tragikon bion*]." Hence "the one who reveals and always moves around [*aei polôn*] the all would correctly be called 'Pan, herder of goats' [*aipolos*], being the double-natured son of Hermes, smooth in the upper parts, and rough and goatish or tragic in form [*tragoeidês*] in the lower parts" (408c5-d2).

Far from ridding the world of monsters, Socrates seems to have allowed speech itself to become infected by a monstrous complexity—and this, in spite of his best efforts to simplify things. In particular, it is clear upon reflection that Socrates' distinction between the true and the false or the high and the low is misleadingly neat. Socrates shows us speech and Pan (or the all) in their multiform wholeness. But from what vantage point does he speak? Viewed from below, speech and his brother Pan are rough and goatlike; viewed from on high, they are smooth and divine. Neither impression, however, is entirely correct. The whole truth about both speech and the all would be accessible to human beings and gods only insofar as they have the power to move from the region of the low to the high or the high to the low. And Socrates' speech reflects just this daimonic power. Socrates gives us an image of speech as something static, with its smooth head in the clouds and its rough feet on the ground; but it is the nature of speech to move between these regions, and it is precisely from this shuttling motion that speech derives its power to speak the truth. Put another way, speech is not partly divine and partly animalic, but is both simultaneously. Were this not so, we human beings would never be able to see the smooth obverse of the rough surfaces that speech, and the all, present to us. That we can see this other side, even though we do not dwell in the smooth region of the gods, is evident in the ambiguity of the word *tragikon*. Such essentially *ironic* words— words whose intrinsic doubleness gives them the power to reveal as well as to deceive—reflect the daimonic and prophetic potential of the human soul: given the duality of the cosmos in Socrates'account, only a daimonic intelligence could divine that that which looks goatish to us is also tragic.

"Tragic" is the "high" meaning of *tragikon*, and Socrates explicitly associates the truth with that which dwells on high. We have just seen, however, that this suggestion is misleading; the truth about the all is not that it is simply smooth, divine, and tragically noble and beautiful. The converse is also true: if we perceived the all only as goatish but never as tragic—if, that is, we could see only the lowest aspect of all things—human life would be unimaginably bestial and ugly. To extend this thought, it would seem that the dramatic genres of tragedy and comedy—which imitate, respectively, human beings who are better and worse, or more noble and more shameful, than those of the present day (cf. Aristotle, *Poetics* 1448a16-18, 1449a32-34, 1454b8-9)—each present us with abstract or one-sided representations of the whole of our experience. There is, however, a dramatic genre that is simultaneously tragic and comic, that is rough and ugly on the outside and divinely smooth and beautiful on the inside, and that in every way plays upon the ironic and daimonic doubleness that Socrates attributes to speech. This genre, whose doubleness is figured in Pan's hybrid nature and appearance, is, of course, the satyr play—the strange drama that each tragedian submitted with three tragedies to make a tetralogy, and that stood between these tragedies and a single comedy in the daily order of performance at the Great Dionysia.

The latter observation helps us to grasp the nature of Socrates' ridiculous performance in the *Cratylus*. It has been argued that the *Cratylus* is a comedy.[41] As a philosophical drama, however, this dialogue is no more akin to comedy than to tragedy. It is obviously not tragic, because tragedies are devoid of humorous playfulness. Socrates justifies a humorous explanation of the name of Dionysus, the god of the theater, with the observation that "the gods too are lovers of play" (406c2-3); the philologist Demetrius, however, rightly states that "laughter is the enemy of tragedy" (*On Style* 3.169). But if we are to judge by the plays of Aristophanes, the *Cratylus* is also not a species of comedy, for its complex,

ironic humor neither simply deflates our philosophical aspirations to divinity nor attempts to deflect these aspirations toward more humble,
earthly pleasures.[42] Put in somewhat different terms, the *Cratylus* is not
purely deconstructive; rather, it dwells on the paradoxical nature of the
daimonic activity of philosophizing in such a way as to spur further
philosophical reflection. The *Cratylus* thus looks most like what Demetrius calls a "tragedy at play": in its strange combination of a laughable exterior and a serious interior, its ironic and paradoxical character,
and its concern with *erôs* and daimonic intermediacy—themes that reach
a crescendo in the satyr-like figure of Pan—it resembles nothing so much
as a satyr play.[43]

Socrates' own resemblance to a satyr has a number of philosophical
implications that I have explored elsewhere.[44] To take seriously Socrates'
Pan-like or satyr-like nature is to call into question the attempt to assimilate Socratic philosophizing to Protagorean sophistry on the ground
that both are simply expressions of the will to power. The circularity of
Protagorean speech is indeed both logically and morally vicious, for it
reduces virtue to the dictates of one's private and arbitrary desires. Pan,
however, symbolizes the alternative posed by Socrates' circle thinking: a
nonvicious, hermeneutical circularity that is rooted in the soul's erotic
response to the difference between the high and the low, the noble and
the base, the beautiful and the ugly—differences that are ingredient in the
nature of the cosmos. The soul can be attuned to these differences, Socrates suggests, because *erôs* is prophetic and daimonic; for the same reason, the soul can fashion and learn from philosophical images. Socrates'
place, in turn, is the place proper to those kinds of beings that help to
make a cosmos out of the all, as he himself does both in speech and in
the deed of a life well lived: it is nothing other than the intermediate region of all things daimonic.

None of this, of course, can be established in argument, for any argument that presupposes prophetic insight into the truth of the proposition
that is to be demonstrated begs the question. Yet if the soul's daimonic
and prophetic nature cannot be *said* in argument, it can nonetheless be
shown dramatically. Only such showing, moreover, can help us to see
that Socratic or satyric irony in speech and deed is a reflection of the
doubleness that inheres in the soul in virtue of its erotic, daimonic
movement. This dramatic exhibition of the soul is precisely what tran-
spires in satyr plays and in their Platonic, philosophical analogues, such
as the *Cratylus*.

Last Words

At the conclusion of the *Cratylus*, Socrates bids his interlocutors to journey into the country (440e). His last words echo the first words of the *Theaetetus*, in which Euclides asks Terpsion if he has come from the country.[45] The three dialogues that take place on the day before the arrival of the Stranger thus turn to face one another in the manner of a hinged triptych. The theme of motion, of journeying to and from the country, also serves as a register of how far we have come over the course of this long day. When we first encounter Theaetetus he is suffering from dysentery; in spite of Socrates' suggestion that motion is good for bodies and souls (*Theaetetus* 153b-c), Theaetetus's life is flowing out of him in a kind of Heraclitean stream. Viewed in this light, Theodorus's comment that Theaetetus's soul flows like olive oil (144b) seems like a bad joke. Yet by the end of the day we have come to appreciate that to be a soul is neither to be fully at rest nor fully in flux. The philosophical dramas *Theaetetus*, *Euthyphro*, and *Cratylus* have shown that the human soul is essentially characterized by the erotic motion of learning. To bring this motion to a standstill would be to cease being human. But this means that human being is, paradoxically, the kind of entity that must move and grow, must *change*, in order to stay the same. The seemingly ridiculous eventuality that Socrates feared early on (*Theaetetus* 181a-b) has come to pass: the truth falls somewhere in between Parmenides and Heraclitus.

One consequence of the paradoxes and ambiguities unearthed in the trilogy *Theaetetus*, *Euthyphro*, and *Cratylus* is that these dialogues are open-ended in a way that invites further critical reflection on Socrates' understanding of what it is to be human and of the relationship between philosophy and politics. The trilogy is in this sense incomplete, as is apparent in its multiple anticipations of both Socrates' public trial and the Stranger's philosophical indictment. During the *Sophist* and *Statesman*, Socrates will imitate the silence of Cratylus in the *Cratylus*, and of the Athenian jury in the *Apology*, as he listens to the Stranger's ostensibly purifying divisions. It may not be easy to tell who is judging whom. Nor should we overlook the possibility that in the philosophic trial the most eloquent silence of all will turn out to be that of Plato.

PART TWO

THE STRANGER

It is necessary for one who aims at the middle ground first to avoid the extreme that is more opposed to it, and just as Calypso advises "keep your ship away from this spray and surf." For of the extremes one is more in error and the other less so. Since, then, it is extremely difficult to hit the mean, we must, as they say, make a second sailing and take the least of the ills, and this will be achieved especially in the way we are describing.

Aristotle, *Nicomachean Ethics*

Chapter 6

The Challenge of Philosophy: The *Sophist*

The reason why certain souls endowed with finesse are not geometricians is that they are not able to apply themselves to the principles of geometry, but the reason why geometricians lack finesse is that they cannot see that which is in front of them.

Blaise Pascal, *Pensées*

Socrates encounters the Eleatic Stranger on the day after he converses with Theaetetus and Theodorus, Euthyphro, and Hermogenes and Cratylus. These earlier conversations, which occur under the shadow of Socrates' impending trial, collectively weave the horizon of dramatic and thematic expectations within which Plato invites us to approach the *Sophist* and *Statesman*. As we have seen, the *Theaetetus*, *Euthyphro*, and *Cratylus* are particularly concerned with the philosophical and political implications of Socrates' manner of caring for human souls. Taken together, these dialogues portray Socrates as a fundamentally intermediate figure who is guided by a deep appreciation of the daimonic wholeness that is our uniquely human unique potential. Put in somewhat different terms, Socrates appears to be an exemplar of *phronêsis*, or what the Stranger will later speak of as nonarithmetical measurement relative to "the mean, the fitting, the opportune, and the needful, and all that is settled in the middle ground and away from the extremes" (*Statesman* 284e6-8). The *Theaetetus* familiarizes us with Socrates, the midwife, who, like Artemis, helps young souls to cross the threshold of human maturity. Socrates' way of life also emerges in the *Theaetetus* as one that traverses the middle ground between Theodorus's apolitical theorizing

167

and Protagoras's antiphilosophical politics. In the *Euthyphro*, the abstractness of the city's manner of caring for its citizens serves as a foil for the concreteness of Socrates' appreciation of the finite contexts of human experience, contexts structured by the legitimate demands of custom and convention as well as nature and by the promise of becoming fully human as well as the obligations of citizenship. Finally, the *Cratylus* confronts the problem of the impurity of Socrates' circle thinking by dramatizing the daimonic intermediacy of the soul and the necessarily prophetic character of philosophical speech. In all three of these dialogues, Socrates demonstrates the soul's ability to find the middle ground and to take its own measure through its erotic openness to the whole of things. In all three, moreover, the measureless alternative of Protagorean sophistry appears as the most serious and persistent rival to Socratic philosophizing.

In the *Sophist*, Protagorean sophistry is once again paired with Theodorean mathematics. Socrates' impersonation of the dead sophist in the *Theaetetus* is subtly answered in the *Sophist* by the Eleatic Stranger's employment of a quasi-mathematical method that obscures the difference between human beings on the one hand and plants and animals on the other. Notwithstanding the Stranger's apparent seriousness, however, there are reasons to believe that he speaks for a philosophical method that flatters both Theodorus and Protagoras in the same manner that Socrates spoke for their ways of thinking in the *Theaetetus*, namely, with the intention of accomplishing an internal critique or refutation. If this interpretation is correct, the presence of the Stranger on the day after their discussion with Socrates gives Theodorus and his students yet another opportunity to become acquainted with the limits of mathematical thinking, or to acquire knowledge about their own ignorance.

I wish to suggest that in the *Sophist* and the *Statesman* the Stranger speaks as one who combines *l'esprit de finesse* with *l'esprit de géometrie*, or who, in Leo Strauss's formulation, is sensitive to both of two opposed charms while refusing to succumb to either one: "the charm of competence which is engendered by mathematics and everything akin to mathematics," and "the charm of humble awe, which is engendered by meditation on the human soul and its experiences."[1] Certain of the virtues of Socratic thinking, as we shall see, shine all the more brightly in the light of the Stranger's implicit *reductio* of technical philosophizing in the *Sophist*. Yet this does not mean that Socrates is free and clear of all charges pertaining to sophistry. For in the fifth division of the sophist (226b-231b) the Stranger violates the rules of his own method of division, and formulates an implicit indictment of Socrates that does not presuppose the philosophical adequacy of this method. This indictment, moreover, has to do precisely with Socrates' lack of measure or *phronêsis*. Nor is the *Sophist* the last word of the philosophical trial. To judge by its title alone, the *Statesman* promises a reconsideration of Socrates' case with a view to more specifically political concerns. And in the *Statesman*, I shall argue, the Stranger still more explicitly confirms both his philosophical kinship with Socrates and, paradoxically, the accuracy of Socrates' prophecy about his punitive intentions.

So as not to get too far ahead of ourselves, let us note here simply that the themes of measure and intermediacy and the issue of sophistry surface immediately in the dialogue's opening passages. These passages pose the question of the Stranger's identity in such a way as to link the questions "Who is Socrates?" and "Who is the Stranger?" with each other, and with the fundamental problem with which the *Sophist* is concerned, namely, "Who or what is the sophist?" The preliminary exchange between Socrates, Theodorus, and the Stranger also alerts us to the range of dramatic possibilities inherent in the *Sophist* and the *Statesman*, possibilities that bear directly on the outcome of Socrates' philosophic trial. It does so in part by allowing us to view the encounter between Socrates and the Stranger through the lens of a richly ambiguous Homeric subtext, and in part by way of a number of deft dramatic touches that resonate with certain themes with which we are already familiar from the preceding dialogues.

Gods, Philosophers, and Sophists

The first lines of the *Sophist* are reminiscent of the first lines of the *Cratylus* in that both call attention, in precisely the same way, to the prelinguisitic visibility of beings. This seems more than coincidental, since Socrates' suggestion at the end of the *Cratylus* that we should learn about beings apart from names turns out to be a practical necessity in the case of the Stranger. Theodorus employs a demonstrative pronoun in introducing the Stranger: "We are leading this here man [*tonde*], a sort of stranger, from Elea in kind [*genos*], a companion of those in the circle of Parmenides and Zeno, and a very philosophic man" (216a2-4).[2] Although the Stranger of whom Theodorus speaks is directly visible to the assembled company in a way that he cannot be to Plato's readers, there is nevertheless some question of just what it is that they see before them. As he will do also at the beginning of the *Statesman*, Socrates reprimands Theodorus for his poor powers of observation. Can he have failed to notice that the companion he has brought with him is, "in accordance with Homer's speech, not a stranger but some god?" For Homer declares that "the god of strangers in particular is a companion to those human beings who share in a just reverent shame [*aidous dikaias*], and looks down upon the acts of hybris and law-abidingness [*eunomias*] of human beings." So perhaps, Socrates speculates, Theodorus has brought with him "some refutative [*elengtikos*] god," who intends to "look over and refute us who are poor [*phaulous*] in speeches" (216a5-b6).

While Socrates suggests that the Stranger has come to judge him, this passage is ambiguous with respect to the verdict he expects to receive. It is possible to read his remarks as a hopeful appeal to a superior court of justice: if Socrates cannot expect a fair judgment from his fellow citizens, perhaps he will receive satisfaction from this Zeus-like Stranger.[3] It is worth noting in this connection that the Stranger later refers to an instance in which Zeus quite unambiguously adjudicated a dispute between Atreus and Thyestes as to who was the legitimate king (*Statesman* 269a). On the other hand, Socrates alludes to two different passages from the *Odyssey* that suggest this *xenos*, this foreign guest and stranger, has come to condemn him. In the first, Odysseus warns the Cyclops Polyphemus to show reverence before "Zeus, the god of strangers, who accompanies reverent strangers" (*Odyssey* 9.269-271); in the second, an anonymous suitor of Penelope rebukes Antinoos for having rudely struck the beggar (Odysseus in disguise): "And the gods, resembling strangers from other lands, take on all shapes and visit cities, looking over the hybris and law-abidingness of human beings" (*Odyssey* 17.485-487). If we are to consider his identity in terms of these Homeric passages, the Stranger resembles either an invisible god who accompanies strangers (such as the foreigner Theodorus) or a human being disguised as a beggar who is mistakenly suspected of being a god. Socrates' allusions are no less ambiguous with regard to his own identity: he compares himself either to an anonymous individual who is about to be slain by Odysseus or to a monster who is soon to be punished by him with the help of Zeus. In either case, however, Socrates figures as a hybristic wrongdoer and the Stranger as someone who will justly punish him for his misdeeds.

Socrates implies that any punishment he might receive at the hands of the Stranger would take the form of *elenchos* or refutation. What is to be refuted, one might well suppose, is a claim that Socrates makes explicitly in the *Apology* and that the action of the *Theaetetus*, *Euthyphro*, and *Cratylus* has helped to support: the claim that he is not a sophist. It is important to remember that we come to the *Sophist* already equipped with some idea of what sophistry is. The paradigmatic example of Protagoras, together with Socrates' present reference to those who are both unjust and poor in speeches, leads us to expect that any accusation of sophistry—regardless of the specific form it may take—will be a two-pronged indictment involving the charge of bad citizenship as well as bad philosophizing. If the Stranger intends to show that Socrates is a sophist, he will have to establish that he is guilty on at least one of these counts.

The Homeric atmosphere in which the Stranger is introduced might be taken to promise a subsequent narrative revealing who or what he is. What the Stranger intends to do, however, is as yet by no means clear. Theodorus, for one, does not suppose that he has come to punish anyone, for "this is not the Stranger's way [*tropos*]; he is more measured [*metriôteros*] than those who are serious about eristic disputes." The Stranger is not a god, he adds, but divine, "for I address all the philosophers as such" (216b7-c1). Theodorus here accomplishes the first division of the *Sophist*. In doing so, he suggests that he stands to learn nothing new from the Stranger's inquiry because he already knows what a sophist is. His distinction between the measured speech of genuine philosophers and the immoderate contentiousness of others is, among other things, a pointed way of praising the Stranger at the expense of Socrates: Socrates' zeal for disputation (cf. *Theaetetus* 169a-b) makes him a sham philosopher or sophist. Theodorus makes no distinction, however, between the sort of disputation that is purely eristic or contentious and the sort that is elenctic or refutative; only the latter, we may note, is pursued by the practitioners of "noble" sophistry who closely resemble Socrates (cf. 230d1). More important, Theodorus assumes that the Stranger exhibits a single and unvarying "way" or "turn" (*tropos*) of character, and that this is the way of the philosopher. He does not entertain the possibility just hinted at by Socrates: that even if he is a philosopher, the Stranger, no less than a (Homeric) god or a sophist, may be a man of *many* ways and turns—a *polutropos anêr*, like Odysseus (*Odyssey* 1.1). If he is, it will not be easy to identify him—or even, as we shall soon see, to understand the point and purpose of his speeches.

Socrates' response to Theodorus illustrates his own capacity for ironic or polytropic speech. The family (*genos*) of philosophers, he explains, is not much easier to discern than that of gods:

> For these men—those who not in a counterfeit way [*plastôs*] but in their being are philosophers—certainly show up in all sorts of semblances [*pantoioi phantazomenoi*] on account of the ignorance of the rest of men, and they "visit cities" [*Odyssey* 17.486], looking down from on high at the life of those below. And to some they seem to be worth nothing, and to others worth everything. And sometimes they take on the semblance [*phantazontai*] of statesmen, and sometimes sophists, and sometimes there are those to whom they might furnish the impression that they are in every way mad [*pantapasin echontes manikôs*]. (216c4-d2)

Socrates introduces in this passage the distinction between image and original around which the search for the sophist will revolve. There are philosophers, and then there are those who are not philosophers even though they may look like them. Paradoxically, genuine philosophers do not look like philosophers to nonphilosophers, but rather like sophists, statesmen, or madmen. Matters are further complicated by the fact that Socrates appeals here to the distorted image of the philosopher with which he flattered Theodorus in the digression of the *Theaetetus*. Like his counterpart in the *Theaetetus*, the "philosopher" Socrates describes here looks down upon human life from a godly vantage point. He also travels from city to city. In both of these respects he resembles Protagoras and Theodorus far more than Socrates (cf. *Theaetetus* 152c, 161c). From Socrates' point of view, Theodorus is arguably a sophist: his abstractly theoretical way of life, we recall, proved to be politically and philosophically hardly less defective than that of Protagoras. It is likely, however, that Socrates' comments are directed more to the visitor from Elea than to the middleman Theodorus, who, for the second day in a row, has introduced Socrates to someone worth talking to. As a member of the Eleatic circle, the Stranger might be expected to hold himself above the perplexity of ordinary mortals after the manner of Parmenides, a thinker whose famous poem "On Nature" presented his teaching as the revelation of a goddess that was delivered to him in her sacred dwelling "truly far from the beaten path of human beings." [4]

Socrates' remarks invite us to ponder the meaning of the strangeness of the Stranger. Among other things, we may wonder how his strangeness is related to Socrates' outlandishness, his oddly provocative quality of seeming to be simultaneously out of place and in place, Athenian and foreign, civilized and yet somehow wild. In his nature Socrates embodies the paradoxical doubleness of irony; although an Athenian, he is genuinely exotic in a way that the *xenos* Theodorus, for example, is not. What about the Stranger? Socrates' speech about those who are "really" or "in their being" (*ontôs*) philosophers did not contradict Theodorus's attribution to the Stranger of a single, consistent *tropos*. Indeed, he appeals only to the ignorance of human beings in accounting for the semblances or false images (*phantasmata*) that shroud philosophers when they visit cities. While Homer makes much of the Olympians' power to disguise themselves by assuming alien looks, Socrates says nothing of this in his comparison of philosophers to gods. If the Stranger is a "philosopher" such as Socrates describes, he is by nature simple and only superficially strange and complex—not inherently polyeidetic or polytropic after the manner of Socrates. In that case, however, we have some reason to believe that Socrates would consider him to be a sophist rather than a philosopher. [5]

Let us pause to see where we now stand. In the dialogue's final division, the Stranger will define the sophist as a maker of false images in speech (265a-268d). If the present interpretation is correct, Socrates has just furnished us with what he regards as a false image of the philosopher. In terms of the Stranger's explicit teaching, Socrates thus appears to be a sophist. Even if warranted by the division in question, however, this inference does not prove that the Stranger believes that Socrates is a sophist. In order legitimately to reach that conclusion, we would have to know that the Stranger is willing to say just what he means and is able to do so within the parameters of his method. Among other things, this means that we would have to know something essential about the Stranger's character—about who he is. But Socrates has just finished emphasizing at length the likelihood that the Stranger's identity or nature is hidden from us. To take the Stranger simply at his word is to suppose, with Theodorus, that he is more like the simple and truth-telling Achilles than the wily Odysseus. We could know this, however, only on the basis of what the Stranger does, not just what he says. "As hateful to me as the gates of Hades is that man who hides one thing in his heart, but says another," Achilles says accusingly to Odysseus in the *Iliad* (9.312-313). In the *Odyssey*, however, Odysseus repeats this same phrase almost verbatim when he appears in Ithaca disguised as a beggar—but his intention on that occasion is to make the swineherd Eumaeus believe that he *is* lying (14.156-157). In sum, Plato leaves no doubt that the *Sophist* cannot be understood without attention to what the Stranger shows of himself in his *deeds* as well as what he says in *argument*. It is hard to think of another Platonic dialogue in which the interpretative priority of drama to explicit argumentation is made so clear.

Unfortunately, the Stranger's deeds are in themselves no less questionable than his speeches. There are several clear indications at the beginning of the *Sophist* that the Stranger fits the picture of the sophist that has emerged in the earlier dialogues of the philosophic trial, a picture that is supported by Socrates' encounters elsewhere in the Platonic corpus with the likes of Gorgias, Protagoras, Hippias, and their students. Interestingly, Socrates asks the Stranger not what *he* believes about the sophist, statesman, and philosopher, but what "those in that place believed about these things and how they named them" (216d3-217a1). The place or region (*topos*) to which he refers is, of course, uncertain; one of the open questions in this connection is what it means to the Stranger to be "from Elea," and whether he thinks of this as a political as well as a philosophical affiliation. At any rate, the Stranger does not choose to shift the terms of Socrates' question in any way, nor does he explicitly suggest that he would not vouch for the speech he is about to give. This speech, however, does not spring from his own intellectual efforts, but is one that "he claims to have heard adequately and not forgotten" (217b7-8; cf. *Meno* 71c-d). Our dawning impression that the Stranger regards teaching and learning as the more or less mechanical transmission of a

logos from the full soul of a knowing teacher to the empty one of an ignorant pupil (cf. *Protagoras* 313d-314c) is strengthened by his preference for an interlocutor who will answer "painlessly and tractably"
(217d1-2). The text also seems to hint that the Stranger's idea of teaching
is more like serving up tasty dishes (cf. *Gorgias* 464b-466a) than inducing psychic labor: Socrates inquires of him "with pleasure," asking him
to speak to his question "if it is pleasing [*philon*] to him" and in whatever
way is "more pleasing," and the Stranger, for his part, is above all concerned to gratify (*charizesthai*) his hosts (216d3, 217c3, e5). On the other
hand, the Stranger is clearly reluctant to go through a long and laborious
speech (cf. 217b). He claims to feel shame at the prospect of putting on
an *epideixis* or "exhibition" (217e2)—a term regularly associated with
the public presentations of the sophists and rhetoricians (*Hippias Major*
282b ff., *Hippias Minor* 363a, *Gorgias* 447a, *Protagoras* 328d)—and he
complies with Socrates' request only because to do otherwise would be
to act in a manner that is "unsuited to a stranger" and "wild" or "savage"
(*axenon ti . . . kai agrion*: 217e6-218a1). Perhaps the Stranger really
means to say that it is Socrates who is behaving in a rude and uncivilized
way. Socrates' earlier comparison of himself to Polyphemus seems apt at
least in one respect: while in the Homeric world the host ordinarily feeds
a *xenos* before asking him who he is (see, for example, Telemachus's re-
ception by Menelaus and Helen in Book 4 of the *Odyssey*), Socrates, like
the Cyclops Polyphemus, immediately begins to interrogate his guest.
The Stranger's reference to wildness may carry a hint of sympathy with
Protagoras's and Theodorus's criticism of Socrates for the pain he typically causes both himself and others in the process of learning (*Theaetetus* 168a-b, 169a-b).

    If anything, the Stranger's subsequent investigation of the nature of the
sophist reinforces the impression that there is something sophistical
about his own manner of inquiry. This can be seen from a cursory inspection of his conclusions. The *Sophist* contains six divisions, each of
which defines the sophist in a different way; hence it will be convenient
to speak of Sophists I through VI, assigning each kind of sophist a number in accordance with the division in which it is identified.[6] Sophist II is
defined as a merchant of learnings (*mathêmata*) who goes from city to
city selling the art of virtue, an art that is not his own product but that he
initially acquired from another (223c-224d). Sophist IIIa differs from
Sophist II in two respects: he stays within the city rather than traveling
from city to city, and he sells some lessons produced by another and
some that he has devised on his own (224d-e). Sophist IIIa subsequently
changes form when the Stranger and Theaetetus summarize their discussion at 231c-e: in this summary he splits in two, showing up both as one
who stays within the city selling lessons that he has purchased from an-

other (Sophist IIIb), and as one who stays within the city selling lessons that he has devised on his own (Sophist IIIc). Neither Sophist IIIb nor Sophist IIIc, we may note, are identical with Sophist IIIa. While we shall soon return to the implications of this interesting fact, let us observe here that, according to the Stranger, where one obtains and sells one's lessons are matters irrelevant to the question of whether one is a sophist. Sophists II, IIIa, IIIb, and IIIc cover all permutations or combinations with respect to the origins and markets of teachings except the case of a man traveling from city to city selling lessons pertaining to virtue that he himself has produced either wholly or in part. But given the Stranger's way of thinking about the matter, there seems to be no good reason to deny that such a man would also be a sophist.

The point at which I am driving is this: the latter description roughly fits the Stranger. The Stranger is a man who travels outside of his own city and exchanges, in return for the gratitude of his auditors (218a; cf. *Statesman* 257a), a teaching about sophistry. Broadly defined, this teaching consists not only in the content of the Stranger's speech about sophistry, but also in the philosophical method (*methodos*) that he employs in hunting the sophist and that he calls the "way of division" (*tropos tês diaireseôs*: 235c8). While the Stranger claims to have heard his speech about sophistry from another, it is unclear whether the same is true of his method. As we have seen, however, the fact that he might himself have fabricated part of his teaching would not disqualify him from being a sophist. Less clear is whether someone who makes no money from teaching can properly be called a sophist. As we shall see, the Stranger implies that the counterfeit character of the sophist's product is more decisive with regard to his identity than the fact that he makes money from selling it. One should also note that, while Sophists I through IV all make money, Sophist V (226b-231b) does not; if anything, he earns his wages in gratitude for having liberated his interlocutors from opinions that stand in the way of learning (cf. 230b-d). Moneymaking may be a common feature of sophistry, but Sophist V shows that it cannot be an essential one. We must next ask whether the Stranger teaches an art of virtue. To begin with, he certainly presents his method of division as an art. The *genos* of the sophist, according to the Stranger, is "difficult and hard to hunt down [*dusthêreuton*]" (218d3); yet the sophist must be hunted because he is a *thêr*, a "wild beast" (235a10). Hunting shows up as an art in the fourth step of the angler division (219e), and the Stranger underscores the artfulness of his own way of division in boasting that it can capture any *genos* (235c4-6). Furthermore, he states that dividing according to natural kinds (*genê*) is characteristic of "the dialectical science" (253d1-3). The Stranger also regards the method of division as an essential component of his teaching. In the

Statesman he tells Young Socrates that revealing the nature of the statesman is less important than "honor[ing] the method itself of the capacity to divide according to kinds [*eidê*]" (286d9). Finally, the Stranger comes close to identifying his artful method of division with virtue. To honor this method, he says, is to honor the excellence of mind (*nous*: 227a-b). Those who possesses the dialectical capacity exemplify the virtue of philosophizing "purely and justly" (253e4-6), as is confirmed by the method's ability to isolate the sophist as an ignorant imitator of justice and virtue (267c ff.).

I do not insist that the Stranger's divisions unambiguously imply that he himself is a sophist. To say the least, however, they do little to alleviate the doubts about his philosophical *persona* that are raised at the beginning of the dialogue. These persistent doubts, moreover, provoke questions about the adequacy of the Stranger's divisions, and raise the possibility that the nature of sophistry might in some important respects be manifested in his own conduct. It may be, in other words, that the Stranger himself dramatically exemplifies the nature of the sophist, and thereby—borrowing a page from Socrates' book—*shows* in the *Sophist* what he fails to *say*. Any account of the *Sophist* along these lines will of course have to explain why Plato chose to approach the matter of sophistry in this seemingly oblique fashion.

In the present chapter I shall pursue the interpretative suggestions set forth above. It seems fitting to preface this task, however, with a consideration of the interpretative circle into which we inevitably enter when we attempt to make inferences about who the Stranger is on the basis of his conduct. We observed earlier that the Stranger's speeches cannot be understood in isolation from his deeds. His deeds, however, are no more transparent with respect to their significance than his speeches. Let us agree that the Stranger acts like a sophist: what follows from this? One might conclude that he is in fact a sophist, except that, as Socrates has already observed, philosophers may sometimes *look like* sophists. Who we think the Stranger is, in turn, will determine what exactly we think he is doing in the *Sophist*. If we suppose that the Stranger is a sophist, his speeches and deeds will mean one thing, but if we think that he is a philosopher, they will mean something else.

The best illustration of the latter point is provided by the *Hippias Minor*, in which the polytropic nature of the philosophical soul occupies center stage. In the course of his debate with Hippias, Socrates links the philosopher with the shifting and shifty figure of Odysseus in a manner that helps us to appreciate the aptness of the philosophic trial's Homeric subtext. Perhaps most important, the *Hippias Minor* corrects Socrates' suggestion that if philosophers look like sophists it is only because of the ignorance of those to whom they appear: in the *Hippias Minor* Socrates

chooses to look like a sophist because it serves his philosophical purposes to do so. I shall argue that the same is true of the Stranger's conduct in the *Sophist*. A brief consideration of the *Hippias Minor* will also
help to attune us to the sophistical character of the Stranger's technical
understanding of the human soul.

Philosophical Polytropism: The *Hippias Minor*

The debate that takes place in the *Hippias Minor* occurs just after the
sophist Hippias has made a display (*epideixis*) on the topic of Homer
(363a-b). Hippias mentions in his very first speech his willingness to answer any question at the Olympic festivals—where he presumably com-
peted as a rhapsode—and by subsequently proclaiming that, "since the
time when I began to compete [*agônizesthai*] at the Olympic games, I
have never yet met anyone who is better than me in anything" (364a7-
9).[7] It is within this distinctly disputatious or eristic atmosphere that Socrates introduces a question about the difference between Odysseus and
Achilles. Hippias answers that Homer made Achilles the best (*ariston*) of
the men who went to Troy, Nestor the wisest, and Odysseus the most
wily or polytropic (*polutropôtaton*: 364c5-7). Socrates agrees that
Achilles is the best. "But," he claims with obvious irony, "when you said
that the poet made Odysseus the wiliest, in this, to tell you the truth, I
altogether do not know what you are saying. . . . Hasn't Homer made
Achilles wily [*polutropos*]?" (364e1-6). Certainly not, says Hippias, and
he cites Achilles' rebuke of Odysseus at *Iliad* 9.312-313 (quoted above)
as proof of the *tropos* or turn of each man's moral character (364e-365b).
Achilles is the better man because he is true and simple (*alêthês te kai
haplous*) while Odysseus is wily and false or lying (*polutropos te kai
pseudês*: 365b4-5). Liars, furthermore, are according to Hippias "very
capable of doing many things and especially of deceiving human beings"
(365d7-8). As such, they are polytropic individuals who "work ills"
(*kakourgousin*) and who are characterized by *panourgia*, the unscrupulous readiness to "do anything" (365e4-9).

   Just prior to the latter clarifications, Socrates observes that since one
cannot ask Homer what he was thinking when he wrote his poems, Hippias must speak on Homer's behalf (365d). Because we confront precisely the same limitation in interpreting the Platonic texts, we cannot be
certain whether Hippias is speaking straightforwardly or deceptively in
praising the simple and true character of Achilles and condemning the
complex and versatile character of Odysseus. At the very least, however,
it seems fair to say that his interpretation of Homer's Odysseus is one-
sided insofar as it abstracts Odysseus's polytropism from its prudential
uses as an indispensable instrument of survival, and indeed of divine jus-

tice, in hostile contexts—including in particular the two Odyssean contexts to which Socrates alludes at the beginning of the *Sophist*. We may note in this connection that the ambiguity of Odysseus's character led poets after Homer to portray him in virtually as many different guises as the sophist assumes in the *Sophist*.[8]

Socrates' interpretation of Homer differs from Hippias's, but is in its own way no less one-sided. As we have already seen, Socrates claims to agree with Hippias that Achilles was the best of the men who went to Troy. Yet he argues that Achilles was best precisely because he, like Odysseus, was a wily liar. In the light of what we know both about Socrates and about Homer's Achilles, it seems clear that Socrates' argument is ironic, or that what he says is not just what he means. Put another way, Socrates defends Achilles in an Odyssean or polytropic manner. Hippias shares this impression of Socrates, but infers that he, like Odysseus, is a base and unscrupulous individual. In particular, Socrates impresses him as one who argues "ignobly" (370e5), "works ill" in speeches (*kakourgounti*: 373b5), and advocates a "terrible" thesis (375d3) just in order to prove to those present that he is the better speaker.

In the *Hippias Minor*, Socrates does indeed beat Hippias at his own eristic game. He does so, moreover, by knowingly employing bad arguments.[9] In other words, Socrates' resemblance to a sophist in the *Hippias Minor* is not just a matter of the ignorance of others. He chooses to behave in a way that he knows will foster the impression that Hippias already has of him, namely, that he is an essentially contentious individual who will do anything to win an argument (cf. 369b-c). In fact, Socrates' explicit denial of the difference between the characters of Achilles and Odysseus is curiously mirrored in the drama of the dialogue, wherein the philosopher and the eristic sophist seem to trade places: it is Hippias, not Socrates, who protests against the use of shameful arguments in the pursuit of victory at all costs.

While Socrates undeniably shows himself to be a polytropic individual, it does not follow that Hippias is right about his character and motives. Hippias's impression of Socrates tells us as much about the former as it does about the latter, as it is doubtless shaped by his own fundamentally agonistic—or better, antagonistic—understanding of argument. To this extent, ignorance about the nature of philosophers, and in particular about their uncommon *erôs*, does play a role in shaping the semblance or phantasm of Socrates as a sophist that presents itself to the mind of Hippias. Yet it is nonetheless true that in the *Hippias Minor* Socrates advances a philosophical criticism of sophistry precisely *by means of* his success in looking like a sophist. Socrates may hope that his criticism will be understood by some of the assembled bystanders (cf. 363a), but, as is the case in other dialogues, the philosophical implications of his speeches and deeds will be most fully accessible to Plato's readers. This does not mean, however, that in the last analysis Socrates did not intend to look like a sophist. It is precisely by looking *like* a sophist—by presenting an image that is, as such, other than the original, but that is nonetheless so similar to the original that some will mistake the two— that Socrates manages to teach us something about sophistry. Read in this way, the *Hippias Minor* constitutes a dramatic defense of philosophical polytropism.

Socrates' philosophical goal in the *Hippias Minor* is to expose the moral and theoretical deficiencies of Hippias's implicit identification of virtue with the possession of technical capabilities. Although Hippias does not claim to teach virtue as a particular art, he does pride himself on his expertise in a great variety of theoretical and productive *technai* (366c-368e). More to the point, his conception of his own distinctive excellence, an excellence that shines forth most fully in the arena of competition, is rooted in his possession of technical knowledge. Thus he has been heard to boast that he is "altogether the wisest [*sophôtatos*] of all human beings in the greatest number of arts" (368b2-3), and he does not dispute Socrates' repeated identification of wisdom (*sophia*) with technical expertise (368b-c; cf. 364a, 372b-c). As is confirmed by his inability to block the shameful consequences of Socrates' argument, Hippias understands virtue to be the mastery of many *technai*. In the *Hippias Minor*, Socrates indirectly attacks this common sophistical identification of virtue with *technê* by showing that it leads to the absurd conclusion that the good man is he who willingly goes wrong and does shameful and unjust things.[10]

Some may be inclined to reject this interpretation of the *Hippias Minor* on the ground that Socrates himself is regularly presented as seeking a *technê* of virtue.[11] I would reply that this common impression of what Socrates is doing in the dialogues goes to the heart of my disagreement with orthodox Plato scholarship, insofar as it is rooted in habits of reading that are more appropriate to treatises than to philosophical dramas. Socrates' treatment of virtue in the *Hippias Minor* is in my view a paradigmatic illustration of Platonic irony. A full defense of my interpretation of the *Hippias Minor* would require a careful study of the ways in which Platonic irony is at work in the many other dialogues in which virtue appears to be modeled on *technê*. Fortunately, David Roochnik has recently authored just such a study.[12] Perhaps it is sufficient to add that our ability fully to appreciate the philosophical significance of Socrates' speeches and deeds depends upon our willingness to acknowledge the fundamentally polytropic character of Platonic writing.

Socrates' debate with Hippias proceeds as follows. Hippias initially identifies the truthful man and the good man, and asserts that the truthful

(*alêthês*) man and the lying (*pseudês*) man are "most opposite to one another" (366a5-6). He admits, however, that liars are "capable and prudent
and knowing and wise in the things in respect to which they lie" (366a2-
4), since they are able to speak falsely and deceive others in these things
whenever they wish to do so. It is at this point that Socrates introduces
technê as a model of knowledge. To be a consistent liar about the matters
with which a given art is concerned, one must be knowing and capable in
that art, for otherwise one might unwillingly speak the truth. But one
who is knowing and capable in an art is good in that art, and is able to
speak the truth about the matters to which the art pertains. Socrates thus
forces Hippias to admit that, with respect to a given art, the truthful and
good man—the man who is technically capable, and who therefore has
the power to speak the truth about the matters with which his art is concerned—is the same as the liar. On this basis, Socrates asks whether it
does not follow that "if Odysseus was a liar, he becomes also truthful,
and if Achilles was truthful, he becomes also a liar, and the men are not
different from one another, nor opposites, but similar?" (369b4-7).

Presumably because he has grown used to thinking of virtue according
to the model of technical knowledge or capability, Hippias does not
counter Socrates' crucial, unsupported move from capacity to disposition, or from the technical to the moral sense of goodness. Hippias thus
agrees that justice is a certain power (*dunamis*) or science (*epistêmê*), or
both (375d-e). In this respect it resembles archery (375a ff.), an analogy
that is cleverly chosen by Socrates because the word that literally means
"to miss the mark" (*hamartanein*) also means "to go wrong." Does it not
follow, Socrates argues, that just as the archer who willingly misses the
mark is better in archery than the one who does so involuntarily, the soul
that willingly does wrong is better than the one that does wrong involuntarily, because it is more capable and knowledgeable in justice? And
does this not mean that the one who willingly goes wrong (*hamartanôn*)
and does shameful and unjust things has a good soul and so is the good
man (376a-b)? While Hippias objects to this conclusion, his conception
of justice as an artful power leaves him no means to argue against it. In
the end, Hippias proves unable to cure Socrates of this "seizure"
(*katêbolê*) of shameful belief—a pathological condition (*pathêma*) of the
soul for which Socrates significantly blames "the preceding speeches"
(372e1-4). The sophists, it seems, offer no remedy for the ethical diseases they help to induce.

Socrates' behavior in the *Hippias Minor* beautifully illustrates the
practical implications of Hippias's sophistical conception of virtue as
technical capability. In the course of his argument with Hippias, Socrates
advances an interpretation of the characters of Odysseus and Achilles
that Homer's text obviously does not support: "Odysseus, the wily one,

nowhere evidently lies, but Achilles appears to be someone wily . . . he lies, at any rate" (369e5-370a2). Socrates cites as evidence of Achilles' "artful contriving and lying" (371d6) the fact that in the *Iliad* he tells Agamemnon and Odysseus that he will return home to Phthia (1.169-171, 9.357-363), but later, when speaking to Ajax, implies that he will remain with the army (9.650-655). Hippias responds with the reasonable suggestion that these passages merely reflect Achilles' uncertainty about what he will do (371d-e).[13] In pressing his reading of Homer, Socrates knowingly "misses the mark," just as he willingly goes wrong in advocating the unjust and shameful thesis that the good man willingly does shameful and unjust things. And although he is most unwilling to accede to the argument's conclusion, Hippias, in turn, is compelled to admit that shameful consequences follow from his own views (cf. 375d with 376c). Measured by the technical standards for which he argues—standards that really belong to Hippias—Socrates proves to be better than Hippias in the arena that matters most to the sophist. Socrates' deeds seem to harmonize completely with his speeches.

But what does Socrates in fact *do* in the *Hippias Minor*? Hippias infers from the look of Socrates' speeches and deeds that he is an eristic sophist. This is an inference, not just about Socrates' particular purposes on the occasion of their conversation, but about his comprehensive desire or desires. It is furthermore an inference that is conditioned by Hippias's own eristic nature.[14] As I have attempted to show, however, a different intuition about Socrates' *erôs* leads to a very different interpretation of the *same* sophistical look. One of the main lessons of the *Hippias Minor* is that philosophers, no less than sophists, are polytropic, so that to distinguish their various looks is not the same thing as to grasp their purposes. Yet it is only on the level of purpose, the level of the soul's guiding erotic orientation and the whole way of life that follows from it, that we may catch sight of the fundamental differences between the philosopher and the sophist.[15]

Dramatizing Sophistry:
The Stranger's Way and the First Five Divisions

At the beginning of the *Sophist* Socrates presents us with a tentative divination about the Stranger: he might be a refutative god. On its surface, the *Hippias Minor* provides good evidence of the hybristic injustice in speech that Socrates supposes the Stranger has come to punish. The *Hippias Minor*'s deeper implication for our reading of the *Sophist*, however, is that we cannot understand the meaning of the Stranger's speeches and deeds independently of a prophecy or divination about his intrinsic nature. We need not agree with Socrates' guess about the

Stranger's identity, but we are nonetheless obliged to follow his interpretative example.

The *Hippias Minor* is relevant to the *Sophist* in other respects as well.
Socrates is able to obscure the difference between Odysseus and Achilles, and to misrepresent the characters of both men, only because he considers artful power or capacity (*dunamis*) independently of the overall
disposition of the soul of the one who possesses this power. The method
of division employed by the Stranger in the search for the sophist proceeds along the same lines: the sophist is to be identified by the nature of
the art that he practices (221d).[16] What is more, the method is unsuited to
the evaluation of character because it is by official declaration value-free:
in trying to understand "the kinship and lack of kinship of all arts"
(227b1) it is supposed to honor all of them equally and to discriminate
like from like without attention to the difference between the better and
the worse. The absurdity of employing this method in the search for the
sophist is suggested by a fact with which we shall soon become better
acquainted, namely, that the Stranger finds it necessary at crucial points
to violate the latter rule. But we now have another way to make the same
point. If someone using the Stranger's method were to describe Socrates
as he is portrayed in the *Hippias Minor*, he would show up in the left-
hand branch of the last step of the fourth division of the sophist (225d-e),
and would be separated from Sophist IV—a practitioner of eristic disputation—only by the fact that he does not make money. To understand
Socrates in this way would be to see him just as he appears to Hippias's
undiscriminating eyes.

Our intuitions about the Stranger's identity do not depend on the
Sophist alone. As we shall see, the Stranger's procedure in the *Statesman*
is more explicitly Socratic in character than in the *Sophist*. And the
Stranger does not in any case consistently adhere to his method in the
search for the sophist. I therefore venture the following hypothesis: the
Stranger is not a sophist, but, like Socrates in the *Hippias Minor*, imitates
the sophist for philosophical and pedagogical purposes. He thereby gives
us a dramatic demonstration of, as well as a *logos* about, the nature of the
sophist. Only in the light of the drama of the *Sophist* can we understand
the defective character of its divisions: the Stranger's definitions of the
sophist are compromised precisely to the extent that they are produced in
a sophistical manner. We gain philosophical insight, however, insofar as
we understand in what respect the Stranger mimetically exemplifies
sophistry. And we gain still deeper insight insofar as we are able to appreciate why the Stranger's teaching about the sophist is shown in this
complex way rather than simply said. The reason, the Stranger himself
suggests, is that to learn about the nature of a human soul through speech
is necessarily to engage in an act of philosophical divination on the basis

of images. In its most fundamental implications, the *Sophist* converges with the *Cratylus*.

The Way of Division: Parmenides, Theodorus, Protagoras

The preceding suggestions will be developed in due time. We return now to the text of the *Sophist*, resuming our investigation just prior to the point where the Stranger introduces his method. The Stranger, we may note, has already had occasion to speak with Theodorus and Theaetetus (cf. 217b, 218a), and it is no doubt on this basis that Theodorus formed such a favorable impression of him. Although he was not willing during this earlier discussion to speak about the sophist, statesman, and philosopher, the Stranger now yields to Socrates' request. One suspects that his earlier reticence is due to the fact that his speech is intended primarily for Socrates' ears. At any rate the Stranger, like Theaetetus, seems to have been impressed by Socrates' reputation prior to meeting him: "In now associating with you for the first time," he tells Socrates, "some reverent shame [*aidôs*] holds me in its grip" (217d8-9). Just before the Stranger makes this comment, Socrates mentions the pedagogical procedure of question and answer employed by Parmenides on the occasion dramatized in the dialogue *Parmenides*—"when I was young, and he was very old indeed" (217c6-7). Uttered in this context, the Stranger's remark calls to mind Socrates' earlier recollection of the shame he felt when he met Parmenides, who then appeared to him to possess "an altogether noble depth" (*Theaetetus* 184a1). These details suggest that Socrates, now himself an old man, elicits from the Stranger something like the reverential respect that he himself once accorded to Parmenides. Perhaps Socrates has fulfilled the philosophical promise that Parmenides saw in him as a young man (*Parmenides* 130e); if so, however, he has done so in his own independent fashion, and without embracing Eleaticism. Socrates thus exemplifies a standard of learning as independent growth that we are implicitly invited to apply to the Stranger in relationship to his teacher Parmenides, and perhaps also in his relationship to Socrates. In the *Sophist*, the Stranger does indeed choose to question Theaetetus much as Parmenides questioned young Aristotle during the long exercise of the *Parmenides* (cf. 217c-d with *Parmenides* 137b-c).[17] If anything, the importance of Socrates' example of independent learning is underscored by the fact that this Aristotle later became one of the Thirty Tyrants (*Parmenides* 127d).

The Stranger tells Theaetetus that their investigation will be a joint effort. The two of them will begin from the sophist, seeking and making evident in speech "whatever he is." For in regard to the sophist they now hold in common only the name, but each might by himself privately possess the deed or work (*ergon*) on account of which they name him "sophist." And, the Stranger asserts, it is always necessary in regard to anything to have reached an agreement about the matter itself (*to pragma auto*) through speeches. But the tribe (*phulon*) or family (*genos*) of the sophist is "harsh and hard to hunt down," and everyone has long opined that it is best in such a case to practice (*meletan*) on smaller and easier matters before tackling "the greatest ones." Hence it seems best to make a practice run (*promeletan*), first selecting something trivial and attempting to establish it "as a paradigm of the greater." The lowly angler, in particular, promises to offer a method (*methodon*) and a speech (*logos*) suited to their purpose (218c1-219a2).

In the foregoing mention of practice we hear a verbal echo of Socrates' notion of care (*meletê*). But the Stranger does not in fact speak for Socrates when he claims to speak for "everyone": while he is concerned to make things easier for Theaetetus and to shield him from the painful experience of sophistry (cf. 234d-e), Socrates confronted the youth with the most challenging of questions without any preparation at all (cf. *Theaetetus* 148c). The Stranger seems concerned to offer his interlocutors an alternative to the harshness and perplexity of an encounter with Socrates. Yet his regular use of paradigms—the angler being but the first of many that will be introduced over the course of the *Sophist* and *Statesman*—may nonetheless point toward a deeper philosophical and pedagogical kinship with Socrates. The word *paradeigma* contains the same ambiguity as the word "model": it can refer either to a replica or image (a model airplane) or to an exemplar ("the very model of a modern major general").[18] Regardless of this ambiguity, a paradigm—like a metaphor, simile, or analogy—does not directly bespeak the being to which it pertains. Rather, it stands alongside of (*para*) another thing so as to bring to light (*deiknunai*) some actual or potential feature of the other's nature. Paradigms thus appeal to the soul's capacity to think through images, or to divine the connection between an illustrative speech and the unspoken nature that it is meant to illuminate. In introducing paradigms into his divisions, the Stranger method seems to combine precision with prophecy.

The preceding suggestions will be further developed when we come to the Stranger's treatment of images. I now turn to some other features of his preliminary remarks. The method of division must be understood in connection with the problems it confronts in attempting to yield a definition of the sophist. The words "family" and "tribe" indicate that the sophist is a living being, with a nature that is independent of our perceptions of it. One must also assume that the sophist reveals his nature in his speeches and deeds, for otherwise the attempt to reach agreement about who or what he is would make no sense. Yet we cannot begin to examine the nature of the sophist directly, but must instead start with the perception, the "work" or "deed" of the sophist, that each of us possesses privately. These private perceptions, in turn, are not the same as the work of the sophist in itself, but—as the Stranger's dynamic language suggests— are in part shaped by the soul's own activity. Socrates alluded to this problem earlier when he mentioned the semblances of the philosopher produced by the ignorance of human beings: sophistry and philosophy affect different souls in different ways. Perhaps most significantly, some are deceived by the speeches of the sophist and some are not.[19]

The fact that the method of division must begin from private perceptions compounds the difficulty of getting a firm grip on the sophist (cf. 226a, 231c, 235a-c). The Stranger nevertheless proposes by means of division to grasp our various private perceptions of the sophist *via* a single common speech, and in such a way as to show forth the sophist's nature as it is in itself. We have already touched upon the two major steps involved in this process. First, the Stranger narrows the subject of investigation by turning from our perceptions of the sophist as a living being, and in particular as a certain kind human being with a particular disposition of soul, to our perceptions of the sophist's art. Second, the Stranger "purifies" our perceptions of this art by separating off any estimates of worth they may contain. The purpose of this twofold process of abstraction is to arrive at the core of common content in our private perceptions about which we may reach public agreement in speech. This common core embraces the formal elements of the sophist's art, which elements may in quasi-arithmetical fashion be divided and then summed by the method of division. About these countable formal elements, the Stranger implies, there will be no disagreement—or, at any rate, we will come to agree if we look closely enough.

That Theodorus prefers the Stranger to Socrates is no surprise, given the affinity between the method of division and arithmetic. Like arithmetic, the Stranger's method lays claim to universal applicability. Any determinate thing may be regarded as a unit and hence may be counted; similarly, the method of division is designed to enumerate the formal elements of any being. By division, the Stranger boasts, he can capture any *genos* (235c). The method also claims to produce accounts that can be publicly certified by common agreement, just as arithmetic does (cf. *Euthyphro* 7b-d). Finally, the method of division, like arithmetic, abstracts from differences in the intrinsic worth of things. All determinate things are equal in the eyes of arithmetic, for they are all equally countable. Things may be numerically unequal, but numbers are multitudes of identical units; as such all are intrinsically alike, and none may meaningfully be said to be "better" or "worse" than any other. So, too, the Stranger's method regards all beings as equal, for their forms are all equally knowable by means of the systematic enumeration of their elements.

In virtue of its ostensible reliability as a way of arriving at knowledge, its definite, precise, and publicly certifiable results, its analytical character, and its neutrality with regard to value, it seems fair to characterize the Stranger's method of division as a technical way of philosophizing. At stake in the success or failure of the application of this method to the characterization of human types is the larger question of whether knowledge about human life can assume a technical form. By his own example, Socrates implies that it cannot.

Let us first note that the Stranger officially disregards the issues of character and erotic orientation that serve in other Platonic contexts to distinguish the sophist from the philosopher.[20] Arts, like bodies, are also formally more stable and internally complete than souls. This point deserves special emphasis. Arts *are* in a way that human souls, which are always coming to be, are not. If—as Socrates regularly suggests—the human soul is essentially characterized by erotic striving, is incomplete or unfinished, and seeks completion through its openness to the whole of things, then it cannot adequately be grasped by a philosophical method that is specifically suited to the articulation of the nature of unchanging beings. To begin with, *erôs* makes the soul polytropic: like a sophist, it is capable of taking on many different (and even inconsistent) looks. The soul's erotic motions and transformations are a resourceful response to its perpetual neediness; because it never ceases to experience lack and longing, however, any list of the elements that make up the look of the soul is necessarily incomplete and provisional. Put another way, the soul has no *eidos* in the specific, technical sense of a stable structure composed of countable formal elements, from which it follows that it cannot be known scientifically or with quasi-mathematical rigor.[21] Perhaps most important, the Stranger's value-free method cannot understand *erôs* in its own terms or from the inside: while such an understanding would involve an appreciation of the beauty, nobility, or goodness of the object of erotic striving, the method of division proceeds as if Protagoras's "human being is the measure of all things" held true for all judgments of worth. In the *Cratylus*, Socrates grounds his philosophical way of life in the daimonic nature of *erôs*. Such Socratic or genuinely hermeneutical self-knowledge, however, is unavailable by means of the method of division. This means that the Stranger cannot consistently make a nonarbitrary case for either the worth of philosophy or the worthlessness of sophistry, which is to say that a slavish adherence to his method would force him ultimately to concur with the Protagorean and Aristophanean analysis of philosophy as merely a peculiar inflection of the will to power. From a Socratic point of view, the Stranger's method represents the capitulation of philosophy to sophistry.[22]

Parmenides taught that "it is necessary [for what is] to be altogether or not at all," and his student Zeno attempted to prove the impossibility of motion.[23] The Stranger's Eleatic heritage is visible in his method's attempt to bring the soul to a standstill, as well as in its godlike disdain for the lowly, impure, distinctively human business of estimating beauty, nobility, and goodness—impure because such estimates are prophetic, and therefore also tentative and imprecise. The Socratic criticism set forth above, however, implies that there is a fundamental incongruity between the method of division and the domain in which the Stranger attempts to apply this method in the *Sophist* and *Statesman*. Thus, in the *Republic*, Socrates differentiates between the activity of mathematics and its objects. This distinction allows Socrates to use geometry as a paradigm of philosophic intuition or acquisition: those geometers who speak "as though they were acting and making all of their speeches for the sake of action, uttering sounds like 'squaring,' 'applying,' 'adding,' and all such things," are mistaken, he says, "for the whole study, I suppose, is pursued for the sake of knowing." "Geometrical knowing," he adds, "is of what is always" (527a6-b1, b7-8). Such a distinction between the activity of knowing and its objects seems to be untenable, however, when the method of division is applied to human souls; in this case, the results at which the Stranger arrives appear to be *produced* by the operation of the method rather than *acquired*. If Socrates is to be judged a sophist because he is a producer of false images, so too is the Stranger.[24]

Another way to formulate the preceding Socratic criticism of the Stranger's method is to say that the unique potentiality or freedom of human beings eludes definition *via* an enumeration of formal elements.[25] This point is confirmed by the image of hunting. Just as the angler is a hunter of fish, the sophist is a hunter of wealthy youths (222a). The implication of this comparison is that the sophist treats young men not as human beings or as ends in themselves but merely as subhuman objects that are to be mastered for the sake of his own gratification. While this is surely an accurate description of the behavior of a sophist like Protagoras, it must not be forgotten that the Stranger also represents his own philosophical procedure as a kind of hunting (235a-c, 241b). In part, the Stranger means to suggest that, like the angler's prey, the sophist is a "slippery and iridescent being."[26] But the deeper point of this comparison is that the method of division treats human beings as if they were animals—or, in the terms employed earlier, as if they were plants. Like the plants Protagoras claims in the *Theaetetus* to farm, animals lack *erôs* (as distinguished from mere sexual appetite) and are not autonomous or free in the way that human beings seem to be. Of course, what it is to be human may still be an open question. Viewed from a certain angle, the Stranger's method harmonizes with his general pedagogical procedure, and may be read as an implicit endorsement of Protagoras's claim that Socrates is wrong in treating human beings as if they were something other than plants.

We shall return to the latter suggestion in due course. At present, however, we can dwell only briefly upon the political implications of the method of division. For in attempting to define the sophist, the Stranger engages in a practical or political enterprise no less than a theoretical inquiry. He emphasizes this point by stressing that the investigation is a common activity that aims at agreement (218b-c). Yet while the Stranger insists that the *results* of the investigation must be commonly agreed upon (cf. *Statesman* 258d), the *way* in which he proceeds is not determined by shared reflection. The Stranger is the guide, tracker, and leading hunter in the pursuit of the sophist. He requires of an interlocutor only that he be tractable enough to follow him without difficulty, and if no one of this sort is available, he can just as well proceed on his own (217d). While this fact may strengthen our doubts about the validity of his definitions, it is important to notice that the problem of the intrinsic nature of the sophist is not in itself politically significant. What counts, the Stranger implies, is the "work" or effect of sophistry in individual souls. Seen in this light, the Stranger's inquiry is of direct political relevance, for it attempts to replace the many different and potentially conflicting effects of sophistry in human souls with another "work": a publicly agreed-upon speech about the sophist. Socratic inquiries, we may note, typically fail to yield anything as positive or tangible as this.

Outfoxing the Sophist: The Angler and Sophists I through IV

In the preceding pages I suggested that the Stranger's style of inquiry furnishes a dramatic illustration of a certain kind of sham-philosophizing or sophistry, and that the philosophical deficiencies of the Stranger's speech are rooted in the incongruity between his technical, quasi-mathematical method and the nature of the human soul. A brief examination of the dialogue's first divisions will help to confirm these points.

The Stranger suggests that the attempt to isolate the angler will in its content as well as its form provide a paradigm for the search for the sophist. With regard to content, Seth Benardete has suggested that the formal elements isolated by the method of diaeresis can express human erotic striving only insofar as they are employed as images of that which human beings in their intermediate condition aspire to be—that which they literally are not but nevertheless are like.[27] The general notion that the Stranger's divisions may function as metaphoric images of the soul and its activities helps to shed much light on the meaning of many details in the *Sophist* and *Statesman* that would otherwise seem irrelevant. In particular, this insight furnishes a key to our understanding of the angler division (219a-221c, figure 1).

Several peculiarities of the angler division suggest that the Stranger's method produces results that are far less definite and precise than they might at first appear to be. Let us start with the distinction between production and acquisition in step two. In giving examples of acquisition, the Stranger distinguishes between the mathematical species of learning (*to mathêmatikon eidos*) and familiarity or acquaintance (*to tês gnôriseôs*: 219c2-3). This seems to be a tacit acknowledgment of the difference between the Stranger's method of knowing souls and that of Socrates (see above, chapter 4). As the Stranger describes it, however, acquisition looks rather like a mode of the poetic or productive art (*poiêtikê*): the arts of acquisition all involve mastering objects by deed or speech (*cheirousthai*), or, more literally, getting them "in hand" (219c5-6). But such mastery presumably transforms the conquered object: a bird in the hand—its wings held fast and its flight arrested—looks otherwise than a bird in the bush. Furthermore, the Stranger uses the same term in the third step of the division when he distinguishes exchange from conquest (*chierôtikon*: 219d7). In other words, exchange (under which branch the Stranger locates Sophists II, IIIa, IIIb, and IIIc) is also a mode of conquest (under which branch he locates Sophists I and IV).[28] Both steps two and three thus fail to meet reasonable standards of technical precision. The same is true of step six, which entirely overlooks birds of the air, and step seven, which associates the hunting of waterfowl with the whole of bird hunting (*ornitheutikê*).[29] In these respects, the Stranger's own procedure shows us (rather than simply saying) something important about sophistry, namely, that it may disguise vagueness and ambiguity beneath a veneer of technical precision.

Step four identifies hunting as conquest by stealth. To hunt is to conceal oneself from one's prey. The sophist's disguise, as we shall see, is that of the wise man. The method of division, however, hunts the sophist, from which it seems to follow that the method, too, camouflages itself. If so, what disguise does the Stranger employ? The answer suggested by our reading up to this point is that the Stranger imitates the sophist in cloaking his method in the appearance of knowledge. This suggestion is borne out by a consideration of the remainder of the angler division. Ancient authors observed that the sea is populated by creatures of exceptional cunning intelligence or *mêtis*, most of whom both hunt and are hunted. Fishing is therefore an art of exemplary *mêtis*: if the angler is to be successful, he must hunt with even greater shrewdness and deploy more clever stratagems than his prey possesses. In this crucial respect,

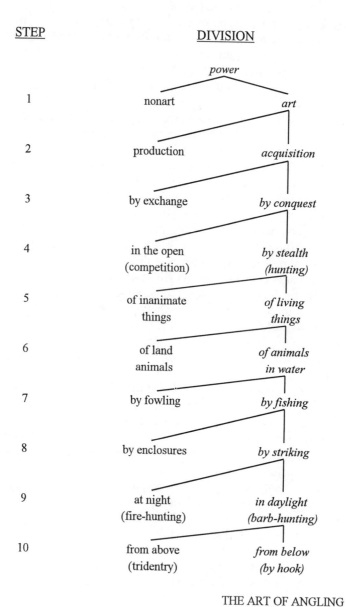

Figure 1. The Angler (219a-221c)

both the angler and his prey closely resemble the shifty sophist.[30] The
same must obviously be true of the hunter of sophists. While the angler
uses a baited hook, the Stranger uses a net of words (235b) and therefore
hunts by means of enclosures rather than by striking (step eight). But the
net, a pliable, polymorphous, invisible trap, is "one of the favorite weapons of *mêtis*," just as the cunning deployment of webs of words is the
hallmark of the sophist, "who knows how to interweave (*sumplekein*)
and twist together (*strephein*) speeches (*logoi*) and artifices (*mêcha-
nai*)."[31] This is not all. At the beginning of the dialogue's second division
the Stranger claims that the sophist parted ways with the angler in step
six of the previous division, where hunting land animals was separated
from hunting animals in water (222a). But the angler, who conceals a
hook within tasty food so as to strike his prey from below "around the
head and the mouth" (221a1), seems to offer an apt image of the sophist's mode of hunting youths. Unbeknownst to their prey, the angler's
bait and the sophist's food for the soul are only the visible tip of a craft-
ily concealed chain. So, too, the angler division itself functions within
the dialogue as a kind of bait: once Theaetetus has taken it into his soul,
he finds that it drags with it a whole series of speeches. And while the
Stranger must have planned things in just this way, he feigns surprise at
the seemingly accidental connection of the angler with the sophist
(221d).

Theaetetus expressed doubt when the Stranger distinguished the hunting of inanimate objects from that of living things in step five of the angler division (219e).[32] The Stranger omits this step altogether when reca-
pitulating the first steps of the angler division in the course of setting
forth the division of Sophist I (221d-223b, figure 2). This may be another
dramatic indication that the Stranger's method cannot adequately address
the soul, by whose presence living things are differentiated from
nonliving beings; even so the Stranger, like the fisherman who jiggles his
line so as to cause the hooked worm to bounce and move, can perhaps
give his results a kind of artificial animation. Step two of the division of
Sophist I, in which human beings are identified as tame animals, is also
problematic: if the sophist is a "beast" (*thêr* or *thêrion*: 226a7, 235a10;
cf. 231a, 241b), he is wild. Although these terms are as yet unanalyzed, it
seems clear that human beings can be or become wild as well as tame.
Once again, and by no means for the last time, the potentiality of the human soul presents problems for the method of division.

Like the angler, who cannot track fish in the murky depths but must
instead make them come to him, the sophist must find some means of
enticing his prey into the trap he has laid. The bait that Sophist I deploys
to lure rich young men (cf. 222a) is virtue or excellence (*aretê*: 223a3).
That the opportunity to learn virtue is indeed a ruse is clear from the

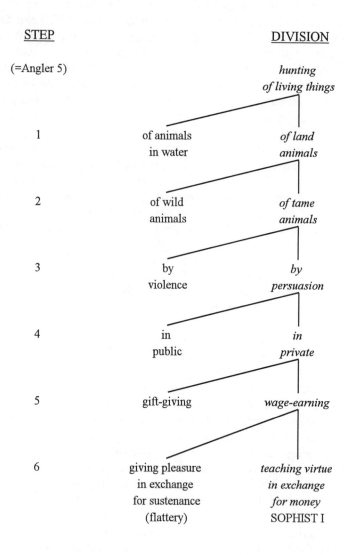

STEP   DIVISION

(=Angler 5)   *hunting*
                                              of living things

1   of animals   *of land*
               in water   *animals*

2   of wild   *of tame*
               animals   *animals*

3   by   *by*
               violence   *persuasion*

4   in   *in*
               public   *private*

5   gift-giving   *wage-earning*

6   giving pleasure   *teaching virtue*
               in exchange   *in exchange*
               for sustenance   *for money*
               (flattery)   SOPHIST I

Figure 2. Sophist I (221d-223b)

Stranger's reference to the sophist's art as one of "seeming-education" (*doxopaideutikê*: 223b5). The sophist looks like one who possesses the knowledge of virtue—the wisdom that Socrates is perpetually seeking. But he makes money by cheating his customers, for he offers them a false image of virtue. That he is an ignorant imitator, in turn, is evident from the fact that a virtuous man would not engage in such base deception—base not just because it is dishonest, but especially because the sophist corrupts young men in making them think they are virtuous when they are not.[33] The sophist hunts tame youths, but there is reason to believe that he helps to make them wilder.

The fifth step of the present division, which distinguishes the gift-giving, erotic branch of private persuasion from the wage-earning branch, may contain an implicit reference to Socrates.[34] If so, it is an open question how the "gifts" offered by the philanthropic Socrates relate to virtue.[35] We may note, however, that Socrates at one point tells Theaetetus that the "wage" (*misthos*) they will earn is either to find that which they seek or "to less believe that we know what we in no way know" (*Theaetetus* 187c1-3). In the event, it is the latter, inherently negative gift—a belief that is meant to nurture moderation (*sôphrosunê*) and to make Theaetetus "tamer" (*Theaetetus* 210c3)—with which Socrates claims to leave the lad. So, too, as we have seen, Socrates tries to give Euthyphro a gift by taking some harmful things away from him, including bad qualities of character as well as bad beliefs. Yet it is not open to everyone even to recognize that these are gifts, much less to be able to receive and profit from them; to do so, one must know the "small thing" that Socrates claims for himself—how "to take a speech from another who is wise and accept it in a measured way" (*Theaetetus* 161b4-5).

It is by now evident that the sophist's art involves manufacturing and trading in deceptive images. The commercial dimension of sophistry receives more emphasis in the next two divisions (223c-224e with 231d, figures 3 and 4). Since we have already briefly discussed Sophist II and the three versions of Sophist III, I shall restrict my comments to the transformation of Sophist IIIa into the forms of Sophists IIIb and IIIc in the summary at 231c-e. This odd multiplication of sophists dramatically underscores two closely related points. First, the sophist cannot be nailed down by the method of division because he is constantly changing his shape. Second, the method of division is so far from producing a technically accurate account of the sophist that it cannot even yield an unambiguous enumeration of its own definitions: it is unclear—and, to commentators, remains so—how many sophists the Stranger and Theaetetus ultimately identify (cf. Theaetetus's count at 225e with the list of six at 231c-e).[36] We may add that the last step of these divisions, which sepa-

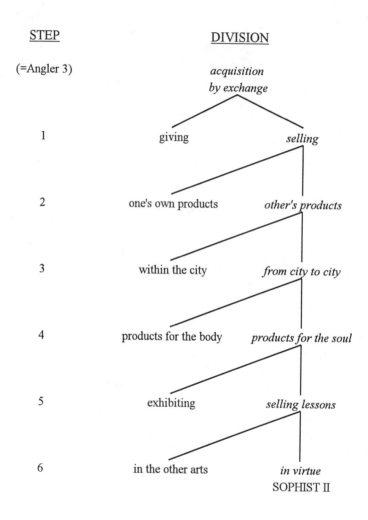

STEP   DIVISION

(=Angler 3)   *acquisition*
                                      by exchange

1   giving   *selling*

2   one's own products   *other's products*

3   within the city   *from city to city*

4   products for the body   *products for the soul*

5   exhibiting   *selling lessons*

6   in the other arts   *in virtue*
                                          SOPHIST II

Figure 3. Sophist II (223c-224d)

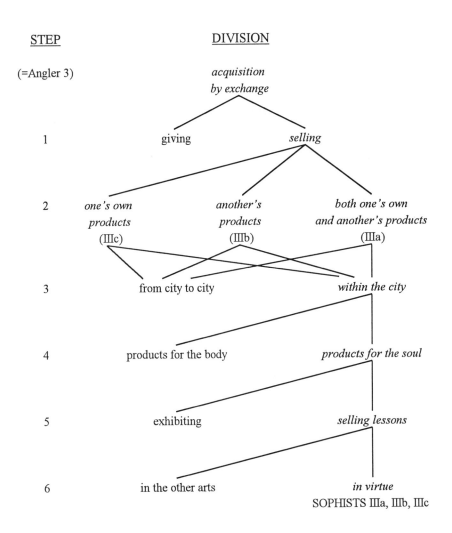

Figure 4. Sophists IIIa, IIIb, and IIIc (224d-e, 231d)

rates the selling of lessons in "the other arts" from lessons in virtue (224c1-2), makes it clear that the virtue taught by the sophists assumes the form of an art.

It is not obvious that we are getting closer to the real nature of the sophist as we move through successive divisions. But it does look like we are getting closer to Socrates. The division of Sophist IV (224e-226a, figure 5) contains the clearest reference yet to Socrates, and those of Sophists V and VI seem to hone in on him to an even greater extent. The Stranger's description of the kind of eristic wrangling "about just things themselves, unjust things, and the whole of the rest of things" (225c7-8) that takes place in private and for profit accurately picks out such soph- ists as Euthydemus and Dionysodorus as Plato depicts them in the *Euthydemus*. One should note that the comprehensiveness of sophistry, which is now no longer restricted to speech about virtue, comes into view here for the first time in the dialogue. The artful eristic speech that is isolated in step four, and that comes under the contradictory (*anti- logikon*) branch of verbal disputation by question and answer, nonethe- less emphasizes justice and injustice. In this respect, it calls to mind the debate between the Just (Stronger) and the Unjust (Weaker) Speeches that Aristophanes stages in the Thinkery of Socrates—a debate that is supposed to teach Pheidippides how to "speak against [*antilegein*] all the just things" (*Clouds* 888). As the *Hippias Minor* shows, Plato's Socrates also knows how to ask and answer questions in such a way as to make the weaker speech the stronger. Step five further strengthens this con- nection, for the sophistry that makes money from such disputes is con- trasted with "idle chatter" (*to adoleschikon*), the kind of talk that "is careless [*ameles*] of its private affairs [*tôn oikeiôn*] on account of the pleasure it takes in passing the time in such things, and in its speaking is heard without pleasure by many of its auditors" (225d7-9). In the *Apol- ogy*, Socrates admits to having no leisure to attend to the affairs of his family (*tôn oikeiôn*: 23b9) and to displeasing his interlocutors (23c-d) while engaging in an activity that is, he admits, "not unpleasant" (33c4) —presumably for himself as well as his young auditors. In the *Theae- tetus*, moreover, he laments his "idle chatter" (*adoleschia*: 195c2), and in the *Clouds* his Thinkery is described as the "home of the babblers" (*tên oikian tôn adoleschôn*: 1484-1485).[37]

In the definition of Sophist I, Socrates arguably appears in the left- hand branch of the penultimate step. In the definition of Sophist IV, he appears in the left-hand branch of the final step. These near misses might be taken positively as a confirmation of the difference between philoso- phy and sophistry—except that the Stranger's next attempt to isolate the sophist seems in crucial respects to hit Socrates head on. Let us now turn to this remarkable division.

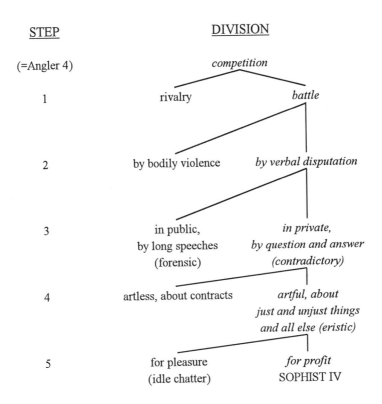

Figure 5. Sophist IV (244e-226a)

Sophist V: The Stranger's Socratic Indictment of Socrates

The definition of Sophist V at 226b-231b (figure 6) stands apart from the other divisions of the sophist in several ways. It is the only one that does not begin from a branch of the angler division. In this respect, we literally do not know where it stands with regard to the other definitions of the sophist. It is also longer than any of the other divisions in the *Sophist* (the division of Sophist VI being next in length). In addition, as Stanley Rosen notes, only in this division does the Stranger engage in a "lengthy treatment of a section that is about to be discarded," namely, the purification of the body.[38] Finally, and most important, the Stranger makes it clear that this division articulates the difference between his own philosophical method and that of Socrates. For all of these reasons, the definition of Sophist V merits special attention.

The present division also marks the beginning of a fundamental transformation in the Stranger's conduct. As if to acknowledge the deficiencies of his method, the Stranger here speaks in a distinctly Socratic voice about the soul's erotic motion, and in particular about its potential for virtue, beauty, and happiness. So pronounced is this change that the Stranger's brief digression on his value-free approach to definition is apt to strike one as little more than a foil for his subsequent imitation of Socrates' prophetic mode of discourse. On the surface, this transformation registers as a mimetic echo of the sophist's polytropism; on a deeper level, it confirms my earlier suggestion that the Stranger imitates sophistry for philosophical and pedagogical purposes.

The division begins with the art of separation (*diakritikê*), examples of which are straining or filtering, sifting, winnowing, and discerning (*diakrinein*: 226b5-6). Step one distinguishes the nameless separation of like from like from the kind of discernment (*diakrisis*) that sets the worse apart from the better, which is said to be a sort of purification (*katharmos*: 226d10). In step two the Stranger distinguishes the purification of the body from the purification of the soul, and quickly divides the former in two successive substeps (226e-227a). The soul once again creates problems for the Stranger, for it reappears in the first substep as that which divides animate bodies from inanimate ones. It is noteworthy also that Theaetetus, perhaps feeling a bit overwhelmed by having rushed through several different kinds of sophists, suggests that he has not the leisure to help the Stranger at this point (226e3-4). This is a nice touch, since in the *Theaetetus* Socrates emphasized the scholarly leisure (*scholê*) of philosophers by contrasting it with the unleisurely press of business in courts of law (172c-e). The Stranger's present speech, Plato hints, is a philosophical version of forensic oratory.

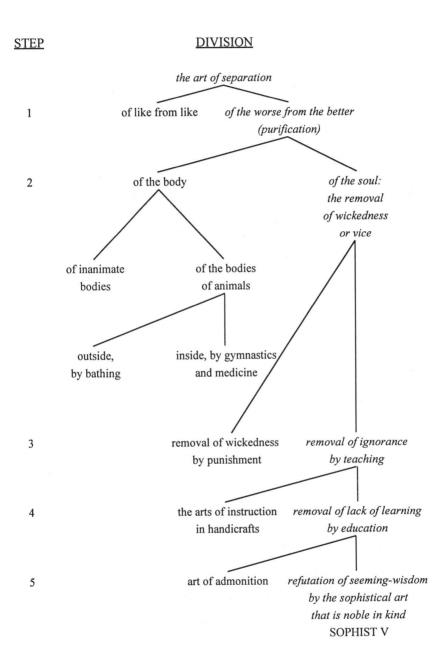

STEP DIVISION

the art of separation

1 of like from like   *of the worse from the better*
(purification)

2 of the body   *of the soul:*
the removal
of wickedness
or vice

of inanimate   of the bodies
bodies   of animals

outside,   inside, by gymnastics
by bathing   and medicine

3 removal of wickedness   *removal of ignorance*
by punishment   *by teaching*

4 the arts of instruction   *removal of lack of learning*
in handicrafts   *by education*

5 art of admonition   *refutation of seeming-wisdom*
by the sophistical art
that is noble in kind
SOPHIST V

Figure 6. Sophist V (226b-231b)

Having spoken of such "seemingly laughable" matters as bathing and cosmetics (227a5), the Stranger interjects some remarks about his method. "The pursuit of speeches," he explains, "in no way at all happens to care either less or more for sponge-bathing than for drug-drinking, whether or not the one benefits us little by its purifying and the other greatly." Rather, "for the sake of the acquisition of intellect [*nous*], it attempts to understand the kinship and the lack of kinship of all arts, and with a view to this honors all of them equally." For this reason, he adds, the practitioner of the art of generalship or strategy (*stratêgikê*) is no more august (*semnoteros*) than the practitioner of the art of lice-killing, but he is more puffed up with vanity (227a7-b6).

The preceding speech is just the sort one might expect from a god or godlike philosopher, from whose lofty perspective human beings must look like insects. It is in some respects reminiscent of the moment when Parmenides gently chastises Socrates for claiming that there are Ideas of the just, the noble, and the good, while being unwilling to honor such "laughable" things as mud, hair, and dirt with Ideas of their own (*Parmenides* 130b-e). The Stranger's method, it seems, corrects for certain distortions of human understanding which stem from what he seems to regard as an unjustifiable sense of our self-importance. We attach greater worth to medicine than to bathing because we value health more highly than the mere appearance of health. Similarly, we attach great worth to the art of strategy because we value political freedom. The word *semnos* or "august" also suggests that the general regards his office as holy. Implicit in these distinctions are the notions that it is better to be alive than dead, human than animal, free than enslaved—better, in part, because there is something divine in free human life. In denying the relevance of these perceptions to philosophical understanding, the Stranger in effect demotes the soul to a rank equal to that of the body; this is why his brief digression on method comes immediately after he formulates step two of the division. It follows that lifeless bodies are in no way inferior to ensouled ones: if medicine is on a par with bathing, it is also on a par with the fuller's art.

It is nonetheless true that the Stranger's words do not harmonize with his deeds. The Stranger implicitly assumes that it is better to be educated than to be ignorant. Beyond this, he implies that from the point of view of philosophical education it is best to proceed by dividing like from like without regard for the better and the worse. Put another way, step one of the present division is itself an implicit purification that separates inferior ways of teaching and learning—including in particular that of Socrates—from superior ones. The Stranger's procedure is therefore paradoxically tainted by the impurity of the inferior activity of purification. The cathartic moment Socrates predicted in the *Cratylus* has now arrived.

The Stranger speaks both of the purification of thought (*dianoia*: 227c4) and of the soul. This produces a certain ambiguity, since the purifications he goes on to describe work on one's character as well as one's intellect. Purification of the soul, he explains, involves the removal of wickedness (*ponêria*) or vice (*kakia*). Step three distinguishes the removal of wickedness from the removal of ignorance by teaching. Wickedness, in turn, is compared to illness in the body, while ignorance is compared to ugliness. Illness, the Stranger explains, is a kind of *stasis*, the term used to denote the seditious "standing still" of a faction of the body politic whereby the concerted movement of parts that constitutes the health of the political whole is disrupted. Psychic illness, or the variance of opinions with desires, anger with pleasures, and the like causes the soul to miss the proper target (*skopos*) of its motion, but the soul can miss its mark also because of the lack of measure (*ametria*) that constitutes ugliness. In this case, the whole soul moves in unison, but because of its internal disproportion it goes wrong—and does wrong—in spite of its best intentions. Ignorance (*agnoia*), which occurs when understanding (*sunesis*) misses the mark, is a case in point. Here the Stranger makes a small correction to step two: ignorance by itself should perhaps not be called vice.[39] It is at any rate clear that those who seek to purify the soul by removing its ignorance are concerned with the well-being of the soul as a whole, and so with moral and practical matters as well as theoretical ones. Psychic illnesses such as hybris, injustice, and cowardice are dealt with by the medicine of the art of punishment (*kolastikê*) which is closely related to justice, while the art of teaching (*didaskalikê*) treats the ugliness of ignorance in a manner akin to the way in which gymnastics attempts to correct the body's lack of measure or proportion (227d-229a). On the basis of the close resemblance between these passages and *Gorgias* 464b-466a, we may infer that the removal of ignorance by teaching is akin to legislation.

In step four the Stranger separates a "big and difficult kind of ignorance" from "all the rest of its parts" (229c1-3). The latter parts of ignorance evidently have to do with a lack of skill in the crafts of manufacturing, for the relevant arts in this case are those of instruction in handicrafts (*dêmiourgikai didaskaliai*). The former kind of ignorance is "seeming [perhaps to others as well as to oneself] to know something while not knowing it." "It is probably through this," the Stranger adds, "that all the slips we make in thought occur for everyone" (229c5-6). This kind of ignorance is lack of learning (*amathia*) and it is removed by way of education (*paideia*: 229c8-d3).

We are now in familiar Socratic territory. *Paideia* has to do particularly with the rearing of the young, as is evident in the fifth and final step of this division. Education is an art of instruction by means of speeches, and, like speech itself as imaged in the figure of Pan, has a rougher and a smoother part. One part is the "time-honored and paternal" art of admonition (*nouthetikê*) which is applied to sons when they go wrong. The other begins from the recognition that no one is willing to learn anything if he believes he is already wise. Fatherly admonition therefore accomplishes little insofar as it does not address just this presumption of the young, to which the Stranger later gives the name "vain seeming-wisdom" (*mataios doxosophia*: 231b6). Those educators who feel the force of this point proceed along a different path (229e-230b).

The Stranger's description of the latter path identifies a class of sophistry that seems to have only one member: Socrates. The allusion seems clear enough, even though the Stranger's characterization of Socratic pedagogy beautifies or purifies a process that we know to be frequently rather ugly.[40] By means of questioning, he explains, those who pursue the remaining branch of education examine their interlocutors in such a way as to make manifest to them the contradictions in their opinions. The result is that the interlocutors "are vexed with themselves and grow tame toward the rest of men" (230b9). The Stranger adds that those who are relieved in this way of their great and rigid or sclerotic opinions undergo the most "pleasant" and "stable" of all riddances (230c1-3). And just as physicians believe that bodies can derive no benefit from nourishment before internal obstructions or impediments are removed, the purifiers (*hoi kathairontes*) believe that the soul will derive no benefit from proffered lessons (*mathêmata*) before someone, by way of *elenchos* or refutation, "puts the one refuted into a state of shame, having thrown out the opinions that are impediments to the lessons, and shows him forth pure [*katharon*] and believing that he knows only the things he does know and no more" (230c4-d4). This, the Stranger adds, is the greatest and most authoritative of purifications, "and we must believe that the unrefuted one, even if he happens to be the Great King [the Persian emperor], if he is unpurified in the greatest things, has come to be uneducated and ugly in the things in which it is fitting for one who is going to be truly happy [*eudaimona*] to be purest and most beautiful [*kalliston*]" (230d6-e3).

The present division of the sophist thus concludes with what looks like a ringing endorsement of Socratic pedagogy. This impression seems to be confirmed by the manner of the Stranger's discourse as well as its content: the Stranger here abandons value-free speech in favor of prophetic talk about psychic beauty (or nobility) and ugliness, the soul's purposive activity, its virtues and vices, and its potential for happiness (*eudaimonia*). Why, then, does the Stranger—however hesitantly—identify Socrates' way of education as a kind of sophistry? And does this accusation of sophistry involve a charge of bad citizenship, bad theorizing, or both?

Let us start with the obvious differences between Socratic midwifery and the art of refutation that the Stranger describes, differences that effectively highlight the deficiencies of Socrates' educational practice. The Stranger's pedagogical style, as we observed earlier, is gentler than that of Socrates. While the Stranger gives Theaetetus a trial run in the search for the sophist and in other respects tries to shield him from harsh experiences (cf. 234d-e), Socrates immediately forces him to undergo painful labor in thinking through the most difficult questions. Yet the Stranger presents Socratic education as something pleasant, not painful. Then, too, Socrates' interlocutors frequently grow angry with him rather than with themselves. In the *Theaetetus*, Socrates notes the ill-will young men often feel toward him when he disposes of their wind-eggs, and he asks Theaetetus not to become wildly angry (*mê agriaine*) if the same should happen to him (151c-d). In this respect, Socrates' interlocutors often become wilder toward others—not tamer, as the Stranger suggests. Nor is Socratic purification always stable, since some of Socrates' young companions regress after they leave him (*Theaetetus* 149e-151a). Furthermore, Socrates does not limit his art of refutation to the young, but often applies it to their fathers as well. This too produces ill-will. Although the Stranger does not say so, the preceding considerations suggest that the refutation of seeming-wisdom is the "rougher" of the two paths of education by speeches: it is both harsh in itself and productive of harshness in others.[41] Aristophanes, after all, got it right when he predicted that the Athenians would do violence to Socrates. In the *Clouds*, moreover, Strepsiades' murderous anger was a paternal response to harsh treatment by a son who spent time in Socrates' Thinkery.[42]

The matters of harshness and gentleness, tameness and wildness are further emphasized by the Stranger's remarks immediately after he completes the last step of the division. The Stranger hesitates to call the practitioners of the art he has just defined "sophists," because he does not want to accord them too great an honor. But it is unclear whom he means by "them" (*autois*: 231a3). And when Theaetetus maintains that the things said resemble "someone of such a sort"—again, the reference is ambiguous—the Stranger replies: "Yes, and a wolf [bears a resemblance] to a dog, the most wild or savage [*agriôtaton*] to the most tame" (231a6). He nonetheless decides to employ the name "sophistry," thereby reinforcing an impression first formed when Socrates associated himself with Artemis in the *Theaetetus*, namely, that while Socrates is not simply wild—not undomesticated by political community and hostile to his fellow citizens—he is also not altogether tame.[43]

There is another, quite telling way in which the Stranger's description of the art of refuting seeming-wisdom differs from Socrates' practice. The Stranger presents this art as if it were preparatory to the application of positive lessons. In the first instance, he suggests, the lessons in question are those that fathers intend to teach their sons (cf. 230a), in which case Socratic refutation would be a kind of negative propaedeutic to fatherly admonition. Given the Stranger's apparent praise for such refutation, however, one wonders if the *mathêmata* he has in mind may include those produced by his own method of division. The analogy he draws between Socratic refutation and medical purification or purging is at any rate at odds with Socrates' pedagogical activity (as well as with his earlier comparison of the treatment of psychic ugliness with gymnastics). The crucial point is this: while medical catharsis makes it possible for the body to derive nourishment from food, Socrates rejects as essentially sophistical the notion that the learning with which he is concerned—wisdom in the fullest sense, including self-knowledge and knowledge about the best way to live—can be acquired by the soul in anything like the automatic and mechanical way in which one ingests servings of bread or meat. What is more, to have learned from Socrates is to regard with deep suspicion anyone who claims to address the soul's deficiencies—be they in the form of illness or ugliness (lack of measure)—by means of ready-made lessons.

If the preceding observations are well-taken, the fifth division of the sophist may be read as a philosophical version of the public indictment of Socrates for bad citizenship. In particular, there is truth in the public perception that Socrates does wrong by interfering with the process by which fathers attempt to educate their sons. Socratic catharsis renders useless the application of lessons by means of fatherly admonition, and not only for the reason just mentioned. Besides casting doubt on the worth of ready-made lessons (lessons that unreflectively reiterate *ta patria*, the traditional ways and beliefs of the fathers of Athens), Socrates applies his art of refutation to fathers themselves, and thereby directly undermines their educational authority. Indeed, the Stranger suggests, Socrates pursues the business of refutation with such zeal that he would not hesitate to cross-examine the Great King himself—a man, as Aeschylus portrays him in the *Persians*, who was regarded by his subjects as a god (80, 151-158; cf. 623-680). One wonders whether the Persians would continue to receive the Great King's pronouncements with worshipful reverence if they could witness a conversation between him and Socrates. This brings us to a further implication of the Stranger's indictment: Socratic catharsis also negates the benefit of other, positive political or philosophical lessons that are meant for the young (including such as might be conveyed by the method of division). To benefit from or be "nourished" by such lessons, young men must be sufficiently tame or docile to acknowledge the superior authority of the speaker. But Socrates makes young men wild in just this respect. His claim to tame the young by helping them humbly to believe that they do not know what they do not know (*Theaetetus* 210c) is thus ultimately misleading. Such humility, I have suggested, is in Socrates' view the fruit of the manly and spirited independence or self-reliance in inquiry that he encourages in his interlocutors. If present at all, it therefore goes hand in hand with a kind of troublesome peevishness toward those whose mode of instruction in matters pertaining to virtue and wisdom requires a significant degree of tractability on the part of their auditors.

Read in this way, the fifth division of the sophist answers Socratic refutation with an *elenchos* of its own—just as Socrates predicted upon meeting the Stranger. Socratic discourse, which is meant to address psychic ugliness, is itself ugly or lacking in due measure. It is important to observe that the Stranger implicitly corrects Meletus's accusation of intentional wrongdoing or wickedness (*Apology* 25d): Socrates does wrong but is not vicious, because he makes a concerted effort to achieve a truly praiseworthy end. Indeed, the Stranger explicitly violates the strictures of his method in revealing his estimation of Socrates' purposes. To call Socrates' art "noble" sophistry is to articulate an intuition about his character and the nature of his *erôs*: Socrates' way of education is both better than other, ignoble modes of sophistry, which *are* vicious, and worse than philosophy and politically responsible education in general. The Stranger, moreover, does what Socrates says Meletus *ought* to do if he corrupts the young involuntarily: "take me aside in private to teach and admonish [*nouthetein*] me" (*Apology* 26a3-4).

In spite of the latter textual echo, the Stranger's elenctic speech is in certain crucial respects closer to Socratic refutation than to fatherly admonition. The Stranger seems to agree with Socrates that admonition is ineffective insofar as it does not address the vain presumption of wisdom that lies at the root of errors in thought. If Socrates takes aim at such vanity, so too does the Stranger. As we have seen, the present division includes a digression on method in which the Stranger attacks our human sense of self-importance. And in the end, the Stranger suggests, Socrates is guilty of just the sort of vain seeming-wisdom that his refutations are meant to expose. Socrates supposes that his elenctic art is on the whole good for human beings. In this he is mistaken. In other words, he is ignorant of what he assumed he knew. Socrates has failed to understand human nature, or at least to form an accurate notion of the harmful political consequences of his philosophical activity. Put most succinctly, Socrates lacks *phronêsis*.

The latter accusation, presented here only in outline, will be further developed by the Stranger in the *Statesman*. At present, we may observe simply that this is a theoretical criticism as well as a practical one. Even while acknowledging that Socrates is guilty to a lesser degree than his ignoble peers, the Stranger's indictment of him for sophistry includes both the charges of bad theorizing and bad citizenship.

What is the Stranger's alternative to Socratic refutation? This is not an easy question to answer on the basis of what we have seen so far in the *Sophist*. The criticism of Socrates that we have teased out of the present division is an internal critique that is fundamentally Socratic in spirit, and that could not have been formulated without violating the rules of inquiry that govern the Stranger's method. Apart from this blatant contradiction, it would be tempting to regard the method of division itself as the Stranger's theoretical and practical alternative to Socrates' way of philosophizing. Our appreciation of the Stranger's criticism of Socrates, however, can only strengthen our sense of the method's philosophical inadequacy.[44]

Perhaps we are meant to see in the Stranger's self-contradictory procedure a dramatic illustration of the tension between philosophy and the political community. A certain kind of bad theorizing, the Stranger suggests, might nonetheless make for good politics. Put more strongly, statesmanship may *require* noble lies, or speeches that are sophistical just insofar as they intentionally present a false image of the truth. The Stranger's playing at being a sophist would then serve not only as a spoof of technical philosophizing but also as a serious illustration of what it is to be a statesman. But if this is correct, it is important to see that the Stranger must also be doing more than simply elucidating the conflict between philosophy and statesmanship. I said earlier that the Stranger's criticism of Socrates is theoretical as well as practical. Yet this criticism is in some respects inconsistent. To the extent that the Stranger's procedure implicitly confirms Socrates' credentials as a philosopher, his criticism underscores philosophy's contradiction with *itself*. It is perhaps this inevitable self-contradiction, moreover, that accounts for Plato's dramatic bifurcation of the philosopher into the two characters of Socrates and the Stranger—a split that is echoed also in the method of bifurcatory division.

We shall find some confirmation of the preceding views in the definition of Sophist VI, and more when we take up the *Statesman*. At present, let us note only that the Stranger ultimately leaves fatherly admonition more or less untouched, both because his value-free method is officially neutral with respect to questions of better and worse, and, more significantly, because his criticisms are directed at what the division identifies as the sole rival of this archaic mode of education. The Stranger thus appears to favor a kind of political conservatism—an impression that will also be confirmed in the *Statesman*.

Speech as Image:
Socratic Measure in the Final Division of the Sophist

The final division of the sophist begins soon after Sophist V has been isolated, but includes a lengthy digression on the problem of false speech that runs roughly from 236d to 264e and takes up most of the remainder of the dialogue. While space prohibits a detailed treatment of the whole digression, I wish to focus fairly closely on two related dimensions of the remainder of the *Sophist*. The first is the distinctly Socratic style of pedagogy that characterizes the Stranger's treatment of Theaetetus after the definition of noble sophistry. The second has to do with the division of Sophist VI and the Stranger's treatment of images. Here, too, in the philosophical emphases of his inquiry no less than his pedagogical style, the Stranger evinces a Socratic orientation. Yet if anything, the Stranger's manner of characterizing the sophist as a maker of false images highlights the tension between Socratic philosophizing and the political community that we began to explore above.

The Stranger's Pedagogy

Confronted with the multiplicity of guises in which the sophist has so far appeared, Theaetetus finds himself in a state of perplexity (*aporia*) about what he is "in his being" (*ontôs*: 231b9-c2). In view of the many different arts that have come to light as sophistry, the Stranger is forced to admit that they cannot yet have adequately understood the unifying essence of the sophist's *technê*—"that toward which all of these learnings look" (232a4-5). He therefore proposes to begin again from the beginning (*ex archês*) in a different way, namely, by considering the sophist's capacity as a contradictor (*antilogikos*) and teacher of contradiction. The Stranger points out in particular the comprehensive nature of the sophist's art of disputation, which encompasses argument about invisible, divine things; the visible, natural world; becoming and being; laws and all of the political things; and all that pertains to the arts. In other words, the sophist has the capacity effectively to dispute about everything (232b-e). The latter observation triggers a question that the Stranger emphasizes with an oath: Can any human being know everything? If that were the case, Theaetetus allows, "our *genos* would be blessed" (233a4). The sophist therefore possesses a "science of seeming [or a 'seeming-knowledge': *doxastikê epistêmê*] about everything, without being in possession of truth" (233c10-11). The new beginning made by the Stranger and Theaetetus springs from a Socratic recognition of ignorance.

From this point on in the *Sophist*, the Stranger and Theaetetus will attempt to characterize the nature of the sophist's seeming-wisdom. The

Stranger now finds himself once again in the Socratic position of refuting pretensions to wisdom, a task that must inevitably draw him into further reflections upon the soul's power both to learn and to be deceived. What is to be grasped is how sophists produce in the young the opinion "that they themselves are wisest of all in everything" (233b2). The Stranger offers as a paradigm of the sophist's comprehensive *technê* the mimetic art of painting. The painter can make images of any visible thing. When viewed from afar by foolish young children, moreover, these images will be mistaken for originals of the same name. The painter can therefore trick children into believing "that he is perfectly capable of bringing to completion in deed anything whatsoever that he wishes to do" (234b9-10). By analogy, the sophist exhibits spoken images of all things to youths "who stand even further from the truth of things [*tês alêtheias tôn pragmatôn*] . . . so as to make them seem to be truly said, and the speaker seem to be the wisest of all in regard to everything" (234c2-7).

The latter analogy effectively endorses Socrates' earlier suggestion that names are akin to pictures in that they imitate the intrinsic being of the things named (*Cratylus* 423e, 430b ff.). Like Socrates, the Stranger presupposes that the originals imaged in *logos* are accessible to intellectual perception independently of speech. In the painting analogy, the originals are well known but the images are far away. The reverse is true in the case of the sophist: the problematic visibility of truth or intrinsic being, which is literally invisible, is here metaphorically figured as a vast distance that makes things hard to see. This "distance," the Stranger indicates in the immediate sequel, is partly a function of the inexperience of youth. The sophist exploits this inexperience by inverting the function of philosophic *logos*, which is to lead the soul as near as possible to the originals—precisely what the Stranger is trying to do for his young interlocutor (234c-e; cf. *Theaetetus* 166a, where Protagoras objects to Socrates' having deceived a "little child").

As I suggested in the preceding chapter, images perform their psychagogic function by provoking reflection on the connection between themselves and the originals of which they are images. Such reflection, which presupposes that the spoken image is understood to be nothing other than an image, turns upon the power of the soul to divine the connection between the image and the original. If a speech is an image, to speak about the connection between image and original is merely to provide another image. The aptness of a speech to the original that it bespeaks must therefore remain unspoken, which is to say that philosophical speech necessarily appeals to the soul's power of prophetic recollection. Like a painter tricking children, however, the sophist attempts to conceal even the fact that his speeches are images, let alone that they are bad ones. The Stranger's analogy suggests that the sophist is a counterfeiter or forger of things themselves, not just of their tokens (like money or paintings): he attempts to close off philosophical reflection by passing off his speeches as if *they themselves* were nothing other than "the truth of things." The painting analogy thus directly anticipates the sophist's denial of the possibility of false speech. Implicit in this Protagorean move is a rejection of the difference between what is *said* to be and what *is*: the sophist advocates the thesis that there are no images, only originals (239e-240a).

The sophist has now shown himself to be a practitioner of deceptive enchantment (*goês*), a conjurer or "wonder-worker" (*thaumatopoios*), and an imitator (235a8, b5). This wild beast (*thêr*) is to be located as quickly as possible within the art of image-making by the Stranger's "royal speech" (235c1), a phrase that underscores the political relevance of the present inquiry. To this end, the Stranger distinguishes two kinds of imitation. *Eikastikê* is the production of likenesses, or images that faithfully reproduce the proportions and colors of the original (here called a paradigm). *Phantastikê* is the production of semblances, or images in which the proportions of the original have been altered so as to suit the perspective of the viewer. In clarifying the difference between these arts the Stranger emphasizes the beautiful, *to kalon*. When molding or painting a "big work," he explains, the sculptor or illustrator does not seek to reproduce "the true proportion or symmetry [*summetria*] of the beautiful things," for if he did the resulting image would appear asymmetrical or ugly. Such craftsmen therefore produce in their images "not the proportions that are beautiful but those that seem to be so." The resulting image is a semblance (*phantasma*)—that which merely "seems to be like the beautiful because it is seen from a position that is not beautiful." The production of semblances, in turn, is present "throughout painting and all of imitation" (235d-236c).

Oddly, the Stranger is uncertain whether the sophist is a maker of likenesses or semblances (236c). His uncertainty seems to be connected with the difficulties that arise when the percipient soul is taken into account, as it must be in the case of beauty. A huge sculpture of a woman that accurately reproduced her proportions might look beautiful to a Brobdingnagian but would seem ugly to Gulliver, who would find the legs too large and the head too small. This means that Gulliver requires a semblance in order to perceive that which is conveyed to the Brobdingnagian by means of a likeness. For the beauty of beautiful symmetry consists in the *look* of symmetry, and it is just this look that is accurately (re)produced by an artful semblance that takes into account the conditions of visibility under which it appears. Semblances, while inaccurate in themselves, may therefore be more accurate than likenesses with regard to the soul's experience of "big works."

What does this image convey to us about the search for the sophist? The sophist, the Stranger has already suggested, is one of the "biggest" things (218d1-2; cf. d9). The truth about the sophist's nature is also one of the things that young men like Theaetetus perceive from a "distance." Given these circumstances, the Stranger must fashion a semblance in order to teach Theaetetus who or what the sophist really is. This semblance will consist in words, not visible shapes and colors, since the being of the sophist is invisible. Beyond this, however, the particular nature of the semblance he will choose to employ depends upon his notion of teaching and learning. To teach might be to fashion images for a soul, wherever it may happen to be standing, in such a way as to require no movement— no improvement of perspective—on its part. This would assume that to learn is to acquire a semblance that has been fitted to one's soul in such a way as to produce an accurate impression of the original. But the Stranger rejects this assumption, for he seeks to lead Theaetetus closer to the beings (*ta onta*) and the truth of things, deeds, or events (*ta pragmata*: 234c-e). The latter notion of what it is to teach and learn harmonizes with Theaetetus's claim that beings are "those things toward which the soul itself stretches itself" (*Theaetetus* 186a4), and finds further confirmation in a similar remark by Socrates in the *Phaedo* (65c). A different sort of semblance would be suited to this task, namely, one that provokes motion on the part of the soul. Finally, I have already suggested that the sophist produces yet a third kind of semblance—one that neither produces an accurate impression of the original nor leads the soul closer to the truth.

The first model of teaching and learning mentioned above has obvious defects. It presupposes that the teacher is wise, and it does not invite active reflection on the part of the learner. It is thus a useful model for sophists, since it increases the likelihood that their deception will go unnoticed. The image that the Stranger offers in order to clarify the difference between semblances and likenesses, however, confirms his endorsement of the second model, for this image is itself a semblance whose deficiencies provoke the sort of philosophical reflection that can advance our understanding of the sophist. The Stranger's account of image in terms of the reproduction of the proportions of the original favors a quasi-mathematical understanding of the being of the original as a kind of ratio. Insofar as a likeness exactly reproduces this ratio, it is in the decisive sense *identical* to the original.[45] The Stranger's account thus suppresses the imagistic nature of philosophical speech—but not entirely, since the image of speech as a sculpture or a painting also calls attention to the inadequacy of this quasi-mathematical understanding of being. Sculptures and paintings of a human being necessarily differ from the original insofar as they freeze motion—and the sophist, in spite of the

Stranger's wishful thinking (235b), will not stand still. In defining noble sophistry the Stranger spoke about the disproportion or lack of measure of the soul, but that discussion proves the point at hand: the soul's due proportion (*summetria*) or lack of it (*ametria*) has to do with its ability to hit or miss the mark at which its erotic motion aims. Put otherwise, one cannot discern the beauty or ugliness of a soul without seeing it in action. The Stranger's divisions are speeches that resemble sculptures and paintings, whereas what is called for are speeches that resemble dramas. Read in this way, the Stranger's distinction between images and likenesses looks like a tacit endorsement of the Platonic dialogue.

An unspoken question that is raised by the Stranger's account of likenesses and semblances has to do with the speeches of the statesman. If the statesman produces noble lies, does he not fashion spoken images of the same general sort as those produced by the sophist—semblances that neither produce an accurate impression of the original nor lead the soul closer to the truth? Later steps in the division of Sophist VI will raise this question explicitly. At present, however, the division is interrupted after only one step, for the Stranger now pauses to examine the problem of false speech—a digression that will take almost thirty pages of dialogue. My primary concern with the digression has to do with what it reveals about the Stranger as a teacher and a learner. For as we shall see, what I have characterized as the Stranger's Socratic treatment of Theaetetus is tightly intertwined with his reconsideration of the doctrines of Parmenides, the leader of the Eleatic circle of philosophy who was the Stranger's own teacher when he was a boy (237a).

At the beginning of the *Sophist* the Stranger asked for a tractable interlocutor, but he now seems to have changed his mind. After he observes that the sophist has fled into a region where he is hard to track, he takes Theaetetus to task for his perfunctory assent (236d). The speech, he observes, allows for "appearing and seeming, but not being" (236e1-2). It thus boldly says that that which is not (*to mê on*) is, thereby directly challenging the repeated prohibitions of Parmenides. The Stranger therefore proposes that he and Theaetetus (presumably as agents of the royal *logos*) "put to the torture" Parmenides' speech (237b2; cf. 241d6). Parmenides is described by the Stranger as *megas*, "great" or "big" (237a5). While he looms large in the imagination, he may resemble one of those big statues that looks beautiful when viewed from far away but reveals its ugliness upon closer inspection. Parmenides himself may be a candidate for Socratic refutation.

The Stranger soon confirms the latter hunch. Speech about that which is not involves a contradiction, since it implicitly attributes being to *to mê on* in addressing it as some one thing (237c-238c). This fact taints even Parmenides' prohibition against such speech, since one is compelled to mention that which is not in attempting to prevent further discussion of it. The Stranger now finds himself entangled in the same contradiction: "I set it down that that which is not must not share in either one or the many, but then and now I have spoken of it as one in just this way. For I say 'that which is not'" (238d9-e3). His speech recalls Socrates' earlier use of the phrases "we know" and "we don't know" (*Theaetetus* 196d-e), but is if anything more blatantly self-contradictory: Socrates' way of speaking could in principle be justified after the completion of his inquiry into the nature of knowledge, but it is hard to see how the Stranger's way of speaking could ever be justified. "Whatever could one say about me?" he asks Theaetetus. "For one would find that I've been defeated for a long time, as well as now, in the refutation of that which is not" (239b1-3). The Stranger, too, seems to be one of those who are *phaulos* or poor in speeches (216b4; cf. *Theaetetus* 197a4).

In the *Theaetetus* Socrates imagines a "contradictor" (*antilogikos*) who will chastise him for his impure and shameless speech. In the face of this challenge, Socrates proposes to speak boldly about what he thinks knowledge is (197a1-4). The situation is much the same in the *Sophist*. The sophist, having turned the tables on his hunters, threatens to trap the Stranger and Theaetetus in a contradiction (241a-b). The only way forward, however, is the bold path upon which the pair has already embarked. They must speak about not-being if they are to show that both false speech and false opinion are possible (240a-e). And they *must* show that these things are possible—they must take up the question that Theaetetus and Socrates failed to resolve on the previous day—in order to establish that the sophist is anything other than a wise man. The inquiries of the *Theaetetus* and the *Sophist* are closely related: the possibility of philosophy stands or falls with the possibility of sophistry, understood as false speeches or semblances that generate false opinions. Parmenides' speech must be put to torture for its own sake, because its silence about not-being amounts to an ugly capitulation to sophistry.

The Stranger's recognition of the problem of not-being coincides with the shift in pedagogical style that we noted earlier. From shortly after the conclusion of the fifth division of the sophist until the end of the dialogue, the Stranger remains consistent in his Socratic encouragement of Theaetetus's philosophical spiritedness. After Theaetetus gives a list of kinds of images when asked for a definition, the Stranger requests that he speak to the one thing that makes all of these items deserving of the name "image" (239d-240a). He simultaneously encourages Theaetetus to stand his ground against the sophist (240a). A bit later, Theaetetus doubts that the sophist can be grasped, yet he forcefully declines the Stranger's invitation to "go soft and stand aside" (241c4). And when the going again gets rough, the Stranger once more exhorts Theaetetus to take courage with a speech that the youth finds beautiful (261b-c).

The boldness of both Theaetetus and the Stranger is nowhere more evident than when it comes to their treatment of Parmenides. In spite of the Stranger's initial appearance as a champion of reverent awe and an enemy of hybris (216a-b), he turns out to be even more shameless than Socrates: while the latter respectfully refrained from examining Parmenides' thought (*Theaetetus* 183e-184b), the former does not balk when confronted with the same opportunity. The Stranger's repeated emphasis upon refutation (*elenchos, elenchein*: 241e1, 242a8, b1, b2) suggests that his examination of Parmenides' speech amounts to a Socratic attempt to expose seeming-wisdom. What is more, Socrates' application of *elenchos* even to the fathers of Athens is paralleled here in the Stranger's quasi-parricidal attack upon the "paternal" speech of "our father" Parmenides (241d5, 242a1-2). The Stranger requests that Theaetetus not take him for a parricide, and he subsequently asks the lad whether "a kind of hesitation" will prevent them from being so bold as to take on Parmenides (241d, 242a1-3). Theaetetus, one should note, enthusiastically favors such parricidal boldness. The Stranger then worries that he may appear "mad" (*manikos*) in undertaking a challenge that has always defeated him in the past, and he stresses that Theaetetus is responsible for the direction that the inquiry is now taking (242a-b). Philosophers, we may recall, sometimes seem to be mad (216d). Perhaps the willingness to change direction by abandoning unfruitful intellectual allegiances—even if such a change seems to oppose filial devotion—is a genuinely philosophical trait. The Stranger's reference to *mania* may also hint at the daimonic character of the inquiry he is about to undertake, an inquiry that pays due heed to the erotic arc of the developing soul.

Let us briefly step back from the text to reflect on the larger significance of this dramatic moment. I suggested earlier in this chapter that the Stranger's ability to move beyond the teachings of Parmenides would be a sign of his Socratic independence as a thinker. But we have already seen the outlines of the Stranger's refutation of Socrates, and the picture will become still clearer in the following chapter. How is the Stranger's emerging Socratic character to be squared with his critique of Socrates? I suggest that the answer lies in the extraordinary richness of Socrates' philosophical example. Perhaps the sincerest imitation of Socrates' capacity for independent growth would consist in the generation of a fruitful criticism of his manner of philosophizing. In "imitating" Socrates by critically distinguishing himself both from him and from his intellectual father Parmenides, the Stranger shares in Socratic philosophizing in a way that enables him to become more than an image. Viewed in this way, the Stranger proves that Socratic philosophizing *can* be shared, that it is somehow both unique to Socrates and separable from him, and that the pursuit of the examined life after the manner of Socrates allows one to come into possession of one's individual being as something greater than and prior to the being of an image.

The Stranger's philosophical parricide is also bound up with the issue of measure that was introduced at the very beginning of the *Sophist* and that played such an important role in the definition of noble sophistry. While the act of parricide might be taken to betray a lack of measure, it is needed in order to open up the middle ground of human life that appears to be denied by Parmenides.[46] This middle ground is the region of becoming that stands between being and not-being and that partakes somehow of both, just as images do (240b-c). The Stranger's philosophical parricide thus enables a measured understanding of human life. This connection is brought home by the fact that the Stranger and Theaetetus agree on the necessity of parricide at 242a-b, a passage that stands at the exact midpoint of the *Sophist*. The midpoint of the *Theaetetus*, one should recall, coincided with the digression at 172c-177c, which also concerned the middle ground of human life. This pattern, as I noted in connection with the *Theaetetus*'s digression, will be repeated in the *Statesman*, wherein the Stranger introduces the notion of the nonarithmetical mean at the very center of the dialogue.

The Stranger's sense of due measure is further attested by the emphases of the ensuing inquiry, which seem to counterbalance the quasi-mathematical character of the first half of the dialogue. He begins anew (cf. 242b) not by means of the method of division, but with various ontological myths that then get woven into the fabric of his own mythic, philosophical "gigantomachy" (246a4). In the first instance, the Stranger's characterization of these pre-Socratic ontologies as *muthoi* (242d6) emphasizes the extent to which their authors have treated others as little children (cf. 242c). More to the point, these pre-Socratics show their contempt for human beings by effectively omitting human life from their philosophical accounts of the whole of things. "In looking down upon us, the many," the Stranger tells Theaetetus, "[they have] excessively despised us" (243a6). This is a striking comment, given Socrates' initial characterization of the Stranger as a god who looks down upon human beings as well as the latter's inclusion of the Eleatics among the mythmakers he is now criticizing.

Neither of the armies ranged against each other in the gigantomachy—neither the earthborn materialists, who deny the being of that which is without body, nor the godlike friends of the forms (*eidê*: 248a4), who identify being with intelligible, motionless, immaterial kinds and associate becoming with the Heraclitean flux of bodies—leave any place in their ontology for the living soul, which moves but is without body. And it is by presupposing or *beginning* from the being of a soul with the distinctively human potential for virtue and vice, intelligence and foolishness, that the Stranger persuades both sides to agree to a compromise. The better sort of materialist—the tamer kind who will answer questions, if one can imagine such (246c-d)—will concede that the soul, justice, intelligence, and the rest of the virtues and vices have being, even though these things are invisible.[47] They can therefore also be brought to agree to the proposition that "the things that are [*ta onta*] are not anything else but power [*dunamis*]" (247e3-4). So, too, because the friends of the forms trust that being can be known by the soul or that the soul cognizes and beings are cognized, they will concede that both soul and the beings share in the power of being affected or affecting. And if motion and life and soul and intelligence are in this way "present to" (*pareinai*: 249a1) that which is, both motion and that which is in motion must be counted among *ta onta* (249b). The Stranger subsequently refers to this compromise as a "prayer of children" (249d3), as if to emphasize that it expresses such faith in the possibility of philosophy as springs from a prophetic understanding of the human soul—an understanding, as he stresses, in which the "better" sorts of human beings are capable of sharing but the "worse" are not (246d; cf. 247c). It is especially because it involves such impure and imprecise thinking, one suspects, that the Stranger's mediating or peacemaking speech about "being and the all" (249d3-4) is cast in the form of a myth.[48]

I conclude this discussion of the Socratic character of the Stranger's treatment of Theaetetus with some final observations. The position of the friends of the forms as articulated by the Stranger at 248a is roughly the one that was reached earlier by Theaetetus when he distinguished the objects of perception from the imperceptible truth and being at which the soul itself takes aim (*Theaetetus* 184b-187a). By developing the ontological implications of the soul's intellectual activity, the Stranger builds upon Socrates' previous work with Theaetetus. Later, the Stranger claims to understand the way in which Theaetetus's nature will advance on its own (265d-e)—a comment that is reminiscent of previous remarks by Socrates and Parmenides (*Theaetetus* 163c, *Parmenides* 130e). And in the course of his discussion of the nature of speech, the Stranger observes that *anthrôpos manthanei*, "(A) human being learns," is "the smallest and first speech" (262c9-10). It is, to be sure, an *example* of the smallest meaningful speech because it contains a noun and a verb and nothing more (cf. 262a-c); in this respect, however, "Theaetetus sits" would have served just as well (cf. 263a). But the specific statement *anthrôpos manthanei* is presumably the "first" speech because it is, for the Stranger as well as for Socrates, *the* fundamental presupposition from which philosophical discourse begins. It is therefore implicit in every other philosophical speech. *Anthrôpos manthanei* bespeaks the power of speech to reveal the way things are even as it articulates the most fundamental thing we need to know and remember about ourselves.

Sophist VI: Semblances of Socrates and the Stranger

The Stranger twice suggests that the perplexity associated with speaking about that which is (*to on*) is no less than that associated with that which is not (*to mê on*: 243c, 250e). He further expects that these two will come to light in tandem, or not at all (250e-251a). In the end, however, the Stranger does not provide a way to talk about *to mê on* as the altogether not or nothingness. Instead, he reinterprets that which is not as otherness or difference (258b-c). If *to on* is truly as perplexing as *to mê on*, there is perhaps a sense in which being is also unutterable, so that what gets articulated in speech is something that stands to being as a distorted image or semblance—roughly as otherness stands to nothingness.

One ineffable dimension of being is wholeness or integrity—both that of individual things, which they must possess in order to be or become at all (245d), and that of the Whole itself. Consider the most pertinent example, that of the wholeness of an individual human being such as a philosopher or a sophist. One could pick out the individual by uttering his name, but a name is not a speech. Even the shortest speech requires a noun and a verb, and in this sense is at least two, not one. And as was suggested by Socrates' attempts in the *Cratylus* to give an analytical account of *logos*, the wholeness of a speech—the coherent meaning that runs through its many parts and binds them together into a unity—is not fully contained within the speech itself, but is partly a function of the larger context in which it is uttered or written. Because their being is not a ratio or proportion—because they are erotic, unfinished creatures—we must think of the wholeness of human beings along similar lines. Indeed, human beings paradoxically achieve a certain wholeness only at the moment when vitality departs and they become a heap of elements. It thus seems safest to count no man a philosopher until he is dead: we would judge Socrates very differently if he had decided to take up Crito's offer of escape from prison, or if he had wailed over the hemlock. But even in the case of Socrates, whose life we can in some sense see whole because it is finished, speech cannot fully bespeak what we see. At best, a speech may possess a certain literally unspoken but intuitively accessible wholeness that imitates, and so helps one to divine, the wholeness of an individual human being. Put another way, speeches about human beings can only be better or worse semblances. Indeed it cannot be otherwise, given the artifice with which *logos* separates and then recombines or reweaves things that exist naturally only in concrete wholes. "Theaetetus is an ugly Athenian boy" may be true in one sense, but it is false in another. There never was a boy who was ugly and Athenian and nothing else—not smart or stupid, tall or short. Yet the speech presents Theaetetus as if he were just such an individual. Every speech about Theaetetus, every speech about a concrete individual, falsifies things in this way, and must for this reason alone be a semblance.[49] Beyond this, the speech at hand is a poor semblance indeed, for "ugly," "Athenian," and "boy" are all featureless abstractions that hardly begin to hint at the rich complexity of Theaetetus. A fuller speech—a Platonic dialogue, for example, or a series of dialogues—may constitute a better semblance, but will still inevitably be abstract and incomplete. Finally, we should recall here a main implication of the Stranger's ontological myth: just as we see ourselves in the light of our perceptions of the Whole, we see the Whole in the light of our perceptions of what it is to be human. For this reason, too, a speech about the Whole cannot be other than a semblance.

With the preceding points in mind, we are now ready to turn to the Stranger's resumption of the division of Sophist VI (265a-268d, figure 7). In the earlier divisions the sophist presented semblances of himself (*ephantazeto:* 265a8); for the first time, however, he will now be sought under the branch of production rather than acquisition. In step two, the Stranger separates divine production or *poiêsis* from human production. This step reflects the Stranger's choice with respect to an alternative that is posed in the form of a question: Does nature generate things "from some spontaneous [*automatês*] cause that grows them without thought [*aneu dianoias*], or from some cause that comes to be with reason [*meta logou*] and divine science [*epistêmês theias*] from a god" (265c7-9)? Theaetetus is uncertain about the answer, but concurs with the Stranger's beautiful opinion (cf. *kalôs*, 265d5); the *Statesman*'s myth of the reversed cosmos, we may note parenthetically, suggests that the truth is both more complex and more ugly. In any event, the Stranger says he "will set it down that the things said to be by nature are produced by divine *technê*" (265e3).

Step three distinguishes between the divine production of "natural" things and images and the human production of artifacts and images. The class of divine images includes dreams, shadows, and reflections in water, and therefore encompasses semblances as well as likenesses (266b-c). One should also note that both divine and human images can be images either of human artifacts or of natural entities. As for human images, the Stranger goes on to separate likenesses from semblances in step four. In step five, he distinguishes two modes of the production of semblances: one proceeds by means of instruments or tools (*organa*), and the other occurs when "the very one who is producing the semblance

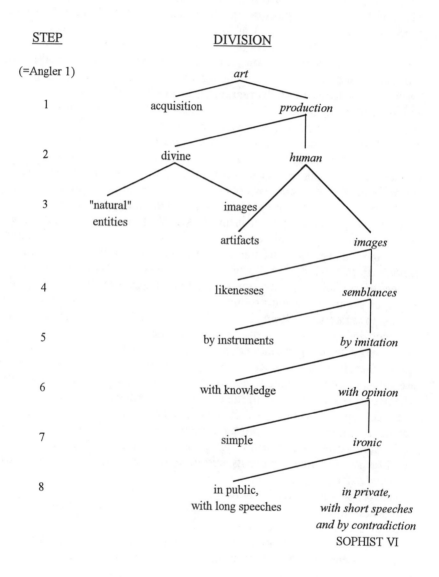

Figure 7. Sophist VI (235c-236c, 265a-268d)

furnishes himself as an instrument" (267a3-4). He illustrates the latter, which is called *mimêsis* or imitation, with the examples of someone's use of his own body or voice to imitate Theaetetus's figure (*schêma*) or voice. This particular example suggests that the Platonic dialogues would appear under the left-hand branch of step five, since Plato produces a semblance of Theaetetus but uses instruments to do so. In a nice Socratic touch, the Stranger corrects one implication of his mention of dreams in connection with divine images: the art of imitation is to be assigned to ourselves (267a), that is, to human beings, from which it follows that Homer was wrong to portray the gods as beings who change their shapes and deceptively take on looks other than their own.

Step six distinguishes imitation that is accompanied by knowing familiarity or acquaintance (*gnôsis*) from imitation in a state of ignorance (*agnôsia*: 267b7-9). It is noteworthy that the Stranger speaks here of *gnôsis* rather than *epistêmê*. His first example involves the knowing imitation of Theaetetus's voice and figure. But the Stranger goes on to mention the figure (*schêma*) of justice and virtue, as if to suggest that these things, too, are known nonscientifically, just as individual human beings are (267c). Perhaps the Stranger means to suggest that we come to know justice and virtue, to the extent that we do come to know these things, only through being in some manner acquainted with individuals who are themselves just and virtuous. At any rate, the Stranger observes that many are ignorant of virtue but nonetheless have an opinion about it, and eagerly try "to make to show forth [*phainesthai*] in them that which seems to them [to be virtue], imitating it as much as possible in deeds and speeches" (267c3-6). *Phainesthai*, to show forth or to appear, is ambiguous in this context: it may or may not suggest that these ignorant imitators of virtue attempt merely to seem virtuous without being virtuous. Put another way, the Stranger does not make it clear whether it is the ignorance of the imitator of virtue or his superficiality that makes his imitation a semblance. Strictly speaking, it cannot be his ignorance, since knowing imitation is *also* a branch of the production of semblances. To complicate matters further, however, the Stranger illustrates knowing imitation with the example of someone who impersonates Theaetetus's voice and looks, *not* someone who imitates virtue. Presumably such knowing imitation comes under the branch of semblances rather than likenesses because the image produced thereby is a superficial one. But what if someone imitated Theaetetus's *virtue*, and did so in a nonsuperficial and sincere way? Would his speeches and deeds nonetheless be semblances—perhaps because speeches and deeds are always potentially misleading as to the inner orientation of soul that constitutes the being of virtue? At issue here is whether the class of ignorant imitators of virtue might include someone like Socrates, who may be ignorant of virtue but is sincere in his attempt to instantiate it in his own life. I strongly suspect that it does.

In formulating step seven the Stranger splits the ignorant imitator of virtue in two "as if he were iron" (267e7). Given that this division separates the ironic (*eirônikos*) imitator of virtue from his simple (*haplous*) counterpart (268a), it is tempting to see the Stranger's image as a reference to Alcibiades' opening up the ironic Socrates in the *Symposium* as one might open a hinged statue of Silenus (215a ff.). Still, the irony to which the Stranger refers is less hard-edged, less hybristic and contemptuous, than that which Alcibiades takes himself to be revealing. The simple imitator believes he knows that about which he has merely an incorrect opinion, whereas the ironic imitator fears that he is ignorant of "the things that he has made a figure of [*eschêmatistai*] before the rest of men as if he knew them" (268a3-4). Considering the multiple figures or *schêmata* that he has produced in the *Sophist* in accordance with the method of division, one wonders whether the Stranger means to include himself in the latter group. Again, I strongly suspect that he does, since we have seen ample evidence that the Stranger is aware that his method conveys a false impression of one virtue in particular: that of philosophical intelligence. If this is correct, the Stranger's identification of ironic imitation would itself be aptly ironic.

The Stranger concludes this division by dividing irony. This was to be expected, since irony stands opposed to simplicity in that it involves doubleness. Step eight separates those imitators of virtue who are ironic in public and by means of long speeches from those who compel their interlocutors to contradict themselves in private and with short speeches (268b). The latter is the sophist, who, "being an imitator of the wise man [*tou sophou*], will clearly get some name derivative of his [i.e., *sophistês*]" (268c1-2). Once again, the Stranger seems to have honed in on Socrates, who admits at his trial that he has gotten the name of being a wise man (*Apology* 23a). His clear implication is that Socrates himself has (or should have) doubts about that with respect to which he seems to be most confident: the virtues of philosophical midwifery, or, more generally, the moral excellence of his philosophical way of life. The sixth division of the sophist thus amplifies the suggestion of the fifth.

There is one moment near the end of the division that deserves special consideration. After the Stranger has set forth step eight, he asks Theaetetus whether the maker of long public speeches is a statesman (*politikos*) or a public speaker (*dêmologikos*). Theaetetus chooses the latter (268b7-9). I wish to suggest that he made the wrong choice, and that the art of statesmanship as understood by the Stranger involves just the sort of dissimulation or irony identified here, namely, the public production of semblances of virtue by leaders who know that they are ignorant of the originals but believe that it is best to conceal this fact. The ending of the *Sophist* thus leads smoothly into the beginning of the *Statesman*, wherein the Stranger will clarify the picture I have just sketched.

It is appropriate that at the very end of the *Sophist* Socratic philosophizing stands opposed to statesmanship but on a par with it. Both pursuits are thus duly accorded equal honor. A further implication of the final step of the last division of the sophist is that we will not have adequately grasped the Stranger's criticism of Socrates until we acquire a better understanding of the nature of statesmanship, and therewith both its kinship with, and opposition to, Socratic philosophizing. Let us begin directly.

Chapter 7

The Paradox of Politics: The *Statesman*

They were offered the choice between becoming kings or the couriers of kings. The way children would, they all wanted to be couriers. Therefore there are only couriers who hurry about the world, shouting to each other—since there are no kings—messages that have become meaningless.

Franz Kafka, *The Castle*

The *Statesman* is the last act of our Platonic drama. It is in this discussion of politics that the knotted issues of Socrates' philosophic trial achieve their denouement. The *Statesman* is philosophically one of the richest Platonic dialogues, yet it is also one of the more difficult from the point of view of interpretation. Certain interpretative challenges arise from the seemingly self-contradictory nature of the Stranger's procedure and from the subtlety and indirectness of his speech. In these respects, the *Statesman* bears a close resemblance to the *Sophist*. The difficulty of the *Statesman*, however, is also a function of the complex and perhaps intractable problems with which it is concerned, problems that come fully into view only when philosophy and politics are considered in the broadest possible context.

The broadest context is that of the Whole itself, and perhaps the first thing to be said is that the *Statesman* is fundamentally about the whole of things in all of its complexity—about the body and the soul, political community, nature, the gods, and the cosmos. In the *Statesman* weaving is an image of speech (cf. 267a-c, 278b) as well as the work of statesmanship (279a ff.), and over the course of the dialogue the Stranger manages to weave together disparate elements into an intelligible whole.

223

In doing so he exemplifies a Socratic sense of due measure, in that his *logos* attempts as far as possible to find the middle ground between opposites that otherwise threaten to confront each other as extremes. It is not always easy to see that this is the case, for the *Statesman* resembles a patchwork quilt whose overall pattern is visible only at a certain distance. Thus, although the Stranger begins the search for the statesman by means of the method of bifurcatory division, he reverses course in midstream. Interrupting his divisions in order to offer an extraordinary myth about the cosmos, he abandons technical language in favor of something more like child's play (268d). This myth is a microcosm of the *Statesman* as a literary whole as well as of the Whole itself, for in tying together seemingly unrelated stories into a unified speech (cf. 268e-269c) it displays the cosmos as a unity of opposed cycles. It is also, as Griswold has observed, a joint that links the two halves of the dialogue.[1] To mention only the most important differences between these halves, the myth accomplishes a shift in emphasis from the acquisition of *nous* or theoretical intelligence as the goal of philosophy to the acquisition of *phronêsis* (272c; cf. 261e and 278e with *Sophist* 227b), and it is fittingly followed by the Stranger's introduction of measurement relative to the nonarithmetical mean and by his insistence upon the subordination of *technê* to *phronêsis* with respect to the governance of human life (284a-e; cf. 292d, 294a-b, 297a).

All of this reflects a way of thinking and talking that is especially appropriate to the nature of human life and the human soul as Socrates understands it.[2] But it would be rash to conclude from the Socratic character of the Stranger's inquiry that he has no further quarrel with Socrates. Both of these men agree that the soul must be understood in its relationship to the Whole, to which it is open by reason of its *erôs* and about which it has a prophetic understanding. They seem to disagree, however, about the nature of this relationship or about its most important implications. In particular, the Stranger speaks about the human lot in a way that brings sharply into view the tension arising from the fundamental oppositions—theory and practice, acquisition and production, body and soul, the necessary and the best—that run throughout the philosophic trial of Socrates. This permanent and ineliminable tension is reflected in the doubleness of human life that the Stranger articulates in the two cycles of his myth, and it provides the framework for his critical appraisal of the political implications of Socrates' philosophical activity.

The Stranger's sense of due measure is most delicately expressed in his clarification of the problem of reconciling the Socratic love of that which is best and highest in human life and with the prudent awareness of political necessity. His final position with respect to Socrates is complex, but may be summarized as follows. Political science (*politikê epistêmê*) is ultimately equivalent to *phronêsis*, or sound judgment about human life as a whole. *Phronêsis* is both the goal of philosophical inquiry and the prerequisite of the best care for human beings; it is, moreover, fully accessible only through Socratic inquiry. Yet Socrates' philosophical practice is deficient in *phronêsis* precisely insofar as his unrestrained devotion to inquiry unravels the constitutive bonds of political community. The Stranger's verdict reflects a disturbing paradox: Socrates turns out to be a sophist just to the extent that he embodies pure philosophic zeal. Put another way, the most perfect available instance of the *genos* or kind "philosopher" is no longer a philosopher. Conversely, we may infer, a philosopher who attempted to correct this error would fall short of perfection in suppressing his philosophical nature: he would forgo the full acquisition of *phronêsis* in the name of *phronêsis* itself. The philosopher is thus a radically paradoxical being: he is one whose own nature properly leads him to retreat from his own nature, or who becomes what he is only in being less than what he is. And whatever we may say about the philosopher, this conscious self-suppression, this wise acceptance of what is only second-best, and, in particular, of the substitution of law for the direct rule of *phronêsis* in the governance of political communities (300a-c), is the mark of the genuine statesman.

The details of the Stranger's dialectically evolving judgment of Socrates will emerge more clearly in the following pages. Let us note here that the *Statesman* is also enriched by the Odyssean subtext of the philosophic trial, which provides a dramatic path into the issues raised above. At the beginning of the dialogue Socrates explicitly introduces the question of kinship with respect to Theaetetus and Young Socrates, one of whom shares his looks and the other his name (257d-258a). As Mitchell Miller observes, the task of "testing to discover kinship" plays upon a "well-established motif in Greek literature," that of *anagnôrisis* or recognition. Miller also remarks that Odysseus's first encounters with Penelope and his father Laertes after he has slain the suitors provide a close analogue to the dramatic situation at the outset of the *Statesman*.[3] If this is correct, the scene has now shifted significantly from the beginning of the *Sophist*, in which Socrates' Homeric allusions made him out to be a hybristic enemy of the Zeus-like or Odysseus-like Stranger. But as we have seen, the Stranger's conversation with Theaetetus establishes that he is not simply hostile to Socrates. So, too, Socrates seems to view the ensuing search for the statesman primarily as an opportunity to explore the emerging philosophical kinship between himself and the Stranger.

Another implication of this Odyssean subtext comes into view when it is connected with the theme of homecoming that is introduced in the *Theaetetus*'s prologue: the *Statesman* stands at the end of a long voyage of deepening self-knowledge. In the course of his wanderings Odysseus seems to go everywhere and to encounter every kind of being, including gods, monsters, and enchantresses, men wild and tame, and even the shades in Hades. He is able to make his way back home in part because he is steadfast in resisting repeated opportunities to settle for easy alternatives to a distinctively human life—including, as a final temptation, the opportunity to enjoy a pleasant and carefree existence among the Phaeacians, who dwell far from the toils and troubles of the rest of humanity and are "near of kin to the gods" (*Odyssey* 5.35). The intelligent steadfastness that makes possible Odysseus's homecoming is visible also in the speeches and deeds of Socrates and the Stranger, who themselves become exemplars of a certain Odyssean turn of mind by virtue of Plato's having inscribed their characters within a philosophical allegory that answers to Homer's epic poem. Just as Odysseus leaves behind once and for all an "unreal, dreamlike world" when he finally returns to Ithaca to confront the dangers that await him at home, both Socrates and the Stranger ultimately repudiate the alluring siren songs of sophistry as well as the beautiful simplicities of theoretical abstraction in favor of a richer, if more problematic, humanity.[4] That Socrates does so is already obvious; that the Stranger does so as well is evidenced by the *Statesman*, in which his clear-eyed movement away from geometrical abstractions and toward an articulation of the concrete fabric of human life makes possible the philosophical recovery of his own identity as well as the more paradoxical identity of Socrates. The token of philosophical kinship that the Stranger offers Socrates is thus also the means whereby their differences come to light.

Odysseus's return is the return of the legitimate king to Ithaca. The political significance of this fact must be viewed against the backdrop of Odysseus's adventures as a whole, and in particular his sojourn with the Phaeacians. The Phaeacians are ruled by *Alkinoos* and *Arêtê*, King "Mighty-Mind" and Queen "Prayed-For" (*Odyssey* 7.54-55)—names that express a beautiful, humanly impossible hegemony of intellect and virtue. As depicted by the Stranger, in turn, the best human ruler is more like Odysseus than the godlike Alkinoos. Indeed, it would not be misleading to describe the *Statesman* as an extended meditation on the political and philosophical consequences of the absence of wise rulers in human life.

One other issue deserves mention before we turn to the text itself. Given that the *Statesman* contains what has recently been described as the Stranger's "punishment" of Socrates, to what extent is it possible to identify the Stranger with Plato?[5] This question arises also in connection with the matter of the "missing" dialogue *Philosopher*. It could be argued that the *Philosopher* is in fact the *Apology*, the dialogue that immediately follows the *Statesman* in the dramatic sequence of the octology. As we have seen, however, a public discussion of the nature of philosophy such as that which Socrates feels compelled to undertake in the *Apology* is bound to be philosophically inadequate. Nor does the latter identification take into account the Stranger's contribution to the definition or identification of philosophy. Alternatively, the *Philosopher* may be contained within the *Sophist* and the *Statesman*; the *Philosopher* was, after all, to have been the Stranger's answer to the third part of Socrates' question at *Sophist* 217a. Yet Socrates introduces a different expectation when he implies at the beginning of the *Statesman* that he himself will interrogate Young Socrates after the Stranger is through with him, so that each man will in the end have had an opportunity to speak personally with both of the young mathematicians (258a).[6] These conflicting expectations once again suggest that the work of clarifying the nature of the philosopher somehow belongs to *both* Socrates and the Stranger. This notion is also consistent with the paradoxical verdict of the Stranger as sketched above, from which it would follow that the paths of philosophizing pursued by Socrates and the Stranger in some sense correct each other's inevitable deficiencies. In the last analysis, however, these considerations point toward the figure of Plato, who has fashioned both of these literary characters together and whose dialogues—writings that he once attributed to a Socrates "grown beautiful and young" (*Second Letter*, 314c3-4)—offer an intriguing alternative to their speeches.

We shall briefly explore some of the philosophical and political implications of Platonic writing in the Epilogue. The next three sections of the present chapter are devoted to a close reading of the opening lines of the dialogue, the initial division of statesmanship (258b-267c), and the myth that follows (268e-274e). The fourth and fifth sections explore the resolution of major themes and issues in the last half of the dialogue. I turn now to the *Statesman*'s opening speeches, which are no less suggestive than those of the *Sophist*.

Beginning the *Statesman*: Tests of Kinship

The exchange between Socrates and Theodorus at the beginning of the *Statesman* recapitulates the conflict between Socrates' way of philosophizing and the Stranger's method of division. Socrates starts by saying that he owes Theodorus much thanks for making it possible for him to get to know Theaetetus and the Stranger (257a). Yet he never mentions the Stranger's divisions of the sophist or the need for an account of the statesman and the philosopher. He suggests instead that the conversations of the *Theaetetus* and *Sophist* have been worthwhile primarily insofar as they have provided an opportunity for acquaintance or familiarization (*gnôrisis*) with other individual souls, as opposed to the *epistêmê* of kinds of souls at which the Stranger's divisions aim. This implicit contrast between *gnôrisis* and *epistêmê* (cf. *Sophist* 219c) looks forward toward the ensuing conversation as well as back toward the previous dialogues: Socrates remarks a little later that the conversation of the *Statesman* should address the need to "refamiliarize" ourselves with those who are akin to us in soul (*anagnôrizein*: 258a3).

Theodorus, however, hears what Socrates neither said nor intended: he understands him to be offering thanks for the Stranger's account of the sophist. "But perhaps, Socrates," he responds, "you'll owe three times this thanks, when they finish working up [*apergasôntai*] for you the statesman and the philosopher" (257a3-5). Theodorus assumes that Socrates must acknowledge the philosophical value of the Stranger's definitions, and he presumably regards his companion's quasi-arithmetical divisions as a vindication of his own intellectual dignity. For this reason, he relishes the opportunity to be the middleman in the exchange of the Stranger's knowledge for Socrates' recognition. His talk of production and payment, however, serves to remind us of Sophist II, the itinerant merchant of another's lessons (*Sophist* 223c-224d).[7]

Socrates exploits the latter resemblance in a way that implicitly challenges the Stranger. He chastises Theodorus, whom he calls "most authoritative in calculations and geometrical matters," for equating the worth of the sophist, the statesman, and the philosopher, "who stand apart from one another in honor or value [*têi timêi*] more than according to the proportion [*tên analogian*] of your art" (257a7-b4). According to Socrates, the *timê* of these men—the honor one bestows upon them, and so, in this case, the rate at which one values speeches displaying their natures—should reflect the differences in their intrinsic worth. Theodorus makes no distinction between the worth of the sophist and that of the philosopher or statesman. Socrates' language suggests that he objects not only to this implication, but, more generally, to the application of arithmetical reckoning to the matter at hand. These three kinds of souls, he implies, are of incommensurable worth, so that the difference in their values, like an irrational number, cannot be expressed by *any* arithmetical proportion or ratio. Theaetetus, we recall, dealt indirectly with irrational numbers by means of geometrical images. Socrates' remark suggests that a similar indirection is required when speaking of human souls. He thus prepares the way for the Stranger's comparison of human nature to the square root of two, an irrational number (266b).

Does Socrates also mean to suggest that the statesman and the philosopher are incommensurable in worth? If so, he would appear to be commenting on the Stranger's suggestion that his manner of philosophizing is profoundly at odds with the political community. Socrates' attempt to awaken his fellow Athenians to the examined life does indeed seem to invite a conflict between incommensurable goods. Those who have become reflective human beings by associating with him will agree that they have received a gift of immeasurable value, but those who remain plants will believe that he corrupts, and both would appear to be right: what is good for us *qua* plants is not good for us *qua* human beings and vice versa, and there seems to be no common ground upon which to settle *this* dispute. One could perhaps try to defend Socrates by claiming that plants are in fact compelled to become human beings. One might point out in this connection that the unexamined life, the life that is unreflectively lived in accordance with tradition, inevitably comes into conflict with itself (as Socrates shows in the *Euthyphro*) just because the tradition is not monolithic. And one might conclude that even those who live like plants are forced to choose between fundamental alternatives, and that in order to do so they must examine life. This argument, however, seems to presuppose what it attempts to prove. To be sure, in order to choose *intelligently* one must examine life. The question at hand, however, is whether there is any political necessity for human beings to be able to make intelligent, distinctively human choices. The answer is by no means obvious. Protagoras, for example, presents himself in the *Theaetetus* as a godlike figure who is capable of giving all of the members of a political community the same beliefs about what is just, good, and noble (166d-167d). Protagoras implies in this context that it is irrelevant whether these beliefs are true, but that it is both necessary and sufficient for a political community merely that they be *shared*. For Socrates, this is not enough. But Socrates aims at a community of reflective human beings, such as one finds in the community of dialogue that grows up around him in the course of the *Republic*—and possibly nowhere else than in philosophical dialogue. If, moreover, a political community requires shared beliefs, and if its members will never be united by a common perception of the goodness of philosophical reflection, then the case for *paideia* as the mass production of citizens (as opposed to the midwifery of individual souls) begins to look stronger—perhaps even in the eyes of one who shares Socrates' sense of the unlivable character of the unexamined life.

We shall return to these issues in due course. For now, we may note that the Stranger's political teaching, particularly insofar as it may be gathered from the myth of the reversed cosmos, bears at least a superficial resemblance to that of Protagoras. His mythical description of the harsh beginnings of human life in the current cycle (274b-e) is similar to the sophist's own mythical account of our origins in the *Protagoras* (320c-322d). Beyond this, the Stranger's description of life in the counter-cycle of the cosmos provides us with an imaginative representation of Protagorean politics, or of the nurture of human beings as plants. And while this image is in general a negative one, it is nonetheless woven into the Stranger's understanding of politics as a whole. In these respects, and especially in emphasizing the priority of the protection of the body to the perfection of the soul, the Stranger gives philosophical legitimacy to certain elements of the Protagorean worldview.

At all events, Socrates' criticism of Theodorus is on target: the mathematician erroneously takes his mistake to be one of calculation, and promises to extract from Socrates the correct payment in gratitude at a later date (257b). Theodorus, moreover, speaks as a self-appointed representative of his "more measured" Eleatic guest (*Sophist* 216b8). His confidence in setting prices for the Stranger's lessons reflects his perception that the measure employed in their production, like that of their valuation, is fundamentally arithmetical. And this perception is by no means entirely unjustified, given the quasi-arithmetical nature of the Stranger's philosophical method. The latter's willingness to violate the rules of his method, however, has escaped the notice of Theodorus, although it cannot have escaped that of Socrates. In chastising Theodorus, Socrates underscores the incongruity that results from applying the method of division to human souls, and thus indirectly calls upon the Stranger to dissociate himself still more fully from the sophistical semblance of philosophy that the geometrician confuses with the genuine article. Socrates has in a sense turned the tables on his Eleatic guest: while he himself is not yet free and clear of the charge of sophistry, neither is the Stranger.

Theodorus states that the Stranger's lessons are "worked up" or fabricated. This is in fact a fair description of what is accomplished by the method of bifurcatory division when it is applied to human souls: in this case, division produces what it claims to acquire. Yet the Stranger begins his inquiry into the statesman by employing this very method. Why does he do so?

It will be helpful in addressing this question briefly to consider the two leading interpretations of the *Statesman* currently available in English. In *The Philosopher in Plato's Statesman*, Mitchell Miller provides a comprehensive account of the way in which bifurcatory division mediates between Young Socrates' theoretical yet initially nonphilosophical consciousness and genuinely philosophical reflection. Miller's guiding interpretative hypothesis is that the Stranger is a Socratic philosopher who arrives as Socrates' philosophical advocate just as his public trial is getting under way.[8] In his own study of the *Statesman*, Stanley Rosen criticizes Miller's approach because it neglects the Stranger's intention to punish the Athenian philosopher.[9] On Rosen's reading, the "concept construction" of the method of division is integral to the Stranger's transformation of the free, essentially acquisitive science of the philosopher

into a kind of practice—a transformation necessitated by the fact that
"the science of the free person leads to the loss of freedom unless it is
extended to practical tasks."[10] The Stranger acts from an appreciation of
the need "to give priority to the body over the soul in the domain of politics," or "to make self-defense primary in view of the hostility of nature."[11] Although Rosen does not say so explicitly, he allows us to infer
that one manifestation of this hostility is the violence that the philosopher
is about to suffer at the hands of the Athenians. The final outcome of
Socrates' public trial supports the Stranger's view that the philosopher
can defend himself only as a citizen. The Stranger then punishes Socrates
in advance for his inability to defend himself before the city.[12] Yet Rosen
also observes that in the *Statesman* Socrates "has the last laugh," in that
the Stranger "comes closer and closer to Socratic doctrine, until . . . one
can scarcely distinguish between the contents of their speeches."[13]

In my view, the latter observation allows for a rapprochement between
the interpretations of Miller and Rosen. While the Stranger's intentions
are doubtless punitive, his criticism of Socrates nonetheless develops out
of his own essentially Socratic orientation toward the goal of *phronêsis*,
and so reflects a paradox at the heart of Socratic philosophizing itself. I
also believe that Miller is right in claiming that the Stranger attempts to
speak simultaneously to the pit and the stalls, or to find the middle
ground between philosophical pedagogy and politically useful rhetoric.[14]
This point can furthermore be used to support and extend Rosen's reading. For the exhibition of this middle ground has a significance that goes
beyond pedagogy and politics: as an act of *phronêsis*, it is a critical
philosophical gesture that is directed above all at Socrates.

Socrates in fact seems to invite just such a gesture. At the beginning of
the *Statesman* the Stranger seems eager to trade interlocutors. "What
must I do," he asks, "about this here Theaetetus? . . . Are we to give him
a rest, and exchange him for his companion in exercises [*sungumnastên*],
this here [Young] Socrates?" (257c4-8).[15] Socrates, again acting as a
matchmaker (cf. *Sophist* 217d), approves this suggestion, and adds that
"they both run the risk [*kinduneueton*], Stranger, of having some kinship
with me from somewhere or other." For one looks like him, Socrates explains, and the other has the same name, "and we must always be eager
to refamiliarize ourselves with our kin through speeches [*tous ge sunge-
neis . . . anagnôrizein*]." Socrates adds that he himself has already spoken
with Theaetetus and has listened to him answering the Stranger's questions, but that he has yet to observe Young Socrates in either of these
ways. He suggests, then, that they now let Young Socrates speak with the
Stranger, and let him answer his own questions at a later time (257d1-
258a6).

After this speech Socrates falls silent; although he is present in the
dialogue as a listener and observer, we never hear from him again. His
last speech contains an explicit request, namely, that the Stranger talk
with Young Socrates for the purpose of helping him to determine
whether the young man's soul is akin to his own. The language in which
Socrates formulates this request reminds us of the prosecutorial intentions of the Stranger as well as his impending public trial: in suggesting
that Young Socrates and Theaetetus both run a risk because of their possible kinship with him, he seems to have clearly understood the implication of the Stranger's definition of noble sophistry.[16] In spite of his emphasis on the importance of knowing one's kin, however, Socrates does
not appear to be primarily interested in examining Young Socrates' nature. If he were, one would expect him to be eager to examine the youth
himself (cf. *Theaetetus* 144d-e), especially since there is a good chance
that he will not have many more opportunities for such discussions. Socrates' request for a test of kinship, I suggest, is instead directed toward
the Stranger, and is a natural complement to the philosophical challenge
he has just issued.

If the latter suggestion is on the mark, why doesn't Socrates talk with
the Stranger himself? One can only conclude that he views the Stranger's
pedagogy as crucial to the matter of their possible kinship. Most important, this way of proceeding allows the Stranger to show by example his
own concrete response to the risks or dangers posed by Socratic philosophizing. For the Stranger has already suggested that Socrates may en-
danger not only himself but also the political community as a whole. By
speaking with youths in the presence of Socrates the Stranger can accomplish two tasks at once, for he can convey his accusation while at the
same time demonstrating the responsible rhetoric that he envisions as a
positive alternative to Socrates' pedagogy. This arrangement presumably
suits the Stranger as well, for a more direct criticism of Socrates in the
presence of youths who are not yet philosophically mature might itself be
politically irresponsible. And if the latter consideration is operative
within the fictive framework of the dialogue, one might also expect it to
pertain to Plato's unknown readers. Perhaps the *Statesman* is a kinship
test for our souls as well.

In emphasizing throughout this study the subtle and indirect character
of the dialogues of the philosophic trial, I have put much weight upon
Plato's Socratic provocation of active reflection on the part of the reader.
This same subtlety, this preference for a certain kind of self-concealment,
is evident in the primary Odyssean model for the kinship test that is
played out in the *Statesman*. Let us pause briefly to consider this Homeric analogue.[17]

Penelope is unsure of Odysseus's identity because his various appearances do not match her memories of him. She wonders in particular how a man who looks so much like a beggar could be her husband (*Odyssey* 23.95, 115-116). In consideration of the formidable power he displays in slaughtering the suitors, she takes him to be a god in disguise—and indeed, Athena finally makes him look like one (23.62-64, 156-163). Penelope reassures her son Telemachus, however, that "if indeed he really is Odysseus, and has come home, surely we two will know one another [*gnôsometh' allêlôn*] much better, for we have signs which we two alone know, as they are hidden from others" (23.107-110). Socrates, it seems, is in a similar position with regard to the Stranger. His Odyssean allusions at the beginning of the *Sophist* implied that the Stranger was either the god Zeus or Odysseus disguised as a beggar. The supposition that the Stranger might be a refuting god is supported by the method of division, which looks down on generals no less than lousecatchers. Yet Socrates' exchange with Theodorus at the beginning of the *Statesman* makes it clear that this particular version of philosophical godhood is in his estimation something rather low or beggarly. In speaking of a kinship test, Socrates implicitly invites the Stranger to repudiate his base looks, or, alternatively, to cast off his cloak of philosophical godhood. Socrates' indirection, in turn, underscores the necessary secrecy of such a test. In this respect as well, the situation of Socrates and the Stranger parallels that of Penelope and Odysseus. To prove to Penelope who he is, Odysseus recounts for her the secret story of how he fashioned their bed from the standing stump of an olive tree (23.181 ff.). This token of his identity is, of course, also meant to test Penelope. The ever-cautious Penelope's recognition of her husband on this basis establishes her fidelity to him beyond the shadow of a doubt: she knows it is Odysseus because no other man (or god) has ever seen their nuptial bedstead. Similarly, the validity of the test of philosophical kinship that Socrates offers the Stranger seems to depend upon the hiddenness even of the test itself, for the Stranger's ability to perceive Socrates' challenge is itself one of the signs by which their kinship may be established.

At first blush, the Stranger's resumption of the method of division seems like a clear token of opposition to Socrates. Upon closer inspection, however, the Stranger's procedure appears rather to reflect his Socratic sense of due measure in the activities of teaching and learning. It has been well observed that Young Socrates may be expected to share Theodorus's narrow, mathematical understanding of what counts as knowledge, and that the division of the statesman prior to the myth confirms the youth's intellectual prejudices.[18] The method of division is accordingly the instrument of a Socratic, internal critique, whereby the Stranger draws the unacceptable consequences of Young Socrates' theoretical orientation with regard to politics.[19] The myth then provides the means to correct Young Socrates' mistakes.

A qualification is in order here. For the preceding remarks are not meant to minimize the genuine disagreement between the two philosophers, which is reflected in the Stranger's style of teaching as much as in the content of his speeches. An example will help to illustrate this point. Young Socrates exhibits a combination of mathematical intelligence and spiritedness (*thumos*). This youth is in fact superior to his agemate in point of philosophical zeal: whereas both Socrates and the Stranger discovered that Theaetetus needed encouragement, the Stranger finds it necessary to suppress the manliness (*andreia*) that Young Socrates exhibits in attempting to distinguish human beings from beasts in a way that is not sanctioned by division (262a; cf. 263d). The Stranger later makes it clear, however, that he agrees with Young Socrates' intuition about the distinctive nature of human beings. Why, then, does he seek to restrain his *thumos* in this instance? I shall argue that he does so in order to restrain Young Socrates' misplaced pride in human intelligence, and that this gesture is also meant as an implicit criticism of Socrates' own overestimation of the power of thought in the economy of human souls. In order for Young Socrates to understand the nature of statesmanship, the Stranger suggests, his spiritedness will have to be moderated no less than his penchant for theoretical abstraction. This musical attunement of intellect and spiritedness is analogous to the interweaving of moderation and courage that he later identifies as the specific task of statesmanship (306c-311c; cf. *Republic* 410c-412a). The Stranger's speech about statesmanship is thus a dramatic intimation of the work of statesmanship itself.

Socratic Reflections:
Division and the Search for the Statesman

Once we have embarked upon the path of division, it is natural to wonder why the Stranger introduces the myth of the reversed cosmos. In part, he does so because he and Young Socrates have in their divisions lost sight of the statesman's nature. More generally, the myth is a commentary upon the things that are passed over in the first part of the dialogue (258b-268e) as well as a development of the themes introduced therein. As we study these pages, we shall therefore pay no less attention to the things the *logos* leaves out of account than to those that it takes into consideration.

A few preliminary observations are in order. The myth is only the most vivid and comprehensive attempt to return to the origins of things in an inquiry that involves more fresh starts and new beginnings than even the *Theaetetus* or the *Euthyphro*.[20] The question of the proper *archê* or rule of political communities necessarily leads to a concern with the *archai* in the sense of origins or beginnings. These origins, in turn, may be understood both in terms of the historical beginnings of a political community and in terms of the regime's animating conception of its ends. With its frequent reversals and repetitions, the dramatic movement of the dialogue reflects the deeply problematic character of a philosophical archaeology of politics. Let us pause to enlarge upon this point. According to the myth of the reversed cosmos, political life is characterized by a falling away, in various senses, from its beginnings. Publicly and politically, the increasing distance of a city from its foundations is bridged largely by the artifice of myth or story telling: political communities understand their origins in terms of the historical act of founding, and are sustained by the common recollection of this act that is preserved in the poeticoreligious tradition. But the statesman understands this act in a different way. The statesman does not derive his authority from the contingent historical beginnings of the community, but from his knowledge about the nature and purposes of a political community as such. Statesmanship aims at the human good, and so requires knowledge of human souls. But the *acquisition* of such knowledge is rendered problematic by man's unfinished nature, as well as by the indispensable *production* of citizens out of the natural material of human souls—indispensable because the various traditional practices, customs, laws, and myths that structure the life of a political community and that weave the fabric of souls are needed as a bulwark against the otherwise unbearable harshness of nature. The multiple reversals of the *Statesman* reflect the resulting theoretical difficulty: the inquiry involves repeated beginnings and includes a founding myth because the ultimate beginnings of political life are too obscure to be understood fully.

The following examination of the portion of the *Statesman* prior to the myth is unfortunately highly detailed. Yet this close reading is necessary for an understanding of the dialogue as a whole, and will, I believe, confirm the Socratic dictum that the beginning is the greatest part of every work. So as not to lose sight of the forest for the trees, however, it will be helpful to anticipate the main conclusions of the present section. Statesmanship emerges in the following pages as a productive *technê* that is guided by nontechnical wisdom. Surprisingly, the critical example of architecture indirectly underscores the nontechnical character of statesmanship and in particular the importance of *phronêsis* in political rule. *Phronêsis*, however, is invisible to a philosophical method that favors arithmetical measurement. The method of division, moreover, effectively suppresses the politically crucial phenomena of *erôs* and *thumos*. But the role of *phronêsis* in statesmanship is complicated by the necessarily partisan and productive work whereby the statesman in effect manufactures citizens. This productive work is imitated by the Stranger's application of the method of division, a point that is reflected especially in the so-called "longer" and "shorter" roads (265c-266e).

Architecture and the Autepitactic Man

We turn now to the initial division of statesmanship (258b-267c, figure 8). The statesman is said to be "one of the knowers [*tôn epistêmonôn*]" (258b4). As with the sophist, we shall attempt to isolate the statesman (*ho politikos*) by defining his art (*hê politikê*).[21] Once again, the Stranger overlooks the considerations of the statesman's character, education, and so forth, with which Socrates is so concerned in other contexts (most notably the *Republic*).[22] Here, however, the Stranger speaks of *epistêmai*, not *technai*, as if to emphasize the superiority of the statesman's genuine knowledge to the artful seeming-wisdom of the sophist. He also divides the sciences in a way that differs markedly from the first division of the arts in the *Sophist*. The Stranger prefaces this first step with the following speech:

> Which way, then, will one discover the political straight-of-way [*atrapon*]? For we must find it, and having separated it off from the rest put as a seal upon it one look [*idean*], and by assigning as a distinguishing mark one other kind [*eidos*] to the rest of the turn-offs, we must make [*poiêsai*] our soul think of all the sciences as being two kinds. (258c3-8)

This passage breaks up the work of division into two stages: first we discover different ways or paths, and then we stamp that which we have discovered with a look. Division, in other words, is both acquisitive and productive, and the Stranger suggests that the dimension of production is crucial to our possession of knowledge that is public and held in common. In this connection one should note that he speaks of our *soul*, not our *souls*. Furthermore, he speaks as if the knowledge of politics were one of two basic kinds of sciences: we are to stamp the political science with one look, and all of the other sciences, taken together, with another. Finally, his talk of straights-of-way and turn-offs suggests that political science is a kind of measuring rod for the other sciences. In these ways, the Stranger anticipates both the combination of production and acquisition in statesmanship and the statesman's subordination of the other arts to the ends of politics (305d).

In step one of the division the Stranger separates cognitive science (*gnostikê*) from practical science (*praktikê*). As examples of cognitive science, he mentions arithmetic and its kindred arts; as examples of

STEP   DIVISION

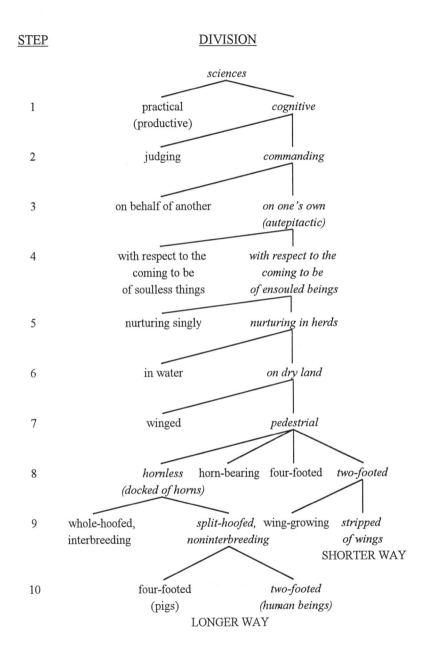

Figure 8. The Royal and Political Art (258b-267c)

practical science, he mentions only manufacturing arts: carpentry and all of handicraft.[23] The former provide only knowing (*to gnônai*) and are "stripped of actions," while the knowledge embodied in the latter "inheres naturally" in their practical (productive) activity, whereby they "bring to completion bodies that come to be by their agency and did not exist before" (258d8-e2). While this step bears some resemblance to the initial separation of the arts in the *Sophist*, there are several noteworthy differences. Production has been renamed "practice" (without any of the connotations, however, of Aristotelian *praxis*) and acquisition, which involves mastery or the prevention of mastery, has become "cognition." By comparison with their counterparts in the *Statesman*, moreover, the two basic branches of art in the *Sophist* include an exotic variety of pursuits (cf. *Sophist* 219a-c). It has been observed that the Stranger identifies the art of politics with the method of finding the art, and the present passage seems to support this insight: the Stranger paves the road, so to speak, to political science with what amounts to a purge of the arts that serve the soul and the body.[24] This purge presents an extreme ordering of the arts. Statesmanship gives order to the arts by fitting their employment to the good of the whole. In this crucial sense, statesmanship is indeed a straight-measure for the arts. But if the measure of statesmanship is understood to be purely mathematical, its ordering may coincide, absurdly, with a wholesale elimination of precisely those nonmathematical aspects of human existence that give political life its distinctive character—including in particular the phenomena related to *erôs* and *thumos*. The first step of the present division makes no mention of arts that serve or pertain to the desires for money, honor, or victory and mastery of all sorts, to sexuality and the care of the body, or to imitation, all of which are included in the corresponding division of the *Sophist*.[25]

The Stranger next lumps together the statesman, king, household manager, and slavemaster (258e). There is one royal science, he asserts, and whoever possesses it—even if he is a private man—is royal (*basilikos*). The royal science is furthermore a universal science of rule, for which the figure (*schêma*) of a large household and the bulk (*ongkos*) of a small city are essentially the same (259b). These geometrical terms suggest that the difference between the public and private spheres of human life is merely one of dimension; the quasi-mathematical science of rule presupposes the calculable and commensurable natures of these realms. There is one science of rule, the Stranger concludes, which we may indifferently call royal, political, or household managing (259c). Significantly, this passage makes no mention of the statesman, but instead speaks of the king (*basileus*); this identification of statesmanship with the royal science (*basilikê*) will persist throughout the dialogue. Furthermore, the assimilation of royal rule to the management of slaves suggests that the distinctively political dimension of human life in which the Greeks took so much pride, the shared participation in common affairs that distinguishes the free citizens of the *polis* from the subjects of barbarian empires, has dropped out of view. Mastery has reappeared in the division of the arts, and we have taken a big step toward the Stranger's eventual characterization of statesmanship as the care of herd animals.[26]

The Stranger goes on to make an observation that leads Young Socrates to locate the royal science in the branch of cognition, but that briefly emphasizes the active, practical dimension of rule. "It is clear," the Stranger says, "that in holding down his rule, every king is able to do little with his hands and all his body in comparison with the intelligence [*sunesin*] and strength [*rhômên*] of his soul" (259c7-9). Because the Stranger does not explain whether maintaining one's power is an end in itself or simply the precondition for achieving some other end, this passage indirectly raises the question of the goal of statesmanship. The latter question will soon come more sharply into focus. The Stranger also introduces here the distinction between the body and the soul. The body's strength is undoubtedly useful in holding onto political power, but more useful still is the quick comprehension and the mettle or manliness of the soul.[27] The Stranger's earlier reference to the bulk of a city is relevant in understanding this point. In actually exercising statesmanship, the statesman must move massive things, namely, the souls and bodies of whole groups of human beings. To do so, he needs to know when and how to act. He therefore needs both intelligence and a certain force of spirit—neither of which, one supposes, can be taught or learned in the manner of a *technê*. The limitations of the Stranger's method are once again apparent, for we may conclude that merely holding power—let alone using it well—involves more than simply knowing an art.

That statesmanship, like philosophy, is not a *technê* is implicit also in the immediate sequel. Since the powers of the ruler's psyche are more important than those of his body, Young Socrates agrees to lump together "as one" under the heading of cognitive science statesmanship and the statesman, the royal man (*basilikos*) and the royal art (259d). The Stranger now indicates that within the branch of cognitive science there is a natural joint (*diaphuê*) or a natural bonding and separation of arts that is reflected in the connection between *logistikê* (the art of calculation) and architecture (259d-260b). The joint the Stranger wishes us to consider is one that links the commanding (*epitaktikon*) and the judging or critical (*kritikon*) parts of cognitive science, which he distinguishes in the second step of the division (260a-b). The Stranger thereby calls attention to the presence of two elements in the epitactic art of architecture: calculation and rule over others. One might at first suppose that the architect's superior knowledge of calculation is what gives him authority over the rest of the builders, while the actual exercise of this authority—the practical application of calculation to the task of building—is what distinguishes the architect from the skilled calculator. In that case, however, the difference between the commanding and judging branches of cognitive science would be a matter not of cognition but of action—even though the cognitive sciences are as such "stripped of actions" (258d5). Is there no *cognitive* difference between the activities of calculating quantities of materials, room dimensions, and the like, and directing the construction of a building?

It seems clear that there *is* a cognitive difference between these activities, but that it is obscured by the mathematical orientation of the division. The *architektôn* is so called because he is a ruler (*archôn*) of builders. As such, his task is "to keep on charging each group of workmen with what is fitting for them, until they should finish up the work that was ordered" (260a6-7). The knowledge involved in this task is not simply mathematical or logistical; rather, it is a knowledge of how to make timely, opportune, and fitting use of calculation in building a structure. In other words, arithmetical measurement and measurement according to the nonarithmetical mean are linked in the productive work of architecture. The architect is distinguished from the carpenters he employs by his comprehensive knowledge of the house, and this comprehensive knowledge of the end at which building aims is also the beginning or *archê* of the work of housebuilding (cf. Aristotle, *Metaphysics* 7.7.1032a32-b14). To anticipate, we may say that the architect knows the becoming of the mean in housebuilding (284c). The architect has a certain kind of technical *phronêsis*: he knows both the purposes a house and all its parts are meant to serve, and the timely steps by which the sort of structure that best fulfills the *telos* of a house may be brought into being in *these* concrete circumstances. It is this joint between arithmetical measurement and nonarithmetical measurement that the Stranger seems to have in mind when he distinguishes the judging branch of cognitive science from the commanding branch.

The example of architecture also indirectly helps us to grasp the extraordinary difficulty of nonarithmetical measurement in the case of statesmanship, which is concerned not with a narrow range of activities but with human life as a whole. To say that politics is an architectonic science (as Aristotle does explicitly at *Nicomachean Ethics* 1.2.1094a27) is to make use of an analogy. Architecture is itself subordinate to statesmanship, and the goods toward which it directs the work of its own subordinate arts—the protection of the body and of other material things from the harshness of nature, the production of spaces that do honor to the gods, and so forth—are only partial goods. For this reason, however, the work of architecture is fairly clear and specific: finished, well-built structures that do the job for which they were intended—a fact that even nonexperts can easily appreciate—are for the most part the necessary and sufficient proof of the architect's qualifications as a ruler of builders. But this kind of universally acknowledged public evidence is absent in the case of statesmanship. The problem here is twofold. Let us provisionally accept Rosamond Kent Sprague's claim that the statesman produces "good men."[28] In the first place, it is not obvious to everyone what a good man is. This is because it is not obvious to everyone what a good soul is. And while the members of a given political community might generally agree about what it is to be a good man, this agreement— which invariably assimilates being a good man to being a good Spartan, or Athenian, or what have you—is always itself a *consequence* of the work of statesmanship. This brings us to another, thornier difficulty. Like houses, political communities protect ensouled bodies; but souls and bodies are also the *material* out of which political communities are made. The analogy of statesmanship and architecture no longer holds at this point, and the same may be said of the paradigm of weaving that the Stranger introduces later. Anyone can see that architecture and weaving are legitimate *technai*, because they fit their protective coverings to stable, finished, determinate entities (bodies) in view of which their work may be judged. But statesmanship, in fashioning a political community as a kind of house or cloak (cf. 311c), fashions also the thing that this artificial "covering" is meant to fit. As the Stranger will later indicate, the statesman is a weaver of the fabric of *souls*: he supervises the binding and plaiting by "educators and nurses" of the elements of "a fitting character" (308e5-7)—one that shares, as far as possible, in moderation as well as manliness (308d ff.).

The importance of *phronêsis* and nonarithmetical measurement in statesmanship is implicit also in what follows. The Stranger and Young Socrates next agree that the royal man must be set down in the commanding part of cognitive science, since he is a lord or master (*despozôn*) rather than a spectator (*theatês*: 260c1-4). The commanding art, in turn, is also divisible along the line suggested by two analogous distinctions: "just as the art of retailers has been divided off from the art of those who sell their own work, so, too, the royal family [*genos*] seems to have been separated off from the family of heralds" (260c7-d2). Those who sell their own work engage in two consecutive activities: manufacture and marketing. Similarly, the royal man first thinks thoughts and then issues them as commands. It is in the thinking that he differs from the herald, who passes on his thoughts (*noêmata*) as commands much as retailers sell the works of others (260d). How is thinking like manufacture? The manufacture of marketable items itself involves two distinct activities: knowing and making. The successful artisan is therefore also a spectator or *theatês*, for his production is guided by his perception of the mean in the work at hand. So, too, the analogy implicitly corrects the Stranger's distinction between masters and spectators: in thinking thoughts that can be successfully retailed as commands, the royal man articulates the mean that he perceives in his capacity as a *theatês*. The herald, on the other hand, need only reissue the royal man's injunctions as commands. The Stranger's analogy, then, suggests that royalty and heralds are to be distinguished by the presence or absence of the knowing perception of what is fitting to the work of statesmanship.

The present passage goes to the heart of the political and philosophical concerns of the *Statesman*. The problem of sophistry enters most directly into politics when one is ruled by a herald who poses as a king and issues his own commands. How can one tell a knowing ruler from an ignorant one? One might well doubt that the method of division will resolve this difficulty, since those who issue orders with knowledge are formally indistinguishable from those who do so in ignorance. Note, too, that the Stranger's analogy asks us to compare a distinction between arts with a distinction between families (*genê*) or tribes (cf. *to kêrukikon phulon*, 260d7). These terms suggest that the distinction between royalty and heralds is not a technical one, but is rooted in a difference in their natures. Beyond this, it is an open question whether there *are* any knowing rulers such as the Stranger envisions. Nor is it obvious that the absence of such rulers is in every instance a political problem. So long as he is faithful to the commands of the ones who know—be they gods or wise human beings—why would it matter if one were governed by a herald? This issue will resurface when we turn to the rule of law. As we shall see, the Stranger presents law as a kind of impersonal herald of political intelligence, so that to submit to the ultimate authority of law is in a sense to be ruled by the ignorant mouthpiece of genuine royalty. Of course, this general characterization of law begs the question of the intelligent basis of any particular set of laws. If in fact there are only heralds in this world, and no kings (divine or otherwise) from whom they could receive their commands, our human lot is indistinguishable from that of the various orphaned children of Kafka's literary universe. But according to the "orphaned" myth of Protagoras (*Theaetetus* 164e3), this fact is politically insignificant. The myth of the reversed cosmos will force us to reflect further upon these difficult issues.

To return to the division, the Stranger next asks Young Socrates whether they should mix together the royal art with the arts of the interpreter, boatswain, soothsayer, herald, and all others related to these, or should separate off the royal family as the *genos* of "self-commanders" or "independent commanders" (*to tôn autepitaktôn genos*), and, overlooking all the rest, leave it up to someone else to set down another name for them (260d11-e8).[29] The name "autepitactic," the Stranger adds, is to be understood as paralleling the earlier analogy of those who sell their own work (*hoi autopôleis*), since the branch of commanding in which the royal family is to be located "happens to be pretty much without a name" (260e3-5). Step three of the division is now complete.

What is suggested by the Stranger's designation of certain kinds of individuals as "autepitactic"? The term implies independent rule over oneself as well as others. This implication should be considered in the light of the Stranger's emphasis on the productive character of statesmanship. While the statesman's nature is necessarily fashioned by the political community in which he grows to maturity, he is autepitactic only to the extent that he can reflectively detach himself from the artifact of community in judging its significance for human souls. The statesman's independence is thus a philosophical independence. These reflections anticipate distinctions that will be introduced only later in the inquiry. For all we know, the autepitactic individual is a divine being: while the boatswain and herald speak for human beings, the soothsayer speaks for the gods, and the interpreter (*hermêneus*) may speak for either.

The Stranger in fact makes it clear that step three is inadequate. While he justifies his neglect of the branch of nonautepitactic commanders (whom he does not even name) by observing that "the inquiry was for the sake of the one ruling, but not his contrary" (260e8-261a1), he later suggests that the method of division cannot illuminate one contrary without illuminating the other (262e-263a). And his claim that the ruler has been "defined by the difference of what belongs to another in comparison with what is one's own" (261a4) is blatantly tautological. Furthermore, in introducing the next step of the division, he speaks of cutting "the part of cognition that is commanding" (261b10-11)—as if the distinction between autepitactic individuals and their contraries had never been accomplished. This oversight is repeated at 263e8-9, where he speaks of "all of the commanding part of the cognitive science" as belonging to the family of animal-nurture.

In sum, the Stranger has not succeeded in separating the royal man from the many who resemble him. Nor will he be able to address this problem in the course of the present division, because in subsequent steps he turns his attention away from the ruler and toward the objects over which the ruler exercises his art. This problem will run through the *Statesman* like a loose thread. While it helps to motivate the Stranger to tell the myth, it is explicitly taken up only much later in the dialogue (289d ff.).

Excess and Deficiency: Moderating Young Socrates

It is impossible to read the *Statesman* without being struck by its "deep
vein of irony, or rather of satire."[30] Satire, the Stranger suggests, has a
proper place in the study of politics. The connection between the laughable and the excessive or deficient provides us with a way to understand
this suggestion. The Stranger calls attention to the issue of due measure
at the beginning of the section of text now at hand, when he ask whether,
as a result of the previous steps, the ruler now stands apart from other
men "in a measured way" (*metriôs*, 261a3). Soon thereafter, he mentions
phronêsis for the first time in the dialogue, and associates it with the
avoidance of excessive seriousness with regard to names (261e). I suggest accordingly that when the comic excesses or deficiencies of the subsequent steps of the division are viewed within the tapestry of the
Statesman as a whole, they help to illustrate the sense of due measure
that characterizes political wisdom.

Let us begin with the method's humiliation of human beings, which
culminates in the comparison of them to pigs. In itself this denigration of
our species is excessive, but this excess may lead to a deeper sense of
due measure insofar as it helps Young Socrates to recognize the limitations of his narrowly mathematical orientation toward politics. Beyond
this, the Stranger's deflation of our species' sense of self-worth may reflect the tendencies of a prudent politics. Seth Benardete touches upon
this point when he distinguishes "human" from "human being": "The art
of ruling finds it safer to regard men as beasts than as nonbeasts. Human
beings are only potentially human."[31] This prudent understanding, which
keeps in sight the body as well as the soul and the necessary as well as
the good, is an essential dimension of the statesman's *phronêsis*. Nor has
the inquiry altogether lost sight of the soul and its potential humanity,
because Young Socrates reminds the Stranger of our mental superiority
"most eagerly" (*prothumotata*: 262a5)—literally, with his "*thumos* to the
fore." Young Socrates' spiritedness here bespeaks his intellectual pride.
This pride is also visible in his easy acceptance of the notion that the
statesman is capable of attaining scientific knowledge of human affairs—
a view that overestimates the theoretical powers of a human ruler no less
than the notion of ruling as herding underestimates the dignity of human
beings in general. And it is this pride—and by extension the more complex pride of the old Socrates, who in his own way overestimates the
power of human souls—that the Stranger seeks to moderate by means of
the method's reduction of human beings to animals. For his part, the
Stranger seeks the mean by leaning toward the other extreme (cf. Aristotle, *Nicomachean Ethics* 2.9.1109a30-b1). The truth about human beings lies somewhere in the middle ground between pigs and gods.

We return now to the text. Having completed the third step of the division, the Stranger begins to speak of the activity of dividing as "cutting" (261a-b) and to emphasize that this process is one of bifurcation (261b-c, 261e-262a). This language gives the subsequent steps an air of technical precision. Yet just as the Stranger earlier referred to a natural joint but did not mention cutting, he now speaks of cuts but nowhere claims that they are being made at natural joints. Indeed, at 266a1-2 the Stranger speaks of animal (*to zôion*) as "having been chopped up into pieces [*katakekermatistai*]," which suggests a rather indiscriminate process—the more so because he had earlier warned Young Socrates not to make his cuts too finely (262b). One might go so far as to suggest that the process of inquiring into the nature of living beings (such as the sophist and statesman) by means of the method of division involves the philosophical equivalent of butchery, except that the butcher cuts animals at their joints rather than chopping them into bits. To put this point in terms that the Stranger will soon introduce, the present division makes distinctions between parts rather than discovering natural kinds. The same thing, however, is true of the statesman, who cannot do otherwise than accept the separation of human beings into such artificial categories as "Athenian" and "barbarian." Perhaps the cuts of the present division should be understood as a mimetic reflection of the necessarily partisan, productive work of political intelligence.

The latter suggestion is indirectly supported by the fourth step of the division. All rulers, the Stranger says, are concerned with coming to be (*genesis*). The productive dimension of statesmanship is now explicit. The Stranger and Young Socrates go on to divide the commanding part (*to epitaktikon meros*) of cognitive science by "ordering one part of it to range over [*tattontes . . . epi*] the coming to be of soulless things, and one over that of the ensouled" (261b13-c1). This procedure exemplifies the work of the art now being sought: the method of division, like statesmanship, issues injunctions. Strikingly, Young Socrates is uncertain whether the statesman supervises the *genesis* of ensouled or soulless things (261c). In responding to his question, the Stranger once again violates the principle of value-neutrality: unlike architecture, the royal science is never in charge of soulless things, but "is more noble [*gennaioteron*], always possessing its power in the case of living beings and about these very things" (261c7-d1). We may note that the Stranger here employs the same word that he used in speaking of "noble" sophistry (*Sophist* 231b8).

We are now at a critical point in the search for the statesman. If statesmanship is concerned with the coming to be of human beings, how are we to understand this *genesis*?[32] Ensouled beings are higher than soulless things. Are we to make a further distinction of rank in the case of ensouled or living things? The Stranger later states that nonarithmetical measurement has to do with "the indispensable being [*anangkaian ousian*] of *genesis*" (283d8-9). But the mean, the fitting, the opportune, and the needful come into view only with respect to the good at which *genesis* aims, that is, only in the light of the end or purpose of that which is coming to be. The quasi-arithmetical method of division, on the other hand, officially disdains such imprecise and prophetic judgments as are implicated in evaluation according to the mean. Hence it will approach *genesis* not with a view toward its end but solely with an eye toward its beginning. Put another way, the method is at home with efficient causation of a mechanical sort, but not with final causes, and so not with the teleological development of organisms.[33]

If one considers only where human beings come from, the Stranger implies, there is no reason to separate them from the rest of the beasts; the Stranger would reject the separate, providential creation of human beings described in the Bible's book of Genesis. This is in itself an important philosophical lesson that will be amplified in the myth. But the result of approaching the coming to be of human beings in this way is that they are shown to be on a par with pigs and sheep, just as their caretaker—the statesman—is on a par with the herdsman. Pigs, however, are cared for by human beings, who are members of another species. Therefore either the statesman is a superior being—a *daimôn* or a god—or ensouled beings, as the myth will suggest, must again be divided in such a way as to reveal the power of human beings to care for themselves.

The Stranger now considers distinct modes of care or nurture. In formulating step five of the division he separates "nurturing singly" from "the common care of the nurslings in the herds" (261d4-5). The Stranger goes on to suggest that the statesman is not a "private nurse" (*idotrophon*) but is instead engaged in "the common nurture of many together," like a horse-feeder or cattle-feeder. He then complicates the contrast between solitary and herd nurture when he asks Young Socrates whether they should speak of the statesman's activity as "herd nurture" or "some kind of common nurture." Young Socrates is indifferent, and the Stranger praises him for not taking names too seriously (261d7-e7).

The passage summarized above deserves careful consideration. It is noteworthy that the Stranger does not distinguish between nurture (*trophê*) and care (*epimeleia*). This, too, is a mistake that will have to be corrected later: for whereas *epimeleia* may signify caring for the soul as well as the body, *trophê* means the nourishment and rearing of young bodies—activities in which the statesman does not engage (cf. 275d-e). If anything, Young Socrates should have paid *more* attention to names, since the Stranger later puts his finger on just this distinction between nurture and care when he says that the statesman "escaped by way of nomenclature" (275d5-6). Step five may also allude to Socrates in its separation of the private or individual nurture of human beings from the nurture of many together. At issue here is not so much the question of whether human beings are herd animals or solitary animals, for it is obvious that they can be both: sometimes they travel in packs, as it were, and sometimes they show up as hermits. More important is the question of how they should be cared for.[34] In this connection we may observe that "common nurture" (*koinotrophikê*)—a term that the Stranger later uses in place of herd nurture (264b6-7)—seems to hint at a kind of care that treats human beings neither as solitary individuals nor as members of a herd. A herd is an undifferentiated multiplicity, whereas a community (*koinônia*) is a unity of many individuals. And if in fact statesmanship is the common care of human beings, it would follow that certain kinds of regimes are illegitimate—namely, all those in which human beings are treated simply as herd animals. Had the Stranger pursued statesmanship under the heading of common care rather than that of herd nurture, the Greek *polis* would have proved to be superior to barbarian empires.

The preceding observation may give us a clue as to why the Stranger chooses the path of herd nurture. As it turns out, he goes on to allude both to the Greek cities and to the barbarian empires in order to criticize distinctions that reflect political partisanship. Significantly, the Stranger mentions wise judgment just prior to formulating this criticism: he tells Young Socrates that he will show up "richer in *phronêsis* into old age" if he guards against taking names too seriously (261e5-7).[35] Young Socrates goes on to display a certain intelligence in being "eager" to state that the next step should separate the nurture of human beings from the nurture of beasts (*prothumêsomai*: 262a3). The Stranger remarks that he has made this distinction "in a most spirited [*prothumotata*] and manly [*andreiotata*] way" (262a5-6). This is his first explicit recognition of Young Socrates' philosophical boldness. In addition, the reference to manliness prepares us for his subsequent criticism of the youth's partisanship: *andreia* (manliness or courage) is the quality not of an *anthrôpos* simply but specifically of an *anêr*, or a politicized human being.

The Stranger objects to Young Socrates' division of human beings from beasts on the ground that this cut separates off one small part (*morion*) from many large ones, and thereby does so "apart from kinds." He explains that one can better hit upon looks (*ideai*) and divide more beautifully in two and according to kinds (*kat'eidê*) if one cuts through the middle, and he gives several examples to illustrate this point. Dividing human beings from beasts is like dividing the family of human beings into Greeks and barbarians, or dividing 10,000 from all the other numbers. In the latter case, one should begin by separating even from odd; in the former, male from female. Only then should one go on to split off Lydians or Phrygians, for example, from everyone else (262a-263a). A bit later, the Stranger adds that Young Socrates incorrectly inferred from the name "beasts" that there was in fact a single family to which it referred (263c).

In this passage the Stranger underscores the difference between political self-understanding and the scientific thinking that characterizes the method of division. Every political community dignifies itself at the expense of all others. But because their intrinsic being does not justify such behavior, the Stranger implies, political communities as they are understood by their members are parts as opposed to kinds. So, too, nature does not justify the pride that leads human beings to distinguish themselves directly from all other beasts. The Stranger does not maintain that human being, Lydian, Phrygian, and so forth are not in fact kinds, but he does insist that in order to understand them as *eidê* or *ideai* one must proceed more reflectively than Young Socrates has.

Stated in this way, the Stranger's criticism seems justified. Yet the path of bifurcatory division is clearly not up to the task of correcting Young Socrates' overly eager distinction. The analogy of numbers is quite suggestive in this connection. It makes a big difference to human beings whether they are grouped together in a medium-sized *polis* of 10,000 or an empire of 10,000,000. Numerical units, on the other hand, are in their being entirely unaffected by the quantities they comprise. Indeed, numerical units are all identical. As we have already observed on several occasions, bifurcatory division treats human beings as if they were numbers—entities that are without having come to be.[36] Among other things, this introduces errors with respect to the matter of sexual *genesis*, as is clear from the Stranger's recommendation for isolating Lydians or Phrygians: first divide human beings into male and female, and only then split off the Lydians or the Phrygians. But we would then have to locate these communities under *both* branches, for Lydians are neither all male nor all female—and indeed, could neither have come into being nor continue to exist if they were. The method of division was supposed to clarify the statesman's rule over the coming to be of human beings, but it abstracts from *erôs*, and hence from the most basic preconditions of *genesis*.

The Stranger's recommendations are also open to a deeper criticism with respect to the coming to be of the soul. Stated generally, it is not clear how it would be possible in the inquiry at hand to make adequate distinctions according to kinds rather than parts. This difficulty has to do with the peculiar conditions of the *genesis* of human beings *qua* human. By nature, or in the absence of the work of thoughtful caretaking, human beings are only potentially different from beasts. Potentialities, however, do not in themselves constitute distinct kinds, nor can the insight involved in the political work of forming souls be grasped as a matter of "encounter[ing]" *ideai* or dividing "according to" *eidê* (262b7, d7). To articulate only actual differences between human beings and other species, as the Stranger does in the subsequent steps, is therefore to speak about the form of the body while overlooking the potentiality of the soul. The results of such speech are themselves parts apart from kinds.

Young Socrates' manliness is philosophical as well as political in character, as is evident from the question he next raises: How is it possible to tell when one is dealing with a part (*meros*) instead of a natural family (*genos*)? The Stranger's initial utterance—"Best of men [*beltiste andrôn*]!"—makes it clear that he is impressed, but he does not answer the question. Instead, he tells Young Socrates only that while an *eidos* is always a part, a part is not necessarily an *eidos* (263a-b). Interestingly, he also treats Young Socrates as a herald of this notion, commanding him "always [to] assert that I speak in this way rather than the former" (263b9-10). One is reminded that the Stranger was initially presented as a herald of the ideas of the Eleatic circle (*Sophist* 216d-217b). In the present context, the Stranger suggests that in leading the discussion he is somehow ruling—and therefore caring for—Young Socrates.

The Stranger concludes his discussion of Young Socrates' mistake by setting forth an analogy. He asks the youth, whom he now calls "manliest of all," to imagine that some other intelligent (*phronimon*) family of animals such as cranes were to make a similar distinction. The *genos* of cranes, "making itself august" (*semnunon*, 263d7; cf. *Sophist* 227b4), might lump human beings together with all the rest of animals and call them all "beasts," and this would clearly be an error on their part (263d-e). This analogy, however, hardly supports the Stranger's case against Young Socrates' division of human beings from beasts. The Stranger appeals to the youth's perception that the cranes will have made a mistake in failing to distinguish us from the rest of the beasts, but this is a mistake only because we understand that we are in fact superior to the rest of the beasts in virtue of our intelligence. The imagined behavior of the cranes underscores the natural sense that intelligence has of its own distinctness, its own character as something *semnos* or holy. And it is this sense of self-worth—however unanalyzed it may be—that arouses Young Socrates' *thumos*. The correct response to the error of the cranes would therefore be to include cranes and human beings on the same side of a split between animals that possess *phronêsis* and those that do not. But *phronêsis* is not discernible by a method that favors arithmetical measurement.[37]

The preceding line of thought may be summarized as follows. Human beings unreflectively exalt themselves both as a species and as members of distinct political communities. The method of bifurcatory division cannot correct these defects, for it effectively obscures just those distinctions about which we require a better understanding. The Stranger's use of the method may help to moderate Young Socrates' excessive and therefore politically imprudent pride in the superiority of human beings to beasts. Beyond this, however, the vanity of unreflective partisanship must be addressed not by quasi-arithmetical thinking but by a reflective understanding of the necessarily partisan character of human political existence that is guided by *phronêsis* and due measure.

Taming Human Beings: The Longer and Shorter Roads

It turns out that the Stranger and Young Socrates made another mistake earlier in the division by failing to distinguish domestic (*tithasa*: from *than*, "to suckle") or tame (*hêmera*) animals from those that are wild or savage (*agria*). This distinction should have been stated explicitly, since it was implicit in their talk of animal nurture. The Stranger's definition of tame and wild animals, however, is interestingly ambiguous: "those that are in their nature capable of being domesticated [*tithaseuesthai*] must be addressed as tame, and those that are not willing as wild" (264a2-3). But many creatures that are unwilling to be domesticated are nonetheless tamed by force. Further distinctions are needed between animals that submit easily to domestication, animals that are unwilling to be domesticated but, like horses, can be "broken," and animals that are both unwilling to be domesticated and incapable of being broken. It is also noteworthy that this definition refers to the natures of animals *prior* to the act of taming: to be "tame" in the Stranger's sense is to be capable of being transformed by human activity in such a way as to acquire a second, gentler nature. As applied to human beings, the Stranger's distinction between tame and wild is thus prepolitical. Prior to political taming, human beings are like young horses: they are capable of being domesticated but must be broken.

The Stranger's examples of the domestication of fish on the Nile and the feeding ponds of geese and cranes (264c) admittedly muddy the waters, so to speak. For one may well doubt that the natures of these animals have been altered in any significant way. Is a fish tame because it will eat food provided by human beings? Then every fish that strikes at a worm on a hook is tame. Do I tame a fish when I put it in an aquarium? Then the tiger in the zoo is tame just because it is in a cage. By provoking such reflections, these examples serve indirectly to make the point that a genuinely *tame* human being is one that does not *need* to be kept in a cage, and that the moderation or self-control that marks one as tame is a quality of the soul that cannot be produced merely by means of a certain way of nurturing the body. If—as the Stranger here implies, and as

the myth makes still clearer—politics can fairly be described as the supervision of the *genesis* of tame human beings, then politics cannot be
simply the exercise of force.[38] This anticipates the second major correction to the division that the Stranger will make after the myth: just as care
must be distinguished from nurture, forcible caretaking must be split off
from voluntary caretaking (276d-e). Yet the distinction between tameness and wildness appears to be especially problematic: although in the
passage at hand the Stranger calls special attention to the earlier omission
of this step, he again overlooks it in two subsequent summaries (267b,
275c-d). Perhaps the harshness or savageness of human beings must be
kept in mind all the more vividly because it easily escapes notice in the
urbane settings of philosophical inquiry. One should not forget that the
octology begins with a wartime death and ends with an execution.

The preceding reflections raise a question about subsequent steps of
the division: Do these steps, which seem merely to describe the bodily
form of our species, isolate human beings in their political or their prepolitical state? I suggest that they do neither, but that instead the two
paths now set forth by the Stranger—the so-called longer and shorter
ways (265a-266d, 266e)—imagistically represent the transformation or
taming of human beings that is now understood to be the primary work
of political caretaking.[39] Let us therefore take up these steps with an eye
toward their possible metaphorical significance.

The strongest clue that the subsequent steps of the division function as
images is provided by the privative terms introduced by the Stranger.
Although at certain points he implies that human beings are wingless and
hornless by nature, he also calls this implication into question. On the
longer way, the Stranger, having just asserted that the division of horn-
bearing and hornless herds is "natural" (*phusei*), goes on to say that "the
king grazes some herd that has been docked of horns [*kolobon . . .
keratôn*]" (265d3-4). And although one might assume from the longer
way that human beings are understood to be born without wings, on the
shorter way the Stranger cuts the two-footed herd by the difference between "the stripped [*tôi psilôi*] and the wing-growing" (266e6-7). These
passages portray human beings (or at least some of them) as having had
their "horns" and "wings" *removed*.[40]

We begin to explore what this might mean by starting with step six, in
which the Stranger distinguishes the nurture of herds on dry land from
those in the water (264d). Once again, birds of the air are overlooked (cf.
Sophist 220a). But whereas in the *Sophist* birds were included under the
branch of animals in water (220b), step seven of the present division
splits the nurture of herd on dry land into winged and pedestrial animals
(264e). In connection with the discussion of birds in the *Sophist*, we
noted that Plato regularly associates wings with the soul's erotic motion.

This suggestion may help to shed light on the present passage. Cranes, a high-flying, far-seeing bird (cf. Aristotle, *Historia Animalum* 6.9.2), have already been associated with *phronêsis*. Conversely, the Stranger now seems to link the branch of pedestrial, nonwinged animals with the absence of *phronêsis*: he asks Young Socrates whether he does not believe that "even one most lacking in *phronêsis* [*ton aphronestaton*], so to speak," would hold that political nurture must be sought under the branch of pedestrial animals (264e8-10). In the cave image of the *Republic*, the prisoners are said to be in a state of *aphrosunê* or folly, whereas philosophical ascent from the cave is associated with increasing *phronêsis* (515c, 518e-519a). In the *Phaedrus*, Socrates implies that *phronêsis* is fully "visible" only on the level of the hyperuranain beings (250d), and wings are directly connected with the erotic, recollective ascent by which a soul may be vouchsafed such a vision. The Stranger's remark that political nurture is to be sought in the region of pedestrial, nonwinged animals is thus a subtle indication that politics is on the whole the care of souls that lack the power of philosophical ascent—earthbound or cave-bound souls, in the terms of the *Phaedrus* and the *Republic*.

The eighth step of the division is also metaphorically suggestive. The Stranger now divides horn-bearing animals from hornless ones (265c). Yet he later replaces "hornless" with "docked of horns," and subsequently speaks of the hornless herd as "smooth" or "soft" (*leia*: 265e4), a term that carries a hint of effeminacy. The implication is clear: the statesman's work involves the alteration of human nature in such a way as to suppress excessive aggression or *thumos*.[41] Human beings, it appears, are not naturally fit to live together in political community, but must be made so. The ninth step of the division, which separates whole-hoofed and interbreeding herds from split-hoofed, noninterbreeding herds (265e), may speak to this point as well: it is tempting to see the transeidetic sexual *erôs* of horses and donkeys as an image of unrestrained appetite, such as is necessarily limited and ordered in a political community. Significantly, the Stranger goes on to state that dogs—a kind of split-hoofed, hornless animal—do not deserve to be counted among herd-nurslings (266a). There may be many reasons for this: dogs interbreed, they are sometimes solitary and sometimes travel in packs, and, once tamed, they can nonetheless revert to savage wildness. In these respects, however, dogs bear a close resemblance not only to wolves (cf. *Sophist* 231a) but also to human beings.

The tenth and final step of the longer way accomplishes the division of split-hoofed, noninterbreeding herds into four-footed animals (pigs) and two-footed ones (human beings). The Stranger observes with apparent seriousness that this result, which might seem ridiculously to put the statesman on a par with the swineherd, reiterates the method of division's lack of concern for the difference between that which is more august (*semnoterou*) and that which is not (266d; cf. *Sophist* 227a-b). Still more absurdly, he claims that pigs are "the noblest [*gennaiotatôi*] and at the same time the most accommodating family of the things that are [*genei . . . tôn ontôn*]" (266c5-6). Their *erôs* and *thumos* having been restrained, the Stranger suggests, human beings will end up being close kin to the pigs with respect to their docility as well (266c-d). Indeed, this kinship suggests a resemblance between these human beings and the members of the community that Glaucon calls a "city of pigs" (*Republic* 372d)—human beings who are notably deficient in *erôs* and *thumos*. But the mathematical analogy that the Stranger offers by way of clarifying this step—an analogy that appeals directly to Theaetetus's and Young Socrates' mathematical discovery of "square" and "oblong" numbers (*Theaetetus* 147c-148b)—actually calls attention to a fundamental difference between pigs and human beings. The nature of human beings, he suggests, is analogous to "the diameter two foot in power [*dunamis*]" (266b1-3), that is, the diagonal of a square whose sides are one unit in length. (*Dunamis*, it will be recalled, is mathematically speaking the root that is capable of generating a square of a certain area.) As is shown by the Pythagorean theorem, the length of the diagonal of a square whose sides are one unit long is the square root of two; hence this diagonal can itself form the side of a square of two units in area. The nature of pigs, in turn, is analogous to "the diameter of our power" (266b5-7), that is, the diagonal of a square of two units in area. That diagonal is two units long, and can form the side of a square of four units in area. The upshot of this complicated analogy is as follows: the "ratio" between human beings and pigs on the physical level—as manifested, the Stranger suggests, by the number of legs each possesses—is two : four. This is the same ratio that obtains between the areas of the squares that can be formed when the mathematical *dunamis* associated with each species is multiplied by itself. But this means that the commensurability of these two families on the level of the body conceals their *incommensurability* on the level of the soul, or of "power" (*dunamis*) in a nonmathematical sense—for the Stranger's mathematical analogy for the power of human beings, the square root of two, is an irrational number. Put another way, the physical manifestation of the power of pigs is commensurable with this power itself, just as four is commensurable with two. The body of the pig is thus a direct measure of (the power of) its soul; what you see, so to speak, is what you get. The physical manifestation of the power of human beings, on the other hand, is incommensurable with this power itself, just as two is incommensurable with the square root of two. The body of a human being is thus *not* a direct measure of its soul. At best, as the last steps of the division show, it may be an indirect image of the human soul in a manner analogous to the way in which a geometrical figure can furnish a visible image of an irrational number.

The shorter way (266e), which Young Socrates has also asked to hear about, is not consistent with the longer way; as the Stranger says, one cannot go both ways at once (265a). The Stranger indicates that the shorter way starts from the pedestrial branch of nurture on dry land in step seven, but this cannot be the case because winged animals are isolated two steps *later*: the Stranger concludes the shorter way by splitting two-footed animals into those that are wing-growing and those that have been stripped of wings. What is more, the shorter way leaves out the split between horn-bearing and hornless animals, as well as the division between whole hoofed/interbreeding and split-hoofed/noninterbreeding animals. In other words, the human beings of the shorter way are a relatively aggressive and appetitive lot. We may note in this connection that their king is described as being "set up over the herd like a charioteer" (266e9-10), as if he ruled in a manner akin to the way in which one might drive yoked animals into battle. If the longer way leads to the equivalent of the *Republic*'s City of Pigs, the shorter way leads to a peculiarly warlike and tyrannical version the Feverish City that follows it (*Republic* 372e-374a). And just as neither the City of Pigs nor the Feverish City hits the mean, a distinctively human regime of citizens who are both free and moderate—if such is possible—must lie somewhere in the middle ground between the longer and the shorter ways.[42]

The Challenge of the Men of *Technê*

Although Young Socrates is quite satisfied with the results of the division (267a), the Stranger is not. He first gets his interlocutor to agree that human beings, a unique herd, are served by the political art, a unique art of nurture (267d). This precise way of putting the matter prepares us for the counterclaims of a group that I will call "the men of *technê*." Kings or statesmen, the Stranger explains, are in an odd position: of all herdsmen, they alone are confronted by challengers to their title. The men of *technê*—merchants, farmers, foodmakers, trainers, and doctors—assert that they themselves take care of human nurture, including the nurture of the rulers as well as human beings in the herd. In pressing their claim, moreover, they "would all together [*sumpantes*] fight through to the finish in speech against the herdsmen of the human things, whom we call statesmen" (267e9-268a1). The men of *technê* clearly dispute the uniqueness of statesmanship: they maintain that there is no single art that nurtures human beings all by itself. What is more, they seem to believe that their own arts *alone* have a share in nurturing human beings, so that there is no work at all left over for the statesman. The Stranger explains that these men contend with the statesman for "joint-nurture" or "joint-grazing" (*suntrophos, sunnomês*: 267e5, 268c8). These phrases are ambiguous: do they claim to share herdsmanship with the statesman or exclusively among themselves? The latter is almost certainly what the Stranger has in mind, since the men of *technê* raise the question of what the statesman does that is not done by merchants, farmers, foodmakers, trainers, and doctors. In support of this interpretation, we may note that these men are not portrayed as presenting their case peaceably. On the contrary, they "fight to the finish" with the statesman and are joined in "swamping" him (268c8) by "ten thousand others" (*muriôn allôn*: 268c2) —by the city as a whole, as it appears. In sum, the men of *technê* are represented as rebelliously contesting the statesman's authority to rule, as though from the fact that statesmanship is not an art of nurture it follows that it cannot be any sort of political knowledge at all. The problem they raise is no less political than theoretical.

The theoretical problem that underlies the rebelliousness of the men of *technê* is one that we have already touched upon several times in the course of our study: the relative invisibility of the soul, which may be usefully contrasted with the visibility and technical accessibility of the body. No one doubts that the arts represented by the men of *technê* are indeed useful sorts of knowledge, for the nature of the body is sufficiently evident and open to technical analysis to allow for common public acknowledgment of the means by which it may be nurtured as well as the ends these means serve. So, too, no one disputes with the cowherd concerning his art, because his methods in achieving the obviously worthwhile end of raising cattle are evidently quite adequate (268a-b). The situation of statesmanship is different, for the statesman cares for embodied souls. And whereas knowledge of the soul is nontechnical, to the men of *technê* and to the city as a whole knowledge is nothing other than technical knowledge. The statesman must therefore come to grips with the problem that his comprehensive care of human beings has no authority as knowledge in the eyes of human beings themselves. The Stranger himself, in fact, must face this problem in the person of Young Socrates. As the myth will make clear, human beings are initially compelled by harsh necessity to view care in terms of the body; Young Socrates, however, is predisposed to do so by his mathematical orientation toward knowledge. The youth's satisfaction with the results of the present division (whose steps reflect the suitability of the body to technical analysis) indicates that he suffers from a certain blindness with respect to the human soul. This diagnosis is confirmed by Young Socrates' sympathy with the men of *technê*: he asks whether these men are not speaking correctly (268a).

The challenge posed by the men of *technê* also concerns the differences in soul between the statesman and the rest of human beings. The Stranger wonders how the previous speech can be made to appear "correct and undefiled [*akeraios*]," and he goes on to suggest that they will not have worked up the statesman with precision until "stripping off the men who have swamped round him" they "show him forth pure [*katharos*] and alone" (268b8, 268c8-10). The Stranger thus represents the men of *technê* and their ten thousand allies as simultaneously contaminating and concealing the statesman: the image of stripping off those who have swamped round the statesman suggests that human beings *themselves* are the source of his obscurity.

As the Stranger later observes, political communities differ from beehives in that no one arises in the former who is "straightaway exceptional in his body and his soul" in the way that a queen bee is (301e2). If the true statesman is to be acknowledged as such, human beings must either be educated about the nature of the soul, or they must be persuaded by semblances that have the effect of elevating the statesman in their eyes. The Stranger seems to pursue the latter strategy in his initial characterization of statesmanship as an *epistêmê*.[43] But as I have tried to show in the preceding pages, it would be more accurate to say that he attempts to speak in such a way as to accomplish both ends simultaneously. This, I contend, is also the aim of the statesmanlike mixture of prophetic, mythical speech and analysis that the Stranger sets forth in the remainder of the dialogue. This mixture—which, like the cowherd's gentle and enchanting tunes (268a-b), is "pretty near to child's play" (268d8; cf. 308d)—is the charming music whereby the statesman may be ennobled in the eyes of his herd: by separating off parts of "a big myth," the Stranger says, he and Young Socrates will "arrive, at the summit, at the thing being sought" (268d8-e2). As we ascend, however, we should not forget that the sophist was also described as an "enchanter" who "share[s] in child's play" (*Sophist* 235a6, a8).

The Human Lot: The Myth of the Reversed Cosmos

The myth is the Stranger's response to the need "to proceed again from a different beginning [*ex allês archês*] on some other way" (268d5-6). At this point the inquiry changes course in a manner akin to the reversal of the cosmos itself: the Stranger takes Young Socrates back toward his childhood with a tale that begins like a bedtime story.[44] He starts by speaking of an omen or portent (*phasma*) that occurred during the legendary strife between Atreus and Thyestes over the throne of Mycenae. Young Socrates takes him to mean the sign of the golden ram, but the Stranger in fact has in mind the change in direction of the setting and rising of the sun and other stars that was brought about by "the god [Zeus] when he bore witness for Atreus" (269a1-5). The Stranger proposes to tell Young Socrates of the cosmic event or affect (*pathos*: 269c1) from which arose this story of the sun's reversal, as well as many other ancient legends. His mythical account of this event is analogous to Zeus's heavenly sign, in that "having been said, it will be conspicuously suited to the showing forth [*apodeixin*] of the king" (269c2). As a philosophical token of the true king, moreover, the myth will attempt to reproduce in speech the vividness and magnificence of Zeus's portent (cf. 275b, 277b).

The first tale to which the Stranger adverts in introducing the myth nonetheless raises doubts about the myth's ability to help us identify the true statesman. Legend has it that during the dispute between Atreus and Thyestes Hermes caused a golden ram, a token of royalty, to appear among the flocks of Atreus. Thyestes then stole the ram (which had initially been stolen from its mother by Pan), whereupon Zeus, in vindication of Atreus, reversed the course of the sun and other stars (cf. Euripides, *Orestes* 995-1012, *Electra* 699-744). This story reiterates the problem that gives rise to the myth: the golden ram stands out from the rest of the flock, but the legitimate ruler of the human herd is in no obvious way distinguished from the rest of men. Yet the political implications of the story of Atreus and Thyestes are disturbing, as are those of the two other families of legends of which the Stranger reminds Young Socrates: the tales about life during the rule of Cronos (the "Golden Age" that Hesiod describes at *Works and Days* 109-120) and about the earthborn men (269a-b). As Pierre Vidal-Naquet has observed, the potential for human savagery is implicit in all of these legends. In an article on this subject, Vidal-Naquet comments in the brute force associated with earthborn generations (cf. *Sophist* 246a-d.), discusses at length the ambiguous mixture of peace and savagery (including cannibalism) associated with the Age of Cronos, and aptly notes that "Plato did not have to mention those strange 'shepherds,' Atreus and Thyestes, nor was he obliged to recall the miracle that had taken place in favor of the organizer of a cannibalistic feast."[45] Beyond this, the thefts of the ram exemplify the potential deceptiveness of "proofs" of the legitimacy of political authority. Indeed, the very portent by which Zeus is said to have decided a question of earthly kingship points toward the questionable legitimacy of his *own* paradigmatic political authority, for the reversal or *metabolê* (269a1) that he brings about in the motion of the heavenly bodies is also a magnificent image of the political *metabolê* or *coup d'état* by which he overthrew Cronos. In sum, the Stranger begins the myth by subtly but forcefully underscoring the potential for chaotic violence among gods and human beings and by raising the question of where in the cosmos one might find any support for legitimate political authority.

The Stranger nonetheless goes on to address the latter question by way of a kind of demythologizing. He tells Young Socrates that the legends mentioned above, along with "thousands of others still more astonishing than these," all spring from the same cosmic event. "On account of the length of time," however, "some have been extinguished, and some, having been dispersed, have been told separately, apart from one another" (269b5-8). This momentous event, then, generated a rich and relatively unified group of myths, whose original order has broken up over time as the cosmos moves toward chaos (cf. 273c-d). The history of oral tradition thus follows cosmic history: the Stranger's speech about the reversal of the cosmos will explain the origin and cyclical history both of myths and of the events they relate—"the many things told of anciently [that] happened and will happen again" (268e8-9). In this way, he will weave together a fragmented group of legends into a unified whole.

The ensuing myth is indeed an imaginative synthesis of various stories, and moreover one that begins with an account of the reversal of the cosmos (269c-270a) that purports to be a more or less scientific explanation of an event that appears much distorted in current *muthoi*. Although it is itself part of a myth, this account—which strikes Young Socrates as "very likely" (270b1)—is in fact a kind of demythologizing. Perhaps most important, the Stranger's explanation of the reversal of the cosmos goes against the grain of traditional myths in all but eliminating the possibility of strife among the gods, and between them and human beings. The motion of the various gods, like that of the cosmos, is determined by their relative divinity, it being "fitting for only the most divine of all things always to be the same, and to remain in the same relation to the same things" (269d5-6). The peculiar motion of the cosmos is due to the fact that, although "it has partaken of many blessed things from its generator, nonetheless it has shared in body as well" (269d8-e1). From its generator, demiurge, or composer, the cosmos possesses "all beautiful things," whereas it owes to the disorder intrinsic to its corporeal component "everything that comes to be harsh and unjust in heaven" (273b4-c1). The most important consequences of this mode of explanation are political. The cycle of tyranny and revolution exemplified in the traditional succession Uranus-Cronos-Zeus becomes the cycle of cosmic "revolutions" necessitated by divine law (*themis*: 269e7) and the nature of matter.[46] Similarly, the political cunning of Zeus and the scheming of Cronos are transformed into the *phronêsis* by which the cosmos rules itself, in accordance with the instructions of the demiurge, during the current cycle (269c-d, 273a-b), as well as the care (*epimeleia*) of the helmsman for the cosmos as a whole and of the lesser gods or *daimôn*s for its parts during the counter-cycle (271d, 272e-273a).[47] The Stranger thus Socratically corrects the traditional tales about the violence of the gods—"the greatest lies about the greatest things" (*Republic* 377e6-7). If we may judge by his example, good statesmanship involves subtly reweaving the poeticoreligious tradition so as to amplify its power to protect souls against the ubiquitous harshness and savagery alluded to at the beginning of the myth.

While the myth may have an exemplary protective function, it is not philosophically opaque. If the Stranger's gods, like those of Socrates, are "not the cause of all things, but of the good things" (*Republic* 380c8-9), they nonetheless do not provide any direct support for the work of the statesman. To be sure, life in the current cycle is made possible by the direct involvement of the gods in reversing the disorder of the all during the counter-cycle and thereby fashioning it into a *kosmos* or ordered whole that has a certain "repaired" or "artificial" (*episkeuastês*) immortality and is "deathless and ageless" (270a4, 273e3-4). It is thus by virtue of the activity of the gods that the cosmos partakes of the nature of that which is divine. Yet the Stranger also makes it clear that the gods have withdrawn from the cosmos during the present cycle, thereby leaving human beings to care for themselves (272e-273a). Kings cannot look to Zeus to vouch for their authority, but they need not fear his punishment either. The Stranger's claim that human beings received "fire from Prometheus, arts from Hephaestus and his coartisan [Athena] and seeds and plants from others" (274c6-d2) is at best a noble lie to comfort us in our abandonment.[48]

The preceding considerations raise the question of whether any of the kinds of care presented in the myth provides a useful analogue to the work of statesmanship. During the counter-cycle, the helmsman who rewinds the cosmos and who appears to be identical to the demiurge (cf. 273d-e with 270a) supervises divine shepherds, each of whom grazes his own families or herd of animals (271d-e). During the current cycle, the cosmos is an independent authority (*autokratôr*) over its own movement, and each part of the cosmos must similarly govern itself (274a-b). Can political rule be modeled after the care of the helmsman for the cosmos as a whole, the care of divine shepherds for their herds, or perhaps the care of the cosmos for itself? These questions lead us to consider the different modes of life in each of the cycles of the cosmos.

Man's Doubleness: The Two Cycles

The myth, some commentators have argued, represents in its pair of cosmic cycles two coexisting aspects of one and the same world.[49] If this is correct, the bifurcations of the method of division have now given way to a prophetic illumination of the fundamentally bifurcated unity of human life. The soul's daimonic imperfection, or the coexistence in the human psyche, as in the cosmos, of wholeness and fragmentation, would then be exemplified in the myth as a kind of wakeful dream about the Whole (cf. 272d5: the myth is "awakened" by the Stranger). Indeed, the myth explains what the Stranger later identifies as our fundamental experience (*pathos*) concerning knowledge—the fact that "each of us, knowing everything as if in a dream, runs the risk in turn of again being ignorant of everything as it is in waking" (277d2-4)—as a consequence of the event (*pathos*) of cosmic reversal. Yet this very explanation of our ignorance or forgetfulness in terms of the internal fragmentation of the Whole also exemplifies the soul's power of prophetic recollection.[50]

The myth's depiction of the two cosmic cycles turns upon its presentation of human forgetfulness and of the significance of recollection with respect to self-knowledge. For it is self-knowledge, the Stranger implies, with which the myth is most fundamentally concerned. What is more, the myth corrects the basic presupposition of the method of division in suggesting that self-knowledge is not equivalent to a knowledge of formal structures. The recollection that the Stranger associates with self-knowledge is not of an *eidos* or *idea*; we may note in this connection that there are no Platonic Ideas in the cosmos as it is described in the myth. This omission, I suggest, is part of the Stranger's punishment of Socrates, for the Ideas are the highest objects of the philosophical *erôs* that the Stranger wishes to moderate out of a concern for the well-being of the political community. At any rate, self-knowledge in the terms of the myth depends upon a prophetic recollection of life in the other cosmic cycle. One of the implications of this point, as we shall see, is that while the analysis of formal structures may be possible during the counter-cycle, human self-knowledge is not.[51]

While the human beings of both cycles are alike in being forgetful, the nature and causes of forgetfulness in each cycle are quite distinct. Memory is severely limited during the counter-cycle: human beings spring from the earth without any recollection of those who preceded them, and they grow more and more like newborns both in soul and in body as time passes (272a, 270e). There are no regimes in the counter-cycle, the Stranger tells us, and without sexual reproduction there are no families either. Interestingly, the Stranger links the absence of these institutions to deficiencies of memory, a point to which we will return below (271e-

272a). In the current cycle, on the other hand, families and regimes both exist, but—as one might infer from the fate of the ancient myths—their integrity is threatened by the growing forgetfulness of human beings, which accompanies the increasing forgetfulness and disorder of the cosmos itself (273c-d). One could say that in the current cycle human beings experience history as increasing loss, whereas in the counter-cycle everything that is, is preserved, and there is no history at all—only the eternal recurrence of the same.

Recollection of one's cosmic counterparts is possible in the current cycle in a way that it is not in the counter-cycle. Thus, even if only distorted fragments of their stories survive, our first ancestors in the current cycle "were the heralds to us" of speeches about life in the counter-cycle (271b2).[52] And in spite of the Stranger's suggestion that the residents of the counter-cycle may have enjoyed "stories of such a sort as the ones that are now related about them" (272c7-d1), it is difficult to see how collective recollections of life in our cycle could be preserved by individuals who advance toward infancy as they age. Yet our literal superiority in this regard is the surface of a deeper, philosophical amnesia. For our ancestors who fought tooth and nail simply to survive during the initial violence and harshness of the cosmic transition (cf. 273a with 274b-c), stories about their cosmic counterparts must have seemed like a beautiful dream; this is surely why they were passed down through successive generations. Little has changed over time: in our various myths about the Golden Age or the Garden of Eden, we human beings continue to dream of another life that looks like paradise. But such dreams, the Stranger suggests, reveal the depths of our self-forgetfulness.

One can best appreciate the latter point by considering the nature of life in the counter-cycle. During that cosmic period, the herds or families (*genera*) of living beings were grazed by divine shepherds, each of whom was sufficient for his own group. As a result of this care or in connection with it, even the beasts that were harsh in their natures were not savage (cf. 274b-c); the animals did not feed on one another, and there was no war or sedition. The earth spontaneously sent up an abundance of different fruits, so there was no farming. And since the seasons were a mild and painless mixture, human beings needed no clothing, and slept in the open air on beds of soft grasses that grew without cultivation (271d-272b). There was thus no need for architecture or weaving, or for the art of politics with which these *technai* are associated. Indeed, human beings possessed no technical knowledge at all during the counter-cycle, as "no need had previously compelled them" (274c3-4). Nor, we might add, would it have been possible for them to acquire and retain such knowledge in the absence of memory.

The Stranger's description of life in the counter-cycle is most interesting for its implications with respect to the soul. Our cosmic counterparts are human beings in body only. They truly *are* cousins to the pig, in
that their bodies are directly commensurate with their souls. Their souls
reflect the atomic discreteness of their bodies, for they are entirely closed
in upon themselves and closed off from larger wholes. As we have seen,
these beings lack *thumos* as well as the capacity to reproduce sexually
(although nothing prevents them from getting pleasure from copulation).
Their lack of sexual *erôs*, whose procreative power surpasses mere sexual pleasure, is an indication that they also do not experience *erôs* more
generally as self-transcending desire. Although they are ruled by
*daimôn*s, our counterparts are not themselves daimonic: they do not
strive for self-transcendence because they are utterly unaware of their
own finitude. They do not experience death as a limit to their lives, since
death is preceded by a sleeplike state of infancy (cf. Hesiod, *Works and
Days* 116). Having no perception of the meaning of death and lacking
any recollection of those who lived before them, they cannot comprehend what it would mean for others to remember them—much less feel
the need for such memorialization. Their forgetfulness is in turn closely
connected with their suppressed *thumos*, for they do not share in what
Diotima calls "the desire to become renowned and to lay up a store of
undying glory for all time" (*Symposium* 208c4-6). Thus they lack the
most fundamental psychic reasons (not to mention the physical means)
for the generation of, and participation in, families and regimes. Families
and regimes, in turn, are more than sums of independently existing parts:
they are wholes constituted by a common life in which individuals may
partake. The absence of these institutions among the human beings of the
counter-cycle is a symptom of their inability to fashion or participate in
any genuine community whatsoever. In certain respects, the divine caretakers of the counter-cycle are more like Protagoras's farmers of plants
than shepherds: the herds they graze spring up from the earth like shoots
and lead lives that exemplify the discontinuous, dimensionless, purely
private existence to which human beings would be condemned if Protagoras's Heraclitean ontology were literally true, an existence utterly
lacking in the public space or middle ground of common life. Nor are our
cosmic counterparts in any sense distinct individuals, as are the members
of a family: taken together, they are an undifferentiated multitude. If in
fact they have their own names, they deserve them no more than would
individual stalks of corn.
    In the counter-cycle human beings are on the same level as the beasts.
It is truly a world in which one could say that "pig is the measure of all
things" (cf. *Theaetetus* 161c). The longer and shorter ways to one side,
this is not the case in our cycle, as the Stranger admits when he states

that we are a "more divine animal" than the herds we now graze (271e6-7). Speaking roughly, the Stranger's description of the counter-cycle suggests either that human beings live like beasts, or that human beings and beasts live like gods. The latter possibility is raised by the fact that the denizens of the counter-cycle have two advantages that we do not enjoy: "much leisure, and power to associate through speeches not only with human beings, but also with beasts" (272b9-c1). In the counter-cycle, speech is not unique to human beings. But under the conditions of the counter-cycle, could speech be anything other than emotive noise, or the essentially uncommunicative expression of private, bodily affections and desires?

The Stranger implicitly raises the latter question when he inquires about the relative happiness (*eudaimonia*) of human beings in each cycle (272b-c). If *eudaimonia* is understood literally as a state of being well-off (*eu*) with respect to one's *daimôn*, it might seem that those who live in the counter-cycle win hands down—for they alone are cared for by divine beings. Yet they themselves are in no way daimonic. Indeed, the withdrawal of the gods at the end of the counter-cycle first opens up a space within which our humanity may flourish, and so coincides with the birth in human beings of daimonic striving toward that which is divine.[53] And although *logos* was overlooked in the previous division of the human herd, the Stranger now strikingly connects the capacity for speech with the issue of *eudaimonia*—a term that is introduced here for the first time in the dialogue, and that subsequently becomes one of the criteria for judging the adequacy of political rule (301d, 311c). In the Stranger's view, everything depends upon whether human beings in the counter-cycle, in associating with the beasts and with one another, employed their leisure and extended power of speech "for philosophy . . . learning by inquiry from every nature whether any, having some peculiar power, perceived something different from the rest for the gathering together of *phronêsis*" (272c1-4). If they did so, the Stranger suggests, then they greatly exceeded us in happiness, but if they simply ate, drank, and told stories to one another—if, in sum, they lived the life that Hesiod attributes to those of the Golden Age, and that many in our cycle continue to associate with paradise—then they obviously fell far short of our happiness (272c-d). It is important to notice that the Stranger does not simply describe life in the counter-cycle, but that he utilizes these descriptions as value-laden paradigms for our own lives. And while he does not explicitly indicate which description holds true, he does imply that human beings of the current cycle stand in the middle ground with respect to *eudaimonia*.

Young Socrates is incapable of answering for himself the Stranger's question about happiness (272b), and the Stranger refuses to speculate about whether human beings philosophized in the counter-cycle. Yet even a little reflection on this question brings sharply into focus the most fundamental difference between us and our cosmic counterparts, for it is precisely *phronêsis* that our counterparts lack and cannot possibly acquire. *Phronêsis* is simply the fullest self-knowledge: it is the "intelligence" by which the cosmos steers itself in the current cycle (*phronêsin*: 269d1) and presumably it is also the power by which we human beings, in imitation of the cosmos, are to govern ourselves (cf. 274a-b, d-e). But the residents of the counter-cycle cannot possibly come to know themselves, much less how *we* are to lead *our* lives in the current cycle. And these two kinds of knowledge, the Stranger suggests, are inseparable. His illuminating comparison of human beings in the two cycles reminds us of a basic philosophical principle that is reflected in the method of division as well as the dramatic juxtapositions of the philosophic trial, namely, that we come to know each thing best in its opposition to relevant others. Now the method of division aims at *nous* (*Sophist* 227b), whereas the Stranger makes it clear that philosophy—which he mentions at 272c1 for the first and only time in the *Statesman*—aims at *phronêsis*. While the method of division seeks knowledge of kinds, *phronêsis*, as intelligent insight into the contexts of speeches and deeds, is the knowledge of due measure.[54] Correspondingly, philosophy is to be conducted, not by the application of a method, but through dialogue with "every nature" (*pasês phuseôs*: 272c3). In the counter-cycle, however, "natures" must refer to the various species of animals, and these species are in several crucial respects distinct from those in the current cycle. In the first place, the species have been largely *denatured* by the conditions of divine shepherding. As a result, they have been rendered equal and are treated as equals; the lion is no longer the ruler of the jungle, nor do any other hierarchies remain in what we in our cycle call the "animal kingdom." Hence the philosophical "dialogue" to which the Stranger refers—assuming that it is possible at all—would issue in an uncritical or value-free catalogue of the powers and perceptions of all of the various kinds of animals. Philosophy would then be equivalent to zoology, a notion already familiar to us from the preceding division of the human herd. In sum, the counter-cycle describes the peculiar conditions under which one might identify philosophy with the method of division, and it does so precisely in order to show that this identification is mistaken.[55]

The fact that human beings in the current cycle dream longingly of a life such as is lived in the counter-cycle suggests that the Stranger's depiction of our cosmic twins illustrates a potentiality of the human soul. To put this point in more familiar terms, the counter-cycle is a pure (and therefore exaggerated) representation of human beings as plants. The unexamined life of a plant is always an option for human beings, but the

Stranger makes clear that it is inferior to the reflective life that is possible for us in the current cycle. Why is a distinctively human life possible only in the current cycle? In pursuing this question one sees that the soul stands in a dialectical relationship to the conditions of the world. Human beings live like plants in the counter-cycle in large part because there is no necessity that compels them to do otherwise (cf. 274c). The predominant feature of nature in the current cycle, on the other hand, is its hostility and harshness toward us. Only in the current cycle are human beings compelled to attend to their literal and metaphorical nakedness, or to the vulnerable conditions of their psyches as well as their bodies, and this compulsion is a spur to the acquisition of technical knowledge as well as to the whole range of erotic and spirited activities that characterize human life in its present form.[56] The transition between cycles is itself quite violent (270c-d, 273a), nurture is no longer "spontaneous" (*automatês*: 274c2), and the weather becomes a source of trouble. In addition, at the beginning of the current cycle the aggression of human beings and other animals that was suppressed during the counter-cycle is now released: "as many [beasts] as were harsh in their natures, became savage" (274b6-7). Violent death is now a frightening prospect, the implications of which are all too clear: "Having become weak and unguarded, human beings were torn apart by the beasts" (274b7-c1). The new needs of human beings can be read off from the legendary "gifts" of the gods that the Stranger mentions—fire and the arts associated with Hephaestus and Athena (including ironworking, warfare, and weaving) as well as agriculture (274c-d). In the current cycle, our species cannot survive without weapons, clothes, and food. The arts that produce and use these items transform parts of the natural world in order to fashion a space within it that is somewhat more hospitable to human beings. But the world will inevitably become more disordered, and things in general more "harsh and unjust" (273c1), as time goes on and the cosmos runs down.

Conspicuously absent from the preceding list of *technai* is the art of politics. This omission is especially striking if one compares the Stranger's myth with the myth about the origins of human life that is told in the *Protagoras* (320c-322d). In that dialogue, Protagoras draws a similarly Hobbesian picture of the harshness of nature and explains that, even with the aid of the arts of Athena and Hephaestus, human beings could not survive in the absence of the political *technê* (322b). The reason is that none of the other arts moderates the harshness of the human soul itself. Zeus was therefore compelled to save our species by endowing us with justice (*dikê*) and reverent shame (*aidôs*: 322b-c). Particularly when viewed in the light of Protagoras's myth, the Stranger's account of life in the current cycle suggests that the most fundamental work of politics is survival itself, or the protection of the body. This is confirmed by the weaving of wool, which the Stranger later offers as a paradigm of politics (279a ff.). In his division of the art of weaving, the Stranger locates woolen cloaks under the category of "defenses for the sake of not suffering or being affected" (*ta de tou mê paschein amuntêria*: 279c8-9). Like weaving, in other words, politics modifies nature in order to preserve intact that which for the most part already exists by nature: as the Stranger implied in setting forth the longer and shorter roads, politics protects the body by altering the prepolitical nature of the soul.[57] Yet his reference to happiness and his description of the empty existence of the bodies in the counter-cycle also suggest that the most fundamental work of politics is not its only work.

The latter observation helps us to appreciate the most essential difference between the political teachings of Protagoras and the Stranger. In Protagoras's myth, human beings are saved by the direct intervention of Zeus. According to the Stranger, however, there is no Zeus for us: the gods left the cosmos when the current cycle began. Yet Protagoras assimilates human beings to gods, whereas the Stranger maintains the difference between gods and human beings that is the precondition of daimonic striving and hence of happiness. Put another way, the Stranger teaches that "there *is* a god who *has withdrawn*."[58] The withdrawal of the gods nonetheless brings us back to the question whether the myth of the reversed cosmos provides us with any useful paradigms of statesmanship that might guide us in acquiring knowledge of the art of politics.

Cosmic Paradigms of Statesmanship

We start with the care of the divine or daimonic shepherds for their herds. The problem with this paradigm is implicit in the Stranger's statement that "a god himself was set over them [human beings] and grazed them, just as human beings now, being another, more divine animals, graze other genera lower than themselves" (271e5-7). Immediately after concluding the myth, the Stranger mentions two mistakes in the previous division of the statesman. The "much bigger and more extensive" mistake (274e7-8) was to speak of the king and statesman as if he were a shepherd from the counter-cycle, and a god instead of a mortal. The figure (*schêma*) of the divine shepherd is "too big to be in accordance with a king," he explains, because the king resembles the ruled in his nature, education, and nurture much more than the divine shepherd resembles his herd (275b8-c4). The smaller mistake was to fail to distinguish between care (*epimeleia*) and nurture (275d-276c). Care, the Stranger implies, differs from nurture only in the current cycle. This cannot be simply because the body now needs new arts of protection from the harshness of nature, for political care is not identical to any of these arts or to all of them together. Political care must be care for souls as well as bodies, and indeed for a community of ensouled bodies. But as we have seen, the herds of the counter-cycle are aggregates of more or less identical animals, not communities of individuals. There is, in short, nothing *political* about the care exercised by the divine shepherds. Beyond this, these shepherds can presumably look for guidance to the god who rules the circling of the cosmos as a whole (271d), but there are no gods available to instruct human rulers.

At the conclusion of the myth, the Stranger states that human beings are to imitate the care of the cosmos for itself (274d). Curiously, the Stranger calls the cosmos an autocrat (*autokratôr*: 274a5), yet he also says that it receives instructions from its "demiurge and father" (273b1-2). Like the divine shepherds, the cosmos is heraldic, not autepitactic. This brings us to a further difficulty. The Stranger indicates that in the current cycle the cosmos rules itself by *phronêsis* (269c-d). But the intelligence whereby the cosmos strives to remember and to apply with precision the instructions of the demiurge clearly differs from that by which human beings are to rule themselves *without* the benefit of divine guidance. Far from being the original that human self-rule imitates, the *phronêsis* of the cosmos is itself a technical version of the sound judgment that would characterize the best human rule.[59] Yet the conduct of the cosmos also anticipates the second-best rule of law: the recollection of divine instructions is much like the preservation of sacred laws. Perhaps the self-rule of the cosmos is a paradigm for human rule after all.

We shall return to the preceding suggestion in due time. Having considered the form of rule that characterizes each cycle of the cosmos, we now take up the paradigm of the care of the cosmos as a whole by the "greatest *daimôn*"—the "helmsman of the all," who, in grasping the "rudder" of the cosmos, prevents it from going down in the "limitless sea of dissimilarity," and who cures "the things diseased" by "working it up into an undying and undecaying thing" (272e4-273a1, 273d4-e4). Lest we miss the political import of these metaphors, the Stranger later insists that "the noble helmsman" and the "physician equal in worth to many others" are "images . . . to which it is always necessary to liken the royal rulers" (297e8-12). The image of the helmsman is admittedly misleading, for the change or motion that takes place both in the cosmos and in the political community does not aim at a final destination. The captain succeeds by bringing his ship safely into port, but the voyage of the ship of state, like the rotation of the cosmos, never ceases. Yet in certain respects the helmsman is the most promising paradigm of the statesman that we have so far encountered. In the first place, he is genuinely autepitactic. His work, like that of the weaver, is to fashion an ordered whole out of fragmentary elements. Furthermore, he is concerned with the motion of the cosmos in both cycles. Roughly speaking, he values the potentiality of the soul no more than the preservation of the body. In the current cycle, however, he does not exercise rule directly; in this respect he resembles the wise ruler who departs after having left behind written laws (295b-c).

The myth's paradigms of rule influence the subsequent inquiry in a subtle but important way. After the myth, the Stranger complains that he and Young Socrates have behaved like inexpert statue-makers in raising up "great paradigms" of the king that are bigger than they should be (277a-b). And although the outlines of the demonstration (*apodeixis*) of the king are now present, it lacks the "vividness" that comes from "pigments [*pharmakois*] and the mixture of colors" (277c2-3). Shortly thereafter, the Stranger introduces the paradigm of weaving. One could playfully say that the Stranger, having fashioned a godlike image of the king that resembles a huge statue, proceeds to clothe it with the paradigm of weaving (much as the Athenians clothed the great statue of Athena with a woven robe during the Great Panathenaia). I put the point this way for two reasons. First, I wish to recall a related passage in the *Sophist* in which the Stranger used big statues and paintings to illustrate the difference between a likeness and a semblance (235d-236c). In the present context, however, the Stranger does not directly attempt to lead Young Socrates closer to the truth. If the youth is to acquire an accurate understanding of the statesman's true proportions, he must do so by means of his own reflective efforts. Although the Stranger suggested just prior to the myth that his aim was to strip off that which concealed the statesman's nature (268c), he now wraps the statesman in a cloak of knowledge on the model of weaving, and thereby "fills up the soul" of Young Socrates (cf. 286a) with a great and beautiful paradigm of the statesman as a scientific knower.[60] This godlike figure (cf. 301d-e, 303b) has a political function akin to the cosmic function of the divine helmsman: his knowledge, as we shall see, legitimates the heraldic authority of the laws, just as the divine helmsman's knowledge grounds the autarchic motion of the cosmos. Woven robes, we may note, can beautify or adorn (*kosmein*) as well as protect the body (cf. 282a). Yet the Stranger nonetheless allows us to see the cosmetic dimension of his speech; as in the myth, he weaves a web of words that is politically protective while still being philosophically diaphanous for those with eyes to see. Second, I wish to suggest that the Stranger employs the paradigm of weaving in conscious opposition to the unraveling of the political fabric by Socratic inquiry, which has a way of showing things and human beings in their nakedness (cf. *Theaetetus* 162b).[61]

Let us now turn to the Stranger's final criticism of Socrates. In what follows I shall not attempt to offer a thorough analysis of the text, but

rather to pick out and tie together those themes of the last half of the
Statesman that bear directly on the philosophic trial.

Phronêsis, Technê, and Law:
The Stranger's Second Sailing

Perhaps it is not surprising that the Stranger's political disagreement with
Socrates is rooted in a profound philosophical agreement about the acquisition of *phronêsis*. The myth indicates that we human beings need
phronêsis in order to govern ourselves, but that we must acquire it on our
own; *phronêsis* is not given to us by nature, nor will the art of politics
come to us as a gift from the gods. The Stranger further indicates that
phronêsis can be obtained only in an essentially Socratic fashion. Consider once again his question whether our cosmic counterparts employed
their leisure "for philosophy . . . learning by inquiry from every nature
whether any, having some peculiar power, perceived something different
from the rest for the gathering together [*sunagurmon*] of *phronêsis*"
(272c1-4). What activity would be equivalent to this in the current cycle?
In our epoch *logos* is restricted to human beings, and the potentially dialogic diversity of the many species of animals has been narrowed to the
diversity of the families or kinds of human souls. What is more, in the
current cycle human nature has been altered by laws and customs, which
later emerge as instruments of the political *technê*. Thus the Stranger at
one point remarks that the characters of the citizens must be "nurtured
through laws [*dia nomôn*] so as to grow according to nature [*kata phu-
sin*]" (310a2). This paradoxical combination of nature and production,
nomos and *phusis* in human life also helps us to see why the acquisition
of *phronêsis* involves more than gathering together perceptions: it requires that one critically sift through opinions in order to separate that
which is justified by nature from that which rests upon custom and convention alone. *Phronêsis* must be empirically acquired through dialogical
inquiry into the origins of the desires, powers, and thoughts of human
beings, or into the relationship between the various kinds of souls and the
productive work of politics. This teasing apart of the rich fabric of human life is precisely the sort of inquiry that Socrates undertakes in examining the ordinary, everyday activities and aspirations of his fellow
citizens and foreign guests: in the *sunagurmos* or "gathering together" of
phronêsis we hear the name of the *agora* or marketplace.[62] In sum, the
philosophical zoology of the counter-cycle finds its cosmic counterpart
in a distinctly Socratic anthropology. Socratic inquiry turns out to be
necessary for statesmanship as well as philosophical self-understanding.

Socrates and the Nonarithmetical Mean

After the myth, at the very center of the dialogue (283c-285c), the
Stranger speaks of nonarithmetical measurement in such a way as to
further increase our estimation of the worth of Socratic philosophizing.
He begins by introducing the topic of excess and defect (283c), which
arises after a long discussion of the nature of weaving (279a-283b). The
Stranger now divides the art of measurement into two parts, one concerned with "the relative sharing in bigness and smallness," and the other
with "the necessary being [anangkaian ousian] of becoming [geneseôs]"
(283d7-9). Arithmetical measurement is relative in the sense that it treats
the greater as "greater than nothing other than the less," and the less, in
turn, as "less than the greater and nothing else" (283d11-e1). Nonarithmetical measurement, on the other hand, is relative to the mean, and has
to do with the coming to be of speeches and deeds whereby bad (kakoi)
and good (agathoi) individuals are differentiated from one another
(283e3-6, 284e6-8). What is more, the Stranger now asserts that "the arts
themselves as well as all their actions or products [erga]," and in particular the political art and the art of weaving, would be destroyed in the
absence of measure relative to the mean. For it is only keeping a watch-
ful eye on the mean, "not on the ground that it is not [hôs ouk on] but on
the ground that it is difficult," that the arts "produce everything good and
beautiful" (284a5-b2). In the search for the sophist, the Stranger continues, he and Theaetetus found it necessary to compel "that which is not"
(to mê on) to be; so too, he and Young Socrates must now compel (pro-
sanangkazein) the greater and the less to become measurable not only
with respect to one another but also with respect to "the coming to be of
the mean." Otherwise the statesman cannot possibly claim to be "a scientific knower concerning actions [peri tas praxeis epistêmona]"
(284b7-c3).

It is obvious that all productive and practical technai utilize nonarithmetical measurement: a shoe is made to fit the foot and to suit the needs
of its wearer. But the present passage also helps us to see that estimates
of worth are integral even to the sort of theoretical analysis undertaken in
the method of division. If I am to enumerate the elements of any particular kind of thing, I must decide in advance what counts as an example
of that eidos or genos. And this decision is not value-neutral. To provide
a conceptual explication of the eidos "horse," for example, I must take
my bearings by a whole and healthy member of the species—not, say,
one that is deformed, or is so sick that it cannot stand up. The Stranger's
reference to the anangkaia ousia (283d9) of becoming is not misplaced:
the very being of that which becomes is visible only in the light of the
nonarithmetical mean.

The digression at the center of the *Theaetetus* aimed at clarifying the nature of the middle ground between politics and philosophy. At the center of the *Sophist*, the Stranger found it necessary to violate Parmenides' prohibition in order to shed light on the middle ground of human life. The Stranger now explicitly connects the present discussion of the middle ground with the previous effort to speak about that which is not. The being of the mean, he suggests, is problematic or "difficult" just to the extent that the mean *is not*, but is instead perpetually *coming to be*. The mean is a feature of reality that comes into being through human purposive activity and that varies from context to context.[63] Hence it cannot be known scientifically, after the manner of unchanging beings. Knowledge of the mean is a matter not of *epistêmê* but of *gnôsis* or familiarity. What counts, moreover, is not the possession of a particular body of knowledge, but a capacity to hit the mean that is developed only through longstanding acquaintance with the contexts in which judgment is called for. In the case of politics, these are the concrete contexts of human life, such as Socrates has made it his business to study. And the capacity to hit the mean, not in shoemaking or weaving but in living, is *phronêsis*.[64]

Of particular interest to us is the relevance of the Stranger's discussion of the mean to his judgment of Socrates. In the *Sophist*, the Stranger was able to compel not-being to enter into a relationship with being only by treating *to mê on* not as the altogether not but as otherness. In other words, the Stranger's account of not-being was a *tour de force* that related or rendered commensurable two items that are in themselves wholly incommensurable. In speaking of the nonarithmetical mean, the Stranger hints that a similar kind of ontologically distorting compulsion may be a necessary component of the work of *phronêsis*. The greater and the less, he indicates, are not in themselves commensurable but must be compelled to be so.[65] So, too, Socrates has suggested that the sophist, the statesman, and the philosopher are in themselves of incommensurable worth. Might not the Stranger's final judgment of Socrates, his ultimate display of *phronêsis*, involve a certain distortion of the being of the philosopher just insofar as it holds the philosopher to the measure of the statesman?

The Stranger's account of nonarithmetical measurement is followed by what looks at first to be an unqualified defense of the superiority of the rule of the king who possesses *phronêsis* to the rule of law. This defense forms part of a section of the dialogue wherein the Stranger, having distinguished the possessor of the royal art from slaves, merchants, heralds, priests, diviners, and others (289c-290e), turns his attention to a family (*genos*) that is "of every tribe" (*pamphulon*). The latter group includes men who resemble lions, centaurs, and satyrs, and who "swiftly ex-

change with one another their looks [*ideas*] and capacity [*dunamin*]"
(291a8-b3). Instead of speaking of this whole *genos*, however, the
Stranger goes on to consider only "the greatest enchanter of the sophists," who "is extremely difficult to remove from those who are in their
being [*ontôs*] statesmen and royal men" (291c3-6). Such sophists, whom
the stranger identifies with "the chorus that deals with the doings [*pragmata*] of the cities" (291c1) and later with the politicians who share in all
of the nonscientific regimes (303b-c), are among those who "pass themselves off as statesmen and persuade many, but are not in any way."
They must therefore be separated from "the intelligent [*phronimou*]
king" (292d5-7).

Roughly ten pages later, the Stranger makes it clear that "the greatest
imitators and the greatest enchanters" who are "the sophists of sophists"
(303c3-5) have been separated from the king, along with the previously
mentioned band of centaurs and sophists. What is more, this has been
accomplished "just like a drama" (303c8). I wish to suggest that Socrates
is purged along with these sophists, and that the drama in question is also
the last act of the philosophic trial. A small but perhaps not insignificant
indication of the Stranger's intention in this stretch of text is furnished by
his mention of the sacrificial duties of the King Archon just prior to his
introduction of the band of beasts and sophists (290e). Let us now see
how the Stranger's verdict unfolds.

The Sophistry of Philosophy

Although "political *epistêmê*" is an odd name for what is essentially a
nonscientific, gnostic capacity, the Stranger repeatedly emphasizes that
the true king is distinguished by his scientific knowledge of statesmanship. Thus the usual criteria by which regimes are differentiated—
whether the rulers rule by force or with the consent of the ruled, whether
with or without law, and whether they are poor or rich, few or many—
are in themselves irrelevant: what matters is only whether they govern
with political *epistêmê* (291c-292d). The distinction between the few and
the many is nonetheless not entirely off the mark: because no multitude
(*plêthos*) could possibly acquire such a difficult science, "the correct regime" (*hê orthê archê*) will be a monarchy or an aristocracy (292e-293a).
All regimes besides the one that keeps the political community safe and
improves it "by employing science and justice" are "not legitimate and in
their being are not [*oud' ontôs ousas*]," but instead imitate the correct
regime in more or less beautiful or ugly ways (293d8-e5). The possessor
of political science seems to be the original to which all other rulers are
related as images.

Political *epistêmê*, the Stranger explains, is rooted in *phronêsis*. "It is clear that legislation is in some manner a part of the art of kingship," the Stranger admits when Young Socrates expresses concern about the prospect of a lawless regime. Nevertheless, "the best thing is not for the laws [*tous nomous*] to have power but for a kingly man with *phronêsis*" (294a6-8). In explaining this point the Stranger equates law and *technê*. "Law," he observes, "would never be able, in comprehending with precision the best and the most just thing for everyone simultaneously, to enjoin [*epitattein*] that which is best" (294a10-b2). The reason is that the extraordinary complexity and variability of the human things do not allow "any art whatsoever" to make universal, unchanging, and simple declarations about them, as does the law (294b2-6). While the human things are "never simple," the dictates of law—like the rules and codified procedures of a *technê* no longer animated by a living intelligence—are "simple through all time" (294c7-8). In its foolish obstinacy, the law allows no one to contradict it or "even to ask a question" (294c2-3). In these respects the laws are like writings that have been abandoned by their author (cf. *Phaedrus* 275d-e).

The latter passage leads one to wonder why the Stranger claims that legislation is a part of kingship, and why he asserts that the best imitation of the correct regime will have "good laws" (293e3-5). Indeed, in describing the royal and political art in the last pages of the dialogue the Stranger speaks of a regime that has been structured by a "legislator [*nomothetou*] king" (305b5; cf. 305c-e). In this regime, the laws play a crucial role in the educative work of weaving the fabric of individual souls out of the warp of manliness and the woof of moderation, as well as fashioning the bonds of shared opinion that bind the citizens together into a political whole (306a-310a).[66] What accounts for this unexpected development? The Stranger's understanding of law becomes clearer in the light of his remark that exceptional kings simply do not arise in cities as in beehives (301d-e) and that the correct regime stands apart from all the rest "like a god from human beings" (303b4). The correct regime— ostensibly the best conceivable *archê* of political community—is in other words humanly impossible, because the political wisdom that animates this regime is not fully accessible to human beings. Nor would it be possible for the possessor of such wisdom to prescribe what is suitable for each individual while ruling many at once (cf. 295a-b)—as it would be in the counter-cycle, where there are no individuals.

The latter reflections suggest that the relationship between the correct regime and its humanly possible images is more complex than meets the eye.[67] But we must not rest content with noting the impossibility of the correct regime, for it is doubtful that this regime would be desirable even if it were possible. The possessor of the fullest political *epistêmê* would be a godlike or superhuman ruler, who differs from the human statesman roughly as *sophia* differs from *philosophia*.[68] Like a tyrant or ruling *daimôn* of the counter-cycle, a scientific ruler who governed so as to insure the wisdom of all of our actions would take up every inch of what would otherwise be common ground. And just as the withdrawal of the gods from the cosmos first opens up a space for human life, law alone, it would seem, provides the public space necessary for the freedom and dignity that characterizes a genuinely political life. Paradoxically, the correct regime is not even the best regime for human beings.[69]

Those laws that have been written down "from the knowers," the Stranger claims, will be "imitations of the truth" (300c5-7). Given his criticism of law at 294a-c, one may suppose that laws imitate political *epistêmê* in a manner analogous to the (admittedly problematic) way in which Plato's writings or Socrates' recorded speeches and deeds image their souls. But just as there are now no gods in the cosmos, among human beings there is no "knower . . . who in his being [*ontôs*] is a statesman" (300c9-10). How, then, could *any* humanly possible regime be a good image of the best conceivable regime if its laws have not been founded by someone in possession of political science?

The answer to the latter question can only be that the legislator must be a prophet—not officially or literally (cf. 290d-e), but philosophically. The daimonic power of prophetic recollection that animated the myth of the reversed cosmos is also on display, the Stranger suggests, in good laws. In this connection the Stranger is concerned more with the institution of the rule of law than with the content of particular laws. The practice of inculcating in the citizens a reverent respect for written laws and ancestral customs (*patrioi nomoi*), he indicates, reflects a prophetic insight into the care and protection of human souls. In this crucial respect, *nomos* is rooted in *phusis*. The Stranger is by no means a Protagorean.

The Stranger seems initially to be contemptuous of law. Thus he observes that no one in possession of the royal science would "lay down impediments for himself by writing these so-called laws" (295b4-5). To illustrate this point he introduces the example of the physician who goes abroad but leaves behind prescriptions that are to be followed in his absence (295b ff.). Upon his return it would be absurd if he were prohibited from issuing new orders; yet this is precisely the situation with respect to the laws (cf. 294c). In order to do something contrary to the existing laws, one must change them, and that requires persuading the city that the new laws are better (296a). But we admit that the physician who compels his patients to undergo a beneficial procedure acts justly, even though he uses force (296b-c). The Stranger now echoes an earlier point: with respect to intelligent (*emphrones*) rulers, what counts is simply that they act justly and improve those in the city while keeping them safe

(296d-297b). Nevertheless, he surprisingly insists, all regimes other than the one correct regime must imitate the latter by using written laws to "keep themselves safe" (297d6; no mention is now made of justice and improvement), and by imposing severe punishments on those who dare to do anything contrary to the laws. While this procedure is "not the most correct," it is, the Stranger claims, "most correct and most beautiful as second" (297d7, e3-4).

The Stranger goes on to explain the genesis of law in a democracy or an oligarchy in a way that is designed to clarify the logic of his claim that the rule of law is indeed second-best. In its description of the initial condition of the political community, this explanation bears some resemblance to the accounts that Glaucon and Callicles give of the origin of *nomos* in the *Republic* (358e-359b) and the *Gorgias* (483b-c). The Stranger asks Young Socrates to imagine a situation in which physicians or helmsmen behaved violently and arbitrarily. Our response to such injustice might be to give an assembly of the many or the rich, including laymen, the power to inscribe laws on tablets (*stêlai*) and fashion unwritten ancestral customs that govern the practices of undertaking a voyage and treating the sick. What is more, we might hold lotteries in which laymen ruled for the year as helmsmen and physicians, at the end of which time others who are also without special expertise in these arts are to hold an audit (*euthuna*) in order to determine whether these rulers have acted in conformity with the laws (298a-299a).

In referring to a popular assembly, political lotteries, Solonian tablets, and the custom of the *euthuna*, the Stranger is evidently describing Athenian institutions.[70] This observation prepares us for the immediate sequel, in which he picks out Socrates' own activity in relation to the Athenian political community. It will also be necessary to establish a law, he tells Young Socrates, that runs as follows:

> If someone is evidently inquiring, contrary to the laws, into the art of piloting [*kubernêtikên*] and nautical matters or health and the truth of the art of medicine concerning winds and things hot and cold, and is sophistically devising [*sophizomenos*] anything whatsoever about these things, first to call him neither a physician nor a helmsman [*kubernêtikon*] but a hightalker [*meteôrologon*], some babbling sophist [*adoleschên sophistên*], and then those for whom it is possible and who are willing can write up an indictment and lead him into a court of law on the ground that he is corrupting others who are younger and persuading them to apply themselves to the arts of piloting and medicine in a way that is not in conformity with the laws, but instead to rule the ships and the sick as autocrats [*autokratoras*]. And if he should seem to persuade either youths or their elders contrary to the laws and the writings, to punish him with extreme penalties, for one

must in no way be wiser than the laws. For no one is ignorant of medical matters and health or helmsmanship and nautical matters, since it is possible for anyone who wishes to learn the established writings and ancestral ways [*patria êthê*]. (299b3-d1)

This description brings together terms associated with Socrates in the writings both of Plato and of Aristophanes.[71] In accordance with the political images of the physician and the captain, Socrates is here depicted as seeking the kind of knowledge represented in the myth by the helmsman of the cosmos, knowledge that would allow for self-rule in imitation of the cosmos (which is called an *autokratôr* at 274a5). Socrates' aim is nothing other than the political wisdom that would allow for the best possible human life in the current cycle.

Young Socrates is of the opinion that the arts would perish once and for all if they were all governed by law in the manner that the Stranger has described, with the result that life would become unlivable (*abiôtos*: 299e8). The ironic tension in this passage is heightened by the echo of Socrates' famous claim that the unexamined life is unlivable (*ou biôtos*) for a human being (*Apology* 38a). The Stranger does not disagree with Young Socrates, yet he defends just this kind of governance in the arena of politics. Politics is unlike any of the arts that image its work, for it is a remarkable fact that the *polis* endures even under the rule of law without knowledge (cf. 301e-302b). Indeed, the humanly possible alternatives are worse. Nor is it politically relevant that Socrates acts with the very best of intentions. Not to punish a noble sophist like Socrates is to encourage base imitators who will violate the law for the sake of profit or private gratification (300a).

After thus reminding Young Socrates about the anarchic condition of violence that originally gave rise to laws, the Stranger speaks to the youth's view that law is utterly opposed to expert knowledge. The laws, he observes, have been established on the basis of much experience (*ek peiras pollês*); hence he who acts contrary to them misses the mark (*hamartêmatos hamartêma*) to a far greater extent than the writings themselves (300b1-6). The prohibition against anyone doing anything contrary to the laws is therefore a "second sailing" (*deuteros plous*: 300c2) for those who establish them. The latter remark strikingly anticipates Socrates' famous reference to his own second sailing in the *Phaedo* (99c-d). This textual connection suggests that laws serve human beings much as speeches (*logoi*) serve Socrates. As the Stranger has already implied, the paramount political issue raised by Socrates' antinomian inquiries is safety. We recall that Socrates turned to speeches to safeguard his soul from such damage as might result from a direct confrontation with beings along the lines of pre-Socratic physics. The speeches in which Socrates takes refuge in dialogue are in the first instance conventional opinions. But insofar as it prizes apart from the fabric of *nomos* so as to examine these opinions individually, Socratic *logos* conflicts with the analogous defensive function of the laws, whose weave of writings, ancestral customs, and poeticoreligious myths insulates human beings from the harshness of nature. The Stranger's description of laws as a second sailing implies that at least some souls that are unprotected by *nomos* will become damaged in such a way that they will lose their distinctive capacity as souls, much as the eye that looks directly into the sun during an eclipse loses its power of vision (*Phaedo* 99d-e). The measures that Socrates has taken to protect himself are nonetheless insufficient for other souls.

The echoes at 299b-d of the myth of the reversed cosmos help us to put the latter point in terms of Socrates' placelessness or *atopia*. The bonds of true opinion by which the statesman weaves together the citizens within a political community are "divine," and the Stranger calls the family (*genos*) of souls in which these bonds come to be "daimonic" (309c8). In commenting on this passage, Miller observes that the statesman's political weaving responds to the absence of the gods in the current cycle by fashioning the community as a sacred, ensouled organism that cares for itself, and that thus "internalizes towards itself the relation which the god bore towards it in the age of Cronus."[72] Socrates, however, comports himself toward the artfully constructed wholeness of the political community as if he were at home in neither cosmic cycle. He is profoundly reflective, as one could be only in the current cycle. Yet like a resident of the counter-cycle, he is curiously unaffected by current psychological and physiological necessities: he is guarded by a *daimôn* (his private *daimonion*), disdains the protection of woolen garments and other warm clothing even in the coldest weather (*Symposium* 220a-c), and is seemingly oblivious to the unrelenting pace of work and political life (cf. *Theaetetus* 172c). Most important, he treats others as if they were or could be as independent and thick-skinned as he is. Socrates' philosophical anthropology involves the persistent attempt to think *ex archês*, or to uncover the beginnings of the human things. According to the Stranger, however, our natural beginnings are so harsh as to be generally unbearable. In unraveling the interior and civic web of *nomos*, the Stranger implies, Socrates upsets the psychic and political balance of quiet self-control or moderation (*sôphrosunê*) and manliness at which statesmanship aims above all.[73] The latter imbalance, moreover, is "the most hateful sickness of all for cities" (307d7-8), a sickness that leads either to enslavement due to the excessively unpolemical character of the citizenry or to an unending attempt, due to excessive aggression, to conquer and tyrannize over other communities (307e-308a). In either case, the free and leisurely activity of philosophy would be impossible.[74]

Concluding Reflections: Philosophy and Politics

While the Stranger makes it clear that philosophy is impossible apart from a political community that dwells in the middle ground between moderation and manliness, he also suggests that such a community could not long endure apart from philosophy. The Stranger's argument for the "second-best" rule of law is itself philosophical, which is to say that it appeals to a measure of *phronêsis* such as can be acquired only through philosophical reflection. Among other things, a political tradition that left no place for philosophizing would ultimately lose sight of the importance of tradition itself.[75] Yet the Stranger also teaches that philosophical inquiry in its purest form corrodes the political community. Socrates' sophistry is an inevitable consequence of his philosophizing: precisely because he is purely and simply a philosopher, Socrates both is and is not a bad citizen. Philosophy and politics are both at odds with, and dependent upon, each other.

The paradoxical verdict urged by the Stranger may also be expressed in terms of the Homeric subtext of the philosophic trial. It is the Stranger who seems to be most clearly associated with legitimate governance, as it is he who is cast in the role of the returning ruler Odysseus. The figure of Odysseus has philosophical as well as political associations, for Odysseus exemplifies the polytropic, erotic, discursive character of the philosophic soul as it strives to find its home-place in the cosmos. Socrates, however, bears a certain resemblance to Penelope, who during Odysseus's absence kept pretenders to the throne at bay by means of a cunning contrivance (*dolos*) that sprang from her own Odyssean cleverness. Penelope deferred accepting any offer of marriage until the shroud that she was weaving for Laertes was complete, but at night she would unravel the web that she had woven by day (*Odyssey* 2.93-105). Her cyclical activity is a nice image of Socrates' ambiguous relationship to the web of *nomos* and the fabric of human souls. Yet her weaving also images the ceaseless work of statesmanship, which must repeatedly repair the political web that is always unraveling due to the fundamental tensions that characterize human life.

The preceding ambiguities help to underscore the point that Socrates' philosophic trial revolves around a paradox at the heart of human existence that is akin to Theaetetus's problem of irrational roots. Socratic inquiry, the Stranger implies, is *the* route to a fully human life and to the knowledge of statesmanship. Yet it is not safe for most human beings. I suggested earlier that in the Stranger's view Socrates underestimates the fragility of human beings, that he overestimates the power of their psyches, or that in his quest for the best in human life he pays insufficient attention to the constraints of necessity. These formulations, however, are inadequate insofar as they suggest that Socrates would not have missed the mark had he been a bit more reflective. But he could have avoided going wrong in these ways only at the *cost* of reflection. And that was a price he was unwilling to pay. Socrates aspired to live up to the Ideas in the fullest possible way, and he therefore chose to live dangerously. For this most noble aspiration brings to light incongruities at the heart of human existence whose threatening character can be mitigated only by the pursuit of an examined life.

Epilogue

Plato and Socrates

"You speak of an altogether noble pastime in contrast to a poor one, Socrates, the pastime of one capable of playing in speeches, telling stories about justice and the other things you mention."

"Yes indeed, my dear Phaedrus, so it is; but I think that seriousness about them is much more noble, whenever someone using the dialectical art should take hold of a fitting soul and plant and sow in it speeches together with knowledge—speeches that are able to help both themselves and the one who planted them, and that are not fruitless but yield seed from which other speeches, springing up in other characters, are capable of making this a forever undying chain, and make their possessor happy to the furthest possible extent for a human being."

Plato, *Phaedrus*

Our study of the philosophic trial has given us a vivid picture of Socrates as a caretaker of human souls whose overriding concern is the achievement of exemplary humanity through self-knowledge. Socrates emerges in the *Theaetetus*, *Euthyphro*, and *Cratylus* not simply as an advocate for excellence, but rather as a trustee of human souls. Whereas Protagoras and other philosophical and pedagogical rivals (including certain dogmatic philosophers, mathematicians, would-be prophets, and self-appointed saviors of the city, as well as Protagoras's deconstructionist heirs) speak and act in ways that rob individuals of their human *ousia*, Socrates helps young souls to come into possession of themselves *as* selves—as active, reflective centers of responsibility. He also teaches by example that self-knowledge turns upon the possibility of the prophetic

281

recollection of the intermediate domain of human life, a middle ground whereupon theoretical reflection emerges from a serious and continuing engagement with the concrete circumstances of everyday existence.

In the *Sophist* and the *Statesman*, the Eleatic Stranger also shows himself to be a caretaker of souls who is ultimately guided, not by an abstract theoretical method, but by a prophetic sense of the nature of human beings and of the middle ground they properly inhabit. The Stranger dramatically vindicates Socrates' most basic philosophical commitments even in the course of formulating his final accusation of bad citizenship, for this very accusation displays a Socratic self-awareness about the necessary limits of knowledge and a recognition of the supreme importance of virtue. To this extent, the Stranger confirms the essential difference between Socratic philosophizing and sophistry.

The conflict between Socrates and the Stranger is nonetheless serious and substantial. Their disagreement recapitulates, without resolving, the doubleness of human existence that has been the most enduring problem of Socrates' philosophic trial. The trial argues against the Socratic thesis that virtue is one insofar as it makes clear that even the highest virtue is in an important sense opposed to itself. To this opposition there is no solution without remainder: if those who imitate the example of Socrates place the political community at risk, those who side with the Stranger seem consciously to relinquish the personal achievement of exemplary humanity.[1]

Where does Plato stand on these issues? One could argue that he signals his agreement with the Stranger by refusing to take philosophy directly into the public space of the political community after the manner of Socrates. Plato instead withdraws from the agora into the groves of Academia, and turns toward writing as a philosophical medium. But the significance of these gestures bears careful consideration. For even the Stranger implicitly concedes that the fullest knowledge of human beings is available only through the Socratic interrogation of the broadest possible variety of human souls. Is it still possible to regard Plato, not to mention the Stranger, as a legitimate heir of Socratic philosophizing—as an Odysseus to Socrates' Laertes?

Plato himself speaks to this question in one of his letters to Dionysius. "There are no writings of Plato," he maintains in the course of a discussion of the dangers of writing, "nor will there ever be any, but those now said to be his are of a Socrates grown beautiful [or noble] and young" (*Second Letter* 314c2-4). In this sentence the genitive phrase *Sôkratous kalou kai neou gegonotos* is grammatically ambiguous, because it can be read both objectively and subjectively. In translation the weight of this ambiguity—which is identical to that of the title *Apologia Sôkratous (Apology of Socrates)*—is borne by the word "of." The dialogues, in other words, are either by or about a young and beautiful Socrates, or perhaps both.

If we allow full play to the grammatical ambiguity noted above, then in this well-known quotation Plato is both identifying himself as a young and beautiful Socrates and claiming in his writings to have rejuvenated and ennobled his teacher. Read in this way, the quotation invites us to ponder the paradoxical reciprocity of the relationship between Plato and Socrates as student and teacher. On the one hand, Plato affirms his teacher's pedagogical fecundity by identifying himself as Socrates' philosophical heir. On the other, he implies that his distinctively Socratic qualities are manifested precisely in his literary and philosophical beautification and renewal of Socrates himself.

I believe that we can learn from the *Second Letter* while largely steering clear of the question of Plato's relationship to the historical Socrates. In particular, the quoted passage helps us to appreciate the extent to which Plato overcomes the limitations of the character of Socrates in the dialogues as well as those of the Eleatic Stranger.

While Socrates' speech is harsh and confrontational, Plato's writing is less so. Like civic law, the Platonic text is a defensive web of words. The production of rhetorically sophisticated dialogues is an act of *phronêsis* that is designed to protect the integrity of the political community by mitigating the ugly political consequences of Socrates' direct interrogation of his fellow citizens. Yet Plato could never have appreciated the wisdom of the decision to write dialogues had he lacked the opportunity to learn from Socrates' attempt to bring philosophy into the public sphere. This risky experiment was in the last analysis an extraordinary gift from Socrates to his philosophically inclined friends.

The Stranger seems to recapitulate what Plato has learned from Socrates' mistakes. But he also appears to speak for Plato himself when in the *Statesman* he confirms the superiority of Socrates' manner of philosophizing with respect to the acquisition, the "gathering together," of *phronêsis* (272c). Contemporary academicians, whose intellectual lives are all too often no less insular and self-enclosed than those of a Theodorus or a Euclides, would do well to take note of this point. Plato, of course, was the first academician. Yet through the representation of Socrates in the dialogues, he finds a way of illuminating, and to this extent transcending, the limitations of his own philosophical choices. Plato does not interrogate the fathers of Athens in public places, but—in a gesture that is at least partly self-critical—he puts before us the pregnant example of one who does.

The preceding reflections suggest that the nature of philosophy is ultimately exemplified neither by Plato alone nor by the characters of Socrates and the Stranger, but by the speeches and deeds of all three together. Unfortunately, this multiplication of philosophers merely restates, without clearly resolving, the problem with which we began. Most important, Plato leaves it to us to think through the enduring opposition between Platonic writing and reading on the one hand and Socratic conversation on the other. Yet perhaps this outcome is the most that we can reasonably expect, for Plato teaches that the process of weaving together the disparate elements of human life and thereby finding the middle ground is in some measure irreducibly personal. And if we are to follow Socrates' advice in the *Phaedrus*, we will act as farmers of our own souls' potentialities in planting and tending just the sorts of fundamental questions that we have examined in this book. It is only in this way, Socrates suggests, that we may continue to grow toward the light.

Notes

Preface

1. *Plato's World* (Chicago: University of Chicago Press, 1995), 2, 47, 110, 121, 131, 140, 146, 147.

Introduction

1. Most scholars who have commented on this group of dialogues omit the *Cratylus*. I accept D. J. Allan's suggestion (in "The Problem of Cratylus," *American Journal of Philology* 75 [1954], 271-287) that the *Cratylus* takes place on the same day as the *Euthyphro*. For further discussion see below, ch. 5.

2. Unless the context indicates otherwise, "Socrates" hereafter refers to the character of Socrates in the Platonic dialogues.

3. The business of the King Archon "was, in the first instance, to see that the indictment was in proper legal form, to enter the reply of the accused to the charge, take the depositions of the witnesses on either side, and make the other necessary preliminary arrangements for the bringing of the case before a popular jury" (A. E. Taylor, *Socrates* [New York: D. Appleton, 1933], 96). According to Douglas M. MacDowell, *The Law in Classical Athens* (Ithaca: Cornell University Press, 1978), these proceedings did not all take place on the same day. Once a charge was admitted by a magistrate, another date was set for the *anakrisis*, a hearing at which the accused entered his plea and the issues in dispute were clarified (237 ff.). It is not clear whether on the day of the *Euthyphro* Socrates was going to the *anakrisis* or to hear Meletus's first statement of his charge. The important point in the present context, however, is that Plato shows us none of the preliminary proceedings, and puts the *Sophist* and *Statesman* in their place.

4. Mitchell Miller maintains that in the *Theaetetus*, *Sophist*, and *Statesman* Plato presents "a distinctively philosophical version of Socrates' [public] trial" (*The Philosopher in Plato's Statesman* [The Hague: Martinus Nijhoff, 1980], 2), a suggestion that is supported by Joseph Cropsey in "The Dramatic End of Plato's Socrates," *Interpretation* 14.2&3 (1986), 155-175. The view that the Stranger particularly intends his fifth division of the sophist (*Soph.* 226b-231b) to apply to Socrates is advanced in Seth Benardete, *The Being of the Beautiful:*

Plato's Theaetetus, Sophist, and Statesman (Chicago: University of Chicago Press, 1983); Jacob Klein, *Plato's Trilogy: Theaetetus, the Sophist and the Statesman* (Chicago: University of Chicago Press, 1977); Stanley Rosen, *Plato's Sophist: The Drama of Original and Image* (New Haven, Conn.: Yale University Press, 1983); Kenneth M. Sayre, *Plato's Analytic Method* (Chicago: University of Chicago Press, 1969); and Harvey Scodel, *Diaeresis and Myth in Plato's Statesman* (Göttingen, Ger.: Vandenhoeck and Ruprecht, 1987). See also Stanley Rosen, *Plato's Statesman: The Web of Politics* (New Haven: Yale University Press, 1995).

5. Socrates' prophetic insight is a theme in other dialogues of the octology as well. Cf. *Apol.* 39c, *Cri.* 44a-b, *Phd.* 84e-85b. As we shall see, Socrates' knowledge of the human soul is "prophetic"—and therefore, epistemically "impure" —in an extended or metaphorical sense.

6. The *Theaetetus* and the *Sophist* explicitly refer to each other (*Tht.* 210d, *Soph.* 216a) and the *Statesman* explicitly refers to the *Sophist* (257a), so that these three dialogues constitute a widely acknowledged trilogy. This trilogy is a subset of a larger group of dialogues linked together by cross-references, a group that includes the *Euthyphro, Cratylus*, and *Apology.* The *Theaetetus* explicitly refers to the *Euthyphro* as well as the *Sophist* (210d), and the *Cratylus* does so implicitly (396d-397a). And like the *Euthyphro*, the *Theaetetus* begins and ends with references to Socrates' public trial (cf. *Tht.* 142c).

7. Cf. Cropsey's remark (in "The Dramatic End of Plato's Socrates") that the "Platonic corpus contains—perhaps simply is—the appraisal of Socrates" (158). Cropsey also speculates that "the dramatic, thematic, and personal ligatures" of the philosophic trial would, "if carefully pursued . . . include some large part, perhaps all, of the Platonic corpus" (157).

8. Lewis Campbell (in *The Sophistes and Politicus of Plato,* 1867 [New York: Arno Press, 1973]) and J. B. Skemp (in *Plato's Statesman* [New Haven: Yale University Press, 1952]) argue that Plato originally intended to write the *Philosopher*. Paul Friedländer, on the other hand, suggests that those who assume that there should have been a dialogue *Philosopher* are victims of Plato's irony (*Plato,* 3 vols., trans. Hans Meyerhoff [Princeton, N.J.: Princeton University Press, 1958-1969], 1.153). Not surprisingly, neither Campbell nor Skemp have much to say in a noncritical vein about the dramatic dimension of the *Sophist* and *Statesman* (see below, note 16).

9. Jacob Klein, *A Commentary on Plato's Meno* (Chapel Hill: University of North Carolina Press, 1965), 18. The general hermeneutical assumptions that guide the present study are shared by a growing number of Plato scholars. Illuminating explorations of crucial interpretative issues may be found especially in *Platonic Writings, Platonic Readings*, ed. Charles L. Griswold, Jr. (New York: Routledge, 1988), and, more recently, in *Methods of Interpreting Plato and His Dialogues*, ed. James C. Klagge and Nicholas D. Smith, a supplementary volume of *Oxford Studies in Ancient Philosophy* (Oxford: Clarendon Press, 1992).

Stephen Salkever offers a judicious assessment of the importance of the latter collection of essays in *Bryn Mawr Classical Reviews* 3 (1992), 368-375. See also the essays in *Plato's Dialogues: New Studies and Interpretations*, ed. Gerald A. Press (Lanham, Md.: Rowman & Littlefield, 1993) and in *The Third Way: New Directions in Plato Studies*, ed. Francisco J. Gonzales (Lanham, Md.: Rowman & Littlefield, 1995).

   10. Heraclitus maintained that "character [*êthos*] for a human being is destiny [*daimôn*]" (*Hêrakleitou Peri Phuseôs*, fr. 119). As a further point of comparison, the dialogues stand up well to a Midrashic kind of literary scrutiny, because they are written with the same deft economy of characterization and subtle attention to the details of circumstance that distinguish the Hebrew Bible.

   11. See Wolfgang Wieland, *Platon und die Formen des Wissens* (Göttingen, Ger.: Vandenhöck & Ruprecht, 1982), 50-70 ("Der Dialog als Medium des philosophischen Gedankens"). Wieland argues that the dialogues show what cannot adequately be said. Philosophical arguments must be understood within the concrete contexts of discourse that give rise to them, contexts which are themselves revealed in the mode of showing rather than saying. The dialogue form, in turn, is a self-conscious response to the fact that no *logos* can exhaustively capture the content of that which is shown: "Mit Hilfe dieser Form wird etwas gezeigt, was nicht mehr gesagt wird. Auch über das so Gezeigte ist es möglich, begründet zu reden. Aber auch die genauste Rede kann den Inhalt des Gezeigten nicht erschöpfen" (70). In "Plato's Metaphilosophy: Why Plato Wrote Dialogues" (pp. 143-167 of *Platonic Writings, Platonic Readings*), Charles Griswold argues along similar lines that "*showing* (rather than merely *saying* or *asserting*) the viability of philosophizing is a necessary component in the dialogical refutation of the critics of philosophy" (160, emphasis in original). In "Irony and Aesthetic Language in Plato's Dialogues," *Philosophy and Literature*, ed. Doug Bolling (New York: Haven Publications, 1987), 71-99, Griswold provides a detailed discussion of Platonic and Socratic irony that resonates with Wieland's approach. While a Platonic dialogue exhibits dramatic irony insofar as "the meaning of the speeches and/or deeds of one or more of its characters is primarily visible to the reader . . . of the drama rather than to the characters in it," Socratic irony (of which Griswold distinguishes six types) "occurs when the speaker purposely dissimulates his views while in the process of manifesting them either through words or deeds" (78). Irony, then, "is a way of speaking (or writing) which is meant to point to what is not spoken (or written), to what is silent and kept in reserve, as it were, by its originator" (78-79). Because it invites the reader actively to reflect upon and so to put into his own words a dialogue's unspoken core, Platonic irony amounts to the literary equivalent of Socrates' "commitment to conversing in such a way as to lead his interlocutors to find the truth on their own" (82). Finally, cf. Hans-Georg Gadamer, "*Logos* and *Ergon* in Plato's *Lysis*" (in *Dialogue and Dialectic: Eight Hermeneutical Studies on Plato*, trans. P. Christopher Smith [New Haven: Yale University Press, 1980], 1-

20), who observes that Socrates cannot be understood otherwise than through active reflection on that which Socratic and Platonic irony leaves unsaid: "Now the difference between Socrates and the sophists is in no way an obvious one; rather it is a difference evident only to someone who has not only the logos in view but also the ergon" (5).

12. Griswold connects the radically fictitious nature of the dialogues with Platonic irony, and suggests that perhaps the most radical fiction of all occurs in situations in which we must suppose that Socrates' interlocutors are incapable of grasping his irony, so that Socrates "acts as though he were—*per impossible*—addressing himself to the reader" ("Irony and Aesthetic Language," 87). Such cases confirm Griswold's claim, in the same article, that Socratic irony is encompassed and regulated by Platonic irony (78).

13. Orthodox scholars adopt what Kenneth M. Sayre has called the "proto-essay" view of the dialogues, according to which the dialogue form "boils down to a quaint way of presenting the moves in a philosophic argument, serving primarily to accomodate a nontechnical audience" (*Plato's Literary Garden: How to Read a Platonic Dialogue* [Notre Dame: University of Notre Dame Press, 1995], 4). Among his other objections to this view, Sayre emphasizes the fact that the "theories commonly associated with the name of Plato in standard textbooks and histories of philosophy" are never stated in an explicit and well-defined way in the dialogues (7).

14. See, for example, the comparative table assembled by Sir David Ross in *Plato's Theory of Ideas* (Oxford: Oxford University Press, 1951), 2.

15. Such change is usually conceived as "development." This approach to the dialogues "solves" the problem of Socratic philosophizing by dividing or dissolving the character of Socrates. Cf. the introductory remarks of the editor in a recent volume on the philosophy of Socrates: "Few would nowadays dispute Vlastos' central claim that there is more than one Socrates in the Platonic dialogues. . . . If the historical Socrates is to be found anywhere in the Platonic dialogues it presumably will be in Plato's early work when the influence of his mentor remains strong. As Plato begins to philosophically mature, we should expect him to gradually move away from the views of Socrates to his own original positions." *Essays on the Philosophy of Socrates*, ed. Hugh H. Benson (Oxford: Oxford University Press, 1992), 4-5. A more cautious assessment of the problem of the historical Socrates is provided by Barry Gower in his introduction to *Socratic Questions: New Essays on the Philosophy of Socrates and Its Significance*, ed. Barry S. Gower and Michael C. Stokes (London: Routledge, 1992).

16. Consider, for example, the criticisms of the style of the *Sophist* and *Statesman* advanced by Benjamin Jowett, Lewis Campbell, and A. E. Taylor. Of the *Statesman*, Jowett writes: "[Plato's] own image may be used as a motto of his style; like an inexpert statuary, he has made the figure or outline too large, and is unable to give the proper color or proportions. . . . The Eleatic Stranger,

here, as in the *Sophist*, has no appropriate character, and appears only as the expositor of a political ideal" (*The Dialogues of Plato* [Boston: The Jefferson Press, n.d.], 3.513-514). Campbell: "The Eleatic Stranger is like the Sophist he describes, whose 'sense is shut' to everything but the dry light of reason. . . . Speaking at the time when Athens was ringing with the trial of Socrates, he never once alludes to a matter so sublunary" (*Sophistes and Politicus*, xxii). Taylor: "The clash of mind with mind," so conspicuous in the earlier dialogues, "is abandoned for the delivery of a lesson by master to pupil" (*Plato: The Sophist and the Statesman* [London: Thomas Nelson and Sons, 1961], 5). A very different approach is taken by Mitchell Miller, who demonstrates both in *The Philosopher in Plato's Statesman* and *Plato's Parmenides: The Conversion of the Soul* (Princeton: Princeton University Press, 1986) that the "later" dialogues are no less essentially dialogic and dramatic than "earlier" works.

17. And with this dramatic ensemble in view, it becomes evident that Plato's narrative decisions in certain respects challenge our expectations of cohesiveness in regard to the dialogues of the octology. Only the first and last of these dialogues, the *Theaetetus* and the *Phaedo*, are narrated; all the rest are presented in direct discourse. But while the *Phaedo* is told shortly after Socrates' death, the dramatic date of the *Theaetetus* is the occasion of Theaetetus's death years later, and while the former dialogue is Plato's writing of Phaedo's recollection of Socrates' death, the latter possesses a far more complex, multilayered narrative structure that brings to mind such works as the *Parmenides* and the *Symposium*. Between the Theaetetus and the other dialogues of the octology there is, to borrow an expression, a significant narrative and temporal "gap"; cf. Diskin Clay, "Gaps in the 'Universe' of the Platonic Dialogues," *Proceedings of the Boston Area Colloquium in Ancient Philosophy*, vol. 3, ed. John Cleary (Lanham, Md.: University Press of America, 1988), 131-157, esp. 148-149. Depending on how one views the situation, the distance between the end of the *Theaetetus* and the beginning of the *Euthyphro* is either one of the shortest or one of the longest in the entire Platonic corpus.

18. "Re-reading Plato: The Problem of Platonic Chronology," *Phoenix* 45.3 (1991), 189-214.

19. The quotation is borrowed from Eva Brann, "Plato's Theory of Ideas," *The St. John's Review* 32.1 (July, 1980), 29, where it appears in a somewhat different context. I suspect, however, that certain kinds of inquiries that are framed in chronological terms need not be. A study of the methodology of Plato's "later" dialogues, for example, need not depend on chronological distinctions, since methodological differences are intrinsic to the texts themselves.

20. See the paradigmatic deconstruction of Plato in "La Pharmacie de Platon," available in English as "Plato's Pharmacy" in Jacques Derrida, *Dissemination*, trans. Barbara Johnson (Chicago: University of Chicago Press, 1981), 61-171. The comparison between Phaedrus and Derrida is advanced by Charles Griswold in *Self-Knowledge in Plato's Phaedrus* (New Haven: Yale University

Press, 1986), 237-238. Derrida's analysis of the way in which the Platonic texts reveal the decisive absence of the Socratic speaker has recently been extended by Harry Berger, Jr., in "Facing Sophists: Socrates' Charismatic Bondage in *Protagoras*," *Representations* 5 (Spring, 1984), 66-91, and by Jay Farness in *Missing Socrates: Problems of Plato's Writing* (University Park, Pa.: Pennsylvania State University Press, 1991).

21. Cf. Stanley Rosen, *Hermeneutics as Politics* (New York: Oxford University Press, 1987), 77: "Derridean writing . . . becomes a satire on Eros, which is continuously changing its shape. Yet the Derridean soul, because of the absence of a divine gift, is neither erotic nor mantic."

22. *Stsm.* 295b-296a; *Phdo.* 60c-61b; *Second Letter* 314c1-4: the writings of Plato are "of a Socrates grown beautiful [or 'noble': *kalou*] and young [or 'new': *neou*]."

23. Berger, "Facing Sophists," 90.

24. *Self-Knowledge*, 235; emphasis in original. Griswold notes that Derrida's reading of the *Phaedrus* is "extraordinarily arbitrary" in that it "pays virtually no attention to sections of the *Phaedrus* other than the last one in which the speaking/writing issue is raised," "fails to consider in detail all of Socrates' criticisms of the written word," and "takes no account of the fundamental role attributed in the final section of the dialogue to the *question*" (235, emphasis in original). Cf. Rosen's reflection that "it is scarcely plausible that Plato was nothing by intention but a metaphysician of presence, since he certainly wrote, not just the passages that look to Derrida like a metaphysics of presence or its failure, but the poetic or dramatic *context* that renders these passages playful. . . . Were this [i.e., Derrida's] the correct understanding of Plato, then he would have written not dialogues but metaphysical treatises. Metaphysicians of presence are not playful." (*Hermeneutics as Politics*, 72-73; emphasis in original).

25. "Plato's Pharmacy," 97.

26. *Self-Knowledge*, 239, 240.

27. "Plato's Pharmacy," 167, 103; emphasis in original.

28. "Plato's Pharmacy," 123, 127; cf. 111, 166.

29. "Plato's Pharmacy," 127; cf. 98-99: "Plato decides in favor of a logic that does not tolerate . . . passages between opposing senses of the same word."

30. "Plato's Pharmacy," 124, 138.

31. "Plato's Pharmacy," 108.

32. "Plato's Pharmacy," 103.

33. "Plato's Pharmacy," 129, 130.

34. "Plato's Pharmacy," 76, 169, 167.

35. "Plato's Pharmacy," 117.

36. "Plato's Pharmacy," 120, 126-127.

37. The phrase is Drew Hyland's, from *Finitude and Transcendence in the Platonic Dialogues* (Albany: State University of New York Press, 1995), 5.

38. Consider Aristodemus, who goes about barefooted (*Symp.* 173b); the miserable and lugubrious Apollodorus (*Symp.* 173c-e; *Phdo.* 59a-b); and the "manic" and "impetuous" Chaerephon (*Chrm.* 153b2; *Apol.* 21a3), whose association with Socrates is lampooned in Aristophanes' *Clouds* (102-104, 144 ff., 503-504; cf. *Birds*, 1296).

Chapter 1

1. On this point cf. Leo Strauss, *The City and Man* (Chicago: University of Chicago Press, 1964), 13-17.

2. This is noted by Eva Brann, "The Offense of Socrates: A Re-Reading of Plato's Apology," *Interpretation* 7.2 (1978), 1. To call the jurors *dikastai* would suggest that they are competent in the sphere of justice (*dikê*)—an implication that Socrates probably wishes to avoid.

3. Among the many advocates of the former view are Brann, "Offense of Socrates," and Cropsey, *Plato's World*. The latter view is advanced by Thomas C. Brickhouse and Nicholas D. Smith, *Socrates on Trial* (Princeton: Princeton University Press, 1989).

4. On the courts as theater, see Richard Garner's discussion of law and drama in *Law and Society in Classical Athens* (St. Martin's Press: New York, 1987), 95-130.

5. Douglas D. Feaver and John E. Hare, "The *Apology* as an Inverted Parody of Rhetoric," *Arethusa* 14.2 (1981), 205-216.

6. Brann, "Offense of Socrates," 18. "Nothing Socrates thinks," Brann adds, "can be expeditiously conveyed by public deliverance; it must always be slowly engendered in leisurely direct conversation with its accompanying inner dialogue (see *Theaetetus* 172d). Socrates' positive wisdom stated concisely in public would appear simply bizarre" (19).

7. Socrates' rhetorical predicament is overlooked by Brickhouse and Smith, who understand irony simply as intentionally disingenuous and insincere speech. As such, ironic speech always threatens to undermine the effective communication of the truth. Thus we are told that "if irony is to be found in Socrates' presentation . . . it must in no way interfere with the jurors' capacity to judge the case correctly. . . . Those who wish to argue that Socrates was ironic in any particular claim must be prepared to show that he believed such irony was at least as likely as the literal truth to get the jury to see the facts of the case clearly and without prejudice" (*Socrates on Trial*, 43, 45). But Socrates evidently does *not* believe that the jury as a whole possesses the capacity to judge correctly or to appreciate the "literal truth."

8. This is how the passage in question is understood by C. D. C. Reeve, *Socrates in the Apology* (Indianapolis: Hackett, 1989): "Religion gives Socrates one reason to live the examined life, and prudence gives him another" (71). Brickhouse and Smith agree that Socrates is sincere about his duty to the god. Yet

while they cite portions of 37e4-38a8 in *Socrates on Trial*, they provide no analysis of this important passage as a whole.

9. As Mogen Herman Hansen has recently observed, the claim that Socrates is wisest cannot be deduced from what the oracle actually says ("No one is wiser than Socrates," *Apol.* 21a6-7). *The Trial of Socrates from the Athenian Point of View* (Copenhagen: Royal Danish Academy of Sciences and Letters, 1995), 34. Reeve's attempt to make Socrates' claim square with the oracle ("No one is wiser than Socrates just in case Socrates is [the] wisest of men," *Socrates in the Apology*, 22) ignores the logical possibility that a great many human beings may be just as wise (or ignorant) as Socrates.

10. An air of irreverence is certainly detectable in Socrates' comparison of gods with horses (27d8-e3). This comparison should be connected with his subsequent image of the city as a horse (30e4). Perhaps there is an allusion here to Xenophanes: "But if oxen (and horses) and lions had hands or could draw with hands and create works of art like those made by men, horses would draw pictures of gods like horses, and oxen of gods like oxen, and they would make the bodies (of their gods) in accordance with the form that each species itself possesses." *Ancilla to the Pre-Socratic Philosophers*, trans. Kathleen Freeman (Cambridge, Mass.: Harvard University Press, 1977), Xenophanes, frag. 15.

11. Cf. Brickhouse and Smith's claim that Socrates' search for someone wiser than himself is "not an impious attempt to prove the god wrong, but only an attempt to understand what the god sought to convey" (*Socrates on Trial*, 96).

12. *Plato's World*, 146ff.

13. "Irony and Aesthetic Language," 78-79.

14. Concerning Chaerephon's manic character, see 21a3 and *Chrm.* 153b2. Socrates' testimony regarding the Delphic oracle, as Strauss observes, supplies "the sole proof of his believing in the gods of the city" ("On Plato's *Apology of Socrates* and *Crito*," in *Studies in Platonic Political Philosophy* [Chicago: University of Chicago Press, 1983], 44).

15. Cf. Aristide Tessitore, "Aristotle's Political Presentation of Socrates in the *Nicomachean Ethics*," *Interpretation* 16.1 (1988), 3-22, who points out that Aristotle's first statement about Socrates in the *Eth. Nic.* (1116b3-5) occurs within the context of a discussion of the sort of courage exhibited by professional soldiers, and in particular foreign mercenaries. Tessitore observes that "like professional soldiers, Socrates did not appear to be especially attached to the polis, at least not after the fashion of those citizen soldiers whom Aristotle has just finished discussing" (9; cf. *Eth. Nic.* 1116b17-18).

16. Cf. *Tht.* 151a and *Theages* 129e, where Socrates states that his daimonic voice or sign occasionally forbids him to associate with certain individuals.

17. With regard to Socrates' interests, Brann observes that in the *Phaedo* "he gives a vivid topology of the things above and below the earth (198eff.), as he does in the *Republic* and in other conversations" ("Offense of Socrates," 9). Such mythical topologies, it should be noted, do not constitute a secret teaching;

nothing in the *Apology* implies that Socrates ever instructs anyone by transmitting any set of doctrines.

18. Clifford Orwin, "On the *Cleitophon*," in *The Roots of Political Philosophy: Ten Forgotten Socratic Dialogues*, ed. Thomas L. Pangle (Ithaca: Cornell University Press, 1987), 119-20.

19. Kierkegaard, in agreement with Hegel, identifies "the indefensible feature in Socrates' behavior as the moral intervention of a third person into the absolute relationship between parents and children." *The Concept of Irony*, trans. Lee M. Capel (Bloomington: Indiana University Press, 1965), 209; *Hegel's Lectures on the History of Philosophy*, 1892, trans. E. S. Haldane and Frances H. Simpson (New York: Humanities Press, 1974), 1:435-440. Kevin Robb argues along the same lines in "*Asebeia* and *Sunousia*: The Issues Behind the Indictment of Socrates," in *Plato's Dialogues: New Studies and Interpretations*, 77-106; see also *Literacy and Paideia in Ancient Greece* (New York: Oxford University Press, 1994), esp. 197-207.

20. In *The Ancient City: A Study in the Religion, Laws, and Institutions of Greece and Rome*, 1956 (Baltimore: Johns Hopkins University Press, 1980), Numa Denis Fustel de Coulanges notes that when Cleisthenes replaced the old religious tribes with new tribes and demes, the demes "uniformly adopted as their protecting gods *Zeus, the guardian of the walls*, and *the paternal Apollo*" (emphasis in original, 274). Cf. Strepsiades' appeal to *patrôion Dia*, "Zeus, the protector of fathers," when he is challenged by Pheidippides in Aristophanes' *Clouds* (1468).

21. The topic of *erôs* is perhaps touched upon, however, by Socrates' references to his *daimonion*. On the association between Socrates' *erôs* and his daimonic voice or sign see Thomas Pangle, "On the *Theages*," in *The Roots of Political Philosophy*, 170-171. More recently, Francis Coolidge has argued in "Socrates and the Daimonic: On the Voice and Daimonic Sign," an unpublished paper presented to the Society for Ancient Greek Philosophy in October of 1994, that Socrates' daimonion "is his interpretation of the event, or the potential event, of *erôs* failing to unite the soul with what it lacks."

22. *Missing Socrates*, 45, 41 (emphasis in original).

23. *Missing Socrates*, 37, 46. Farness quotes *Republic* 561c-e, along with Derrida's comment that the democratic man Socrates describes in this passage "has no essence, no truth, no patronym, no constitution of his own" ("Plato's Pharmacy," 145).

24. Aristophanes, *Clouds* 348 ff. The Clouds seem to Socrates to mirror the natures of those to whom they appear. This entitles us to ask what aspect of Socrates' *own* nature is reflected in his perception of the Clouds as plastic, imitative beings. A plausible answer is: Socrates' capacity to reflect the natures of his interlocutors, or, in general, his irony. I owe this observation to David Lachterman.

25. Some of these antagonists, like Meletus in the *Euthyphro* and Protagoras in the *Theaetetus*, are not literally present, but are nonetheless intellectually encountered by Socrates.

Chapter 2

1. Dionysius of Halicarnassus, *On Literary Composition* 25; cf. Diogenes Laertius, 3.37. Some highly significant first words are identified by Joan C. Harrison, "Plato's Prologue: *Theaetetus* 142a–143c," *Tulane Studies in Philosophy* 27 (1978), 104 n. 3. See also Diskin Clay, "Plato's First Words," in *Beginnings in Classical Literature, Yale Classical Studies* 29 (1992), 113-130.

2. On the dialogue's probable dramatic date of 369 B.C. see Auguste Diès' introduction to the *Theaetetus* in *Platon: Ouevres Complètes*, vol 8.2, ed. Diès, 7th ed. (Paris: Société d'Édition "Les Belles Lettres," 1976), 120-121. Additional support for this date may be found in John M. Cooper, *Plato's Theaetetus* (New York: Garland Publishing, 1990), 1 and 280, n. 2, and Benardete, *The Being of the Beautiful*, I.184 n. 2. If the prologue can be shown to provide an especially suitable introduction to the octology, the possibility that it is a later, non-Platonic addition to the dialogue (on which see Diès, 121-123) would seem to be remote.

3. Cf. Harrison, "Plato's Prologue," 108 n. 19, which establishes, at least in the case of the *Theaetetus*, that "words meaning 'care' recur with startling frequency in the dialogues dramatically linked with Socrates' death." As Harrison notes, "care" in the form of Meletus "is Socrates' final undoing" (123). Joseph Cropsey also emphasizes the extent to which Socrates "allow[s] his caring to govern his doings" (*Plato's World*, 2).

4. M. F. Burnyeat surmises that Theaetetus is at the time of his conversation with Socrates "a mere youth of sixteen or even less" ("The Philosophical Sense of Theaetetus' Mathematics," *Isis* 69 [1978], 489).

5. Cf. *Cra.* 386e-387a: actions (*praxeis*) are done according to the nature of the beings of which they are the actions. At *Cra.* 400c, Socrates states that the body is the *sêma*, the "tomb," "safe," or "signpost" of the soul.

6. Aristotle, *Metaph.* 1046b29ff. Cf. Stanley Rosen, "Dunamis, Energeia and the Megarians," *Philosophical Inquiry* 1.2 (Winter 1979), 119.

7. Aristotle claims that the Megarian view amounts to an endorsement of the *logos* of Protagoras (*Metaph.* 1047a6). Cf. the following remarks of Harrison: "Time and intentions, passion and insight must, on the Megarian view, be relegated to the domain of non-being. . . . How could the experience of an individual upholding such a view fail to be reduced to atomicity? On such a view must not each moment be seen as self-contained, unrelated to any other?" ("Plato's Prologue," 106-107). The philosophical implications of Protagoras's view will be addressed in detail in ch. 3.

8. Socrates worries early on about appearing thoroughly ridiculous (*katage-lastos*) in disputing against Homer and all those who join with him in asserting that "nothing ever is, but everything always becomes" (153a2-3). Cf. 161e4-6: if Protagoras is correct not only Socrates' art of midwifery but also "the whole business of dialogue" will be ridiculous. In general, Socrates' attempts in the *Theaetetus* to measure his philosophical efforts against those of others seem to result in comedy: a cursory inspection of Leonard Brandwood, *A Word Index to Plato* (Leeds: W. S. Maney and Son, 1976), shows that words associated with laughter and the laughable occur at least nineteen times in this dialogue.

9. Burnyeat reviews the nature and significance of Theaetetus's mathematical accomplishments in "The Philosophical Sense of Theaetetus' Mathematics." See also ch. 3 below.

10. On *anamnêsis* (recollection) and *mnêmê* (memory) in Plato see Klein's discussion in *A Commentary on Plato's Meno*, 108-172.

11. Cf. Klein, *Commentary on Plato's Meno*, 157-166 and esp. 164-165. Klein connects the absence of "positive" learning in the *Theaetetus* with the absence of "the *anamnêsis* thesis" (166).

12. The apt description of Socrates as "outlandish" was suggested by Carl Page, "Philosophy and the Outlandishness of Reason," *Journal of Speculative Philosophy* 7.3 (1993), 206-225.

13. See *Phd.* 84e-85b and *Cri.* 44a-b with Strauss, "Plato's *Apology of Socrates* and *Crito*," 55. Cf. also Socrates' claim in the *Cratylus* that the god Hades is a "perfect sophist" who speaks beautiful speeches as well as a "philosopher" who knows "all noble things" and binds men to his domain by means of "the appetite for virtue" (403d-404b).

14. On the practice of feeding and keeping the *pharmakoi* in the Prutaneum, see Aristophanes, *Knights* 1405, together with the scholiast on *Knights* 1136. Socrates' birthdate is recorded at Diogenes Laertius 2.44. This evidence is cited in Jane Harrison's useful discussion of "The Pharmakos," in Harrison, *Prolegomena to the Study of Greek Religion*, 3d. ed. (New York: Meridian Books, 1955), 95-106; cf. the treatment of the Thargelia in Louis Moulinier, *Le pur et l'impur dans la pensée des Grecs d'Homére à Aristote* (Paris: Libraire C. Klincksiek, 1952), 94-99, and of purification in Walter Burkert, *Greek Religion*, trans. John Raffan (Cambridge, Mass.: Harvard University Press, 1985), 75-84. The expulsion of *pharmakoi* at the Thargelia amounted to the removal beyond the borders of the city of a contaminating poison, pestilence, or sickness, with the result that the old life of the city could begin anew after this purifying separation. For a stimulating discussion of Socrates as *pharmakos* see Derrida, "Plato's Pharmacy," 128-134. One should note in addition that "the yearly *theôria* [religious embassy] to Delos which delayed the execution of Socrates must have taken place in Thargelion, the month of the Delian Apollo" (Holger Thesleff, *Studies in Platonic Chronology* [Helsinki: *Commentationes Humanarum Litterarum* 70, 1982], 26 n. 24).

15. The latter phrase is borrowed from Klein, *Commentary on Plato's Meno*, 149.

16. J.-J. Alrivie finds in these round-trips an echo of Socrates' characteristic, repeated requests to begin "once more from the beginning" (*palin ex arches*). "Les prologues du *Théétète* et du *Parménide*," *Revue de Métaphysique et de Morale* 76 (1971), 15.

17. On the space in which Socratic irony unfolds cf. the remarks of René Schaerer in "Le Mécanisme de l'Ironie dans ses Rapports avec la Dialectique," *Revue de Métaphysique et de Morale* 48 (1941), 181-209: "L'ironiste ne trompe pas pour tromper, mais pour qu'on devine qu'il trompe. . . . Mais une tromperie qui se dénonce elle-même est-elle logiquement concevable? Oui, si l'on admet une dualité au sein du reel. Le terrain de l'ironie est celui de l'antithèse être-non-être, vrai-faux, bien-mal, humain-divin, idéal-phénoménale, mien-tien, implicite-explicite, . . . etc." Schaerer adds that practitioners of irony are "toujours ailleurs et toujours présents, comme Socrate" (185).

18. On the *Odyssey* as Odysseus's quest to "win his soul," see G. E. Dimock, Jr., "The Name of Odysseus," in the *Odyssey*, ed. Albert Cook, Norton Critical Edition (New York: Norton, 1974), 406-424.

19. See Jacob Howland, *The Republic: The Odyssey of Philosophy* (New York: Twayne Publishers, 1993), especially 47-54.

20. Miller, *Philosopher in Plato's Statesman*, 6.

Chapter 3

1. David Konstan, "An Anthropology of Euripides' *Kyklops*," in *Nothing to Do with Dionysus? Athenian Drama in Its Social Context*, ed. John J. Winkler and Froma I. Zeitlin (Princeton: Princeton University Press, 1990), 207-227. A thorough introduction to the structuralist analysis of Greek drama is provided by Charles Segal in "Greek Tragedy and Society: A Structuralist Perspective," in *Greek Tragedy and Political Theory*, ed. J. Peter Euben (Berkeley: University of California Press, 1986), 43-75.

2. Eugenio Benitez and Livia Guimaraes, "Philosophy as Performed in Plato's *Theaetetus*," *Review of Metaphysics* 47 (December 1993), 308. The significance of the latter question is underscored by the *Theaetetus*'s pervasive emphasis on the parent-child relation, which Kenneth Dorter calls "the dominant leitmotiv of the dialogue" (*Form and Good in Plato's Eleatic Dialogues: The Parmenides, Theaetetus, Sophist, and Statesman* [Berkeley: University of California Press, 1994], 76).

3. The quotation is from Benitez and Guimaraes, "Philosophy as Performed," 299.

4. Consider *Soph.* 224e and 231d along with *Prt.* 313d and Socrates' remark at *Tim.* 19e2-5: "The family [*genos*] of sophists . . . wanders from city to city, nowhere having settled habitations of its own."

5. This passage is commonly referred to as a "digression" because at 177b8 Socrates says that the preceding speeches have been *parerga*, "by-products." The reflections advanced below, however, may serve to show that Socrates' remark understates the significance of the passage in question.

6. As measured by Stephanus pages, the midpoint of the *Theaetetus* is page 176 and that of the *Statesman* is page 284.

7. Recent commentaries on the *Theaetetus* generally pay little attention to the digression. Cooper asserts that it "merely, in a quite general way, affirms against Protagoras and others who share his political views that there are standards of right and wrong other than those which particular states happen to enshrine in their legal and other institutions. Nothing more than this can be found in the passage . . ." (*Plato's Theaetetus*, 84-85). David Bostock devotes less than two pages to the digression in *Plato's Theaetetus* (Oxford: Clarendon Press, 1988). In *The Theaetetus of Plato* (Indianapolis: Hackett, 1990), Miles Burnyeat detects no irony in the digression's "impassioned otherworldliness," and suggests that the purpose of this passage is either to emphasize the things worth knowing (including geometry and astronomy) or to call attention to the sorts of things that *can* be known, that is, the Forms (35-37). Ronald Polansky's *Philosophy and Knowledge: A Commentary on Plato's Theaetetus* (Lewisburg: Bucknell University Press, 1992) views Socrates' portrait of the philosopher in the digression as providing a serious if somewhat "exaggerated" defense of philosophy that aims at "enchanting [listeners] with the nobility of the philosophic purpose" (138, 148). Rosemary Desjardins devotes only a long footnote to the digression in *The Rational Enterprise: Logos in Plato's Theaetetus* (Albany: State University of New York Press, 1990), but opens up a more subtle and promising line of interpretation than those advanced in the books cited above. In Desjardins' reading (238-239, n. 13), the opposition between the philosopher and the orator exemplifies the sterile "disjunctive dichotomies" that Socrates advances throughout the dialogue. These dichotomies explicitly exclude alternatives that seek somehow to affirm both disjuncts, but just insofar as they fail to make sense of experience they provoke reflection upon the generative character of mind, which produces "emergent" wholes that dialectically reconcile opposites and are not reducible to their elements. The digression's "false dichotomy between abstract reflection and withdrawal on the one hand, and the involvement of experience on the other" is thus meant "to insist on an ultimate wholeness in which, as mutually opposed but 'fitting' elements, the practical and theoretic will constitute a unity that qualifies as genuine knowledge" (239). Desjardins' suggestion that the digression's abstractions are meant to provoke reflection on Socratic wholeness is echoed and extended in two articles that explore the digression's dramatic and rhetorical contexts: Scott R. Hemmenway, "Philosophical Apology in the *Theaetetus*," *Interpretation* 17.3 (1990), 323-346, and Rachel Rue, "The Philosopher in Flight: The Digression (172c-177c) in Plato's *Theae-*

tetus," *Oxford Studies in Ancient Philosophy* 11, ed. C. C. W. Taylor (Clarendon Press: Oxford, 1993), 71-100.

8. As Rue observes, the latter phrase might also be translated "letting itself down to none of the particulars [*ouden tôn engus*]" ("Philosopher in Flight," 80). The philosopher's one-sided interest in universals is further examined below.

9. See above, ch. 1, n. 24. Note also that in playing the role of the deceased Protagoras, Socrates demonstrates the ability to assume the intellectual posture even of interlocutors who are merely imagined to be present.

10. Socrates' use of Aristophanes' caricature of philosophic extremism in the *Theaetetus* may be compared with his similar employment of this caricature in the *Republic*. See Howland, *Odyssey of Philosophy*, esp. 112-118.

11. Thus the anus does the work of the eye (193-194; cf. 171-174, where a lizard defecates in Socrates' eyes as he is gazing at the stars). And again: Socrates spends much time aloft, but his pale and sickly students resemble the shades in Hades (184-186, 504; cf. 508). Consider also Socrates' perversion of religious rituals: the jumps of fleas and the farts of gnats are described by his students as "Mysteries," and Strepsiades must undergo a rite of philosophic "initiation" before entering the Thinkery (143, 250 ff.).

12. Consider in this connection Aristotle's ambiguous remark that the individual who lives independently of political community is either a beast or a god (*Pol.* 1.1.1253a27-29). The roots of this insight are noteworthy: in stark contrast to Aristophanes' Socrates, Aristotle uncovers the distinctively political nature of human beings by way of a consideration of *logos* (*Pol.* 1.1.1253a1-18).

13. Benardete nicely captures this point: "One's own place is not simply interchangeable with any other place, for the sameness of the measure from Athens to Thebes and from Thebes to Athens does not entail the sameness of the motion in either direction" (*Being of the Beautiful*, I.131).

14. Hemmenway notes that the distinction between men and beasts is one "that not only otherworldly theoreticians ignore, but also sophists like Thrasymachus find helpful to blur." He adds that "ancestry is also crucial to know about, especially if one's twenty-fifth progenitor happens to be Heracles, because that would make your twenty-sixth not the mortal Amphitryon, as Socrates ironically mistakes (175a6-7), but the god Zeus. Thus the Thalean philosopher is oblivious to the divine element in the constitution of man, a fact which could explain his easy confusion of men with beasts" ("Philosophical Apology," 333). We may also note that 174d-e anticipates a similar confusion in the first third of the *Statesman* between rulers and shepherds and men and beasts.

15. See Hemmenway, "Philosophical Apology," 335, together with Rue's arguments to the effect that "justice and piety are not properly attributes of gods, or at least not of Greek gods" ("Philosopher in Flight," 89). (Nonetheless the *aidôs* or reverent awe that is central to piety is occasionally expressed by Greek deities. Consider, for example, the reverence shown by Thetis toward Zeus when

she pleads Achilles' case in Book 1 of the *Iliad* [500 ff.].) These virtues also sit uneasily with Socrates' rhetorical elevation of theoretical activity.

16. Cropsey finds in the *Theaetetus* a key to the philosophical significance of geometry for Plato: "The irrational and the incommensurable in mathematics . . . are the sign that the whole is intractable in itself. Their significance explains why Plato put geometry at the gateway to philosophy" (*Plato's World*, 34; cf. 29).

17. As Edward N. Lee observes, "This entire framework of [up/down and up-right/upside-down] imagery has more relevance to the *Theaetetus* than has yet been suspected." "'Hoist with His Own Petard': Ironic and Comic Elements in Plato's Critique of Protagoras (*Tht.* 161-171)," in *Exegesis and Argument: Studies in Greek Philosophy Presented to Gregory Vlastos*, ed. E. N. Lee, A. Mourelatos, and R. Rorty (Assen: Van Gorcum, 1973), 260, n. 45.

18. The phrase is Rue's: "Philosopher in Flight," 75.

19. Benardete makes this observation in *The Being of the Beautiful*, I.187 n. 51, where he notes that the phrase occurs elsewhere in Aristophanes but nowhere else in Plato.

20. Cf. Lee, "Hoist with His Own Petard," 240: Protagoras's "Man the Measure" motto "applies to man in no other way than as a particular instance of a universal generalization about *any* sentient creature, just insofar as it is sentient. . . . [it] cannot really tell us anything about man *as man*, i.e. in terms of that particular and complex nature through the having of which he is what he is and not any other sort of being than himself" (emphasis in original).

21. Cf. Aristotle's remark that "such views [as those of Protagoras] leave nothing to be 'of necessity,' as they leave no essence [*ousia*] of anything" (*Metaph.* 1010b26-28).

22. This distinctively Greek assessment of slavery is well documented in Paul A. Rahe, *Republics Ancient and Modern: Classical Republicanism and the American Revolution* (Chapel Hill: University of North Carolina Press, 1992), 32-54.

23. This has been well argued by Lee, who helpfully suggests that Protagoras would approach the denial of his assertion that human being is the measure of all things with the detachment of a psychoanalyst talking to an angry patient or perhaps of "an anthropologist describing the *mores* of some alien tribe" ("Hoist with His Own Petard," 246-247 and 246 n. 33). "Protagoras can smile benignly at the man and say 'Yes—that *is* what you think; that is true-for-you.'" But Protagoras's position has a "rebound" effect, for all of his *own* claims are *also* "systematically saddled with . . . relativizers." "And until Protagoras removes his relativizing qualifiers, he will not have actually asserted anything that can significantly be discussed or denied; he has not so much as made a move in the 'game' that Socrates calls *dialegesthai*" (247-248, emphases in original). It is in this way, Lee maintains, that Protagoras comes to be "hoist with his own petard." He goes on to suggest that Socrates likens Protagoras to a plant at 171d in

order dramatically to emphasize the point that Protagoras "cannot involve himself with others in the giving and receiving of any *logos*" (251).

24. Cf. the following remarks of Rahe on the political significance of the concept of the middle ground: "If the body is the ground of privacy, intelligible speech (*logos*) is the middle ground (*to meson*) of publicity. This is why *to meson* comes to be identified with the political community itself, and it accounts for the fact that the middle ground was thought to be the proper sphere in which to weigh and determine what is measured, fitting, timely, needful, and the like" (*Republics Ancient and Modern*, 42; see also 812 nn. 80-86).

25. Despite appearances, Socrates' attempt to embolden Theaetetus is not at odds with his concluding remark that their discussion may make Theaetetus "less burdensome to your associates and tamer, believing moderately that you do not know what you do not know" (210c2-4). Socrates refers here to the intellectual arrogance of an inexperienced youth, which is something different from *thumos* in the service of philosophic inquiry. His treatment of Theaetetus implies that the humbling reflections to which one is led only by genuinely philosophic courage provide the best antidote to intellectual pretentiousness (cf. 187b-c).

26. Hence the aptness of Theodorus's comparison of Socrates to Antaeus and Sciron, criminals of legend who inhabited wild or barbarian regions and from whom there was no escape (169a-b). The former would wrestle men to the point of exhaustion and then kill them on the hot sands of the Libyan Desert; the latter would kick his victims off of the rugged coastal cliffs between Megara and Corinth. The figure of Sciron, however, provides a fitting image of the ambiguous significance of Socrates' harshness, for he was alleged by certain Megarians actually to be a virtuous man (Plutarch, *Theseus* 10 and 25). Note, too, the existence of the Scirophoria, a ceremony involving a *pharmakos* who was apparently represented in a series of icons by the image of Sciron himself (Robert Graves, *The Greek Myths*, 2 vols. [Baltimore: Penguin, 1955], 1.331, section 96.3).

27. According to Brandwood (*Word Index to Plato*, 159), *Rep.* 535b1-2 is the only other place in the Platonic corpus where the term *blosuros* occurs.

28. The statesman first "assays" (*basaniei*) young souls, and then sees to it that the souls of those who pass this test are bound together by a divine bond of true opinion about "the noble and just and good things and their opposites" (*Stsm.* 308d4,309c5-6). He also makes use of the human bond of marriage to ensure the birth of good children (*Stsm.* 310a7ff.). Socrates, too, arranges "marriages": *Tht.* 151b.

29. David Roochnik, *Of Art and Wisdom: Plato's Understanding of Techne* (University Park, Pa.: The Pennsylvania State University Press, 1996), 17-88. The criteria of $techne_2$ are listed on p. 52.

30. A similar understatement is involved in the notion that the rulers of the just city in the *Republic* will be able, like miners, to determine whether the souls

of the children born to its citizens are "gold," silver," bronze," or "iron" (415a-c).

31. The sorts of knowledge identified by Theaetetus include mathematical arts or sciences (geometry, astronomy, logistics, and music) and arts concerned with the care or production of corporeal things (shoemaking, and others sorts of craftsmanship such as carpentry). See 146c-d, and cf. 145d, 146e. All of these kinds of knowledge fall under the rubric of techne₁. As is clear from the Stranger's division of *technai* into productive and acquisitive forms, the distinction between *epistêmê* and *technê* is not hard-and-fast in the Platonic dialogues. Cf. Roochnik's argument, in "Socrates' Use of the Techne-Analogy" (in Benson, *Essays on the Philosophy of Socrates*, 185-197), for the introduction of the phrase "theoretical techne" into "the Platonic lexicon" (186-190).

32. If so, Socratic midwifery—unlike its ordinary counterpart—is in this respect like a theoretical *technê* and unlike a productive one. Cf. Roochnik, "Socrates' Use of the Techne-Analogy," 187: "The value of theoretical knowledge is not instrumental: its worth derives solely from itself."

33. The character of Euthyphro, whom Socrates encourages to "study" with Meletus and who accuses Socrates of distorting his ideas (*Euthphr.* 5a-b, 11c-d), seems to exemplify the peculiar lack of self-consciousness that Socrates associates with false pregnancy. I examine Euthyphro in detail in the following chapter.

34. "The Figure and Functions of Artemis in Myth and Cult," in *Mortals and Immortals: Collected Essays*, ed. Froma I. Zeitlin (Princeton: Princeton University Press, 1991), 195-196. On the associations of "Same" and "Other" in the cited passage, consider that the ritual battle of ephebes before the altar of Artemis Ortheia at Sparta was part of their initiation into the ranks of full-fledged Spartan citizens or *homoioi*—"the equals, the similars, the peers." A brief synopsis of the nature and significance of Artemis with citations of the ancient sources may be found in Burkert, *Greek Religion*, 149-152.

35. "Figure and Functions," 196-197.

36. "Figure and Functions," 197-202.

37. Kenneth Dorter finds here a "direct reminder" of the theory of Forms (*Form and Good*, 91), a view prepared by his earlier observation that "the *Theaetetus* . . . recalls the *Meno* at almost every turn" (71).

38. Benardete, *Being of the Beautiful*, I.86. Klein develops this point in detail in *A Commentary on Plato's Meno*, 157-166.

Chapter 4

1. The conflict between the particularity of Socratic care and the city's demand for abstraction is nicely illuminated by Arlene W. Saxenhouse in "The Philosophy of the Particular and the Universality of the City: Socrates' Education of Euthyphro," *Political Theory* 16.2 (1988), 281-299.

2. The theme introduced here is studied at length by Hyland in *Finitude and Transcendence*.

3. Marlo Lewis suggests "instant mind" as the meaning of Euthyphro's name in "An Interpretation of Plato's *Euthyphro*," *Interpretation* 13.1 (1985), 46. This is the second part of a two-part article; see also "An Interpretation of the *Euthyphro*," *Interpretation* 12.2&3 (1984), 225-259. Lewis suggests that Euthyphro's insight is "instant" in the sense that he is "not used to thinking things through. . . . The motion of which he complains [at 11b] is, at bottom, the discursive activity of reason" (46).

4. The specific nuances of these Greek terms are discussed below. We may note here that *hosion* and *eusebes* are adjectives that generally apply to actions. The nouns *to hosion* and *to eusebes*, "the pious," could be understood as the equivalent of the virtues of *hosiotês* and *eusebeia*, or "piety."

5. On the distinctions between these types of cases see MacDowell, *Law in Classical Athens*, 57-62. Euthyphro's case is peculiar because he is not a relative of the victim. MacDowell argues that Athenian law "did not forbid, though it did not require, non-relatives to bring a case of homicide" (111); on the controversy surrounding this point, cf. the studies he cites at 267 n. 237.

6. MacDowell, *Law in Classical Athens*, 46-47.

7. On the general significance of "place" in the Platonic dialogues see Hyland's discussion of the "privileging of place" in ch. 1 of *Finitude and Transcendence*. "Plato's writing," Hyland observes, "exhibits the conviction that the place of a dialogue is nothing incidental to the content or character of the discussion that ensues therein" (17).

8. The connection between the *Euthyphro* and the *Clouds* is also noticed by Lewis, "Interpretation of the *Euthyphro*," 240-241.

9. Griswold distinguishes between the "Episteme" of the gods in the *Phaedrus*, human methodical "episteme," and "a third sort of knowledge that one might call 'gnosis,' and that characterizes, in my view, 'self-knowledge.' . . . I use 'gnosis' because Socrates, following the Delphic Oracle, speaks of the need 'gignoskein' himself (not 'epistasthai')." *Self-Knowledge*, 261 n. 23.

10. In addressing these questions it will be convenient to speak of Meletus's care for human beings, but we should keep in mind that Socrates draws no distinction in this passage between human beings and citizens.

11. As Saxenhouse notes, "The seemingly reasonable image of the farmer draws us back to the *Republic* and to the traditional myth of autochthony at the basis of the Athenians' self-conception of their own origins; these are men sprung from the earth with neither father nor mother but, as citizens, related to one another by a common parentage in the earth itself" ("Philosophy of the Particular," 292; cf. 296). On the Athenian myth of autochthony, see *Menex.* 237b-238b.

12. Cf. Saxenhouse, "Philosophy of the Particular," 283-284. One should note in this connection that Socrates identifies Meletus by reference to his deme, but

not (as in the case of Theaetetus) by reference to his father (2b). The same is true of Euthyphro, whose father's name we never learn, but who is identified by his deme at *Cra*. 396d.

13. The ordinary translation of *ou biôtos*, "not worth living," misses Socrates' point. He does not mean that the unexamined life is a worthless life for a human being to live, but rather that a human being, *qua* human, *cannot* live such a life—that living an unexamined life is in and of itself incompatible with being fully human. In "Reflections on and in Plato's Cave," *Interpretation* 21.2 (1993-94), 115-134, Joel Warren Lidz observes: "The fact that Socrates here makes reference to humans (when such is normally implicitly understood) only emphasizes his desire to contrast the properly human (rational-deliberative) mode of life with the nonhuman" (118).

14. A good description of the strangeness of Spartan *paideia* may be found in "The Spartan Regimen," ch. 5 of Rahe, *Republics Ancient and Modern*.

15. Cf. *Ion* 533c-535a. As Lewis observes, prophetic receptivity requires that the "mind's power of self-movement . . . be put in suspension" ("Interpretation of Plato's Euthyphro," 47). Socrates notes the etymological relatedness of *mantis* and *mania* ("madness") at *Phdr*. 244b-c; cf. Burkert, *Greek Religion*, 112.

16. "Philosophy of the Particular," 289. Like Meletus, Saxenhouse suggests, Euthyphro displays a certain "adoration of the city and the abstract" (294).

17. Hyland, *Finitude and Transcendence*, 6.

18. Burnet marshals evidence in support of the view that a *pelatês* is a "day-laborer" who worked for hire. John Burnet, ed., *Plato: Euthyphro, Apology of Socrates, and Crito* (Oxford: Clarendon Press, 1977), 104 (note on 4c3).

19. The *exêgêtai* were unelected, unofficial specialists who "possessed a unique knowledge of the [religious] laws and might therefore be asked either to expound points of ritual or to lay down rules of purification, for example in the case of a homicide." Louise Bruit Zaidman and Pauline Schmitt Pantel, *Religion in the Ancient Greek City*, trans. Paul Cartledge (Cambridge: Cambridge University Press, 1992), 52.

20. Nor does he show much real concern for the laborer: Lewis asks "Why, if the laborer's death was as easily foreseen as the prophet indicates, he [Euthyphro] did not take it upon himself to clothe and feed the man, or at least urge his father to do so" ("Interpretation of the *Euthyphro*," 249).

21. Euthyphro's desire for recognition and praise is noted also by Jan Blits, "The Holy and the Human: An Interpretation of Plato's *Euthyphro*," *Aperion* 14.1 (1980), 24, and by Lewis, "Interpretation of the *Euthyphro*, 241.

22. Burkert, *Greek Religion*, 270, 273. According to Zaidman and Pantel, "Everything that was prescribed or permitted by divine law was . . . *hosion*, and the word *hosion* was often associated with *dikaion* ('just'). . . . But the term could also derive its meaning from being opposed to *hieron*; in which case it signified a condition of being liberated from the sacred, desacralized, and therefore free, permitted, profane" (*Religion in the Ancient Greek City*, 9).

23. Burkert writes of *eusebeia* (the equivalent of *to eusebes*): "The sole criterion available is the custom of the ancestors and of the city, *nomos*: 'to change nothing of what our forefathers have left behind,' this is *eusebeia*" (*Greek Religion*, 273). Zaidman and Pantel concur: "The [religious] obligations of the *community* involved above all respect for ancestral tradition (*ta patria*)" (*Religion in the Ancient Greek City*, 13, emphasis in original). They note in addition that "*hosion* was a term applied . . . especially to modes of behavior or to actions that were in conformity with the norms governing relations between gods and men, or between men themselves," and that "to be *eusebês* . . . was to believe in the efficacy of the symbolic system that the city had established for the purpose of managing relations between gods and men, and to participate in it, moreover, in the most vigorously active manner possible" (9, 15).

24. With regard to the centrality of filial gratitude in Greek religion, see Fustel's account of the nature and religious significance of paternal power among the ancients (*Ancient City*, 77-82). About the father, Fustel concludes that "the whole religion resides in him" (81).

25. A case in point: the democratic political innovations of Cleisthenes, which, as Lewis notes, "completed the overthrow of the aristocratic priest class," and therefore "den[ied] the ultimate authority of the ancestral" ("Interpretation of the *Euthyphro*," 234-235).

26. Pheidippides offers a justification for beating his father that abstracts from his status as both a son and a human being: as a free man (*eleutheros*: *Clouds*, 1414), he alleges, he is his father's equal; moreover, chickens and other animals beat *their* fathers (1427-1428).

27. Jacob Klein, *Greek Mathematical Thought and the Origin of Algebra*, trans. Eva Brann (Cambridge, Mass.: M.I.T. Press, 1968), 49 ff.

28. Daedalus, it will be recalled, managed to return home to Athens only because he acknowledged the limitations of his artificial wings while using them to lift him above the region of earth-bound men. This is a nice image of finite transcendence, of Socratic moderation, and of Socrates' daimonic intermediacy.

29. The political cost of philosophic leisure is a major theme of Alexandre Kojève's "Tyranny and Wisdom," in Leo Strauss, *On Tyranny*, ed. Victor Gourevitch and Michael S. Roth (New York: The Free Press, 1991), 135-176.

30. MacDowell writes: "Purification was required because killing was believed to cause pollution (*miasma*). Pollution was a kind of supernatural infection, which was liable to spread from the killer to others who consorted with him. . . . So it was considered very important, for practical religious reasons, that legal action should be taken against anyone believed to be guilty of homicide (*Law in Classical Athens*, 110; cf. *Laws* 871a ff.). With regard to *miasma*, Lewis observes: "Only if the family is a sacral union is it possible for the sins of the fathers to be visited upon the children. Yet if the family is sacred, Euthyphron's action is sinful" ("Interpretation of the *Euthyphro*," 247).

31. Plato at times suggests that the poetic characterization of the gods is itself a projection of what human beings "love," that is, of their deep and socially illicit desires for pleasure and domination. Consider Glaucon's remark at *Republic* 360c3 that the ring of Gyges would allow one "to act as an equal to a god among human beings."

32. At the Great Panathenaia, a festival celebrating the glory of Athens, the Homeric epics were recited in full in an extended competition for rhapsodes. This public recitation played an important role in the festival's recreation or reaffirmation of the city's self-image: "The work performed in the Panathenaia," as Simon Goldhill says, "becomes the shared narrative of all Athenians." *The Poet's Voice: Essays on Poetics and Greek Literature* (Cambridge: Cambridge University Press, 1991), 173.

33. By "catharsis" I mean the act or accomplishment of *kathairein* as this word is used at 3a1, where Socrates speaks of Meletus's "purging" or "cleaning out" the corrupters of the young shoots, and later by the Stranger in the *Sophist*, where it is defined as the kind of separation (*diakrisis*) that "leaves behind" the better and "throws away" the worse (226d5-7).

34. I make the case form this claim in *The Odyssey of Philosophy*, chs. 7 and 8, and in "Socrates and Alcibiades: Eros, Piety, and Politics," *Interpretation* 18.1 (1990), 63-90.

35. *Stsm.* 262d-e; cf. Klein, *Greek Mathematical Thought*, 58-59.

36. Klein, *Greek Mathematical Thought*, 58.

37. Cf. Lewis, "Interpretation of the *Euthyphro*," 231: "The *Euthyphro* is a defense of Socrates' justice. . . . It is Euthyphron, not Socrates, who proposes what could be called a definition of justice: *therapeia*, 'therapy' or 'care.' It is Socrates whose deeds make that definition intelligible and bear witness to its truth."

38. Blits ("The Holy and the Human," 33) and Lewis ("Interpretation of the *Euthyphro*," 246) both suggest that Socrates identifies piety with the activity of philosophizing.

39. Other puns associated with *meletê* are noted by Klein, *Commentary on Plato's Meno*, 157 with n. 150

40. Cf. Lewis's suggestion that the *eidos* of piety is nothing other than the "look" of the whole problem of piety ("Interpretation of the *Euthyphro*," 258).

41. The name *eirôn* first occurs in Greek literature at *Clouds* 449, where Strepsiades uses it in connection with what he hopes to learn from Socrates, and is formed on an Indo-European root meaning "to speak." See F. Amory, "*Eirôn and Eirôneia*," *Classica et Mediaevelia* 33 (1982), 49 with the studies cited in 79 n. 2. Amory concludes his discussion of Aristophanes' usage of *eirôn* and *eirôneia* by asserting that "on stage as in the agora irony was a catchword for any trickiness or slipperiness of character, and particularly for any sophistical and flattering evasiveness of speech, as, e.g., in Socratic professions of ignorance" (52). Cf. G. Markantonatos, "On the Origin and Meanings of the Word

Eirôneia," Rivista di Filologia 103 (1973), 16-21, who maintains that in the *Clouds* the word *eirôn* "is used of a character skilled in many kinds of unscrupulous trickery" (16).

Chapter 5

1. *Lives and Opinions of Eminent Philosophers*, 3.6.

2. Cf. Timothy M. S. Baxter, who observes that "the vocabulary of teaching and learning . . . crops up at various points throughout the dialogue, the first occasion being Socrates' reference to Prodicus's teaching on this very subject of the correctness of names [384b-c]." *The Cratylus: Plato's Critique of Naming* (Leiden: E. J. Brill, 1992), 16.

3. In "Putting the *Cratylus* in Its Place," *Classical Quarterly* 36.1 (1986), 124-150, Mary Margaret MacKenzie has shown that many of the arguments deployed by Socrates in the *Cratylus* bear a striking resemblance to those of the *Theaetetus* and the *Sophist*. MacKenzie stresses the aporetic character of the *Cratylus*, and argues that it belongs in the company of the latter dialogues as a late, critical work of Plato. MacKenzie's article supports the grouping of the *Cratylus* with the *Theaetetus* and the *Sophist* for which I argue on dramatic rather than chronological grounds.

4. See Zaidman and Pantel, *Religion in the Ancient Greek City*, 65, and Burkert, *Greek Religion*, 78, 87.

5. In support of the dramatic placement of the *Cratylus* between the *Euthyphro* and the *Sophist* see the study by D. J. Allan cited in the introduction, n. 1, along with John Sallis, *Being and Logos: The Way of Platonic Dialogue*, 1975, 2d ed. (Atlantic Highlands, N.J.: Humanities Press International, 1986), 230, and Cropsey, *Plato's World*, ix. For the opposing view see Baxter, *The Cratylus*, 28, with the studies he cites at 28 n. 73.

6. Other evidence helps to place the dramatic time of the *Cratylus* somewhere near 399 B.C. Socrates' reference at 398d to "the old Attic pronunciation" (cf. 410c) establishes that the discussion is set at a time after 403-402, when the East Ionic alphabet was officially adopted at Athens; see *The Oxford Classical Dictionary*, ed. N. G. L. Hammond and H. H. Scullard, 2d ed. (Oxford: Clarendon Press, 1989), 47, s.v. "Alphabet, Greek." According to Xenophon, Hermogenes had occasion to speak with Socrates about his trial after Meletus had formulated his indictment (*Mem.* 4.8.4-10). Plato also places Hermogenes at Socrates' execution (*Phd.* 59b).

7. Socrates will later connect *sôma* ("body") with *sêma*, a name that indicates (ambiguously, or in the manner of an oracle) that the body is the tomb, safe, or *sign* of the soul (*Cra.* 400c).

8. In a note on this passage, Sallis observes that "Socrates' introduction of *rhêma* alongside *onoma* . . . indicates explicitly something that was, in fact, already evident in the etymologies, namely that the regress is not simply from one

name to another but also requires, at the very least, the use of certain phrases by which to explain these names" (*Being and Logos*, 265 n. 33). Cf. MacKenzie, "Putting the *Cratylus* in Its Place," 127, and Malcolm Schofield, "The Dénouement of the *Cratylus*," in *Language and Logos: Studies Presented to G.E.L. Owen*, ed. Malcom Schofield and Martha Craven Nussbaum (Cambridge: Cambridge University Press, 1982), 62.

9. On the much-debated "Problem of Cratylus," which concerns the incongruity between Cratylus's Heracliteanism and his commitment to a theory that stresses the fixity of names, see Baxter, *The Cratylus*, 25-30. Baxter suggests that the *Cratylus* "perhaps dramatises the beginning of the end of his [Cratylus's] more youthful belief in moderate flux" (29). Put another way, Plato may have dramatized Cratylus's Heracliteanism by deliberately showing us a Cratylus who is himself in flux. Cf. Sallis, *Being and Logos*, 186-187 n. 3, who observes that Hermogenes' presumed Eleaticism may have originally been inferred from the *Cratylus* itself.

10. These two theses are identified by Baxter, *The Cratylus*, 18. Sallis distinguishes further between positing names by convention and agreement and positing them by law and custom; in the latter case the positing is not just by "any random association of individuals" but has "a broad political character." He also points out that the jumble of alternatives offered by Hermogenes is an early sign of what will later prove to be the elusiveness of the origins of names (*Being and Logos*, 193).

11. Rudolph H. Weingartner, *The Unity of the Platonic Dialogue: The Cratylus, the Protagoras, the Parmenides* (Indianapolis: Bobbs-Merrill, 1973), 18. Nor could it be shown that one has erred in the use of names, so long as the speaker (or writer) who would otherwise seem to be in error avows that he has chosen to rename the thing in question. Cf. Baxter, *The Cratylus*, 18, 21.

12. This point is made by Weingartner, *Unity*, 23. Cf. Sallis, who notes that Cratylus cannot accommodate the activity of teaching and learning through dialogue: "For Cratylus names, themselves, are the teachers" (*Being and Logos*, 291).

13. MacKenzie suggests that "Hermogenes—plaintive at Cratylus' dismissal of his name—looks for an account of naming that will recover his name for him" ("Putting the *Cratylus* in Its Place," 126). The high price he pays for his theory is the Protagorean consequence that his name *is* "Hermogenes," since people choose to call him that, and at the same time *is not* "Hermogenes," since it is also whatever name other than "Hermogenes" Cratylus (or anyone else) may choose to call him.

14. I follow MacKenzie's interpretation of Socrates' somewhat obscure description of Euthydemus's view ("Putting the *Cratylus* in Its Place," 132).

15. The irony of 385b-d is almost universally overlooked in the scholarly literature on the *Cratylus*; see Baxter's discussion of the standard treatments of this passage in *The Cratylus*, 34-37. An exception is Sallis, who detects "some

irony in the fact that Socrates, the one who mediates between whole and parts, does not here mediate at all but moves directly from whole to part" (*Being and Logos*, 195-196 n. 10). On the closely related irony of Socrates' treatment of wholes and parts at *Tht.* 205a ff. see below, n. 17, and cf. n. 21.

16. As Benardete observes, "*pragmata* are the beings with which we deal and are of interest and concern to us; they are not the beings as they are in themselves." "Physics and Tragedy: On Plato's *Cratylus*," *Ancient Philosophy* 1 (1980-81), 130.

17. At *Tht.* 205a7-10 Socrates and Theaetetus agree that the whole (*holon*) is identical to the all (*pan*) and is nothing other than "all the parts." Socrates goes on to illustrate this point with reference to the learning of letters and syllables and then with the example of music. He observes that, as a child, Theaetetus "attempted to become familiar in sight and in hearing with each [letter or element of sound] itself by itself, in order that their placement in being spoken and written might not disturb you" (206a6-8). Yet a full account of the acquisition of language would begin with the observation that children first become familiar with the *whole* of speech: they learn to recognize and correctly to form all the elements of speech—saying and writing "hamburger," for example, instead of "hangerber"—only *after* they have learned to speak tolerably well. So, too, anyone who has no knowledge of a foreign language for the most part perceives only gibberish when it is spoken, as he cannot even hear its phonemes well enough to distinguish them from one another. Socrates' next example works against his explicit point in a similar way. "To have learned perfectly at the kithara-player's was nothing other than to be able to follow each note, and tell what sort of string it belongs to" (206a10-b3). But the case of music seems rather to support the opposite thesis. Being able to recognize and reproduce each individual note that appears in a given musical composition is not equivalent to knowing the composition as a whole. Conversely, someone might have "learned perfectly" how to play compositions for a given musical instrument and perform with great insight and brilliance even while occasionally striking incorrect notes (as, for example, Vladimir Horowitz did during his famous Moscow concert of 1986). Finally, Socrates suggests that one knows a thing when one can list its elements, and he offers the example of a wagon (206e-207a). But a list of elements does not tell us what a wagon is for, and without the knowledge of its use or purpose one surely cannot be said to know a wagon. This knowledge, in turn, is independent of the knowledge of the parts of a wagon, for it is only the wagon as a *whole* that is a vehicle for carrying cargo or passengers. Cf. Dorter's discussion of the priority of wholes to parts in *Form and Good*, 109-118, esp. 114-115.

18. *Being and Logos*, 214.

19. One should note in this regard that Socrates' analogy between the dialectician and the helmsman is suggestive of the image of the ship of state, and anticipates the Stranger's employment of the same analogy in order to illuminate the work of the statesman (see esp. *Stsm.* 297e-299e and cf. *Rep.* 488a-489a).

20. The problem introduced by these two touchstones of correctness surfaces again at 425a4-5, when Socrates speaks uncertainly of composing *logos* "by the art of naming, or of rhetoric, or whatever is the *technê*." Note, too, that the expertise of the lawgiver in fashioning tools for learning is no substitute for the *phronêsis* of the human dialectician or teacher, who must select the particular verbal tools appropriate to each concrete pedagogical context.

21. Socrates states that the analysis of names into their elements is necessary "if we are going to know scientifically in a technical manner [*technikôs epistêsometha*]" (425a7). Yet he does not even know the *technê* in accordance with which these elements are put together in order to compose language (cf. 425a4-5). Note also that at 414c3, Hermogenes accuses Socrates of having proceeded "very shabbily" in deriving *technê* from "possession of intellect [*nous*]" by means of a manifestly arbitrary etymology (414b-c). At 428d1-2, Socrates admits to Cratylus that "I myself have for a long time been amazed by my own wisdom, and I am unpersuaded by it." The irony of this section of the *Cratylus*, and of the previously discussed passage in the *Theaetetus* in which Socrates employs the same "decompositional" or analytical model of explanation, is overlooked by many commentators; see for example Julia Annas, "Knowledge and Language: The *Theaetetus* and the *Cratylus*," in *Language and Logos*, ed. Schofield and Nussbaum, 95-114, esp. 107 and 111 with n. 33. Thus Baxter suggests that Plato desired a philosophically ideal language that would be constructed in accordance with a mathematical model and would function analytically along Russellian lines, "with the structure of sentences mirroring the structure of the world." On the basis of this assumption, Baxter goes on to charge Plato with "underestimat[ing] greatly the range of uses that language is put to, in favor of an overly rationalistic theory" (*The Cratylus*, 54, 55). Victor Goldschmidt argues against a similar view in his *Essai sur le Cratyle: Contribution à l'histoire de la pensée de Platon* (Paris: Bibliothèque de l'École des Hautes Études, 1940), 202-205. Among other things, Goldschmidt notes that the creation of an ideal language would at best be an unnecessary luxury, for it would presuppose that the dialectician had already fully understood the nature of things and had done so "avec la seule aide de sa méthode" (203).

22. The analysis of names in terms of letters also turns out to be circular. Socrates explains that the natures of beings are not directly visible, but that we must give names to the beings "from which it is possible to see them, as well as whether there are in them kinds (*eidê*) in the same manner as in the letters" (424d3-4). Contrary to what Socrates has already suggested, *logos* thus becomes a precondition for the visibility of *ousia*.

23. Thus Minos, a son of Zeus, is supposed to have established the laws of Crete under the tutelage of his father (*Laws* 624a-625a; *Minos*, 319c ff.). Lycurgus is alleged to have established laws for Sparta after consultation with the oracle of Apollo at Delphi (*Laws* 624a, 632d; cf. 634d-e), just as Cleisthenes consulted with the Delphic oracle prior to introducing his reforms at Athens.

24. At 391b-c Socrates notes that Hermogenes' brother Callias controls Hermogenes' patrimony now that his father is deceased, and that Callias has spent a good deal of money on the sophists. Bruce Rosenstock observes that this same Callias is the host of the gathering of sophists Plato dramatizes in the *Protagoras*. "We may say," Rosenstock adds, "that Protagoras dispossesses Kallias of his *ousia* and offers him (in return for a certain sum of money) the semblance (*phantasma*, 386e3) of *ousia* in its place." "Fathers and Sons: Irony in the *Cratylus*," *Arethusa* 25.3 (1992), 402; cf. 399. Note, too, that Homer and Hesiod are said to be Heracliteans at 402b-c; cf. *Tht.* 152d-e.

25. Cf. the references to *adoleschia*, "idle talk," at *Clouds* 1480 and 1485. Socrates criticizes his own *adoleschia* at *Tht.* 195c; cf. *Sophist* 225d.

26. The immediate context reinforces this dramatic echo. Just prior to the passage at hand, Socrates tells Hermogenes that "I suppose that I seem already to have traveled far in the sphere of wisdom" (*porrô êdê oimai phainomai sophias elaunein*: 410e3). This phrase is nearly identical to one Socrates utters in commenting on Euthyphro's prosecution of his father: "I don't suppose that it belongs to any chance man to do it, but rather to one already having traveled far in the sphere of wisdom" (*oimai . . . porrô êdê sophias elaunontos*: *Euthyphro* 4a12-b2). In both of these contexts it is also tempting to hear *sophias*, ironically, as a genitive of separation: "far *from* wisdom."

27. Cf. *Stsm.* 269e-270a. There is also an echo here of the *Euthyphro*'s problem of how, given that the gods are in conflict with one another, one could define piety with reference to their loves and hates.

28. At 413c and context, Socrates comments on the explanatory insufficiency of pre-Socratic natural philosophizing in general and of Anaxagoras's teaching about *nous* in particular with respect to the question "What is justice?"

29. At 428b, for example, Socrates associates Cratylus with the silent, monological activity of writing. Still more tellingly, Cratylus overlooks both the figure of the dialectician and the activity of questioning and answering in wrongly attributing the art of teaching to "the lawgivers, whom you [Socrates] spoke of in the beginning" (429a1).

30. Cf. Baxter, who notes that "Hermogenes is a lover of opinions" (*The Cratylus*, 17). The superficial connection between Hermogenes ("Son of Hermes") and speech is strengthened by Socrates' attribution of the invention of *logos* to Hermes (407e-408b).

31. On the fundamental role played by *eikasia* in the image of the divided line see Klein, *Commentary on Plato's Meno*, 112-125.

32. The language of Mystery initiation is applied to philosophy also in the palinode of the *Phaedrus*. See esp. 249c, 250b-c.

33. "Fathers and Sons," 401-402. The Trojan Hector, of course, was slain by Achilles, and his death doomed his city as well as his young son. Rosenstock adds in this connection that the term *ousia* "perfectly displays the ambiguity of

language: the term which connotes stable identity, essence, and being, also can refer to physical property which can be lost or appropriated by another" (402).

34. Cf. Rosenstock, "Fathers and Sons," 403-404.

35. Cf. *Stsm.* 257d-258a. In "Socrates' Mulishness and Heroism," *Phronesis* 17 (1972), 53-60, Diskin Clay links with the *Cratylus* the implicit comparison Socrates establishes at *Apol.* 27d-28d between himself, mules, and heroes. Since the mule is incapable of sexual reproduction, this comparison may suggest that Socrates cannot reduplicate his own nature in the soul of another, and so will not in this sense leave behind philosophical children. But cf. Plato's claim that his dialogues are "of a Socrates grown beautiful and young" (*Second Letter*, 314c3-4).

36. The irony here is palpable, since *koros* can mean either "lad" (hence the purity of youth?) or "satiety" and the insolence associated with it.

37. Cf. the *Phaedrus*, in which the gods are said to stand on the outer surface of the heavens beholding or "theorizing" (*theorousi*) the beings outside of the heavens in the hyperuranian region (247b-c).

38. *Beyond Good and Evil*, trans. Walter Kaufmann (New York: Random House, 1966), I.9.

39. The *Clouds* suggests that Aristophanes sees philosophy as a spiritualized version of the hybristic ambition that most often manifests itself in war and politics, and that stands at the center of his concern as one who seeks to save the city by means of the political medicine of comic drama. For further discussion see below, n. 42.

40. Note that Socrates compares names to drugs or poisons (*pharmaka*) at *Cra.* 394a.

41. Sallis, *Being and Logos*, 185.

42. The speech Plato gives Aristophanes in the *Symposium* is in fact a microcosm of the comic universe portrayed in his eleven surviving plays, all of which reflect the fundamental conflict within the human soul between the "upward" desires to surpass and dominate others and the "horizontal" desires associated with Dionysus and Aphrodite. In celebrating the bodily pleasures of food, wine, and sexual *erôs*, Aristophanean comedy offers a kind of temporary medicine for the ultimately incurable political sickness that is rooted in or manifested by our upward aspirations—including Socratic philosophizing. I develop this reading of Aristophanes and explore the quarrel between Aristophanes and Plato in "Plato's Dionysian Music? A Reading of the *Symposium*," in *The Sovereignty of Construction: Essays in Honor of David Lachterman*, ed. Daniel W. Conway and Pierre Kerszberg, Rodopi Publishers (forthcoming).

43. Demetrius writes that "nobody would think of writing a tragedy at play [*tragôidian paizousan*], since he will then write a satyr play instead of a tragedy" (*On Style*, 3.169).

44. In "Plato's Dionysian Music?".

45. This point is made by Baxter, *The Cratylus*, 25.

Chapter 6

1. Leo Strauss, *What is Political Philosophy? And Other Studies*, 1959 (Chicago: University of Chicago Press, 1988), 40.

2. The word *genos* is related to *gignesthai*, "to come to be," and it implies that we are dealing with a natural kind or family of beings. Whereas the translations "family" or "kind" might sometimes create unnecessary confusion, "genus" and "species" suggests a taxonomical specificity that seems foreign to the Stranger's use of the term. It will therefore be best often to leave *genos* untranslated.

3. Cf. Friedländer, *Plato*, 3.246; Sallis, *Being and Logos*, 458; Miller, *Philosopher in Plato's Statesman*, 11.

4. *Parmenidou Peri Phuseôs* 1.27.

5. The whole question of strangeness is further complicated by Socrates' Homeric allusions with respect to the matter of homecoming. In the *Euthyphro* Socrates implicitly compares himself to Menelaus, who wrestled Proteus until he learned from him how to get back to Sparta (15d; cf. *Od.* 4.351ff.). But Socrates' allusions at the beginning of the *Sophist* suggest that it is the Stranger, not Socrates, who (as Odysseus) will find his way home. We shall return to this issue when we take up the *Statesman*.

6. Some commentators identify seven sophists. This problem of counting sophists is discussed below.

7. Hippias later uses the same verb for competitive striving, *agônizesthai*, to describe Socrates' participation in their discussion (369c1). On Hippias's likely activities at the Olympic festivals see Mary Whitlock Blundell, "Character and Meaning in Plato's *Hippias Minor*," in Klagge and Smith, *Methods of Interpreting Plato*, 136.

8. On the depiction of Odysseus in the tragedies see W. B. Stanford, *The Ulysses Theme: A Study in the Adaptability of a Traditional Hero*, 1954, 2d ed. (Oxford: Basil Blackwell, 1963), 102-117.

9. Some scholars would dispute this claim; see Blundell, "Character and Meaning," 147 with n. 73 and 160 with n. 128. With regard to Socrates' blurring of the distinction between being capable of doing wrong and being disposed to do wrong, Blundell writes: "We cannot assume that a fallacy so obvious to us or even to Aristotle was equally apparent to Socrates or Plato" (147). I see no reason, however, to suppose that Plato's philosophical competence was in any respect inferior to ours.

10. Sophists regularly identify virtue with *technê* in the dialogues. Protagoras, for example, claims to make men good citizens by teaching them a political *technê* (*Prt.* 319a), and Thrasymachus understands justice as a precise art or craft akin to calculation (*Rep.* 340d-341a). Cf. Gorgias's identification of the *technê* of rhetoric with "the very thing that is in truth the greatest good" for human beings (*Grg.* 452d5-6).

11. Thus Blundell attempts to block the central paradox of the *Hippias Minor* by arguing that, for Socrates, justice is a skill, albeit a special kind that "cannot be used 'badly' . . . since its internal goals are precisely those of morality" ("Character and Meaning," 161; cf. 160 with n. 128, where she claims that Socrates recognized no distinction between functional and moral excellence). Terry Penner offers a similar account of the "science" of justice in his discussion of the *Hippias Minor* in "Socrates and the Early Dialogues," *The Cambridge Companion to Plato*, ed. Richard Kraut (Cambridge: Cambridge University Press, 1992), 132-133.

12. In *Of Art and Wisdom*, Roochnik persuasively argues that *technê* was never a positive model of moral knowledge for Plato, and he supports this claim by showing that Socrates' various uses of the *technê* analogy can be fully accounted for by the pedagogical purposes of critique, refutation, and protreptic.

13. I accept James Leake's recommendation that we read *euêtheias* rather than *eunoias* at 371e1. Cf. Leake's note on this passage in his translation of the *Lesser Hippias*, in Pangle, *Roots of Political Philosophy*, 292 n. 13.

14. In support of this point we may note that Thrasymachus, himself a skilled practitioner of eristic speech, initially shares Hippias's intuitions about Socrates when he first encounters him in the *Republic*. See esp. *Rep.* 336c, 337a, 341a-b; on Thrasymachus's nature see Howland, *Odyssey of Philosophy*, 68-75.

15. This is also Aristotle's view. Cf. *Rhet.* 1355b17-18, *Metaph.* 1004b17-26.

16. Thus the paradigmatic division of the angler, 219a-221c, begins from *dunamis*. I follow Dorter in making power rather than art the starting point of this division (*Form and Good*, 125).

17. This is noted by Sallis, *Being and Logos*, 463; cf. Rosen, *Plato's Sophist*, 68. In Cornford's view, however, the Stranger makes it clear that he will engage in "a genuine conversation" with Theaetetus, as distinct from Parmenides' procedure with Aristotle (Francis M. Cornford, *Plato's Theory of Knowledge: The Theaetetus and the Sophist of Plato* [London: Routledge and Kegan Paul, 1935], 167 n. 1 and 170).

18. Thus at *Rep.* 472d, a painting of a man is said to be a paradigm, whereas at 500e, the word refers to the divine originals toward which philosophic craftsmen look when they "paint" or "draw" images of the virtues in the souls of human beings (cf. 484c-d). But as Rosen points out, a model that is not a copy need not always be an original. See his helpful discussion of paradigms in ch. 5 of *Plato's Statesman*, esp. 81-88.

19. As Rosen mentions in commenting on the passage at hand, "'works,' 'deeds,' and 'events' [are] *already* the consequence of the interplay between cognition and things" (*Plato's Sophist*, 86; emphasis in original). The Stranger later states that thought (*dianoia*) is the silent conversation of the soul with itself (263e; cf. *Tht.* 189e-190a), from which we may infer that cognition shapes its objects at least insofar as it grasps them by means of its dianoetic/linguisitic capacity. In the aviary image of the *Theaetetus* (197a ff.), which seems to antici-

pate certain features of the Stranger's philosophical procedure, the dianoetic capacity is represented as a power of hunting and grasping whereby birds (knowledges) are acquired through learning or discovery. Thought, moreover, is inseparable from the rest of the soul: Socrates' remark that the *dianoia* of the philosopher "flies" (*Tht.* 173e5) should be considered in the light of the central myth of the *Phaedrus*, in which he not only describes the philosopher's *dianoia* as winged (249c4-5) but also explicates its natural union with *erôs* and the rest of the soul in the image of the winged charioteer and horses (246a ff.).

20. This is observed by Dorter, *Form and Good*, 122-124. The cave image of the *Republic*, which presents sophistry as arrested or truncated philosophy, may be added to Dorter's examples. The sophist is a cave-dweller who begins to ascend from the shadows; because of the erotic defectiveness of his soul, however, his upward progress stops at the fire. See Howland, *Odyssey of Philosophy*, 137-141.

21. Cf. Griswold's reflections on the absence of an Idea of the soul in *Self-Knowledge*, 89.

22. Superficially, one should note, the Stranger bears a strong resemblance to Aristophanes' Socrates. Both of these dramatic characters employ the technique of division (cf. *Clouds* 740-742), utilize the relative measurement exemplified in mathematics to the apparent exclusion of due measure according to the mean, pay equal attention to things big and small but seem to ignore the intermediate domain of human things, and obfuscate the distinction between human beings and animals (cf. the Stranger's comment at 227b that the method of division gives equal honor to the general and the louse-catcher, and consider also the inability of the method to distinguish human beings from beasts in the first part of the *Statesman*).

23. *Parmenidou Peri Phuseôs* 8.10; cf. Zeno's fragments in Freeman, *Ancilla*, 47.

24. Note that while Sophists I through IV practice arts of acquisition, Sophist VI practices an art of production. Yet in the division of Sophist V, in which the Stranger's method implicitly appears in the first step under the separation of like from like, it is unclear whether we are dealing with arts of production, of acquisition, or of some combination of the two.

25. See Charles Griswold, "*Politikê Epistêmê* in Plato's *Statesman*," in *Essays in Ancient Greek Philosophy III*, ed. John Anton and Anthony Preus (Albany: State University of New York Press, 1989), 148-149.

26. Friedländer, *Plato* 3.251.

27. "*Eidos* and *Diaeresis* in Plato's *Statesman*," *Philologus* 107 (1963), 200 ff.

28. As if to underscore this point, the step in which exchange is distinguished from conquest is omitted from the summaries of the divisions of Sophists I and IV (223b, 226a). Cf. Rosen's comment on the second division: "The sophist [Sophist II] is the hunter whose victim pays him a salary" (*Plato's Sophist*, 107).

29. The omission of birds of the air in this division may be meant as a reminder of the method's abstraction from the soul's erotic motion. In the great myth of the *Phaedrus*, the human soul is said to have wings with which to fly (246a6-7). In the octology, Socrates repeatedly represents himself as a winged creature: he is a gadfly (*Apol.* 30e, *Phd.* 91c), he is a swan (*Phd.* 84e-85b), and he is akin to Daedalus (*Euthphr.* 11b-d). Cf. *Euthphr.* 4a, where he asks Euthyphro whether he is prosecuting someone who is flying away, and *Tht.* 173e, where he describes the flight of the philosopher's *dianoia*.

30. On the paradigmatic *mêtis* of both fish and fisherman see Marcel Detienne and Jean-Pierre Vernant, *Cunning Intelligence in Greek Culture and Society*, trans. Janet Lloyd, 1978 (Chicago: University of Chicago Press, 1991), 27-54. Detienne and Vernant compare the wiles of the sophist with those of the octopus and the fox (39-42; cf. 33); in this context they also speak of "Odysseus, the *polumêtis* one" (39).

31. Detienne and Vernant, *Cunning Intelligence*, 41, 42.

32. Benardete suggests that "the anonymous class [of hunting inanimate objects] is none other than philosophy, the hidden hunting of the hidden beings or kinds" (*Being of the Beautiful*, II.81).

33. Cf. *Rep.* 493a-c, where Socrates states that the sophist organizes as an art and calls "wisdom" the opinions of the many about the noble and the base, the good and the bad, and the just and the unjust, although he knows nothing about the truth of these matters. Benardete's translation of *doxopaideutikê*, "educates in opinion," harmonizes with this picture of the sophist, although it does not reflect the illegitimacy of the sophist's claims (cf. Cornford's translation of *doxopaideutikê* as "spurious education," *Plato's Theory of Knowledge*, 174).

34. Friedländer, *Plato* 3.252-53.

35. Insofar as the persuasion of tame animals (identified in step three) is a part of hunting, however, it is a kind of conquest and so is necessarily manipulative. The Stranger seems to leave no room for philosophical rhetoric: are his own divisions nothing but a concealed attempt to get the upper hand over his auditors?

36. Dorter, Friedländer, Sallis, and Sayre count seven appearances of the sophist in the *Sophist*; Rosen counts six. On the multiplication of Sophist III, see Rosen, *Plato's Sophist*, 110, 142-143.

37. At *Prm.* 135d5, Parmenides remarks that philosophy is "called by the many *adoleschia*."

38. *Plato's Sophist*, 119. That this discarded section is relevant to our interpretation is suggested by Theaetetus's remark at 226a that we must grip the sophist with both hands.

39. This description of psychic ugliness anticipates Aristotle's treatment of *hamartia*, which I explore in "Aristotle on Tragedy: Rediscovering the *Poetics*," *Interpretation* 22.3 (1995), 359-404.

40. Cf. Benardete, *Being of the Beautiful*, II.98-99.

41. Contrary to Rosen, *Plato's Sophist*, 128; cf. Klein, *Plato's Trilogy*, 23.

42. Aristophanes seems to stand behind the Stranger's criticism of Socrates in other respects as well. In "Aristophanes and Socrates on Learning Practical Wisdom" (in *Aristophanes: Essays in Interpretation, Yale Classical Studies* 26 [1980], 43-97), Martha Nussbaum connects the Stranger's characterization of the purification of seeming-wisdom with Aristophanes' characterization of Socrates' practice in the *Clouds*, and she contrasts this practice with the traditional paternal education described by the Stranger in the present division (43, 74; cf. 81, where Nussbaum states that Aristophanes attacks Socrates for "his lack of a positive program to replace what he has criticized").

43. Cf. Rosen's reading of this passage as a commentary on the difficulty of distinguishing the philosopher from the sophist (*Plato's Sophist*, 131). Both Benardete (*Being of the Beautiful*, II.172 n. 36) and Klein (*Plato's Trilogy*, 24 n. 11) refer us to the *Republic*, where dogs provide an image of the nature of the Guardians. Socrates at one point speaks ironically of the philosophical nature of dogs (*Rep.* 376a-b). He also mentions the danger that sheepdogs may for various reasons become like wolves and turn on their flock (*Rep.* 416a; cf. 422d); one might add that the wolf never becomes tame of his own accord. At *Soph.* 231e, the Stranger remarks that calling the purifier of souls a sophist was a "concession" to the sophist.

44. Sayre notes that Socrates is not "depicted as having any particular ability to *produce* true belief or knowledge in the soul purified of falsehood" (*Plato's Analytic Method*, 151; emphasis in original), and he goes on to argue that Plato intended by way of the present division "to chide" Socrates because he lacked the "science of the Philosopher," which includes the separation of like from like as well as the practice of collection (152 ff.). But as Scodel points out, the Stranger fails to define the method that Socrates lacks: the division of like from like is a part of the art of separation "which remains completely undefined so that we can only speculate about its contents" (*Diaeresis and Myth*, 38). Cf. Scodel's comment on *Soph.* 226a6-8: "If the principle of grasping a *definiendum* 'with both hands' or sides of a division is not limited arbitrarily to species . . . the result will be that the *definiendum* can be located properly only after a comprehensive division of reality" (39). And although the divisions of the *Sophist* and *Statesman* are presented as a scientific discrimination of arts or sciences, the Stranger, as Griswold observes, "never does define *epistêmê* or *technê*" ("*Politikê Epistêmê*," 143).

45. This is noted by Rosen, *Plato's Sophist*, 192.

46. But see Dorter, *Form and Good*, who notes that the Stranger's conclusion that "not-being exists *qua* difference" does not contradict the spirit of Parmenides' prohibition against saying or thinking that not-being exists "*qua* the opposite of *existence*" (159, emphasis in original; cf. 140).

47. Cf. Socrates' appeal to the existence of wise insight (*phronêsis*) and folly (*aphrosunê*) in the course of getting Hermogenes to abandon his essentially Protagorean view of the correctness of names (*Cratylus* 385e-386d).

48. These pages of the *Sophist* resemble the myth of the reversed cosmos in the *Statesman* (268e-274e), which also serves the function of doing justice to the peculiar being of the human soul and the unique character of human life. Although I cannot pause to establish the point here, I would argue in addition that the Stranger's seemingly exact and analytical discussion of the "alphabet" of kinds (252e ff.) is not meant to replace the imprecise context of analysis that is sketched in such myths.

49. Cf. Michael Davis, *Aristotle's Poetics: The Poetry of Philosophy* (Lanham, Md.: Rowman & Littlefield, 1992), 108: "In the world we never encounter a 'man.' . . . To say 'the man walks' we must assume there is such a thing as a man apart from walking. As we read the sentence from left to right, we must attach some meaning to the word 'man' before we learn that he is walking. But what is he doing before we get to the end of the sentence? In treating him as though he could be doing nothing, we treat him as something he is not. We lie. All *logos* has this form."

Chapter 7

1. "*Politikê Epistêmê*," 147.

2. Indeed, in form and function the myth of the reversed cosmos closely resembles the myth about the Whole that Socrates tells in the *Phaedrus* (246a-257a): while the latter corrects Socrates' previous denigration of *erôs*, the former is in part a response to the method of division's inability to do justice to the nature of the human soul (see below).

3. Miller, *Philosopher in Plato's Statesman*, 6.

4. The quotation is from Charles Segal, "The Phaeacians and the Symbolism of Odysseus's Return," *Arion* 1.1 (1962), 17.

5. "Punishment" is Rosen's word (*Plato's Statesman*, 6).

6. Cf. Rosen's observation that it is unclear who could have presented the promised *Philosopher*, given the dramatic structure of the trilogy *Theaetetus*, *Sophist*, and *Statesman* (*Plato's Statesman*, 12-13).

7. On Theodorus's connection with sophistry cf. Miller, *Philosopher in Plato's Statesman*, 124 n. 5 and context.

8. *Philosopher in Plato's Statesman*, 11.

9. *Plato's Statesman*, 51.

10. *Plato's Statesman*, 78.

11. *Plato's Statesman*, 69.

12. Here, too, the Stranger voices a point of view that Plato associates with sophistry. Cf. Callicles' similar criticism of Socrates at *Grg.* 485e-486b.

13. *Plato's Statesman*, 8.

14. *Philosopher in Plato's Statesman*, 12. Rosen unnecessarily exaggerates his differences with Miller. In spite of the ample evidence to which Miller calls our attention, Rosen claims that the Eleatic Stranger "never suggests that he is withholding the truth or accommodating it to the undeveloped understanding of Young Socrates" (3).

15. These passages employ the same demonstrative pronoun, *hode*, that occurs at the beginning of the *Sophist* (216a2) and the *Cratylus* (383a1, a4).

16. *Kinduneuein*, "to run a risk," is formed from the noun *kindunos*, meaning "danger." While it is often translated as a neutral expression of possibility or probability, in the present context *kinduneuein* seems to retain its original connection with danger or hazard.

17. Here I examine Odysseus's reunion with Penelope. I shall comment later on the implications of Socrates' association with Laertes and of the Stranger with his son Odysseus.

18. See Miller, *Philosopher in Plato's Statesman*, 7ff., and more recently Scott Hemmenway, "Pedagogy in the Myth of Plato's *Statesman*: Body and Soul in Relation to Philosophy and Politics," *History of Philosophy Quarterly* 11.3 (1994), 253-268.

19. Griswold observes that "in imitation of Socratic pedagogy, the Stranger has led YS [Young Socrates] up the garden path" ("*Politikê Epistêmê*," 144). Cf. Kenneth Dorter's account in "Justice and Method in the *Statesman*" (in *Justice, Law, and Method in Plato and Aristotle*, ed. Spiro Panagiotou [Edmonton, Alberta: Academic Printing and Publishing, 1987], 105-122) of the Stranger's employment of bifurcatory diaeresis as a way of "introduc[ing] the bridging concept of quality (in abstraction from that of value) into the erstwhile exclusively quantitative *dianoia* practiced by Young Socrates and Theaetetus" (122).

20. Rosen notes that the word *palin*, "back," "once more," occurs thirty-eight times in the dialogue and fourteen times in the myth alone. He observes also that "the emphasis upon errors and new starts is appropriate to a discussion of politics" ("Plato's Myth of the Reversed Cosmos," *Review of Metaphysics* 33.1 [1979], 60-61). Cf. Klein, who contends that the *Statesman*'s "stress on faultiness and inaccuracy in the drama of the dialogue" suits the theme of statesmanship (*Plato's Trilogy*, 161).

21. A *politikos* is literally a "political man." Like our word "politician," it is not necessarily an honorific term. Hence "statesman" is a somewhat misleading translation; the word *politikos* itself expresses the problem of sophistry or seeming-wisdom with respect to politics that will become a major issue in the dialogue. Note too that *hê politikê* may also be translated literally as "the political art."

22. This point is made by Griswold, "*Politikê Epistêmê*," 142.

23. In the present context, the Stranger appears to draw no distinction between *technê* and *epistêmê*.

24. On the identification of the Stranger's method with the art of politics see Campbell, *Sophistes and Politicus*, 5 n. 4, and Benardete, *Being of the Beautiful*, III.74. Rosen infers from the different beginnings of the *Sophist* and the *Statesman* that there is no natural division of the *technai* or *epistêmai*; the results of division are relative to the intentions of the investigator (*Plato's Statesman*, 18, 33).

25. As Benardete notes, "Arithmetic handles beings that are without having become (cf. *Soph.* 219c4-5, 238a10-b1), but statesmanship handles beings that become. It deals with beings that have *erôs*" ("*Eidos* and *Diaeresis*," 201). Rosen observes that the word *erôs* occurs only once in the *Statesman*, and that it is associated in the myth with decadence and destruction (*Plato's Statesman*, 41, 154; cf. 22). Aside from the politically problematic character of *erôs* and *thumos*, the method of division's failure to take *erôs* into account is connected with the Stranger's abstraction in the present context from the art of imitation. Benardete develops the point that the nature of *erôs* is best understood by imagination (*eikasia*): "The likeness and unlikeness of an image is not the otherness and sameness of a magnitude; and hence an image's relation to what is imaged necessarily eludes a method that is most at home with magnitudes and numbers" ("*Eidos* and *Diaeresis*," 200). Poetic images alone, he suggests, can do justice to the erotic intermediacy and polymorphic potential of the human soul; cf. his discussion of man as simply *zôion* (animal), whose "nature in its artfulness can imitate or discover the likeness to himself in any kind" (216). The myth of the reversed cosmos establishes that our very survival depends upon this polymorphism, which finds its expression in various indispensable arts that compensate for our natural nakedness and weakness (274b-c).

26. Cf. Aeschylus's *Persians*, in which the Persian emperor is repeatedly represented as a shepherd and his subjects as slaves and yoked animals.

27. *Rhômê* is used primarily of bodies and armies. Benardete notes Xenophon's reference to the "strength [*rhômê*] of soul" that Socrates displayed in conducting his defense and bearing his sentence of death (*Memorabilia* 4.8.1; *Being of the Beautiful*, III.150 n. 7.).

28. *Plato's Philosopher King: A Study of the Theoretical Background* (Columbia, S.C.: University of South Carolina Press, 1976), 115.

29. Here I follow the B manuscript, which at 260e4-5 has "autepitactic men," rather than Burnet's "autepitactic arts." Among other things, the latter does not square well with *to tôn basileôn genos*, "the family of kings," at 260e5-6.

30. Campbell, *Sophistes and Politicus*, v.

31. *Being of the Beautiful*, III.88. At III.92, Benardete adds that "the ruler of men needs to be immunized from the contagion of human pride."

32. The Stranger actually uses a variety of expressions to characterize the work of statesmanship: he calls it command "for the sake of" (*heneka*) and "over" (*epi*) generation, command "concerning" (*peri*) living beings, and power "in the case of" (*en*) living beings (261b1, c1, c7, c9).

33. I speak here of mechanical causation because, as we shall soon see, the method also seems oblivious to the preconditions of sexual reproduction.

34. One should recall in this context Socrates' statement at *Rep.* 520b that philosophers grow up spontaneously in cities and owe their rearing (*trophê*) to no one.

35. This remark looks forward to the myth in that it answers Young Socrates' question about which cosmic cycle we currently inhabit (271c): it would be impossible to grow wiser while becoming more and more like a newborn child in soul as well as in body (cf. 270e). There is also a subtle joke here, for the Stranger's remark comes just at the point when he and Young Socrates, by choosing to divide herd nurture, thereby decide to treat human beings as if they were identical to the beastly residents of the counter-cycle of the cosmos.

36. Cf. Griswold's reflections on why "a 'gnostic' science similar to arithmetic" should lead the Stranger to conceive of man as a featherless biped ("*Politikê Epistêmê*," 148).

37. Miller argues that bifurcatory division, which seeks to distinguish positive contraries, cannot isolate intelligence: intelligence "has no positive contrary corresponding to it in some other class," and "'intelligent/lacking-this-intelligence' is not a differentiation into positive contraries." Bifurcatory division therefore fails to reveal "the essential character—the *eidos* in the fullest sense of this term—of man," so that "mankind is revealed only through the brutish aspect of its being" (*The Philosopher in Plato's Statesman*, 31, 32; cf. 89, where a similar point is made with respect to the statesman). Miller offers an interesting account, however, of how the technique of bifurcatory division may nonetheless help Young Socrates to learn how to distinguish forms (20 ff.).

38. As Rosen observes, force cannot produce virtuous actions, which must be performed freely (*Plato's Statesman*, 166).

39. I here develop Benardete's suggestion that the "rejected classes" in the subsequent steps of the division are "images of something latent in man" (*"Eidos and Diaeresis,"* 215).

40. Cf. Rosen's translation of *kolobon* as "mutilated" or "cut off" (*Plato's Statesman*, 33).

41. Cf. *Tht.* 174d6-7, where Socrates remarks that kings or tyrants graze "a more troublesome and conspiratorial animal" than do herdsmen.

42. In the present context, the metaphorical implication of the removal of wings from two-footed animals seems to be something like Periander's suggestion to the tyrant Thrasybulus that he rid the city of men whose superior natures lift them above others, just as one might lop off the tallest ears of corn to level a field (Aristotle, *Pol.* 1284a26 ff., 1311a20 ff.).

43. Cf. Hemmenway, "Pedagogy in the Myth of Plato's *Statesman*," 257.

44. The particle *ên* at 268e8 is the rough equivalent of "Once upon a time . . ." (Campbell, *Sophistes and Politicus*, 42 n. 5; A. E. Taylor, *Plato: The Sophist and the Statesman*, 273).

45. "Plato's Myth of the Statesman, the Ambiguities of the Golden Age and of History," *Journal of Hellenic Studies* 98 (1978), 136. Atreus fed Thyestes his own children (Aeschylus, *Agamemnon* 1590 ff.).

46. The cosmos thus "shares imperfectly in the perfect" (Miller, *Philosopher in Plato's Statesman*, 38). We may note in this connection that although the Stranger mentions Cronos by name he does not speak of Zeus, but instead refers to him as "the god" (*ho theos*: 269a4).

47. In the course of the myth the Stranger seems to use the words *theos* (god) and *daimôn* interchangeably (cf. Miller, *Philosopher in Plato's Statesman*, 128 n. 5).

48. Cf. Plato's Protagorean version of the origin of the arts, in which Prometheus ("Forethought") is said to have stolen the arts of Hephaestus and Athena along with fire (*Prot.* 321b-322a). Protagoras's implication is that human beings owe these crucial arts to their own forward-looking intelligence.

49. Vidal-Naquet, "Plato's Myth of the Statesman," 137 (where he quotes with approval a remark by J. Bollack); Rosen, "Reversed Cosmos," 74 ff., and *Plato's Statesman*, 44.

50. Miller observes that in the myth "the Stranger seems to give up self-accountable analysis for the posture of the inspired seer" (*Philosopher in Plato's Statesman*, 36; cf. Rosen, *Plato's Statesman*, 46).

51. Rosen goes further, maintaining that the method of division could not be applied in the counter-cycle because there are no stable looks at that time (*Plato's Statesman*, 56; cf. 49). In support of this claim, it could be argued that the nonteleological nature of change in the counter-cycle renders impossible the recognition of *eidê*.

52. Presumably these ancestors, who were "born at the beginning of this revolution" (271b1-2), related the speeches of their parents, who lived through the violent cosmic reversal (cf. 273a) and thus straddled both cycles.

53. Cf. Miller, *Philosopher in Plato's Statesman*, 51, and Rosen, *Plato's Statesman*, 61. Much the same point could be made in connection with the expulsion of Adam and Eve from the Garden of Eden. One should also note that there is a certain teleology implicit in the myth: Rosen argues convincingly that the counter-cycle exists for the sake of the current cycle (*Plato's Statesman*, 44).

54. Rosen observes that whereas "*phronêsis* sees each individual case as it is," the method of division, "like *nomos*, gathers together many individual cases under a common stamp" ("Reversed Cosmos," 69; cf. 258c4-6).

55. Cf. Benardete, "*Eidos* and *Diaeresis*," 203: "The myth gives the conditions under which the *diaeresis* [i.e., the preceding division of the human herd and the statesman] would be true." Owing to their limited natures, of course, the human beings of the counter-cycle would not engage in philosophy at all. Cf. Rosen's conclusion that "in the absence of memory, experience, Eros, and work, there can be no philosophy" ("Reversed Cosmos," 79). Griswold concurs, and suggests that these human beings would also lack a sense of piety ("*Politikê*

Epistêmê," 151). Socrates' comparison of himself in the *Cratylus* and the *Apology* to heroes, *daimôns*, and mules (see above, ch. 5) points in another way toward the absence of philosophy in the counter-cycle: these mixed beings are generated from the intercourse of different species, and so could not exist under conditions of asexual generation (cf. Benardete, "*Eidos* and *Diaeresis*," 197).

56. Here Plato borrows a page from Aristophanes. Cf. the attempt in the *Plutus* of Penia, "Poverty" or "Need" (as distinct from *ptôcheia* or abject beggary) to prove to human beings that "I alone am the cause of all good things for you, and that you live through me" (468-470). Central to her argument is the claim that "if Wealth [*Plutos*] could see again and distributed himself equally, no one among human beings would pursue either *technê* or *sophia*" (510-512), with the result that human life would be miserable. Note also that in the *Symposium* Penia is said to be the mother of *erôs* (203b-c).

57. Griswold notes that "woolens are necessary when nature is most hostile, in bitter winter. . . . Political science is the art of defending the citizens from a fundamentally hostile nature" ("*Politikê Epistêmê*," 152).

58. Miller, *Philosopher in Plato's Statesman*, 50 (emphasis in original).

59. Rosen distinguishes between two different standards of measurement in accordance with the nonarithmetical mean, namely, technical efficiency and moral virtue (*Plato's Statesman*, 126). This insight offers some support for the notion of technical *phronêsis* that I see exemplified in the intelligence of the cosmos.

60. Just as a woven web is an "all-round covering" (*perikalluma*: 279d6), the Stranger seeks a speech that will "envelop" the statesman (*perikaluptein*: 275e6-7). Cf. Rosen, *Plato's Statesman*, 170: "The myth of the *technê* of politics is designed to exhibit how we may render possible the impossible rule of *phronêsis*. Unfortunately, the *technê* of politics is itself a further myth."

61. Consider also the metaphoric significance of the theme of stripping in Book 5 of the *Republic*. Socratic philosophizing is closely associated with stripping in Aristophanes' *Clouds* (177-179, 497-498, 719, 856-859, 1103, 1498).

62. *Ho agurmos* is a synonym for *hê aguris*, which is in turn an Aeolic form of *hê agora*. See H. G. Lidell and Robert Scott, *A Greek-English Lexicon*, 1843 (Oxford: Oxford University Press, 1985), 16, s.v. *agurmos* and *aguris*. Cf. Rosen, *Plato's Statesman*, 162: "*Phronêsis* cannot rule because it is parcelled out to the individual citizens and prevented from uniting by the boundaries of corporeal existence."

63. The mean, Rosen observes, "does not exist antecedent to our efforts to achieve it." "The metric of excess, deficiency, and mean . . . is ingredient in the structure of an intentional act. But if one does not act, the structure remains in potency" (*Plato's Statesman*, 130; cf. 121, 134). Cf. Griswold: "It seems that the mean must change relative to the context. The '*anangkaia ousia*' (283d8) is *not* an Idea or Form, or even an *eidos* in the Eleatic Stranger's sense. What counts as the 'mean' will depend on the situation; it will be what is timely, suitable, ap-

propriate for the occasion. And in this sense the mean may be said to 'become'" ("*Politikê Epistêmê*," 155, emphasis in original).

64. The main lines of this understanding of *phronêsis* are further developed by Aristotle in the *Nicomachean Ethics*. Yet as Rosen observes, Plato does not separate *praxis* from production, and he does not suppose that man is by nature a political animal (*Plato's Statesman*, 132, 151). The implications of these significant differences are developed in Rosen's study of the *Statesman*.

65. This point is stressed by Pierre Kucharski, whose interpretation of 283c-284e begins from the observation that "le plus et le moins sont conçus comme étant originairement indéfinis ou incommensurables, et que, dès lors, il faut les contraindre à devenir commensurables" ("La conception de l'art de la mesure dans le *Politique*," *Bulletin de l'Association Guillaume Budé* 19 [1960], 466).

66. At 308e5, the Stranger speaks of educators *kata nomon*, "according to law." Cf. 310a1-2: the characters of the citizens are "nurtured through laws."

67. Griswold observes that while the Stranger describes both "the political science suitable for the gods" and "an excellent and occasionally attainable political science suitable for men as they have become," the relationship between the two "is not simply that of best and next best" ("*Politikê Epistêmê*," 143). Cf. Melissa Lane, "A New Angle on Utopia: The Political Theory of the *Statesman*" (in *Reading The Statesman: Proceedings of the III Symposium Platonicum*, ed. Christopher Rowe [Sankt Augustin, Ger.: Academia Verlag, 1995], 276-291), who asserts that "just as, in the *Statesman*, the method of example (*paradeigma*) is not a model-copy relation, so the relation of actual states to the ideal is not a model-copy relation" (287).

68. Dorter argues that in the *Statesman* sophists are defined as "those who imitate the one who knows, but without the science of the mean, by which the latter knows what is good" (*Form and Good*, 220). But if this were correct, the human statesman would be either a sophist or a wise man. Furthermore, the philosopher, who lacks knowledge of the good yet aspires to it, would be indistinguishable from the sophist, who does not aspire to such knowledge.

69. Cf. Rosen, *Plato's Statesman*, 155. The same is true, I argue in *The Odyssey of Philosophy*, with respect to the "correct regime" of the *Republic* (the Kallipolis). On the positive function of law, cf. Miller's observation that "it is only on the basis of laws . . . that the plurality of men is first constituted as a political whole. . . . The laws are the explicit and implicit norms which first permit the gathering and cooperation of men into and as the polis" (*Philosopher in Plato's Statesman*, 95).

70. Cf. Miller, *Philosopher in Plato's Statesman*, 97-98.

71. *Meteôrologon*: *Apol.* 19b-c, *Clouds* 171-173, 194, 225, 1503, 1506-1507; cf. *Tht.* 173e-174a, *Crat.* 401b. *Adoleschên sophistên*: *Tht.* 195c, *Soph.* 225d, *Clouds* 1480, 1485; cf. *Crat.* 401b. *Sophizomenos*: cf. *Clouds* 547.

72. *The Philosopher in Plato's Statesman*, 109. Cf. Miller's account of the work of the true aides of the statesman—the orator, general, and judge

(303d ff.—as assisting the statesman to subordinate appetite (*epithumia*) and *thumos* to reason, and so to establish good order in the "psyche" of the *polis* (105).

73. "This is the single and whole work of royal weaving, never to allow moderate characters to stand apart from the manly ones, but by tamping them down together by means of shared opinions and honors and dishonors and reputations [*doxais*] . . . to entrust to these in common the offices of rule [*archas*] in cities" (310e7-311a2). The political image of weaving is first introduced by Aristophanes in connection with the character of Lysistrata, who best exemplifies within the playwright's dramatic universe the balance between moderation and manliness recommended by the Stranger himself (*Lysistrata* 567-586). Lysistrata's bold plan to end the war by seizing the Acropolis and withholding sex from the men calls for a striking combination of *andreia* and *sôphrosunê*, and effectively subordinates the armor-making of Hephaestus to the weaving of Athena (cf. 274c, 311b-c).

74. Although the Stranger has already implied that Socrates exposes human beings to the prepolitical savagery of their own unbridled *thumos*, his description of the behavior of moderate individuals, who "alone and themselves by themselves [*autoi kath'autous*] mind their own business," whose *erôs* is "more inopportune [*akairoteron*] than it should be," and who "are themselves unpolemical and make the young similarly unpolemical" (307e3-9), is also reminiscent of Socrates. Cf. Callicles' criticism at *Grg.* 485a ff. of what he perceives to be Socrates' shameful softness. This apparent contradiction is mitigated by the observation that while civic courage is rooted in a sensitivity to public shame, philosophic courage goes hand in hand with a lack of concern about how one is perceived by others. In the light of the Stranger's suggestion that Socrates' behavior is inopportune, it is also interesting to note that the concept of the opportune (*ho kairos*) would be inapplicable in the counter-cycle of the cosmos.

75. And as Rosen points out, laws must change in order to suit the changing circumstances of human life—yet such change is perilous in the absence of *phronêsis* (*Plato's Statesman*, 174-175).

Epilogue

1. Some might point to the *Crito* as evidence that I have overstated Socrates' antinomianism, or perhaps that Socrates has at any rate learned from the Stranger's criticism of him in the *Statesman*. Yet in the *Crito* the laws are made to present arguments; for Socrates, the authority of law thus rests on the persuasiveness of these arguments, and no longer derives from tradition. Despite appearances, the path laid out by Socrates in the *Crito* requires the city to answer for itself before the bar of philosophy, and not the other way around. One suspects, moreover, that the apparent success of the Law's arguments in the *Crito* is due in no small measure to Socrates' unwillingness to listen to other speeches

(54d); cf. the *Republic*'s very different approach to the question of what a philosopher like Socrates owes to the city (520a-b).

Bibliography

Allan, D. J. "The Problem of Cratylus." *American Journal of Philology* 75 (1954): 271-287.

Alrivie, J.-J. "Les prologues du *Théétète* et du *Parménide*," *Revue de Métaphysique et de Morale* 76 (1971): 6-23.

Amory, F. "*Eirôn* and *Eirôneia*." *Classica et Mediaevelia* 33 (1982): 49-80.

Ancilla to the Pre-Socratic Philosophers. Trans. Kathleen Freeman. Cambridge, Mass.: Harvard University Press, 1977.

Annas, Julia. "Knowledge and Language: The *Theaetetus* and the *Cratylus*." In *Language and Logos*, 95-114.

Baxter, Timothy M. S. *The Cratylus: Plato's Critique of Naming*. Leiden: E. J. Brill, 1992.

Benardete, Seth. *The Being of the Beautiful: Plato's Theaetetus, Sophist, and Statesman*. Chicago: University of Chicago Press, 1983.

———. "*Eidos* and *Diaeresis* in Plato's *Statesman*." *Philologus* 107 (1963): 193-226.

———. "Physics and Tragedy: On Plato's *Cratylus*." *Ancient Philosophy* 1 (1980-81): 127-140.

Benitez, Eugenio, and Livia Guimaraes. "Philosophy as Performed in Plato's *Theaetetus*." *Review of Metaphysics* 47 (December 1993): 297-328.

Berger, Harry, Jr. "Facing Sophists: Socrates' Charismatic Bondage in *Protagoras*," *Representations* 5 (Spring 1984): 66-91.

Blits, Jan. "The Holy and the Human: An Interpretation of Plato's *Euthyphro*." A*perion* 14.1 (1980): 19-40.

Blundell, Mary Whitlock. "Character and Meaning in Plato's *Hippias Minor*." In *Methods of Interpreting Plato and His Dialogues*, 131-172.

Bostock, David. *Plato's Theaetetus*. Oxford: Clarendon Press, 1988.

Brandwood, Leonard. *A Word Index to Plato*. Leeds: W. S. Maney and Son, 1976.

Brann, Eva. "The Offense of Socrates: A Re-Reading of Plato's Apology." *Interpretation* 7.2 (1978): 1-21.

———. "Plato's Theory of Ideas." *The St. John's Review* 32.1 (July, 1980): 29-37.

Brickhouse, Thomas C., and Nicholas D. Smith. *Socrates on Trial*. Princeton: Princeton University Press, 1989.

Burkert, Walter. *Greek Religion*. Trans. John Raffan. Cambridge, Mass.: Harvard University Press, 1985.

Burnyeat, M. F. "The Philosophical Sense of Theaetetus' Mathematics." *Isis* 69 (1978): 489-513.

———. *The Theaetetus of Plato*. Indianapolis: Hackett, 1990.

Campbell, Lewis. *The Sophistes and Politicus of Plato*. 1867. Reprint ed. New York: Arno Press, 1973.

Clay, Diskin. "Gaps in the 'Universe' of the Platonic Dialogues." In *Proceedings of the Boston Area Colloquium in Ancient Philosophy*, vol. 3, ed. John Cleary (Lanham, Md.: University Press of America, 1988), 131-157.

———. "Plato's First Words."*Beginnings in Classical Literature. Yale Classical Studies* 29 (1992): 113-130.

———. "Socrates' Mulishness and Heroism." *Phronesis* 17 (1972): 53-60.

Coolidge, Francis. "Socrates and the Daimonic: On the Voice and Daimonic Sign." Unpublished paper.

Cooper, John M. *Plato's Theaetetus*. New York: Garland Publishing, 1990.

Cornford, Francis M. *Plato's Theory of Knowledge: The Theaetetus and the Sophist of Plato*. London: Routledge and Kegan Paul, 1935.

Cropsey, Joseph. *Plato's World: Man's Place in the Cosmos*. Chicago: University of Chicago Press, 1995.

———. "The Dramatic End of Plato's Socrates." *Interpretation* 14.2&3 (1986): 155-175.

Davis, Michael. *Aristotle's Poetics: The Poetry of Philosophy*. Lanham, Md.: Rowman & Littlefield, 1992.

Derrida, Jacques. "Plato's Pharmacy." In *Dissemination*, trans. Barbara Johnson (Chicago: University of Chicago Press, 1981), 61-171.

Desjardins, Rosemary. *The Rational Enterprise: Logos in Plato's Theaetetus*. Albany: State University of New York Press, 1990.

Detienne, Marcel, and Jean-Pierre Vernant. *Cunning Intelligence in Greek Culture and Society*. Trans. Janet Lloyd. 1978. Chicago: University of Chicago Press, 1991.

Dimock, G. E., Jr. "The Name of Odysseus." In the *Odyssey*, ed. Albert Cook, Norton Critical Edition (New York: Norton, 1974), 406-424.

Dorter, Kenneth. *Form and Good in Plato's Eleatic Dialogues: The Parmenides, Theaetetus, Sophist, and Statesman*. Berkeley: University of California Press, 1994.

———. "Justice and Method in the *Statesman*." In *Justice, Law, and Method in Plato and Aristotle*, ed. Spiro Panagiotou (Edmonton, Alberta: Academic Printing and Publishing, 1987), 105-122.

Essays on the Philosophy of Socrates. Ed. Hugh H. Benson. Oxford: Oxford University Press, 1992.

Farness, Jay. *Missing Socrates: Problems of Plato's Writing*. University Park, Pa.: Pennsylvania State University Press, 1991.

Feaver, Douglas D., and John E. Hare. "The *Apology* as an Inverted Parody of Rhetoric." *Arethusa* 14.2 (1981): 205-216.

Friedländer, Paul. *Plato*. 3 vols. Trans. Hans Meyerhoff. Princeton: Princeton University Press, 1958-1969.

Fustel de Coulanges, Numa Denis. *The Ancient City: A Study in the Religion, Laws, and Institutions of Greece and Rome*. 1956. Baltimore: Johns Hopkins University Press, 1980.

Gadamer, Hans-Georg. "*Logos* and *Ergon* in Plato's *Lysis*." In *Dialogue and Dialectic: Eight Hermeneutical Studies on Plato*, trans. P. Christopher Smith (New Haven: Yale University Press, 1980), 1-20.

Garner, Richard. *Law and Society in Classical Athens*. St. Martin's Press: New York, 1987.

Goldhill, Simon. *The Poet's Voice: Essays on Poetics and Greek Literature*. Cambridge: Cambridge University Press, 1991.

Goldschmidt, Victor. *Essai sur le Cratyle: Contribution à l'histoire de la pensée de Platon*. Paris: Bibliothèque de l'École des Hautes Études, 1940.

Graves, Robert. *The Greek Myths*. 2 vols. Baltimore: Penguin, 1955.

Greek-English Lexicon. Ed. H. G. Liddell and Robert Scott. 1843. Oxford: Oxford University Press, 1985.

Griswold, Charles L., Jr. *Self-Knowledge in Plato's Phaedrus*. New Haven: Yale University Press, 1986.

——. "Irony and Aesthetic Language in Plato's Dialogues." In *Philosophy and Literature*, ed. Doug Bolling (New York: Haven Publications, 1987), 71-99.

——. "Plato's Metaphilosophy: Why Plato Wrote Dialogues." In *Platonic Writings, Platonic Readings*, 143-167.

——. "*Politikê Epistêmê* in Plato's *Statesman*." In *Essays in Ancient Greek Philosophy III*, ed. John Anton and Anthony Preus (Albany: State University of New York Press, 1989), 141-167.

Hansen, Mogen Herman. *The Trial of Socrates from the Athenian Point of View*. Copenhagen: Royal Danish Academy of Sciences and Letters, 1995.

Harrison, Jane. *Prolegomena to the Study of Greek Religion*. 3d. ed. New York: Meridian Books, 1955.

Harrison, Joan C. "Plato's Prologue: *Theaetetus* 142a-143c." *Tulane Studies in Philosophy* 27 (1978): 103-123.

Hegel, G. W. F. *Hegel's Lectures on the History of Philosophy*. 3 vols. Trans. E. S. Haldane and Frances H. Simpson. New York: Humanities Press, 1974.

Hemmenway, Scott R. "Pedagogy in the Myth of Plato's *Statesman*: Body and Soul in Relation to Philosophy and Politics." *History of Philosophy Quarterly* 11.3 (1994): 253-268.

——. "Philosophical Apology in the *Theaetetus*." *Interpretation* 17.3 (1990): 323-346.

Howland, Jacob. *The Republic: The Odyssey of Philosophy*. New York: Twayne Publishers, 1993.

——. "Aristotle on Tragedy: Rediscovering the *Poetics*." *Interpretation* 22.3 (1995): 359-404.

——. "Plato's Dionysian Music? A Reading of the *Symposium*." In *The Sovereignty of Construction: Essays in Honor of David Lachterman*, ed. Daniel W. Conway and Pierre Kerszberg, Rodopi Publishers, forthcoming.

——. "Re-reading Plato: The Problem of Platonic Chronology." *Phoenix* 45.3 (1991): 189-214.

——. "Socrates and Alcibiades: Eros, Piety, and Politics." *Interpretation* 18.1 (1990): 63-90.

Hyland, Drew. *Finitude and Transcendence in the Platonic Dialogues*. Albany: State University of New York Press, 1995.

Jacoby, Felix. *Die Fragmente der griechischen Historiker*. 3 vols. Berlin: Weidmann, 1923-1958.

Jowett, Benjamin. *The Dialogues of Plato*. 5 vol. Boston: The Jefferson Press, n.d.

Kierkegaard, Soren. *The Concept of Irony*. Trans. Lee M. Capel. Bloomington: Indiana University Press, 1965.

Klein, Jacob. *A Commentary on Plato's Meno*. Chapel Hill: University of North Carolina Press, 1965.

——. *Greek Mathematical Thought and the Origin of Algebra*. Trans. Eva Brann. Cambridge, Mass.: M.I.T. Press, 1968.

——. *Plato's Trilogy: Theaetetus, the Sophist and the Statesman*. Chicago: University of Chicago Press, 1977.

Kojève, Alexandre. "Tyranny and Wisdom." In Leo Strauss, *On Tyranny*, ed. Victor Gourevitch and Michael S. Roth (New York: The Free Press, 1991), 135-176.

Konstan, David. "An Anthropology of Euripides' *Kyklops*." In *Nothing to Do with Dionysus? Athenian Drama in Its Social Context*, ed. John J.Winkler and Froma I. Zeitlin (Princeton: Princeton University Press, 1990), 207-227.

Kucharski, Pierre. "La conception de l'art de la mesure dans le *Politique*." *Bulletin de l'Association Guillaume Budé* 19 (1960): 459-480.

Lane, Melissa. "A New Angle on Utopia: The Political Theory of the *Statesman*." In *Reading The Statesman: Proceedings of the III Symposium Platonicum*, ed. Christopher Rowe (Sankt Augustin, Ger.: Academia Verlag, 1995), 276-291.

Language and Logos: Studies Presented to G.E.L. Owen. Ed. Malcolm Schofield and Martha Craven Nussbaum. Cambridge: Cambridge University Press, 1982.

Lee, Edward N. "'Hoist with His Own Petard': Ironic and Comic Elements in Plato's Critique of Protagoras (*Tht.* 161-171)." In *Exegesis and Argument: Studies in Greek Philosophy Presented to Gregory Vlastos*, ed. E. N. Lee, A. Mourelatos, and R. Rorty (Assen, Neth.: Van Gorcum, 1973): 225-261.

Lewis, Marlo. "An Interpretation of Plato's *Euthyphro*." *Interpretation* 13.1 (1985): 33-65.

——. "An Interpretation of the *Euthyphro*." *Interpretation* 12.2&3 (1984): 225-259.

Lidz, Joel Warren. "Reflections on and in Plato's Cave." *Interpretation* 21.2 (1993-1994): 115-134.

MacDowell, Douglas M. *The Law in Classical Athens*. Ithaca: Cornell University Press, 1978.

MacKenzie, Mary Margaret. "Putting the *Cratylus* in Its Place," *Classical Quarterly* 36.1 (1986): 124-50.

Markantonatos, G. "On the Origin and Meanings of the Word *Eirôneia*." *Rivista di Filologia* 103 (1973): 16-21.

Methods of Interpreting Plato and His Dialogues. Ed. James C. Klagge and Nicholas D. Smith. A supplementary volume of *Oxford Studies in Ancient Philosophy*. Oxford: Clarendon Press, 1992.

Miller, Mitchell H., Jr. *The Philosopher in Plato's Statesman*. The Hague: Martinus Nijhoff, 1980.

———. *Plato's Parmenides: The Conversion of the Soul* (Princeton: Princeton University Press, 1986.

Moulinier, Louis. *Le pur et l'impure dans la pensée des Grecs d'Homére à Aristote*. Paris: Libraire C. Klincksiek, 1952.

Nussbaum, Martha. "Aristophanes and Socrates on Learning Practical Wisdom." In *Aristophanes: Essays in Interpretation, Yale Classical Studies* 26 (1980): 43-97.

Orwin, Clifford. "On the *Cleitophon*." In *The Roots of Political Philosophy*, 117-131.

Oxford Classical Dictionary. Ed. N. G. L. Hammond and H. H. Scullard. 2d ed. Oxford: Clarendon Press, 1989.

Page, Carl. "Philosophy and the Outlandishness of Reason." *Journal of Speculative Philosophy* 7.3 (1993), 206-225.

Pangle, Thomas L. "On the *Theages*," in *The Roots of Political Philosophy*, 147-174.

Penner, Terry. "Socrates and the Early Dialogues." In *The Cambridge Companion to Plato*, ed. Richard Kraut (Cambridge: Cambridge University Press, 1992), 121-169.

Plato's Dialogues: New Studies and Interpretations. Ed. Gerald A. Press. Lanham, Md.: Rowman and Littlefield, 1993.

Plato: Euthyphro, Apology of Socrates, and Crito. Ed. John Burnet. 1924. Oxford: Clarendon Press, 1977.

Platon: Ouevres Complètes. Ed. Auguste Diès. Vol 8.2. 7th ed. Paris: Société d'Édition "Les Belles Lettres," 1976.

Platonic Writings, Platonic Readings. Ed. Charles L. Griswold, Jr. New York: Routledge, 1988.

Platonis Opera. Ed. John Burnet. 1900-1907. Oxford: Oxford University Press, 1979-82.

Polansky, Ronald. *Philosophy and Knowledge: A Commentary on Plato's Theaetetus*. Lewisburg, Pa.: Bucknell University Press, 1992.

Rahe, Paul A. *Republics Ancient and Modern: Classical Republicanism and the American Revolution*. Chapel Hill: University of North Carolina Press, 1992.

Reeve, C. D. C. *Socrates in the Apology*. Indianapolis: Hackett Publishing Company, 1989.

Robb, Kevin. "*Asebeia* and *Sunousia*: The Issues behind the Indictment of Socrates." In *Plato's Dialogues: New Studies and Interpretations*, 77-106.

———. *Literacy and Paideia in Ancient Greece*. New York: Oxford University Press, 1994.

Roochnik, David L. *Of Art and Wisdom: Plato's Understanding of Techne*. University Park, Pa.: Pennsylvania State University Press, 1996.

———. "Socrates' Use of the Techne-Analogy." In Benson, *Essays on the Philosophy of Socrates*, 185-197.

Rosen, Stanley. *Plato's Statesman: The Web of Politics*. New Haven: Yale University Press, 1995.

———. *Hermeneutics as Politics*. New York: Oxford University Press, 1987.

———. *Plato's Sophist: The Drama of Original and Image*. New Haven: Yale University Press, 1983.

———. "Dunamis, Energeia and the Megarians." *Philosophical Inquiry* 1.2 (Winter 1979): 105-119.

———. "Plato's Myth of the Reversed Cosmos." *Review of Metaphysics* 33.1 (1979): 59-85.

Rosenstock, Bruce. "Fathers and Sons: Irony in the *Cratylus*." *Arethusa* 25.3 (1992): 385-417.

Ross, Sir David. *Plato's Theory of Ideas*. Oxford: Oxford University Press, 1951.

Rue, Rachel. "The Philosopher in Flight: The Digression (172c-177c) in Plato's *Theaetetus*." *Oxford Studies in Ancient Philosophy* 11, ed. C. C. W. Taylor (Clarendon Press: Oxford, 1993): 71-100.

Salkever, Stephen. Review of *Methods of Interpreting Plato and His Dialogues*. *Bryn Mawr Classical Reviews* 3 (1992): 368-375.

Sallis, John. *Being and Logos: The Way of Platonic Dialogue*. 1975. 2d ed. Atlantic Highlands, N.J.: Humanities Press International, 1986.

Saxenhouse, Arlene W. "The Philosophy of the Particular and the Universality of the City: Socrates' Education of Euthyphro." *Political Theory* 16.2 (1988): 281-299.

Sayre, Kenneth M. *Plato's Analytic Method*. Chicago: University of Chicago Press, 1969.

———. *Plato's Literary Garden: How to Read a Platonic Dialogue*. Notre Dame: University of Notre Dame Press, 1995.

Schaerer, René. "Le Mécanisme de l'Ironie dans ses Rapports avec la Dialectique." *Revue de Métaphysique et de Morale* 48 (1941): 181-209.

Schofield, Malcom. "The Dénouement of the *Cratylus*." In *Language and Logos*. 61-81.

Scodel, Harvey. *Diaeresis and Myth in Plato's Statesman*. Göttingen, Ger.: Vandenhoeck and Ruprecht, 1987.

Segal, Charles. "Greek Tragedy and Society: A Structuralist Perspective." In *Greek Tragedy and Political Theory*, ed. J. Peter Euben (Berkeley: University of California Press, 1986), 43-75.

——. "The Phaeacians and the Symbolism of Odysseus's Return." *Arion* 1.1 (1962), 17-64.

Skemp, J. B. *Plato's Statesman*. New Haven: Yale University Press, 1952.

Socratic Questions: New Essays on the Philosophy of Socrates and Its Significance. Ed. Barry S. Gower and Michael C. Stokes. London: Routledge, 1992.

Sprague, Rosamond Kent. *Plato's Philosopher King: A Study of the Theoretical Background*. Columbia, S.C.: University of South Carolina Press, 1976.

Stanford, W. B. *The Ulysses Theme: A Study in the Adaptability of a Traditional Hero*. 1954. 2d ed. Oxford: Basil Blackwell, 1963.

Strauss, Leo. *The City and Man*. 1964. Chicago: University of Chicago Press, 1978.

——. *What is Political Philosophy? And Other Studies*. 1959. Chicago: University of Chicago Press, 1988.

——. "On Plato's *Apology of Socrates* and *Crito*." In *Studies in Platonic Political Philosophy* (Chicago: University of Chicago Press, 1983), 38-66.

Taylor, A. E. *Plato: The Sophist and the Statesman*. London: Thomas Nelson and Sons, 1961.

——. *Socrates*. New York: D. Appleton, 1933.

Tessitore, Aristide. "Aristotle's Political Presentation of Socrates in the *Nicomachean Ethics*." *Interpretation* 16.1 (1988): 3-22.

The Roots of Political Philosophy: Ten Forgotten Socratic Dialogues. Ed. Thomas L. Pangle. Ithaca: Cornell University Press, 1987.

The Third Way: New Directions in Platonic Studies. Ed. Francisco J. Gonzales. Lanham, Md.: Rowman & Littlefield Publishers, 1995.

Thesleff, Holger. *Studies in Platonic Chronology*. Helsinki: *Commentationes Humanarum Litterarum* 70, 1982.

Vernant, Jean-Pierre. "The Figures and Functions of Artemis in Myth and Cult." In *Mortals and Immortals: Collected Essays*, ed. Froma I. Zeitlin (Princeton: Princeton University Press, 1991), 195-206.

Vidal-Naquet, Pierre. "Plato's Myth of the Statesman, the Ambiguities of the Golden Age and of History." *Journal of Hellenic Studies* 98 (1978): 132-141.

Weingartner, Rudolph H. *The Unity of the Platonic Dialogue: The Cratylus, the Protagoras, the Parmenides*. Indianapolis: Bobbs-Merrill, 1973.

Wieland, Wolfgang. *Platon und die Formen des Wissen*. Göttingen, Ger.: Vandenhöck & Ruprecht, 1982.

Zaidman, Louise Bruit, and Pauline Schmitt Pantel. *Religion in the Ancient Greek City*. Trans. Paul Cartledge. Cambridge: Cambridge University Press, 1992.

Index

Achilles, 49, 154, 173, 177–178, 180–182
Aeschylus, 204
Ajax, 181
Alcibiades: speech of, in the *Symposium*, 4, 220; tyrannical aspirations of, 122; on tyranny of Socrates' teaching, 33
Alcibiades II, 119, 122
Alfarabi, 23
Alkinoos, 226
allegory of the Cave. See *Republic*
Anaxagoras, 24, 147
angler, 175, 184, 188–193
Apollo, 7, 47, 100
archery, 180
architecture, 235, 239–241, 261. *See also* statesman, *phronêsis*
Aristophanes: *Acharnians*, 43; criticizes Socrates, 7, 73; *Clouds*, 33, 59–63, 100–101, 117–118, 120–121, 196, 203; dangers of Socratic education and, 34; describes Socrates, 59–63, 276; *Euthyphro* and, 100–102; predicts Socrates' death, 203; sees philosophy as the will to power, 186–187; in *Symposium*, 152
Aristotle:, 41, 73, 98, 148, 161, 165, 183, 240, 244
arithmetic. *See* mathematics
Artemis, 82–86, 93, 167, 203. *See also* midwifery
astronomy. *See* mathematics
Athena, 121, 233, 259, 265, 268

Athens: authority of gods and fathers in, 33, 99–100, 117, 204, 213; legal procedures in, 25–27; as measure of human goods, 6; Socrates' care for, 31–32, 96–97, 100; Socrates' outlandishness and, 85. *See also* law
Atreus, 170, 256–257

becoming, 42, 87, 270
beehive, 273
being, 216, 245–46, 270, 271
Benardete, Seth, 92, 188, 244
Brann, Eva, 26

Callicles, 4, 34
care: bad trusteeship and, 70–75; of community for itself, 277; of cosmos for itself, 267; in counter-cycle, 261; different from nurture in current cycle, 246, 266; of divine shepherds, 266–267; education and, 90; forcible versus voluntary, 251; for gods, 126–127; of human beings for themselves, 259; as therapy, 96, 126–127, 133; Meletus' understanding of, 99, 102–104, 106, 112, 130; *nomos* and, 93, 100, 103, 274; piety and, 128–129; Protagoras and Theodorus deficient in, 95–96; as taming, 251. *See also* citizenship, midwifery, statesman

geometry: and Aristophanes'
  Socrates, 59–61; Theodorus
  and, 55–56, 71
Glaucon, 110, 111, 122, 151, 253
gods: Artemis' distance from other,
  84; assimilated to Ideas, 121;
  chorus of orators and, 67;
  compared to the Mafia, 123–
  124; gifts of, 259, 265–266;
  humans stand between pigs and,
  244; madmen and dreamers as,
  71; as models for human beings,
  124–125; motion of, 258;
  names of, 132, 144–145, 154,
  156, 158–160; piety not a virtue
  of, 63, 123; of poets, 120, 158,
  219; proper work of, 127;
  prophecy and, 97, 112, 125;
  Protagoras's desire to mimic,
  65, 68; resemble philosophers,
  63, 122, 123, 172; Socrates as
  maker of, 120–122, 126, 128;
  Stranger resembles, 170–172,
  181, 187, 200, 214; tradition of
  Athens and, 29, 32–33, 98,
  100–101, 121; violence of, 122,
  257–259; withdrawal of, in
  current cycle, 114, 259, 263,
  266–267. *See also* Artemis,
  Athens, care, piety, Zeus
Golden Age, 157, 257, 261
Gorgias, 34, 174, 201
Great Dionysia, 161
Greek tragedy, 53, 161
Griswold, Charles, 15, 30, 224

Hades: Odysseus in, 49; etymology
  of, 145; as Socrates' true home,
  47
Hector, 155
Hemmenway, Scott, 63
Hephaestus, 259, 265
Heracles, 155
Heraclitus: dictum of, 10; doctrine
  of flux, 58, 87, 137, 163, 214; a
  precursor of deconstructionism,
  15
herd: human community as, 247,
  251–254, 267; nurture of, 246–
  247
Hermes, 136, 145, 151, 158–160,
  257

Hermogenes: companion of Plato,
  131; conventionalism of, 143;
  identity of, 134–135; name of,
  154, 158–159; on names of
  gods, 144; on oracles, 135;
  theory about names, 137–139,
  148–149; on Socrates'
  prophecy, 133
Hesiod, 117, 120, 122, 128, 156–
  157, 257
Hippias Minor, 18, 49, 176–182
Hobbes, Thomas, 265
homecoming: exile and, 39, 46–47,
  225–226; as Homeric subtext, 7,
  225–226; and place of
  philosophy in *polis*, 5
Homer: 7, 120, 122, 128, 144–145,
  177–178, 181
Homeric Hymn to Pan, 159
Hyland, Drew, 114–119

Ideas, 122, 200, 260
irony: in *Cratylus*, 131–132; in
  Euclides' transcription, 43; first
  occurrence of in Greek
  literature, 305–306n41;
  intentional, 29, 36; Platonic, 10,
  43–44, 138, 176; proper to
  study of politics, 244; Socratic,
  18, 48, 129, 135–136, 162, 172,
  220, 287–288n11, 288n12,
  295n17, 305–306n41, 307–
  308nn15, 22; Stranger divides,
  220; unintentional, 27–31, 36–
  37
irrational numbers, 64, 228, 253–
  254, 278

justice: gift from Zeus, 265;
  Hippias on, 180; of Meletus'
  indictment, 107, 117, 120; in
  Sophist IV, 196; Stranger on,
  219. *See also* care

Kafka, Franz, 223, 242
Kierkegaard, Søren, 1
King Archon, 2, 99, 134, 272,
  285n3
kinship test, 7, 50, 231–233
Klein, Jacob, 9
knowledge: and art of politics, 266,
  272–273; of beings, 142, 146;

About the Author

Jacob Howland is associate professor of philosophy and Chair of the Department of Philosophy and Religion at the University of Tulsa. He is the author of *The Republic: The Odyssey of Philosophy* (New York: Twayne Publishers, 1993). His articles on Platonic chronology, Plato's political philosophy, Aristotle's *Poetics*, and other philosophical topics have been published in a variety of journals, including *Interpretation*, *Phoenix*, and the *Review of Metaphysics*.